THE LIVING LIGHT DIALOGUE

Volume 6

THE LIVING LIGHT DIALOGUE

Volume 6

❦

Through the mediumship of
Richard P. Goodwin

Living Light Books

The Living Light Dialogue Volume 6
Copyright © 2013 Serenity Association

Through the mediumship of Richard P. Goodwin.

All rights reserved. Printed in the United States of America. No portion of this book may be reproduced—electronically, mechanically, or via internet transmission—without advance, express written permission of the publisher except in the case of brief quotations embodied in critical articles and reviews. No derivative work—games supplemental material, video—may be created without advance, express written permission of the publisher. For information address Living Light Books, P.O. Box 4187, San Rafael, CA 94913-4187.

Cover design copyright © 2013 by Serenity Association
Cover photograph by Serenity Association, 2013; copyright © 2013 by Serenity Association.

www.livinglight.org

Library of Congress Control Number 2007929762

FIRST EDITION

This volume of teachings is dedicated to the spirit friends who brought to Earth the Living Light philosophy. With eternal gratitude, we pray that we may demonstrate these principles and continue to bring to publication these teachings.

CONTENTS

Acknowledgement ix
Introduction xi
Consciousness Class 140 3
Consciousness Class 141 9
Consciousness Class 142 19
Consciousness Class 143 28
Consciousness Class 144 34
Consciousness Class 145 41
Consciousness Class 146 48
Consciousness Class 147 56
Consciousness Class 148 63
Consciousness Class 149 72
Consciousness Class 150 80
Consciousness Class 151 88
Consciousness Class 152 96
Consciousness Class 153 104
Consciousness Class 154 115
Consciousness Class 155 125
Consciousness Class 156 135
Consciousness Class 157 142
Consciousness Class 158 150
Consciousness Class 159 159
Consciousness Class 160 171
Consciousness Class 161 178
Consciousness Class 162 188
Consciousness Class 163 201
Consciousness Class 164 208
Consciousness Class 165 217
Consciousness Class 166 225

Consciousness Class 167 231
Consciousness Class 168 237
Consciousness Class 169 241
Consciousness Class 170 247
Consciousness Class 171 256
Consciousness Class 172 269
Consciousness Class 173 273
Consciousness Class 174 290
Consciousness Class 175 301
Consciousness Class 176 317
Consciousness Class 177 326
Consciousness Class 178 335
Consciousness Class 179 344
Consciousness Class 180 359
Consciousness Class 181 370
Consciousness Class 182 379
Consciousness Class 183 402
Consciousness Class 184 427
Consciousness Class 185 435
Consciousness Class 186 446
Appendix 459

ACKNOWLEDGMENT

Grateful acknowledgement is made to the many friends and associates for invaluable aid in compiling this book, for their helpful suggestions, for their loyal interest and encouragement.

Special acknowledgement is due to those who painstakingly and selflessly transcribed and proofread the text.

INTRODUCTION

[This introduction was written by Mr. Goodwin and originally appeared in *The Living Light*, which were the first teachings of the Living Light Philosophy published in book form. The entire text of *The Living Light* was republished in *The Living Light Dialogue,* Volume 1.]

> "Think, children. Think more often
> and think more deeply."

The teachings in this book were given as a progressive series of lessons to a group of four students who were sitting for spiritual unfoldment with me beginning in January of 1964. The communications were regular until October of that year, when nearly a seven-year silence ensued, and resumed in 1971 to the present. They were received in three ways by me as a channel. The main text was taped from a direct control of my voice in deep trance at special sittings of our group, during which I had no experience of the voice or what was being transmitted. A few scattered verses were given independently when I was privileged to see and hear our teacher clairvoyantly. I have also been a channel for this communicant when speaking from the podium at church and in answering difficult questions at our public seminars.

Nearly all we know about our teacher is contained in the lectures. He reports that he had tried for sixteen years to break through an interference barrier that the channel had to deep trance. When our conditions were in resonance with his patient wisdom, he came through ready to teach his understanding. I have seen him as an old man dressed in white with long flowing white hair. He has blue eyes, slightly smiling and deeply compassionate. I have always called him the Old Man. The students liked to call him the Wise One. He is surely one of those often called a Teacher of Light. I do not know his country, although he indicated at one time that he was from 6000 B.C., and a form of a judge in his time.

The text is often difficult, but it is complete, having been transcribed word for word from the original tapes recording the trance voice. It is presented with a minimum of punctuation to be freer for the individual interpretation of each reader. The lessons given before the long silence are phrased with many allegories often paradoxical. There are repetitions and renewals of theme, but it is explained that if an understanding is not perceived, compassion dictates that it be said again. Some of the topics have but a simple mention with little development but all are revealed, we are told, according to merit.

The Old Man is a fine teacher. He has in a hundred ways intertwined his allegory, progressive explanations, unfolding exercises, and timely references to reach a multitude of levels of individual understanding. A notable change is his more direct style of presentation beginning in 1971.

There is an endearing intimacy of person that can be felt through his lectures, a meaningful and loving encounter with a wise friend. Like an old man, he makes a mistake and conscientiously corrects himself a few paragraphs later. He listens often and carefully to our earnest discussions of his words. He consults with a group of experts on evolution and cites their learning in his lesson. His use of the direct address "children" or "my children" is not patronizing but infinitely loving and supportive.

A word must be said about the teachings. The Old Man makes clear that his lessons are not dogma, a creed or a narrow way, but simply his own understanding offered to us as a form of instruction to aid us in our own individual progression. When he speaks of Laws, he does not refer to man-made rules or moral traditions but to the cosmic and atomic way-things-are, the natural world of what-is, the universal laws of life, part of the original creative design and through which creation is fulfilled. These laws are beyond the possibility of being changed, suspended, transcended, or destroyed but they are ever a tool of mankind, not his master. First, through our awareness of the universal laws and then slowly through our developed understanding, the powers of creation are accessible to us. Not power over men's minds or circumstances, but power over whatever is selfish and imperfect in ourselves is the way up the eternal ladder of progression. When the Old Man cautions us concerning the Law of Responsibility or gives us a thinking exercise to explore the Law of Identity in a dynamic manner, he prepares us to take another step. And all move in accordance with the Law of What Can Be Borne.

Our teacher shows us how the two worlds are drawn together. In his realm, he describes, there is a great diversity of thought, many schools of understanding; but the Light is always known by the Light. Because of the interdependence of the two realms, listening to our discussions helped to clarify his teaching to others on his side of the curtain. His love and gratitude he humbly equates with ours.

The lessons to be perceived are not new, they are very old, but they are new to certain levels of our being. I would personally advise the reader, after reading this volume of discourses in full, to make a daily habit (or when there is a feeling or need) to sit quietly with the book. Open it at random and be guided to the Light by the passage that is there for the day. This technique is still used by the original students who were given the lessons and by many students after them who have studied in unfolding classes with me through these teachings.

Go beyond the words into feeling, into the immediate meanings for you. Touch into the inspiration that flows into the form of this book. It is from the Divine.

RICHARD P. GOODWIN
San Geronimo, California
June 1972

CONSCIOUSNESS CLASSES

CONSCIOUSNESS CLASS 140 ✤

Greetings, students, and welcome to the Living Light Academy.

This evening we shall be most happy to share our understanding on the questions that you have prepared.

Thank you. We are taught that when one procrastinates, one is in fascination. Is procrastination triggered by fear?

The reason that one fascinates and procrastinates, so to speak, is an effort by the human mind to entertain itself with visual pictures in order that it does not have to accept what is rising from its own soul consciousness and dictating what is right to do because it is right to do. Each and every individual is aware of what their path in evolution truly is. Each person is aware of what they must do in keeping with the lessons that are before them. Because of the experiences in evolution that are indelibly recorded in what is known as the memory par excellence, the human mind is aware, to some extent and degree, and therefore in order to try and block out what it knows it must, in time, do, it fascinates into a realm of delusion and procrastinates on what it knows it must do. In time, man will do what he has earned to do regardless of the battle between the created mind and the infinite eternal soul.

Thank you. Why are some healers more specialized or more proficient at working on one part of the body rather than another, or better at working with animals or plants than with humans?

Because, my students, in their evolution in life they have spent more time and directed more energy to those particular areas. And so it is the constant revelation of God's manifestation of variety in creation.

Thank you. What effect does surgery have on the body? Does it have elements in common with psychic surgery?

Surgery is detrimental to the temple of God known as the human body. But its detriment does not have to be long enduring. For it is in the divine plan of the Divine Architect to heal through the power of peace. And peace, the great healer of the universe, once reigning supreme within the human consciousness, brings that great healing and restores harmony to the body, to the mind, and the soul rises and shines in its beautiful light of joy and happiness. We have, for many years, emphasized the importance of the power of peace, for that *is* God. That is the great of the greatest. However, the human mind, in all of its dictates, is also aware that peace is a power supreme to its dictates. And so, whenever you have disturbing experiences, remember that peace is the greatest healer you will ever know.

Thank you. Do some conditions respond more readily to spiritual healing than others?

All so-called conditions respond to spiritual healing. It is dependent upon the recipient of how receptive they choose to be.

Thank you. Will knowledge and instrumentation ever advance to the point where channeling the healing power can be affected by means other than through the human being?

The human being is the temple of God on your earth realm. It is through that, the most evolved instrument on your planet, that God works in all his fullness. That does not mean to imply that God does not work with healing through the plants, the animals, and the other forms of life upon your planet. It does mean that the human being has, in its evolution, the intelligence, the faculty of reason, to use wisely this divine power.

Man, forgetting the source of his life, has, in that forgetting, denied, through his own errors of ignorance, the great healing of not only his own body, but the bodies of all forms of life. When we speak so often on divine will, total acceptance, that, my good children, is the power that will bring unto you the goodness and the happiness that you all are seeking. But you must learn to accept the small things as well as the great. You must learn to accept the small things as well as the great, for, in so accepting, you are freed from judgment, for it is judgment that compares. It is judgment that views the variety of manifestation. Go beyond the manifestation or effects in life. Go to the source that sustains this variety, this manifestation.

Remember that you, the part of you that judges, the part of you that dictates, is effect and not cause. It is fallible. It is born and it shall die. Go beyond that changing form. Go beyond the thoughts of your mind. And when you go beyond the thoughts of your mind, you will find that which is the true you. You will find the united whole which, in truth, you are.

Separate the thoughts that swim through your consciousness. Separate them from you. View them objectively, as part of creation. For they *are* a part of creation—your thoughts—and being a part thereof, they cannot bring you the peace and joy that you truly are seeking, for they are a dual aspect. They will lift you and let you fall, only to rise again and to fall again.

In the midst of this creation, be that which is truly you. That does not mean that you do not direct the divine energy for the accomplishment of good within your lives, but accept, for acceptance rises you above and beyond duality. It doesn't matter where you go, it doesn't matter what you do, for you are not that which you think you are. It is because you think you are that you are deluded by what you think you are. You are that which causes the thought. You are beyond the effect. Remember that, my good students.

Go above and beyond within your own consciousness and look at life, the dream. Look at it in the light and you will see that you have always been, are inseparably united with all, that you will always be. That so-called identity is a thought that you have attached your universal being to. That so-called individuality is an attitude of mind that you, in your errors of ignorance, have attached your true being to.

So much concern is placed, by the human mind, upon its individuality, upon its identity, upon its uniqueness. But you are not that uniqueness. You are not that identity. You are not that individuality, for you are not creation. You are the cause of creation, but you are not creation. You are moving through the thoughts that pass through your mind. You are moving through the attitudes, the feelings, and the emotions. But you are not those emotions. You are not those feelings. You are not that identity. It is fleeting and it is passing. And what it was yesterday, it will not be tomorrow.

Accept something greater than those passing thoughts, for they have run loose in your mind for so very long that they have tricked you into believing that *you* are them. And as you believeth, so you becometh. And to become identified is to lose your freedom, to lose your peace. Use these things. Do not be the victim of these things. Drive your car. Do not become it. Wear your suit of clothes. Do not become it. Use it, don't abuse it. It is through the Law of Abuse that you become attached and blinded and believe that you are those things.

You have the golden opportunity here and now to make the conscious effort to separate truth from creation, to move your true being from these thoughts and patterns. So many souls in many realms and planes of consciousness cry out in seeking, "Who am I? What am I?" When you, in your evolution, open your eyes in awareness to a greater light, you must lose the so-called identities that you have attached yourself to.

And as you evolve, you must lose what you call your individuality. Nothing and no one outside takes that from you. It is a process of evolution that is taking place within you. And as you, in your evolving, pass through these deceiving thoughts of identity and individuality, you will begin to enter the great void. And the first experience that you will encounter is the experience of loss, generated and created by fear. But as you travel on, that fear and that loss shall diminish. And as that loss diminishes, you will begin to view your eternal gain. You will no longer be torn by the duality of conflicting thoughts and feelings and emotions within you. You will know beyond a shadow of any doubt what you must do and you will do it. You will no longer be concerned with what others think, for thought no longer has you in control. You will rise with that quietude and with that faculty of reason above and beyond the discordant and disturbing notes of dual life. You will have united yourself in consciousness and become the whole, which is the oneness, which is the truth that frees you.

So, my good students, as you, in your distant evolution, begin to get these experiences of so-called loss, these fears concerning identity and individuality, remember, it was only your created brain that told you, you were special and unique. For you are no greater, and no lesser, than the sparrow or the ant, in truth. For that which is you is all. And that which is all is, in truth, you. Then you will be freed from the frustrations of unfulfilled desires. Then you will be freed from the dictates and the bombardment of the human mind.

Here, during your earth journey, you have earned, in your evolution, an understanding that *is*. An understanding that will always be. Though called by many names, you cannot change the simplicity and demonstrability of truth. You may have differing views of life, depending, of course, upon your attitude of life, but life itself you will not change. Your view frequently changes, but life does not change, for it is a principle, an essence of the Light itself. It is not created and, therefore, cannot be changed. It is the changeless, the formless, and the free.

Whatever your mind chooses to change, be rest assured, it is of mental substance, for the Law of Change is the Law of Evolution. And God is beyond evolution, for God the Divine is changeless and eternal.

Think, my students, think of this, the moment of your peace. Become receptive to that vibratory wave and listen, listen to the songs of harmony. Listen to the symphony of the eternal spheres. They are playing in the universe without ceasing. But you must first become receptive to the power which can help you to hear them. That is the power of peace. Use the power of peace more often. Man thinks and says many things in the course of a day. And those many things cause him many feelings, so-called good ones and so-called bad ones. It is better to think of peace, to knock at the door and experience heaven, for beyond the door of peace is heaven itself. It is right where you are, but you must first accept it.

If you permit your minds to dictate what it is, then you will establish an opposing law to your seeking it. Whenever you permit your mind to dictate, whenever you permit your mind to judge, you establish an opposition to that which you seek. And so it is on this, the first class of this semester, that we emphasize to you that you may remember frequently the laws opposing what you seek are created by your judgments, by your dictates. And those opposing laws have a greater strength than the laws of your seeking. The reason the Law of Opposition is stronger is because it is fed by human emotion. And that is a great force that leaves your magnetic field.

So remember, good friends, whatever you seek, place peace first. Place God in front of your desire. Never permit the mind and its judgment, its dictates, never permit it the supremacy over peace and over God. For if you do, life will become a living demonstration of failure and obstruction. Let the will of the Divine—the only will capable of bringing what you seek—let that will flow through your consciousness unobstructed. And the key to it flowing freely and unobstructed is total acceptance of each and every moment of your experiences in life. Accept their right of expression and accept your right of peace.

Good night.

MAY 5, 1977

CONSCIOUSNESS CLASS 141

Greetings, students. This evening we shall discuss, for a time, the wheel of experience created by the thought of I.

As man, this infinite, divine expression of intelligent energy, gathers around and about him a so-called identity of experience, he, in time, begins to believe that he is the experience that he is expressing through. Whereas this intelligent energy is designed to express itself and whereas this vehicle through which it is expressing is a dual vehicle, man believes and man doubts. And so this so-called wheel of experience continues to revolve until such time as the true being takes hold of the reins, so to speak, and begins the slow, but sure, process of rising in consciousness in order to still this mental vehicle.

Many different paths have been revealed to man that he may still this mind. And in our teachings, we have repeatedly stated the value, the importance, of peace. For as man makes the daily effort to flood his consciousness with peace, he rises from this level of dual thought and experiences the beauty and the harmony of neutrality. As long as we permit this vehicle to deceive us into believing that we are the mental vehicle, as long as we, from lack of effort, permit that, shall we be the victim of that level of consciousness. So often in the students' efforts they will spend a short time in flooding their consciousness, but the magnetic pull of the earth realm is yet stronger than the limited efforts that have been made.

The great value of this flooding of consciousness is to remove the true being from this dual law, for each thought that passes through the mental process carries with it this duality of expression. It is known as a house divided. Therefore, man, in his Earth experiences—and several yet to come—is, in truth, in a process of refinement and evolution. The process of this refinement is painful because we have yet to accept that there is something greater. Our beliefs are the effects of our experiences. And our experiences are the effects of our errors of ignorance. For he who knows the lighted path does not choose the darkened one. And so it is, my good students, as the centuries before us pass quickly, time, that great illusion, traps untold millions of souls. But in that process, we must also realize that it is a part of creation.

In many different ways have we spoken on the separation of truth and creation, of the soul faculties and the sense functions. Through an effort to bring about a balance with these functions, the faculties awaken, or more correctly stated, reawaken within us. When Earth life has nothing left to offer, we must be filled with the spirit of gratitude, for that which has, to our mind, nothing left to offer is guaranteed to pass.

And so it is in the passing of things are we in pain. It is never in the new experience. It is always in the passing of the old, for the new experiences in life bring temptation, and the sense functions are flooded with anticipation. But those that we have already experienced, we have already judged. And so their going is always painful.

So often we think that the passing of an experience is not painful, that we are so grateful to be rid of that experience. But it is painful in the sense of what you have done with the experience. For if you have not gained the lesson that was offered in the experience, it will repeat itself. For it leaves you in pain, to return in like kind, another day in another way, seemingly and ofttimes its form changed, but the essence of the lesson remains ever the same.

And so it is in these classes and in this understanding that we make the effort to awaken within our consciousness the true purpose of life itself. Everything that you permit to enter into your sphere of action comes to you as a child to be trained, to be disciplined, and to be awakened to that which, in truth, is sustaining it. For each experience within your consciousness is a birth. And that experience is a responsibility that you, and you alone, have incurred, in keeping with the infallible laws of the Divine.

And so on this wheel of experience, the effect of the thought of I, are you, in truth, the mothers and the fathers, bearing the personal responsibility to refine this child, called experience, to help it to grow and to mature and to awaken to that which is its true and only sustenance. We have spoken to you many times on a simple truth: to put God into it or to forget it. For that putting of God in it is your recognition and your acceptance that the experience—whatever it may appear to your mind—is sustained by the very intelligent energy that is sustaining your very life.

And so, my good students, as you in all of your daily endeavors continue to revolve on the wheel of experience, put this faculty of reason into each experience. Place the thought of goodness—no matter what the mind may dictate at the moment. View it for what it truly is: a child that you have called forth from the universe and that you, and you alone, are personally responsible for.

Do not try to orphan your children called experience. For if you continue to try to orphan them, they will grow, out in the jungle of creation, and they will return unto you someday as grown adults. And they will demand their just due. For you, and you alone, are their mothers and their fathers. Place this peace, which is the power of God, in each of your experiences, in each and every moment. Recognize in all of your thoughts and in all of your feelings that they are merely effects. They are children of mental substance. They are sustained by a divine Power, and that divine Power moves ever in keeping with your own judgments.

How does man become freed from this law called judgment? How can man be freed from this identity called creation? Only through your efforts, my good students. Only through your prayers that never cease, through your acceptance of this power called peace. For this wheel of experience upon which you are evolving and revolving has gone on for untold centuries. Now is the time to take hold of this wheel. Now is the time to accept your personal responsibilities for your experiences called life.

If you will make this simple effort to accept the goodness that is hidden within all of these experiences, if you will make the effort to accept that for you and your evolution the experiences have come to serve, for you, a good purpose—for I assure you, my friends, in everything that you encounter, there is good if you will look for it. There is good in all experience. There is good in everything. For all experience and everything is sustained by the power of God. It is our view of life. For in our viewing life we have become the object, instead of the objective. Let us return to our true purpose. Let us return to the objective in life eternal and let us no longer be viewed as the object, for we are more than all of these things. We are more than this great wheel of experience. We are more than the thought of I.

View life and the many changes that you have already made as evolving souls. Look at your days, your weeks, your months, and your years. See how many changes you have already made. Those changes did not pass through your consciousness graciously and harmoniously and peacefully. They passed through painfully. The pain being the deception of the mind, for in its identification, you believe that you are it. My good friends, in these many years and in these many words I can only say that the peace which is yours has never left you, for you are that peace. That which is your true being is inseparably a part of God. The only separation that you experience is when the mind is ruling supreme.

It is through your efforts of bowing the dictates of created substance, called the human mind, that you find your true being. Those moments are fleeting. And some have yet, on Earth, to have those experiences. But for you they will come. And they will increase as you make that effort to flood your consciousness with the power of God known as peace. Why look forward at centuries, working through the wheel of experiences, when you, your eternal being, have earned the opportunity of making the effort today?

So often in life man says, "Well, I will take care of that when it comes. I am interested in this today." But, my good students, as time passes in your realm, the things that you have put off, they are more difficult to face. And so the more that you push them into the so-called future—that you will take care of those things later—the more difficult it is for you to do. Whatever it is in experience in the wheel, face it in the moment. Recognize and accept your personal responsibility for the children that you insist upon creating. Accept it and then it shall pass and, yea, greater doors for you shall open.

But if you insist upon pushing those things aside—that your mind dictates you have more important things to do—then one day this wall created of responsibility, the weight shall be so great—but pray that it never be greater than your love of God. For it is only your love of God that will sustain you. It is only your love of God that will free you, that will bring you the joy and the love and the peace, the happiness that is truly yours.

To pray for things is to guarantee the continuity of experiences. Pray for peace, then all experiences will be a harmonious joy to your eternal soul.

So, my students, though ofttimes we repeat ourselves in these classes, it is that very Law of Repetition that is recording in your consciousness and bringing about the necessary changes in your own life. For although you cannot perhaps often see the changes that you have made, those changes are taking place each and every moment of your life. You no longer view life in exactly the same way that you did, for slowly, but surely, there is, in truth, an awakening.

My heart is often filled with compassion as I speak to students not only on the earth realm, but in my other classes, for I know the centuries that it has taken me. I also know that it is service to this Light, called God, that keeps me free in peace, that passes the understanding of any mind. For once having gained the smallest fraction of that peace, man cannot turn back. He must go ever onward, ever forward. You cannot, once awakening within your consciousness the divine eternal truth that you are an inseparable being of the whole—once having gained that experience—you cannot turn back on any soul or any life, for all life is your life.

It is this thought of I that has separated you from the life of the tree and the life of the animal and the life of all things, for all things live and breathe. There is nothing dead, for there is, in truth, nothing that is stagnant. Everything is in a process of change and therefore everything has life. For without life, without this energy, without this power, there would be no change: all things would be.

And so it is, my good students, awaken within you the life that is you. Go beyond this limited, small sphere of action. Go above and beyond it, that you may know who you truly are.

And so, these illusions of death and birth, these illusions of coming and going—when, in truth, you stand still in the eternal moment—these illusions are called the wheel of experience. You are with a greater responsibility than any form on your planet. You bear this responsibility and, having earned that great responsibility, you must account for all your thoughts and attitudes, acts and deeds. That accounting takes place beyond the control of the human mind.

Remember that this great divine Intelligence is not a judge. It is the mental throne that is the judge. That is what man must face. He must face his educated conscience; then he must face his spiritual conscience. But man leaves this earth realm and a physical body, and he lives in a mental sphere and plane of consciousness. There, he faces the judge that he alone has created.

And so, when it was stated long ago to judge not least ye be judged, we guarantee the judgment from life, for we insist upon judging life. And he who judges shall be judged. He who becomes the vehicle of God's infinite peace shall become the peace. He who seeks the good shall experience the good. And he who finds the goodness in all things shall become the goodness of all things.

So often we have spoken on the great self-control—the control of the mind—its effect being our own freedom. It is the mental world that is our greatest difficulty. It is the mental world that is our greatest struggle. For it is the mental world that is the throne supreme of the functions and the senses of your earthly form. And so, my students, through your efforts each day to go above and beyond the mental sphere, there is your heaven. There is where life truly is worthwhile. There is where honesty reigns supreme. There is where the home of your soul is truly a fulfillment of the purpose of life.

To think or entertain the possibility that it is not for you until you pass through the gates of so-called physical death is a delusion created by the mind in order to keep you where you are in consciousness. I assure you that the process called change takes place in the very moment that you are ready. It takes place in what you call death, for you are dying each moment to something in a mental world, and you are being born each moment to something in a mental world. It is the effort that is needed to be made to go beyond this mental world, to go beyond it, where you can be at home; to no longer rely upon what creation has to offer; to use it and not abuse it; to know that it is not, in truth, your home; to know beyond the shadow of any doubt that you are a visitor on that earthly planet, that your visit may end in the moment or the year, for it is numbered and it is timed by a divine plan and a divine law. And so we follow this plan and this law for we are the followers of the Light. Our light brightens as we brighten. Our life is fulfilled as we fulfill it.

My students, I beseech you to make that effort now: to make that effort to see, to see clearly why you are here in the world that you are. That in seeing here today, you will not stumble along the path tomorrow.

As we progress in this semester, we shall speak a bit upon some of these realms and the varied experiences that await those who come over from your earthly realm, for they vary as the stars in the heavens are varied. But remember, you are the inseparable whole. It is only your thought of I that blinds you from the cosmic consciousness, which is the true you. Remove the thought of I and flow in the beauty, the harmony, and the goodness of all of life.

So often have we spoken on fear, the negative expression of faith. And so we find that man on Earth fears frequently, for man on Earth has much to defend. And so each time a pattern—an attitude of mind that we refuse to surrender to the Divine—each time that it senses a threat to its continuity, fear rises as its defense.

But truth needs no defense. Truth *is*. Therefore man, in truth, has nothing to fear. It is man in falsehood and complexity, that is the man who has much to fear, for that is the man who has much to defend. Defend not and ye shall not be moved from the rock of principle that is the eternal truth. Speak the truth, for when you speak the truth fear does not exist. It is when you speak from mental levels of creation that fear exists. It is when you speak from mental levels of creation that denial exists. But when you speak from your heart, the vehicle of your eternal soul, there is no fear, for there is no falsity; there is only humbleness and truth. And then you shall touch the hem of the garment known as the universality of consciousness.

You may ask your questions at this time.

Thank you. Please explain to us why we feel the Earth has such seemingly destructive and non-productive forms such as ticks, leeches, fleas, and the like.

All forms upon your planet serve, in truth, a good, productive, and useful purpose. And in speaking of those insects known as fleas, try to disassociate yourselves from the proud thought of I and think and feel for a moment how lost the dog would be without his flea. What would he do but lay and sleep and sleep and sleep. Oh no, the flea serves a beautiful purpose for the animal: it keeps it active and entertained.

And so do all these other so-called "non-productive" insects. My good students, take a look at the bee. It looks at you. It sees you and could ask the same question. "Of what value are those forms? They make no honey. They spend their time in ofttimes destruction and disaster, chasing seemingly strange and non-productive things. What do they do to keep the flower in bloom and reproducing? They do nothing."

And so, you see, it is our throne of judgment that views the rest of life, which, in truth, we are a part, as non-productive. Think, my good students, of such a question. Think that we and our mind should rise so supreme over the infinite divine eternal Intelligence that sustains all life—that *is* all life—that we must question the wisdom of the divine Architect that sustains the humble flea.

Thank you. May we please have your understanding concerning the principle of marriage?

For those who have merited the experience called marriage have earned a principle of great responsibility: a responsibility to make great effort to control their personal thoughts and desires, to place each feeling and attitude under the light of reason and consideration, for they have merited a rapport on a very personal basis with another human being. And so, in marriage, without God, without the thought and the acceptance of God, there is no principle to marriage. For one of the very first things that takes place within the human consciousness in marriage is to make their partner their god, therefore creating a false god. And he whoever creates a false god has denied the principle of truth.

And so it is, in marriage, if each one ever remembers that they are an evolving individualized soul, that they are willing, in their relationship, to consider the thoughts and the feelings of their partner, to make the daily effort to understand the evolution of themselves—for without making the effort to understand their own evolution, they cannot qualify themselves to understand the evolution of another. And to make great effort, great effort never to permit another soul to rely upon them, for in that reliance is the denial of the true God that is their sustenance. And so, so very often the principle does not exist in marriage.

Thank you. It can be observed, while playing the Serenity Game, as in life, that some people play competitively and others do not. Is being competitive a desirable or an undesirable trait?

It depends, for that which seems desirable could be undesirable. If the spirit of competition is instrumental in rising the soul faculty of enthusiasm, then it can be—the spirit of competition—most desirable. It can, however—the spirit of competition—rise to a level of personal self-interest and become an emotional disaster.

Thank you. Is there a relationship between aspiration and determination?

Is there a relationship between the soul faculties of aspiration and determination? My good students, we aspire to many things, but without determination we are found wanting for the fulfillment of our own aspirations. Determination is a necessary instrument in bringing about encouragement, in bringing the necessary strength from within our being to carry on, regardless of other levels of consciousness that keep gnawing at us to go astray. On the path of spiritual evolution there are many things that will distract us. And so, without determination to do what is right because it is right to do right, man falls frequently by the wayside. Determination serves us well when it is under the light of reason. And so, this determination, expressed through the beauty and the clarity of the faculty of reason, moves us ever onward and ever upward to our eternal goal.

And before we conclude our class this evening, I should like to spend a few moments in encouraging you to make that effort each day on flooding your consciousness with peace. Do it again and again and again. My good students, there is never a moment that your mind is not filled with thought. In the stilling of the mind is the rising in consciousness. As man's experiences are the effects of what his mind is receiving and giving forth and whereas man, in his present evolution, is not fully aware of the untold millions of thoughts passing through his mind, but is personally responsible for them, it behooves you to flood your consciousness with peace, that your continued experiences may be the joy and harmony that you desire.

Good night.

MAY 12, 1977

CONSCIOUSNESS CLASS 142

Good evening, students. This time, we shall discuss our journey in time.

Some time ago we spoke to you about the Earth planet being the fifth planet in your solar system. And so it is in your journey that you have earned being at this time on the earth realm. Upon that planet you stand in evolution at the crossroads. At the crossroads, so to speak, in the awakening consciously of the bodies that you do, in truth—and are—inhabiting. So many upon your planet have the firm belief in the dense or physical body being their true and only life. And so it is that the awakening opportunity you have earned—to realize beyond a shadow of any doubt that these finer bodies of which you, slowly but surely, are becoming aware, such as your mental body, are the true vehicles that are bringing about the experiences and creating for you your own lessons in life.

As you continue on with your journey, you will become more keenly aware of your mental body, more alert to the power of your thought, more awakened to the forms and the effects that you personally, though through errors, ofttimes, of ignorance, are creating and continue to create. And so it is that the effort that you are making is, in truth, awakening your consciousness to these other bodies that you are, in truth, so very active in.

The control of thought is the discipline and the lesson that all of Earth is offering to you, in keeping with this system of slow, but sure, evolvement. From the denser realms of experience, you have already evolved to the earth realm. And you will continue upon this cycle, this circle of creation, to move.

So often the question is asked, "Why must we rise in evolution, only to once again descend?" It is through this process and natural law that the forms of the planets are refined and evolved. Each time that you ascend into the more refined vibratory waves in creation, you are strengthened in those vibrations. And as you are strengthened, you are guaranteed, in keeping with the natural Law of Duality, to descend. And it is in your acceptance of this natural law that you are freed, through a control of your mind, which grants unto you an objectivity that, in time, you will truly become the witness of things passing by.

For it is your duty in evolution to be the witness and the demonstration; to be a teacher, not a preacher; to be a servant, not a slave. And so it is that as you permit this natural refining process to take place, you shall graciously move harmoniously and peacefully on your journey in time. For it is your acceptance of these natural, infallible laws of life, it is your acceptance of them that permits you to live in peace with them.

Do not continue to struggle against the natural, divine law, for you cannot change law that is. You can, and are, changing the created laws of mental substance. But the law that sustains it, you cannot change. You can, through your efforts, learn how those infallible laws work and, once learning how they work, accept the demonstration that is. And in that shall you live a life more joyous, more happy, and more peaceful than you have yet known.

In these centuries of untold passing experiences, I personally have tried untold thousands of times to stem the tide of experiences that I had encountered. But in time, my good students, you rise to levels of consciousness where you accept the beauty and the clarity, the infallibility and the perfect balance of divine law. And once having reached that state of evolution—and in some areas many of you have touched that realm—there is where you find your purpose of life. There is where you see clearly that many, many years you have already experienced; you have risen and fallen, only to rise again and again and again. And each time you rise and each time that you stumble and fall, you become stronger. There is greater acceptance of something beyond the limited mind. There is a greater joy that rises within the depths of your own heart.

In that process of evolution, you must be alert and on guard not to resign to a so-called destiny that has no enthusiasm, no care, and no consideration, for that is not what we are speaking of. For that type of thinking is a level of surrender to what you call, in your world, "What's the use? I am a failure." That is a mental level of consciousness. As the throne of judgment of the human mind faces the infallibility of divine law, it bows begrudgingly. It experiences the fullness of self-pity. It experiences the fullness of sadness, because that level does not understand that every loss, in truth, is a gain and that every gain, in truth, is a loss.

And so it is your perspective of this flux and flow, of this loss and gain—it is through your faculty of reason that you will view it in its true light: as natural flux and flow and what creation has to offer.

Often we have spoken on the separation of truth and creation. And it is in truth that you really live. This other that you experience will always be a high and low. It will always be that, for it is the illusion of mental substance. And in this, our understanding of a divine principle called God, of a neutrality that is the peace that passeth the understanding of all men, that you find your true home. Your true home is in consciousness. You may experience it this moment or you may establish laws and experience it in centuries yet to be.

The purpose of these classes is to help you, who are seeking, to awaken within your consciousness in this, the eternal moment of now, to awaken to the home of your soul. For there is no divine law that dictates you must wait for centuries yet to pass. There is no divine law that states you cannot experience it now. In these efforts to still the mind, you will have the opportunity, in those moments, to experience the true home of your soul. But in so doing, you must never forget that your soul has, in its own merit, earned the right to return to creation. To return with that awakening that you may, by your own demonstration, separate truth from this dual experience, from the mental contradictions that are the very sustenance of mental life.

My good students, though many words are spoken from our realms, each word is intended to serve the purpose for which it has been designed. And so often we speak to you on many different levels of consciousness, for you are moving in consciousness through so many different levels. So when you experience your disasters and struggles, remember, in the experiencing, that it is not you. It is not you until you permit the delusion of the thought of I. It is in that level of consciousness that the experience becomes a part of you, for you then become a part of it.

And so we must speak, in this separation of truth from creation, on the Law of Personal Responsibility: the ability to respond to each and every law that man creates. For man, and man alone, *is* the creator. Man is the creator of mental worlds of consciousness. God is the sustainer of all those worlds, but man, indeed, is the creator. And so it is that we gave to you, some time ago, that great truth, as you feel this great weight: that the weight of responsibility must never exceed the love of God. For man often feels and experiences a heavy weight upon his shoulders, a heavy weight: the weight of effects of the laws that he alone has established in a mental world. Each time you make a judgment, each time you dictate in that mental dimension, you have an effect, not only upon yourself, but to everything and everyone with whom a rapport has been established.

All vehicles of expression upon your planet have what is known as a mental vehicle, or body, of expression. The human, the plant, the mineral kingdom, all those kingdoms have mental bodies. And so when the thoughts in your mental body, in your mind, are discordant, unhappy, then all mental bodies have a reaction to negative, discordant thought. And so, my good students, it returns unto you in like kind. Therefore, in facing your responsibilities in life, never forget that God alone, the neutral principle of Life herself, is at the helm and can bring a healing balm over any and all disturbance in your life.

The thoughts of men, it has been known for eons of time, affect the weather of the planets. It has an effect upon all of life, for all of life is expressing through these mental bodies. And when you are entertaining your sadness and your grief, when you are entertaining your disappointments and discouragements, remember, in those moments, what you are doing is affecting the whole. And because you are affecting the whole, the whole, in turn, will, and does, affect you.

It behooves all souls to flood their consciousness with the acceptance of divine principle, for in the flooding of your consciousness with the acceptance of divine principle, divine principle being perfect harmony, you become an instrument through which a perfect balance, a perfect harmony, flows unobstructed through you and into the universe. And you, as the instrument for that divine principle, are healed and uplifted and truly move in what is known as the divine flow of God. But you cannot move in that perfect principle and harmony as long as you permit the human mind to dictate, to judge, to believe, or disbelieve.

It is our purpose in the many classes that have been given—and will continue to be given—to reveal to you the home of your soul, to reveal to you a better way, through the effort of upliftment of your consciousness, to something that is worthwhile, to something that is reliable, to something that is the sustenance of your life and, being the very source and sustenance of your life, is, in truth, the only thing worth relying upon.

And so, my good students, when you find your mental universes so active, so flooded with fear, remember there is a way. And it is totally dependent upon your personal acceptance in each and every level of consciousness.

So often man experiences, in his prayers to this divine principle called God—he prays for so many things and then becomes discouraged, dissatisfied, and loses faith because the divine law, he states and judges, is not responding to his pleas and to his dictates. What man, in that level of consciousness, fails to see is that the divine law *is* responding. It is responding to your plea, to your request, to your prayer, or whatever you care to call it. The law is responding. What you fail to see is that in the responding, the mountain of transgressions that you have created are being removed in keeping with the law established. And so man in his prayer, in his efforts, not having the wisdom of patience, is deceived by the slow, but sure, process of removal of the obstructions that he has created.

My good students, it takes discord and dissension in the mind to create obstructions. And dissension and discord in the mind is a painful process. Therefore, in order to remove the obstructions created, it is a painful process of removal. And so it is that patience is, to the mind, painful, because the mind is reliant upon a mental world. And it is a most unreliable dimension. Think of the many experiences you have had with the minds of men. I am sure that you will agree, it has been most unreliable: that the thoughts of men change so frequently, for that is what the mental world has to offer.

And so, my good friends, we continue to move on and on and on and on. We are doing that in this moment. Do not concern yourselves about what is yet to be. Be interested in what is, for in being interested in what is, what is yet to be shall be, indeed, in keeping with the motive that you are establishing. Yesterday's motivations, reaping their harvest today, have come and shall pass. But you have this moment to bring about a more fruitful harvest in your life.

And so, you are never left void, nor are you left alone, for you cannot separate that which is a united whole. And it is a united whole that *is* your life. Your mind sees the variety of creation, but your soul views the oneness of truth. And it is in these years that we serve that oneness, that you may awaken, while yet on your earthly journey, to the oneness which is the true home of your real being.

You may ask your questions at this time.

Thank you. Can you please tell us what the pancreas represents and how does pancreatic cancer relate to that?

At this time, we will speak upon cancer, as we have many times before. It is the effect of negativity. And they are negative cells—discordant to the harmony of the body, created by the attitudes deep within the consciousness of man. And it is an acceptance of peace, an acceptance of harmony, that will bring about the healing balm. At some time in your future, we shall discuss the pancreas and its spiritual meaning.

Thank you. Although one may accept that a desire will be fulfilled in God's way and in God's time, it is my understanding that many obstructions could be standing in the way that must be removed before fulfillment comes to pass. Would you please clarify this?

We have spoken upon these obstructions to one's desires many times and in many different ways. Man desires many things. He moves on in consciousness forgetting his desires ofttimes of yesterday and entertaining constantly new desires. And in man's desiring, he creates obstructions, for the desires are not united in purpose and in motivation. For example, one day man desires to live in a certain area and the time passes for him and he does not move. And then he creates another desire and desires to live someplace else. And these desires come together in a mental world and they battle each other for their fulfillment, for their supremacy. And so man, being the creator, has become a house divided.

If man would view the principle of desire and take control of the desire, if man would view, when he desires a home or a shelter, a willingness to accept what he has earned and, knowing that the divine law knows what he has earned, and accept that, be it a crumb or a mansion, and not deny, by thoughts of envy and jealousy and greed, what another soul has earned in their evolution—There are so many different laws of contradiction involved in man's desires that create these mountains of obstruction. It is also the impatience of man's desires. For example, man desires a home, but he does not desire to wait whatever years it may take for him to have the home in keeping with the laws established. And so man moves from here to there to there to there, never satisfied. It's never enough, for it was not enough in the desire itself.

And so it is with the nature of desire as it passes through the human mind. It does not pass through with the balance of the soul faculties. Now, desire is the divine expression: the expression of God. But in the entertaining of desire, as it passes through your mind and you do not make the effort to bring about the corresponding soul faculties to put it into balance, which is reason, then you create these multitudes of obstructions.

The divine expression known as desire, flowing through the functions of the human mind, not accompanied by the soul faculties, brings about disasters and mountains of obstruction. Now, a student may ask, "Then what are the functions?" The functions, when not balanced with the soul faculties, clearly state: *m-e-s*—mes: money, ego, and sex. Now, money, ego, and sex are not something negative, nor destructive, when they are balanced with the soul faculties. And the soul faculties clearly given to you are faith, poise, and humility. If, in your desires, you make the effort to place the soul faculties corresponding to the sense functions, directing the divine energy equally through the faculties and the functions in the very moment of the thought, then wisdom, flowing through the faculty of patience, will bring you the fullness, the beauty, and the joy of life itself.

But so often with the human being, the divine expression flowing through the mind becomes a judgment, a dictate. It does not have any faculties accompanied with it. It has nothing but a driving force. You see, my good students, the functions are force, the creative principle of nature. The faculties are power, the divine harmonious law of life. And so, when you, through your own awakening and through your own efforts, place the proper faculty with each function bringing about the divine balance in a dual world, God will move the mountain. For God will move the mountain through that perfect balance.

You see, my students, we understand God to be a divine principle of total neutrality. And the positive and negative, the power and the force, must be brought into a perfect balance. When that is accomplished, then you and God become a majority. When you bring about this, what is called 51 percent within your consciousness, God moves any mountain that your mind is capable of creating.

Good night.

MAY 19, 1977

CONSCIOUSNESS CLASS 143 ✤

Greetings, students. At this time, we wish to discuss with you the process of freeing the self from the various thought patterns that have bound the soul to the repetitive experiences that have proven to be not so beneficial to oneself.

Many words have been given on the human mind, the vehicle through which the soul, in its journey, is expressing. And at this time, we shall discuss how these thought patterns not only dissipate the divine energy, but stand as the obstructions to the unfoldment and the fullness of one's life.

Because the nature of mental substance is, in truth, an electromagnetic vibratory wave upon which the eternal soul, once having identified with that vibratory wave, must move in consciousness upon what is known as the stream of life, it behooves man to become aware of the process that takes place in his identification, in order that he may move onward through this magnetic-electric field into a divine neutrality of consciousness, where the stream of life will pass. And he will, once again, become the observer instead of the observed.

As we permit thought to pass through the human mind, we identify in the passing of that thought. And each and every thought that is passing through the mind is reaffirming and re-establishing certain attitudes, feelings, and emotions that were initially identified with in our paths of evolution. All of the experiences that are encountered in your earthly life are the repetitive effects of this identification process in your evolutionary path.

When the awakening takes place within your mind—of what is truly going on—you will make this pause to think in such a way as to guide yourself, slowly but surely and gently from the vibratory wave that is, in truth, utilizing the very energy passing through your being in order to reaffirm and solidify the vibration. In keeping with this process, man, being the instrument of this energy, dissipates, in time, the necessary energies for his own good health, his own prosperity, his own fullness of life itself.

Many, many teachings have been given to mankind in order to awaken him that he may make the continued effort demonstrating the Law of Continuity, for it is the Law of Continuity, used in those vibratory waves, that has him, so to speak, trapped and victimized. Through a constant effort, through a flooding of the consciousness with the power of the universe known as peace, through this constant process, man establishes a new law in this vibratory wave and rises in his own consciousness where harmony, the healing power of the universe, manifests itself in his own life.

It is sometimes seemingly difficult for man to realize that he is, in truth, a sphere of energy, that this energy is in a constant revolving process, that, as this revolving process takes place, moving in a clockwise position consciously, moving in a counterclockwise position subconsciously, creating a friction which is, in truth, his experiences and his reality. It is the friction that man in his mind is aware of. This friction, known as the Law of Duality, known as the Law of Creation, is this cloud of illusion upon which man insists upon moving.

It is the purpose of this philosophy to help you to view objectively these energies which, in truth, you are. Because of this creating process, because of this constant visualization that is taking place within the human mind, and because of a lack of effort upon the individual's part to become aware, man believes that he is the form. And as man believes in this illusion, he becomes this illusion. As man believes the thought that passes through his mind, the belief is the attachment. And so it is that man, slowly but surely, shall learn that he is not his belief; that he is that which is the cause of his belief; that he is not the attitudes of mind, but he is the cause of the attitudes of mind; that he, in truth, is not his thought, that he, in truth, is not his feeling, that he, in truth, *is*. This *is*, and because it *is*, man is free.

And so, my good students, as you make the constant daily effort, the moment-by-moment effort, to flood your consciousness with peace, that will establish the necessary law through which you may free yourself from the constant bombardments of thoughts that flood up from the so-called levels of the subconscious.

Friction is the law through which the soul must evolve. Man cannot escape the path and journey of life through creation. He cannot escape it, but he can, and does—for the law is inevitable—grow through it.

And so it is for every positive thrust forward in evolution, there is an equal pull backward. And through that, man, in time, shall clearly see that peace, that eternity that, in truth, he is, views, as an observer, the passing of all form, the passing of all things, the passing of all thoughts, the passing of all emotions. This awakening, this great peace is beyond the understanding of mental substance. The mind can only grant what the mind is capable of granting. And the mind is a dual vehicle of expression. When you flood your consciousness with the power of peace, you become that peace. When each thought that passes through your mind is cleansed with this power of peace, then you'll become freed from this Law of Friction and evolve to higher realms of consciousness in the here and the now.

It behooves you to make that effort, for the effort made in your moment of what you call today wipes away the centuries that wait before you. So many times students will entertain the thought of "what's the use," will entertain the thought "there must be something better." My good students, the "something better" in life is the awakening that what is better is also worse, as long as you view it from the perspective of a mental realm. For it is the nature of mental substance to be contrary unto itself in order to create the friction which is necessary for life's experiences.

Remember that experience is not life. Experience is the effect of man's view of the Law of Life. And man's view of life is not only constantly changing and very limited, but it lacks the faculty of reason, for it lacks objectivity. It lacks being the observer, for the mind views life from its own realm in its own dimension. And so it views it, always, in dual aspect.

It is in keeping with the efforts that you have already made that you begin to view the benefit of this power known as peace. For those of you who are ready, for those of you who have entered at the door of acceptance, will use this flooding of consciousness and reap the harvest which is beyond mental consideration.

When we have had enough, we will pause to rest. And it is the rest where we free ourselves from so-called life's experiences. And it is a very important factor in evolution, for all life, in truth, pauses periodically to rest and to rejuvenate to revitalize the form through which this energy is passing through. In order to understand this phase of evolution, you will have to give much. You will have to give the cherished opinions, thoughts, and attitudes. You will have to give your dictates and your judgments to the realms and to the rulers of those realms from whence you first, through the Law of Identity, received them. For though, to the mind, they seem to be gifts, they were only loans by the rulers of those realms. And because you have borrowed much from those rulers of those realms, your payments have already been much.

And it is our purpose to share with you a freeing from those rulers of those realms, known, by many philosophies, as the false gods of creation that must, in time, be dethroned. They are not dethroned easily. You have received the illusion of their gifts in errors of ignorance, as you pass through those realms of consciousness. But an error of ignorance is no escape from divine, impartial law. We stated many times in these classes that your greatest gift to life is the gift of self. For it is the self that has added unto itself these so-called gifts which have now become burdens and obstructions in your own evolution.

When you leave the physical body, you become, then, aware, if not before, of your debts to the rulers of these dimensions. Some of you are already aware of these debts. Some of you are already aware of your payments. All of you will be aware in so-called time. As you leave the physical body and you travel on in consciousness in your mental body, there, in those dimensions, will the payment be demanded. Ever in keeping with the energy that you have directed through what is known as thought patterns, judgments and dictates, the dues from you are extracted. This process is already taking place. It has been taking place long before you entered your earth realm. And it will continue to take place until you free yourself, through the power of peace, the flooding of consciousness, which rises your eternal being.

My good students, for each thing that you seemingly receive in life carries a price tag with it. The price tag is not often viewed in the moment that you receive it, but the price is ever extracted from you. Until such time as your faith rises supreme and receives all from the divine, humble Light itself shall you continue to pay the rulers of those realms.

It takes more than the thought of the human mind to accept from what is called God. But it is in your recognition and acceptance of the true source of that eternal Light, through your acceptance of that true source and through the peace that floods over your consciousness, do you free yourself in time. As man, in that state of mind, as man, in that peace and serenity within his being, moves along the river of life, he knows where he is and where he is going. No longer shall he pay the rulers of dual created laws, for he has awakened to the purpose that they serve.

As you entered your earthly bodies, you were fully aware of what lay before you. And that awareness is still with you, but it is deeply hidden by the rulers of mental substance. But truth crushed to Earth shall rise again. And so that light within you, slowly but surely, is burning brighter. And as that light continues to brighten, you will feel the pangs and pain of mental experience. For it must—and it knows it must—let go of the control that it has upon you.

You cannot change the mind by working with the mind. The change takes place in your heart. And it is your heart, the vehicle of your eternal soul, that lifts your soul above and beyond those mental and astral dimensions. It is through your heart that you are healed. It is never through your head. It is through your heart that you are freed. It is never through your head. And so it is that I speak to your heart. There, you feel the gentle breezes of truth that whisper within your consciousness. There, you know and do not have to be told what is right and what is wrong. There, my good students, *is* your joy and your eternity.

Do not be discouraged in the beginning years of your efforts to unfold and awaken. Do not view the stepping stones of unfoldment as the final plateaus of eternal life. Do not view experiences as you. View them for what they truly are: an expression that comes and, in time, shall go—no matter what we may decide. View life in the beauty and the joy that is truly there. Do not continue to choose to suffer, when, through a microscopic effort, you may be free. The law is the Law of Continuity. Use the law to rise up. You are already using the law to remain where you are. It is the same law, just redirected, upward, not outward.

You see, my students, it is the outward direction—the horizontal and parallel law—that binds you to the wheel of experience. It is the outward Law of Continuity that keeps you upon the wheel. It is the upward Law of Continuity that helps you to view and to rise to the paradise that is your true home.

When you entertain a thought, it moves on a horizontal line out into an atmosphere of vibratory waves. It is an energy and it calls forth all similar energies in the universes. When you take that same thought and you direct it upward into a vertical path, it returns unto the divine Source and, there, is harmonized for your greater good by an intelligence that sustains all.

Man lifts his thought by placing Peace, God, the Intelligence of the whole, in it. In his effort to place Peace, God, the Intelligence, in thought, that thought then moves upon a vertical line from his energy field, is harmonized, neutralized, and uplifts his life. One is known as the divine will; the other, the horizontal path, the wheel of experience, as his self-will or the will of his limited mind.

We shall speak more on the parallel laws of life and the vertical laws of life at another class.

Good night.

MAY 26, 1977

CONSCIOUSNESS CLASS 144

Greetings, students. We shall continue on with our discussion of the rulers of the realms.

Man, in releasing energy, divine energy, through the vehicle known as thought, has created, in eons past, an image known as the image of judgment. As the centuries have passed in those mental dimensions, these rulers, known as the rulers of judgment, are sustained and fed the divine energy through this vehicle of the mind known as thought. As man in his mental dictates releases this energy along the horizontal paths of life, these rulers get ever more demanding from those who feed and sustain them with this divine and neutral energy. And so it is that man, in time, becomes, slowly but surely, aware of a thought bombarding his consciousness repeatedly demanding its so-called fulfillment. This is, in truth, the only bondage that man, in his evolution, will ever know.

We spoke in our last class about directing this energy through the vehicle of thought upward, in order that it may be released and return to the divine Source and, therefore, free you from this bondage and this slavery that has been established in mental realms through error of ignorance. As you continue on along the spiritual path of awakening, you will become more and more aware of this process, of these pounding thoughts and demands upon you.

The greatest illusion known to man is the illusion known in your world as time. This illusion is part of the mental deception created by the minds of men. We have spoken to you before about the eternal moment and also about the power of eternity that is in the moment of your awareness. In your daily efforts of mental activity, remember, in order that you may free yourself from what your mind calls mental attitudes and patterns—which are, in truth, the line that binds you to the rulers of the realms.

Now, the question may well arise, "Is this created entity within my head or is this created entity in a realm of its own?" The realm of those rulers is everywhere in the mental world. For example, desire, known as the divine expression, when released upon the upward path, becomes the very instrument, on the horizontal path, to bind man to the slavery and the bondage of the rulers of the realms. Anything that robs man of his peace and his happiness, anything that has been given that much power by man, becomes the false god of man. And the false gods of man are the rulers of the mental realms.

We have often spoken of the strength that you have in your physical bodies, for your physical bodies are offering to you, on your planet, a density that you will not have once you leave those bodies. As it is in your present evolution to most of you upon Earth, you do not see the thoughts that are entertained in your mind. You have some awareness of some of them. You have some feeling accompanying some of your thoughts. But you do not see the ruler that is in charge of that thought. You do not see his realms. When you leave your physical bodies, your mental bodies carry you along the evolutionary path. And your mental bodies see clearly what is in, and has always been in, those mental realms.

Most of you are aware, at times, of the great difficulties that you have in being freed from a certain thought; that once it begins to plague your mind, the great difficulty in thinking of something else. That great difficulty is a revelation unto your eternal soul of how much control those mental rulers have over you. Because, in your evolution, you have earned the exposure and the discussion of these rulers, it behooves you to make a greater effort so that you may be the instruments of peace; that you may be qualified in your strength and your courage to help those who are not yet aware of what is really taking place in these many realms of consciousness.

Much has been discussed on concentration, the key to all power. All men concentrate. All men, in truth, meditate. It is the direction that is the difference. Anytime that man places his attention pointedly and fixedly upon the object of his choice until only the essence remains, man has concentrated. And no student within the sound of my voice can say that they have not, more than once, placed their mind pointedly and fixedly upon the object of their choice.

My good students, awaken in this the moment which is rightfully yours. Awaken to the truth that lies within you. And question, Why does a thought, that which you have formed, have so much power over you? The law states clearly that man is a law unto himself and that law, that man is, is used or it is abused. We often abuse the greatest gift we'll ever know: It's known as the gift of life. The gift, so-called, of life is an eternal movement, moving through a multitude of forms.

So often we ask for a spiritual awakening, but a spiritual awakening, a spiritual awakening is an effect. It is an effect of mental control. Mental control is a process of freeing the eternal soul from the victimization of the false gods known as the rulers of the realms. So seek ye first the control of self, for your greatest gift to God is the gift of self. But you cannot give what you do not control. And you cannot control what you refuse to be aware of. And so, my students, become aware of thoughts, become aware of their rulers. Then you can gradually, slowly but surely, begin to control your thoughts, the thoughts which you, the self, are entertaining. And once gaining the control of self, of your thoughts, give them—your greatest gift—to God.

You may practice a most constructive exercise. It has been given to you before in other ways, but we [have] yet [to] find a student upon your planet who is making that moment-by-moment effort to practice that exercise. We gave it to you in very simple words. And it stated, "Put God in it or forget it." Think of the untold thousands of thoughts passing through your mind in the course of one of your earthly days. How many times do you put God in the thought? The placing of God in the thought of the minds of men is releasing the thought to an Intelligence, called God, who knows what to do with the thought and does not have to be told by the rulers of the realms what to do with the thought.

Whatever it is that you desire, you establish the laws to become. But unless that desire is directed upon the vertical path to return directly, uncontaminated and unpolluted, to the Source, then you must pay the price that is to be extracted from you by the rulers of the realms.

To God, the divine Intelligence, all things are possible. And when you, your eternal being, is in God, all things are possible. The only obstruction between man and God is the mental thoughts of men, for they refuse to give them. The reason that man refuses to give the thoughts he entertains wholly and completely to God is because, in this veil of illusion, created by the rulers of the realms of mental substance, they have convinced man that he is the thought he entertains.

This is the great illusion. And it is supported and sustained by the illusion known as time. To he who is patient, all things shall come. Man has no patience until he frees himself from the illusion of time. As man continues to believe he is the thought he entertains, he continues to support the rulers and pays the price. You are not the thought. You *are* the idea. And remember, as we have stated before: The universe is the law's meditation and man is an idea of it. As man and the law is ever one, so man, his true destiny, is the awakening of so-called cosmic consciousness.

That awakening, slowly but surely, is taking place. And you, as students, would be much more aware of it if you would only demonstrate the separation of truth from creation. Look at your lives in review. And if you still believe that you are the thoughts you entertain, see how many times you have changed. Where is stability? Where is reliability, if you continue to permit your minds to dictate that you are the thought?

In the continuing of these classes and the expansion process of this philosophy, designed to awaken your consciousness, designed to expand that you may live the universality which, in truth, you are. Often we speak on God's will. Often we speak on the infinite variety and demonstration of God's will, called, in this philosophy, total acceptance. Accept the right of a thought. Accept your right to direct it upward to the Source. Accept an Intelligence that sustains your mind. Accept an Intelligence, an Energy, that sustains your very being. Accept the wisdom of that Intelligence and you will be freed from the control of so-called false gods.

My good students, though these teachings are often difficult for the students to understand, the difficulty is in the letting go of the cherished opinions, for the simplicity of truth represents a threat to these patterns of mind, to these rulers within and without. It is the very nature of form to preserve itself. But all of nature teaches us that form is destined to change; that form is born, only to die; that form is to rise, only to fall. Now, the thought of man is form. It rises and it falls.

So, you see, my students, you are not the thought. You are not the form, for you are changeless and free. Your changeless free spirit—its purpose of incarnation is to educate the forms. We have often taught that the human ego must never be annihilated. It is designed to serve a very good purpose as a vehicle through which the eternal soul may express itself. Our teaching is to educate it. Educate your thoughts. Educate your forms, whatever they may be. And the education of form or thought is done by becoming the observer, not the observed; by being a true witness of time, the illusion, passing on.

And once again we speak to you in reference to the witness. Think more deeply on these words that are again given to you [*The Living Light* and in *The Living Light Dialogue,* Volume 1]:

> I'm only a witness of time passing on,
> A witness of things that have come and gone.
> Never the jury or judge shall I be,
> For I am the witness, the life, and the tree.

My good students, you are formless, but you are form. For without form through which your formless free spirit may express, there is no knowingness in mental substance. And it is your personal duty and responsibility to educate the vehicles through which your soul, your free spirit, is now expressing.

Think of your day-to-day world. You waste no time in educating your automobile. You drive it where you choose to drive it. You park it where you choose to park it. You fill it with fuel when you choose to do so. And so, in truth, it serves you well, as you educate it and care for it. The clothes on your back—also forms of creation—are educated in the sense of how you care for them. It is your duty to educate the forms of creation of mental substance. It is your duty, for you have evolved, your eternal being, to a point in consciousness of self-awareness. And because you have evolved to that point in universal consciousness, your responsibilities and duties weigh heavily upon you. But they must never exceed your love of God. For if ever responsibility weighs heavier than your love of God, then you have forgotten God and you have taken unto yourself that which is not yours to take.

Whenever man, in mental dictate, holds to thought and releases not to the source that sustains it, he has taken what is not rightfully his and shall pay his just dues. For the rulers of created substance shall extract those just dues, impartially and in keeping with divine law. And so, my good students, you must not look at the rulers of mental substance as something bad. But you must look at it in keeping with God's divine law of perfect balance. For he who steals, shall be stolen from. And the robber shall go without a home.

Remember that the home of your soul is your heart, not your head, for your heart is the vehicle through which your soul expresses and, therefore, is, in truth, your real home. That which is lasting and enduring is what you feel in your heart, not what you think in your head.

Life indeed is a circle, a circle upon which man eternally evolves. Rising from the allness of one to the variety of many, he returns once again to the allness of one. And so it is as the thoughts of many, passing through your mind, are educated— for they are forms in need of education—as they are educated, they bow their seeming supremacy. They bow in recognition of their true sustenance.

No one and no thing exists for itself or by itself. It is inseparably related in consciousness to all of life. All the thoughts that you think affect, to some degree, the peace and the harmony of the whole. The battle between good and evil is a battle in creation. Beyond that is the sublime peace and joy of true living.

Good night.

JUNE 2, 1977

CONSCIOUSNESS CLASS 145

Greetings, students. Whereas unfulfilled desires are the most common ailment of the children of Earth, we shall speak at this time on the balance that brings the peace over what is, in truth, the divine expression known as desire.

Some time ago we spoke to you on the forty soul faculties and the forty sense functions—and the one divine Spirit—representing the eighty levels of consciousness. We have also spoken to you, of recent date, on what happens to desire when it enters the human mind. We have also spoken on the thought form being released on the vertical path, returning unto the divine Source, and expressing on the horizontal path, in keeping with the Law of Duality of creation.

This divine intelligent Energy, when expressed through the functions, of which the human mind is the throne, becomes a creative force and, in keeping with the Law of Creation, has a dual reaction. As man, entertaining a multitude of thoughts and desires, releases each and every thought along the vertical paths of consciousness, it returns unto the divine Source and returns back to man through the soul faculties.

Now, our teaching has always been, and continues to be, a balance between the faculty and its corresponding sense function. This balance is brought about through the education of the human senses. This educational process is the ability—which is available to all mankind—to release from the human mind the form, which this divine energy, or desire, takes in mental consciousness. As man begins to make that effort, he learns, slowly but surely, the wisdom of patience. For without patience, he stumbles along the path and returns to the level of consciousness known as mental force.

We have also stated many times that man's great struggle are the judgments made by the human mind. When you release this form, this energy, which is brought into form by mental substance, to this divine Intelligence, it becomes neutralized and is returned to you through the soul faculty of inspiration. Man is inspired through total consideration. And total consideration is hand in hand with total acceptance.

So many times have we spoken—not only in your world, but in these other worlds—on the importance and the true salvation, so to speak, of divine will or the totality of acceptance. We all seek the peace that passeth all understanding. But this peace comes to us through our heart, the vehicle of our soul. It is not in the mental realms of duality. It is a soul experience. It is when you truly are at home, for your home is the abode that is built, so to speak, by divine energy released through the soul faculties.

Any and all things that are created shall pass. There is no peace in mental realms, for mental substance cannot offer what it does not contain. And so, in your evolutionary path, many, many things will distract you. But they will ever be the things of the mental worlds. Their distractions are ever in keeping with the refinement processes that are taking place in your consciousness at this very moment.

As these soul faculties, like the lotus, unfold petal by petal, you begin to breathe fresh air, so to speak. You begin to feel the something that is beyond words to describe. Many things are offered in the realms of creation, but they are never without their payments. And so it is that God, divine, neutral, impartial, and totally considerate, is, in truth, your real being. Remember that before unity can truly awaken within you, you must separate the mental realms of creation from the truth which is eternity.

When you are in your mental worlds you question much. When you are expressing through the home of your soul, the soul faculties, you are beyond the need of question, for you know. He who knows is he who accepts, for you cannot know, nor understand, what you do not first accept. Take stock in your daily activities of what it is you accept. You will find that acceptance exists within a boundary of emotional judgments. You will awaken and be amazed at how limited your mental spheres of action truly are. You will also be amazed at the restrictions and the limits that you have placed upon your life's experiences. So often do we think that we are free, free to do what we choose to do. But that thinking is of short duration, for it always finds its own obstruction.

Now, my students, enthusiasm is a soul faculty. When you are enthused you are expressing through your soul. When you are in duty, in gratitude, in tolerance, in faith, poise, humility, in principle, in character, in reason, and all these many soul faculties, then good is what you truly experience.

It seems that students' difficulties are the unwillingness of the so-called self to forget the self. And, in time, as the years roll by, so much takes place, distasteful to the self, that the self begins to make the effort to forget the self. And so, my friends, do not be discouraged in your distasteful experiences. They are the path that your soul is walking upon. And the experiences becoming more distasteful are, in truth, helping you to be free. Some time ago it was stated that every knock is a boost. And remember, what is taking place is boosting you above and beyond those realms that are so unreliable.

It is our search for security that keeps us in the mental realms of activity, for it is the very instinct of the mental body to preserve itself and move in the universes ever seeking the necessary means to do so. And that thirst and search is known as the desire to be secure. To search and desire security one must, in consciousness, have accepted the opposite. The mind which deceives us into the belief in security, prior to that deception, has deceived us into the belief of insecurity. Without fear, man cannot believe or feel insecure. And, not having believed or felt insecure, he cannot go on the search to be secure.

And so it is the revelation—as the demonstration ever is the revelation—that fear is where we have directed the divine energy. Through faith, through the soul faculty of faith, have we accepted the negative, for fear is the effect of faith in the functions of the human mind.

And so it is that we must, in time, go to work on this direction of intelligent, neutral energy in the human mind and the functions that it offers. For in the final analysis, our faith, a soul faculty, directed to the sense functions, has brought us what is known as fear. It is these forms in these mental realms that are the forms of fear. They are the rulers of the realms and they help you, for you, by your presence, have solicited their help and assistance. Some time ago it was stated that presence is the Law of Solicitation. And it is your presence in the mental realms that is soliciting the assistance of the rulers of those realms. And so your payments are ever in kind.

How does man free himself from these realms? By awakening the soul faculty of reason, for reason is the power that will transfigure the form. You all know that faith is inseparable from poise and humility. And so it is a very simple lesson to learn whether or not your faith is directed to the source that sustains all good. For if it is directed to that Source, you will experience poise and humility. If it is not directed to that Source of light, then you will experience pride and judgment. Preceding the soul faculty of faith, poise, and humility, is duty, gratitude, and tolerance.

View your thoughts. Become the observer. And you will know, by your personal living demonstration, whether or not you are the eternal free spirit expressing through the soul faculties, equally balanced in the sense functions.

The teaching is to educate what is called the human ego. But you cannot educate without acceptance. The denials in life are the destinies in life. And we are all present, in our efforts, to make changes in our destinies. It is within the power of the Divine for destinies to be changed. It is not within the power of minds of men.

My good students, so much has already been given, and yet, so much remains to be said. We are going to take a few moments this evening to answer some of the questions that you have submitted, for these questions represent various levels of consciousness. And remember, when you hear these questions, some, you will accept, and some, you will deny. It is ever dependent upon whether or not the corresponding soul faculty to the function you are in is balanced with that function.

So often students will say that it is difficult for them to have tolerance, the first soul faculty. The difficulty is the revelation that the function corresponding to tolerance is far out of balance and refuses to bow from its temporal throne. For each level of consciousness looks down upon the other levels in order to be superior to them. It is called, in some philosophies, as a house divided.

And so it is our purpose to share with you the light that will bring reason and unite, for the common good, your house, that you may express in peace and harmony; that you may consciously become aware of your purpose for being upon the Earth planet at this time. For the journey has already been eons, and eons yet to be. Man shall, in time, learn to be the observer, for he shall, in time, separate truth from creation. He shall, in time, become the witness, for the witness is free, unattached, and unaffected.

Remember, in truth, you are the witness. You are, in truth, free and unattached. And through your continued efforts, you can remain free and unattached. Your only payment is the payment of self, the payment of identity, the payment of judgment, the payment of intolerance, the payment of superiority, and the final payment of all payments: the payment of pride.

When pride goes, humility comes and, with it, poise and faith. Good is the effect of the payment of pride. But the good comes after the humility, after the poise, and in the fullness of faith.

You may ask your questions at this time.

Thank you. Can humility and humbleness be used interchangeably?

Whenever the soul faculty of humility is expressing, the goodness of the soul is evident. And that is known as humbleness.

Thank you. Would you please explain the saying: Fear is the fulfillment of desire?

Yes, indeed, fear is the fulfillment of desire. As man entertains, in his mental realms, the divine expression known as desire and does not redirect that desire or divine expression to the corresponding soul faculty, then man forms the desire by the functions of pride and judgment. Pride, judgment, and denial are the fear, the fulfillment thereof, of desires held in mental realms. And the payment is very, very, very great.

Thank you. How do the functions protect?

The functions protect because the functions, created from mental substance—it is the functions that fear. And they protect by denial, for they deny, they judge, and the false feeling of power called, by the human mind, pride, rises supreme, but temporary, and falls, to rise again. Remember, my students, that the climb is never higher than the fall. So he who climbs not in mental realms falls not in mental realms. Be the observer that views those realms. Be not the participants. And you will have balance and you will have your peace.

Thank you. Is it detrimental to our spiritual, mental, or other bodies to have physical body parts donated after our physical death?

That is entirely dependent upon your attachment to self. Man's great pain and suffering is self, for what is called self garners up and possesses, for a time. It holds a thought and says, "It's mine." And thoughts are forms. And so man, expressing through what is called self, the effect of pride and judgment and denial, garners up many forms. And the forms that he garners up cry to be sustained. And their sustenance is the energy of their creator. And you are their creators.

And so once the mind is permitted to entertain the illusion that the form of the thought is theirs, it becomes responsible unto the law for the sustenance of the form. And the sustenance of the form is the energy of the Divine flowing through the minds of men. And as you entertain thoughts, the more you entertain them, the more the form of the thought grows. And when you try to make a change in thought in mental realms, the forms of the thoughts you have expressed much energy to cry out for their sustenance. And they haunt you and repeat in your mental realms their needs for sustenance.

Not only do they do that, these forms your thoughts have taken, but the rulers of those mental realms extract their payments from you. For you first chose the thought and you first possessed it—and you bear the personal responsibility for it—though in days of error of ignorance. There is no escape from impartial divine law. But you have evolved in consciousness and become aware of the force of thought and the form of thought. And you know how to release the form and the thought along the vertical path to the divine Source. But the choice is, moment by moment, in your hands.

You have, in keeping with your evolution, been given charge over all creation. If you had not, in your evolution, evolved in consciousness to realms above and beyond creation, then you would not have been given charge over all creation. And, in truth, all creation is form. And all form is mental substance, for form is the effect of identity and belief.

The thought of I is the building block of the mental worlds. And therefore it is the thought of I that is, in truth, the building block of the prison of the eternal soul.

When man, in entertaining his thoughts, bows the thought of I associated with the thought passing through his consciousness, the thought, instead of being possessed in mental realms, is released. And man has the fullness of life, no longer is concerned with fulfillment, for he is fulfilled; no longer waits for promise, for he *is* promise, the effect of divine law. No longer does he question, for he *is* the answer. No longer does he search, for home he is living in. No longer does he worry. No longer does he fret. No longer does he turn over the stones of ignorance and find an empty void, for he has accepted. And finally, he lives the fullness of life itself.

Slowly and surely, the wandering children of Earth are returning home. They have viewed much and, yet, have lack. They have gone across the universes of mental horizons and found it isn't there. The search is close to an end. And the end of the search is, in truth, their very beginning.

Good night.

JUNE 9, 1977

CONSCIOUSNESS CLASS 146

Greetings, students. This evening, for our discussion, we shall speak on service and survival.

Reality is experience, and a conscious acceptance thereof is known as fact. Truth is awareness that it is self-created and in a constant process of change. As we have often spoken on the divine, neutral, intelligent Energy, known by man as God, we view, when we are in the soul faculty of reason, that this intelligent energy is the servant of mental direction. And so it is as this intelligent energy passes through the human mind, it is directed and formed and becomes the creative force.

In our previous classes, we spoke on these rulers of the realms. And we spoke on these multitudes of forms that man, when in the mind and reliant upon the mind, is subservient to—these many, many forms. As this intelligent energy, directed by the mind, creates these forms, these forms demand a constant feeding for their survival. And so it is that each form created by mental substance is, in truth, subservient to the forms created by other minds in other times of untold eons ago.

Often it has been spoken, by the philosophers of old, to guard or control the thought before the thought controls its creator. Man, in his unawareness of these mental realms, becomes the servant thereof. And so it indeed behooves man to make the constant effort to be freed from reliance upon his mind and the multitudes that have been created by mental substance.

Peace, as you know, is the power, for as the energy, passing through the human mind, is directed by the mind—when the thought of peace is flooding the consciousness, this intelligent energy goes upward to the Source from whence it has come. And in so doing, man, being the vehicle through which the energy is passing, is healed with this so-called healing balm of peace.

In the early attempts of the students to flood their consciousness with peace, the mental forms of association try to take control of the thought form. However, in time, the peace, flooding the consciousness, becomes formless and free. Man, then, is transfigured by this perfect balance, known as the soul faculty of reason.

Whenever you pause to think, you, in truly pausing, become the strength of your eternal being. And so it is the endeavors of the students should be directed to pause to think.

Often it has been spoken that a house divided cannot stand. When the thoughts of men are in contradiction with each other, the thoughts, being the forms created by mental substance, they go to war and man is depleted of what is known as energy. For these untold multitudes demand more and more of the divine energy in order that they may win their battles and their wars.

And so it is, my good students, that all the goodness of life is the direct effect of energy. All of life is energy. All thought is the effect of your personal choice. And so it is that your reality of the moment, in a constant process of change, someday will pass from your view into the nothingness of mental dimensions from whence it has been temporarily created by you.

Man, having this great power within his grasp, can only use it wisely as he awakens to the truth that frees him. But man cannot awaken without the acceptance of the possibility of something greater than his present realizations.

And so it is that we are here and you are here to awaken within; to flood the consciousness with peace and experience the so-called reality that is greater than your greatest dreams, for what is beyond the dream is the cause of the dream. And that is when man, on his long journey through forms, goes home.

It is that peace, so often spoken of, that passeth and goes beyond all understanding, for to understand a thing man must become that which he desires to understand. And the process and path of understanding is through total acceptance and total consideration. And so it is the peace that passeth all of that, that goes above and beyond.

The awareness of this creative principle, used wisely with reason, brings about the fullness and the fulfillment in so-called creation. The fullness of life is the total acceptance of its constant change. The fullness of life cannot take place in accepting the limitation of form.

It is the nature of the human mind not only to create, but to possess what it thinks it has created. And it is this very possession that causes man his hurt and his rejection, for man, viewing the passing of forms, cannot hold them, cannot, in truth, possess them. But the human mind, designed to gather and to garner, does not know, nor believe, that simple truth.

As man flows in a stream of consciousness and views the shores of creation for what they have truly been designed for—a passing panorama to entertain the human senses—then man will view with objective reason. And it is one of the principal purposes of these classes to help you to awaken and no longer depend and no longer rely upon form for your sustenance. For it is this so-called self-reliance—the reliance upon created self, upon the identity of the thought, which is the form of I—that is the bondage that keeps man from the fulfillment of life.

To accept in your consciousness this peace is to become a part thereof. And in so becoming, you will no longer experience the gain, for you will no longer experience the loss. But you will *be*, for that is the true you.

We stated that presence is the Law of Solicitation. And so I am sure you will all agree that your minds are in a constant process of solicitation. Perhaps it could be best understood in stating that the human mind is constantly asking, constantly seeking, constantly gathering and garnering. Because presence is the Law of Solicitation—and the presence, your true being, is in mental consciousness and is not freed to be objective to the vehicle known as the human instrument called mental substance. Let your presence, your infinite spirit, become the viewer—to view the passing panorama and not to rely upon what it offers, for it is ever fleeting and ever changing. The seeking will cease when peace is once again restored. The questions will no longer be, the solicitations will disappear, and you will find the true beauty and love of life itself.

Remember, my students, that life is not form. It is a stream of consciousness that sustains ever-changing form. When we first came to your earth realm, we brought to you, at that time, a very simple truth: Be ever ready and willing to change. Now think, my good students, in all of your daily experiences, how many opportunities you have to demonstrate your readiness to be free. For when you make the effort and ready yourself to change, then you are no longer held by the forms, you are no longer possessed by those forms.

The illusion of the mind is that you possess things or forms. That illusion is what binds you to creation, for the truth is that that very thought is the device that the forms that you have created use to possess you. You all know that you are not the thought, but you have a vehicle, a mental body, through which the thought was created. And it is the created thought that is, in truth, the possessor. You can easily demonstrate that truth by viewing honestly the thoughts that insist upon repeating themselves in your mind. When the thought is disturbing and you know it is not beneficial and yet it continues to repeat and to dictate and to demand, then you can be rest assured that you are possessed by the thought, for you have lost control thereof. And that that man loses control of, in his mental world, controls man.

For example, when you feel that your health is not up to par and you desire to change it and it does not change, then you know that something called "poor health" is not responding to your wishes. And because it is in your consciousness and because it is in your zone of action, you are affected by it. Whatever man is affected by has power over man. And so it is that we, in this study class, are making the effort to be free from these many things that possess us and control us.

Often it does seem, when one views the mental worlds, that the souls may never be free. But that is indeed far from the truth, for the process of freedom, slowly but surely, is taking place. And as you pause to think and you look within and see how your minds are possessed and you have an ever greater desire within to be freed, that very desire is the instrument through which your consciousness begins to expand, the awakening takes place, and, step by step, you move above and beyond the so-called realms of creation.

Each time that man entertains a thought—thought being the form and form being creation—he has become the instrument of dual forms: one so-called positive and one so-called negative. And so the battle rages. Who shall win? And man becomes the victim of each and every one. And in this evolving process, there is much to be encouraged, for it is through encouragement that you rise up on this long, long, long journey and see the light that shines across the horizon and your ship moves over and returns.

The question could well arise within the mental realms, Why leave the peaceful shores to go into the wars of creation? Because, my good students, in your evolution you have earned charge over creation. And it is in keeping with your evolution that you someday accept the responsibility that you have earned: to face with a joyous heart and a clear mind your responsibilities, not only to yourself, but to all that you have created.

And now, we have some time to answer the questions you have presented.

Thank you. Will it be possible, through the process of cryonics, the science of freezing the body after death, to revive the body at a future time? What happens to the soul? Is it trapped in the frozen body? How can the brain survive without oxygen?

In reference to your question of freezing the human body, whenever the Isle of Hist separates, there is no return of the eternal soul to that particular form. There are times when medical science states that so-called death is a fact, when it is not yet a truth. It takes seventy-two hours for the human soul to be completely freed from the physical form. And we have stated before that within those seventy-two hours the mental body experiences whatever is taking place with the physical body. And so, my good students, if you had thought more deeply, you would already be aware that the separation of the Isle of Hist is not something that takes place in a split second, but takes place over a process of time of seventy-two hours.

Thank you. What is the true meaning of universal consciousness?

Our understanding of the meaning of universal consciousness means a conscious awareness of the universe and all therein. Remember that universal consciousness is not the totality of consciousness, but is limited by the universe in which one is experiencing their so-called reality.

Thank you. If we wish a new home, or whatever, we are told we must release this desire to God that it may be fulfilled. At the same time we have a responsibility to do our part. What is the principle involved in doing our part? And how do we know what effort to put forth in demonstrating our faith?

Doing our part is the releasing of the desire to the Divine. The remainder of the question is the control of the mind to dictate how God, in truth, shall do his part.

Let me speak once more on desire, whether it be a home, a car, or anything else. When man is instructed to do his part, his part is the releasing of the desire to the divine Intelligence. But man, faced with giving up the desire—for the mind makes the judgment—the moment it makes the attempt to do its part, to release the desire to the divine Intelligence, the mind pulls the thought back again.

And so it is that so often when man says, "I release this desire to you, God," a few moments later the desire is, once again, in mental consciousness. Because the mind has not yet bowed to an authority that, in truth, sustains the mind. And so man is plagued—in giving the desire to the Divine, where it may be fulfilled, and entertaining the desire. And so it takes a great deal, so to speak, of the soul faculty of patience, for man views time, for man is locked in mind. And the desire insists upon returning, for man calls it home.

That is where man is not doing his part, for he only loans the desire to God. And calls it back repeatedly. Until so-called time passes and he gives up the desire in disgust and says, usually, "God did a poor job or no job at all." Once again relying upon the authority of his own uneducated ego. And so, my good friends, for each person the fulfillment of desire varies in time, for it is totally dependent upon the true release to the only Intelligence that can fulfill it, in keeping with the laws of obstruction and transgression created by the human mind.

Thank you. Please distinguish between imagination and/or creativity and fascination.

Fascination is being controlled by form. Imagination is the choice of the individual to image and to create. When man is imaging, he has the soul faculty flowing and creates in keeping with his personal choice. When man is in fascination, the forms created in the universe, in his universe, and in all universes that are in harmony therewith, control him.

Thank you. On entering the realms of pride and pity, you were advised by your guardian angel to give complete and total obedience to the rulers of that realm. Would you please elaborate on the principle involved in so doing? Why this would not have meant further bondage?

What man gives, man frees. And so the principle is very simple: what man holds, man binds. What man gives, man frees. And so it is that blessed are the givers in life, for God gives to the givers and takes from the takers. And so, you see, my good students, the questioner has not yet thought, and thought more deeply, in the very basic principle of this philosophy: that in the giving is the freedom. We told you long ago that to forgive—to give forth—is to free, and to hold is to bind. And that that we hold destroys us; that that we give unfolds us.

And so in the realms of pride and pity, there was the givingness to the rulers of the realms and in that givingness was the soul evolved and freed. For as you, in your thought, hold, as you battle, you bind yourself. Truth needs no defense, for truth is a stream of consciousness that nothing can change, for it is beyond change, for it is beyond form.

Truth is formless. And as man, evolving to that formlessness, flows in the givingness of life, God, the divine Principle, gives unto him as freely as he gives. And so, my good students, givingness is freed from thought. Givingness is freed from judgment. Givingness *is*. And because it *is*, truth flows freely.

If you find obstructions to your desires, it is the revelation, for the demonstration is ever the revelation. Remember that the demonstration is the revelation. The obstructions to your desires reveal your lack of givingness in those areas of consciousness. The teaching clearly states that whatever you are seeking is also seeking you. And, indeed, it should be, for whatever you are seeking you are creating. And that that you create ever looks for you for its continued sustenance.

So go beyond, by the greatest gift that you have to give: the gift of self. Take inventory of what you believe yourself is. For what you believe yourself is, is that that you have created. And those created things demand your care. Give your gift of self by forgetting self. And when you forget self, you will be fulfilled with life. It is your thoughts of self that obstruct and keep the goodness from your experiencing. But to forget self is to give up judgment. To forget self is to give up pride. To forget self is to give up fear. But I can assure you, after centuries of effort, my greatest joy was when I finally forgot the thought of I.

Good night.

JUNE 16, 1977

CONSCIOUSNESS CLASS 147

Greetings, students. We shall, at this time, continue on with our discussion of thought forms.

Some time ago we gave to you that simple truth: when you harbor a thought, you are feeding a form. And, in keeping with that truth, we must realize that whatever the mind creates is created by directed energy, through our own choice. And so it is in an understanding of thought forms and becoming the— through error of ignorance—victim of those self-created forms that you have been given the most helpful affirmation ever given to your world, known as the "Healing Power" affirmation. Whenever the guiding hand of peace is directed at the very moment of the thought, the energy, instead of being instrumental in sustaining and supporting the thought form, is released by this power of peace and goes on the upward path that you may be freed from created forms.

In keeping with that understanding is the simple teaching: to separate truth from creation in order that you may experience freedom. And so it is in your endeavors and in your efforts to flood your consciousness with peace, as these demands from the forms of thought, created even years and untold centuries ago, come to demand from you the necessary energy for their sustenance.

To those of you who have made some effort in directing, through your consciousness, this peace of your soul, I know that you are well aware of the difficulties that are experienced in mental consciousness of the struggle because of the demand of the thought form to entertain, which is, in truth, to drain your energy. This seeming struggle will pass as you continue to make the effort over and over and over again to come to the awakening that the mind is in a constant state of activity; that there is, upon the human mind, constant demand by the created forms for your attention. And so it is as you make the effort to bring forth from the depths of your very being this great peace, those demands seem to increase.

It is not, in truth, that the demands increase. It is your awareness of their existence. You all have experienced the demands of these thought forms. But it is when you begin to make the effort to flood your mind with peace that you become more aware of how demanding these forms are upon you. The climb, of course, is never higher than the fall.

And so it is in keeping with your level of consciousness, whenever your consciousness is in creation, then you are aware of this rise and fall, of this payment and attainment. For these dual experiences take place only in mental consciousness, in keeping, of course, with the principle of mental substance, which is creativity. But as you, continuing on with your interest and attention, and rise with this power of peace into the realms of divine neutrality, you witness and are not affected thereby. Learn to become the witness and view this dual aspect of creation. But you cannot become the witness until you are freed from being the judge.

And so it is that God's will is the total acceptance, for in total acceptance there is no judgment. And wherever there is no judgment, there is no duality. Wherever there is total acceptance, there is divine equality. And it is this divine equality, this level of consciousness, that we are, in truth, slowly but surely, all rising to.

To be aware of duality is an indispensable part of your evolutionary journey. To become objective and to view it and be free from it is also in keeping with your evolutionary journey through life. For you, in truth, are the principle of life, passing through a multitude of forms, responsible and, in truth, in charge of all creation. And in keeping with that evolutionary responsibility, your children are indeed very many. And they all come to you—their father and their mother—for their sustenance and for their care. As long as you rely upon the mental worlds for the fulfillment of your desires, you will remain in the realms of judgment and in the levels of dual experience. In time, you shall evolve through those realms. But remember, it is your reliance upon the mental world that brings you, as an effect, the duality that that world has to offer.

Whenever you accept—and you accept wholly, completely—then the seeming experiences in life will be without the pain and without the pleasure. But you, in turn, will be freed from frustration. You, in turn, shall be freed from anxiety. And you, in turn, shall be the living, healing balm.

Let us remember, and ne'er forget, that our true being is not dependent upon form. The goodness of life is not dependent upon created substance. Its existence—this, the true you—is forever and forever, for forever is what you really are.

In order to awaken to the truth of eternal existence, of eternal consciousness, you must first be freed from mental substance. And those steps to free you from those realms are through the soul faculties that you have already been given. And if you feel that your progress to date, so to speak, is not satisfactory to your mind, then take another view, my students, from another level of consciousness, for what is not pleasing to the mind is dependent upon the judgments the mind has already made.

Much has been spoken in this semester on judgment, rejection, and bondage, for it is in keeping with the necessary steps to move ever upward and ever onward. You will note in all religions and all philosophies the teaching is ever onward and upward. The teaching is never outward and downward. We have spoken to you in these classes of energy released on a vertical path and energy released upon a horizontal path. We have also spoken on how you can release this energy upward on the vertical path under the guiding hand of peace, for it is peace that takes the energy upward and accomplishes the good in your life.

We have also spoken on fear, the mind's control of the eternal you. Without fear, there would be no judgment. Without fear, there would be no duality. And so it is, you become aware of duality by the mental aspect of fear and you judge accordingly, in keeping with your efforts to preserve what you have judged you possess. The outward physical possessions of man are not the problem. It is the inner possessions. It is the mental forms, for what man believes he possesses, in truth, possesses him. And in keeping with that possession, energy is demanded from him, that the illusion of possession may be sustained.

It behooves all children to accept, to accept totally, for in total acceptance there is freedom from fear. And this freedom from fear is also a freedom from judgment. And he who is freed from fear is freed from judgment, is freed from rejection, and is freed from denial.

You have a beautiful truth given to you in one of your church hymns and it clearly states, "Destiny at my command." For destiny, in truth, has always been, is, and will always be, at your command. For your denials in life are at your command, and your denials in life are your destinies of life. And so it is that you can broaden your horizons, for you have created your horizons. You can change your destiny, for you created your denials. And if you will study honestly these classes—and especially the principles that have been revealed to you this evening—you will indeed free yourself from these boundaries and limitations, which bring lack and insatiable, unfulfilled desires into your life.

Patience, we all know, is the wisdom of the Divine. So often man speaks about the circle of life. And he puts it so clearly and simply when he says, "What goes around, comes around." But so often, my students, the disturbance is when it comes home, when it returns. You cannot change what has been, but you can change what shall be. Take inventory of your denials and you will know your destiny in life, for your destiny is ever in keeping with the throne of judgment called denial.

The transformation, the expansion of consciousness, is, in truth, taking place this moment. It is taking place on levels of consciousness which most people are not yet aware, consciously, of. But in keeping with the Law of Evolution, which is, in form, constant change, it is taking place. It is bringing about, through your own endeavors, a conscious awareness of that process that can indeed be most beneficial to you. Place your attention upon what you accept and in so doing shall your acceptance be broadened. And in the broadening of your acceptance, known as the will of God, will you be freed from the reliance upon limitation and form.

Take control of the harness. Let not the mind run rampant, for it is like an adolescent child. It has not yet been educated and, therefore, does not yet accept its position: its responsibility as a servant of your eternal soul. The reeducation of the human mind, called the ego, is to place it in its proper perspective as a servant of your true being. But it is a very clever instrument and it has deceived untold multitudes for untold centuries. It is formed of creative substance and knows that it was born and it shall die. And so, in working with the education of your ego, you must use total consideration. You must understand that it fights for survival. You must understand that it is, in truth, an instrument, a vehicle, that the true you is using to express the true you in the dimension of which you are consciously aware.

To accept the simple truth—that it is not you—takes great effort on your part. But the demonstration that it is not the true you is constant. The thoughts are constantly in a process of change. The beliefs are in a constant process of change. The fears are in a constant process of change. And all that the mental world has to offer is in a constant process of change.

Whenever you judge, you command. And your command is responded to by the forms you have created. They can only do what they are capable of doing in the world in which they were created—a world of duality. They promise you anything, they promise you everything, in order to be fed. But their promises are like piecrust: they easily crumble.

The promise of God is the law, the essence. That is something that is not created. That *is*. But the judgments of the mind have risen and, in so rising, are guaranteed to fall. So what does it behoove man to rely upon substance that he knows shall rise and he knows shall fall?

When man, in mental desire, does not have the desire fulfilled in keeping with the dictates of time that he has judged it shall be fulfilled, he makes new judgments in order to justify and to support the authority of his original judgment. Because, my good students, unless these forms, created by mental substance, justify, they cannot support the original created entity. The original created entity, this thought form, is the king of kings in mental consciousness, a realm that is very real whenever we are in it, which is most all of the time.

Now, you have heard in some philosophies and religious teachings about the fall of the angels of God. You've heard much discussion about Satan, about the Garden of Eden, and about the serpent that beguiled Eve. Now, you must ask yourself the question, Is this Garden of Eden—this story that is not exclusive to the Christian world, but may be traced back untold eons of time into very, very ancient philosophies and religions. Supposedly Adam, man, had everything. Supposedly in this Garden of Eden was beauty unsurpassed. From whence cometh the desire of Adam? What inside of Adam—he who supposedly had everything—could record loneliness? For in keeping with this story of old, Adam was in a Garden of Eden; everything was beautiful. And all the animals and trees and everything were there for Adam. But Adam became lonely.

We understand in this philosophy that loneliness is nothing more, nothing less, than self-pity in poor disguise. Now, my good students, you cannot pity self until you become aware of self. And it is in the awareness of self that man loses the universal consciousness which he is in truth. And so it is that we have brought to you over these years the teaching of sel*fless* service. Now, what does sel*fless* service truly mean? It means service minus, or less, the self. Now, that is what sel*fless* service really means. It means service without the self. How does man do service in life minus the self? By forgetting the self and becoming totally absorbed in the service.

We have a teaching in this philosophy that clearly states: Put God in it or forget it. God, the universal divine consciousness, cannot get into your efforts and endeavors until you can forget self. For as long as self is entertained, the fullness of divine consciousness, your soul, cannot get in.

Now, my students, whenever you are blessed with the opportunity of service less the self, you have indeed merited a golden opportunity to experience the fullness, the goodness, and the beauty of life itself. And whenever, on the path of service, all are easily distracted, for all are easily tempted. And on that path of service, whenever your mind rises, you can be rest assured, self is in and service is out.

And so we view many who come and we view many who go. But the Light never fails to shine, for the Light is not dependent upon the viewer. It is the viewer who is dependent upon the Light.

So once again we ask that you, in your acceptance, open your heart and close your eyes, for the heart needs not the senses to awaken.

Good night.

JUNE 23, 1977

CONSCIOUSNESS CLASS 148

Greetings, students. We have spoken with you many times on energy and on the vehicle known as thought, which passes from your universe out into the greater universe. And this evening, we should like to speak a bit more on this energy.

We spoke to you in one of our other classes on directing the thought on a vertical path, rather than the habitual horizontal, or path of creation. And so it is when a man, entertaining thought, creates the vehicle through which this divine, neutral energy moves, when man releases this vehicle on the upward or vertical path, it releases what is commonly known as prana, a substance from the human aura. As it moves in this upward direction, it returns back to man. And it leaves his aura as a vapor or vaporous substance. On the horizontal path of creation, this vehicle called thought, bearing this divine, neutral energy, is formed into a rigid form, goes out into creation attracting unto itself like forms that continually demand this energy or prana for their survival.

And so it is that each moment we are in a constant so-called battle or struggle within ourselves: knowing, in truth, what is right for us to do and the strong magnetic pull of creation to once again take us out upon the path of duality.

Much has been spoken in our teachings on peace, the power that healeth. And so it is that peace—whenever the student makes the smallest effort to entertain that state of consciousness, there is the great hue and cry and call of creation. What, in truth, is the call of creation but the forms of life demanding their sustenance for their survival? For whatever is formed is under the Law of Preservation. And it is this Law of Self-preservation, the preserving of the form—though it is destined to change and to pass—it still demands its continuity.

The continuity of form is ever in keeping with the evolutionary path of the formless, divine, free Spirit. But remember that the true you is the immortality. The continuity is the constant change of the form. And so it is our payment and our pain, in keeping with our own attachments to form, that we suffer in our lives, that we limit our view and cannot see clearly the freedom and the joy that is awaiting our simple acceptance.

For several years, we have repeated certain basic laws and teachings to you, in our efforts to ever expand the consciousness, in our efforts to bring to you a simple truth that may be accepted at least on one of the many levels of consciousness. It is like a seed planted in fertile soil: an idea is something that man must nurture, must water, and care for. And how does man care for an idea that floods up from his eternal being (for ideas are the effects of inspiration)? But man is inspired by his eternal being when man is freed from the entertainment of form in his consciousness.

And so it is that when we, in our efforts, gain, slowly but surely, some degree of control of these many forms that live within our consciousness, as we gain control of them, we, in that moment, are freed from them. We are freed from their dictates. We are freed, in those moments, from their demands.

But remember, my good students, these forms and entities and things are not the cause of anything outside of your control. They are not caused by things outside. They are the direct effects of our choices within. And so we have often counseled you, as students, whenever you are facing an important decision in your life, to weigh it carefully in prayer, in acceptance, for a minimum of seventy-two hours. To weigh something in consciousness for seventy-two hours is not to think about it now and then. It is a seventy-two-hour process of facing objectively the various levels of consciousness.

So often, in making important decisions in our evolution, we make them in the errors of ignorance. We make them from levels of consciousness that dictate to us, that deceive us. And time, the illusion, passes in our consciousness and then we have the desire to make other decisions.

Look at life, my friends, the experiences that you have already encountered. Look at the many times you have made decisions. Look at the many times you've lived in regret. So often when we face these seeming obstructions within ourselves, we face them with levels of emotionalism, we face them in levels of darkness. We must honestly ask ourselves the question, "Who am I? What am I? Am I the things with which I identify? And if I am, then I am constantly changing."

I—the I of the thought—is the great deceiver over the eternal you, for the I of thought is the Law of Identity. And in the Law of Identity is the limitation and is the bondage, is the attachment, and is all of the things that cause the struggles of life.

And so man can use impartially this Law of Identity which takes him on the path of personality, that deceives him into the false belief that he is a unique entity in consciousness. There is no unique entity in consciousness except the illusion created by mental substance. For the true being is a universal consciousness, inseparable from the great whole.

When this identity law, which brings the eternal being into creation—when man fully believes in this identity law, man becomes it in its fullness. To become one thing is to deny all things, for in becoming one thing the Law of Self-preservation annihilates anything outside of its I.

And so we find this eternal struggle of identity and universality. We find the eternal being constantly moving to and fro in the realms of creation. For man to entertain a thought of peace in levels of consciousness governed by the dual Law of Creation is to guarantee its opposite of peace and war. And so we find the students—a few moments of mental peace and much time of emotional war, so to speak.

In rising from those realms to realms of spiritual, eternal substance into the humble and simple Light that exists within all, man not only knows, but is aware in its fullness of his own divinity. For his divinity is an inseparable part of the Divinity. But in rising to those levels of consciousness, we lose the curtain of illusion of identity, for we have gained in those moments the totality of acceptance. And in that totality of acceptance are the horizons broadened to encompass the allness and goodness of the Divine.

My good students, along this eternal path you are trodding. Some of you will be here in your classes in years yet to be. There will always be someone. But remember that wherever you go in this great eternity, it has recorded indelibly into your consciousness: the eternal truth that you are indeed a part of all. And no matter how the Law of Identity and the delusion called the thought of I takes reign and rules over your eternal being, there is a light that has awakened within you, and that light, though ofttimes will it flicker, it shall never ever go out.

So be of good cheer in all your endeavors and remember that in keeping with laws well established are you trodding along the evolutionary path of life. Spend more time encouraging yourself that you may experience the beauty and the goodness that life, in truth, has to offer to all of its children. But never forget you are not the form, you are not the things, and you are not the thoughts. You are greater than all that creation has to offer and you are experiencing everything that is necessary to free your true being. Without these steps, there cannot be that which, in truth, is your divine right.

You are home in consciousness when you choose to be there. Awaken in this moment, my students, and view what creation really is. Awaken and go home in consciousness. Let the armies of creation return to the substance from which they were gathered and garnered. No longer seek to gather the things that your senses view. No longer garner in consciousness. And when you let go of all of those things, the goodness which is, in truth, the true you will rise in its joy and in its beauty.

But you must, you must give the thought of I. For with the thought of I is all the changing, created forms that you have garnered and gathered unto that great illusion. Those are the things that must be given. But I assure you in that giving of that illusion, you will rise to the heavenly heights in your eternal moment. And, once having risen, those forms of creation will not again have control over you. You will no longer be serving these multitudes of forms, for you will have risen above them. And, having risen above them, you will be freed from fear.

It is fear, the mind's control over the eternal you, that is the prison in which you live. Remove fear by giving each thought, each emotion, each experience to God. We brought to you some time ago a simple truth: to put God in it or forget it. To forgive, we know, is human. To forget is divine.

And so, if you feel that you are not yet strong enough to put God in it, then pray to forget it, for in so doing you are freed from serving these untold, complex realms of mental substance known as creation. For God, the infinite, divine, intelligent eternal Spirit, has granted unto you, in the forms of Earth, has granted unto you, your eternal being, charge over all creation. It is your divinity, your divine birthright, to take charge over all creation.

It is not in keeping with the divine, infinite plan for you to be the victim of creation. For your eternal souls entered your earthly realm to take charge over mental substance called creation. And for you to be the victims of that realm is directly opposing to your divinity. Think over your thoughts, your attitudes, and your experiences, and you will soon become aware how many times those mental realms have ordered you to do so many different things. There is no fulfillment in the realms of the mental world, for they offer only opposition. For it is in opposition that they survive, for that is the law in which they exist.

However, you can—and some day you will—view it as it really is. You can, and you will, once again rise up and accept your divine birthright. It is only those forms created by your own mind that blind you to your divinity. For they know—they have the intelligence of your mind, having been created by your mind—they know if you rise up in truth that they will no longer exist. They are fighting within you for their very survival. They are fighting for the preservation of self, for they have judged that there *is* a self and that they *are* that self.

Now, those created forms that you have created are in opposition to each other. And this is why you experience, in your days, you experience what you call good feelings and good thoughts and you experience what you call bad feelings and bad thoughts. And so they battle. They battle over you. Now, the reason that they battle over you is because they are fighting for what they have judged is the source of their life. And so that is your revelation to the path of freedom.

View not form for your fulfillment and you will be freed by the principle of truth. And if you continue to view form for your fulfillment, then you will continue to be confused, to be not at ease, to be in discord, not in harmony. And the final effects of these battles within, the final effects are called disease. Disease is not in the divine plan. Disease is a transgression, an obstruction to the Law of Harmony. And so it is in keeping with this philosophy that each and every disease can quickly, readily, and reasonably be traced to a pattern of mind established in your present evolution or carried over on your eternal path.

There is instantaneous healing whenever the light of reason shines over the level of consciousness that has transgressed the Law of Harmony. And so it is that we encourage you in these classes to flood your consciousness with peace, the epitome of harmony. To flood your mind and consciousness is to renew your life. It is the great healing balm that calms the waters and restores you to perfect health, to perfect wealth, to perfect happiness.

If you find, in your present experiences, that you are not filled with health, wealth, and happiness, then be honest with yourselves: Go deep within and you will find the transgression that, through an error of ignorance, stands between you and your divine right.

Accept your right, for acceptance is the first step in becoming. But you must first accept. So often in this teaching of divine will, the will of God, total acceptance, so often man says on one, perhaps even three or four, levels of consciousness, "I accept." But what about the other seventy or so levels of consciousness? You can easily tell whether or not you accept by taking conscious view of your desires. And in taking conscious view of your desires, you will experience whether or not you accept the experience that you presently have as a direct effect of the law or whether you have judged, and continue to judge, how it shall be. Through your acceptance are the doors of heaven opened, but not until you do accept will they open for you.

You may feel free to ask your questions at this time.

Thank you. How can a student attain the state of consciousness known as the plane of purification?

We have spoken on attainment through acceptance. Through the totality of acceptance is man freed from the realms of mental creations. And in that freedom does he enter the realms of purification.

Thank you. Would you please explain what causes muscular tension and how this may be eliminated through spiritual efforts?

Muscular tension is the direct effect of a discord within the consciousness, created and caused by unfulfilled desires, commonly referred to as frustrations.

Thank you. Please clarify the difference between showing an interest in and fascinating with something or someone.

Whenever man truly shows interest in any thing, place, or person, he is, in showing interest, freed from judgment. However, when man is in fascination, he is totally controlled by the throne of judgment and always dictates the final so-called end.

Thank you. What would a sudden onset of mediumship mean in the evolvement of an individual?

That that is sudden is only an illusion to those who are not yet aware of the slow, but sure, process of divine law. What does that which is suddenly experienced by the human mind cause to the human mind? There are many different effects. One of the very common effects is a state of shock to the human mind, for the human mind is an instrument designed to preserve whatever is fed into it. And so it is that anyone experiencing a sudden change in consciousness must pray without ceasing for guidance of the Divine.

Thank you. Why do we need creation to evolve? Don't we evolve on the other side as well as in creation?

Creation is not something that is limited to your physical world. Creation is form and form is everywhere, until you rise in consciousness to the formless free spirit, which, in truth, you are. And when you rise to that consciousness, you view forms objectively. You become, then, the observer, not the observed. The observer is not affected by experiences known as creation. It is the observed that are affected. So, my good friends, you see, when you are the observer, you are not affected. But when you are the observer and identify with what you are observing, you then become the observed. And that is when you are affected.

Thank you. When the mind is not under control, acceptance of one's own judgment can be mistaken for experiencing acceptance, the divine will. Would you comment upon this, please?

Well, the question reveals that a judgment has already been made in reference to the statement. If you are, in truth, in total acceptance, there is no concern whether or not you are in your mind or you are in total acceptance. For when you are in total acceptance, the mind is not active.

Thank you. In this country, much emphasis is currently being placed upon the study of the iris of the eye. What is the spiritual significance of so doing?

Well, the spiritual significance of the eyes is the awareness of truth. The eyes have always been known as the looking glass, or reflection, of the eternal being. And because the eyes not only represent awareness, but they represent deception, man must listen to the still small voice of his heart, the vehicle through which his true soul is expressing. For that that reflects, deceives. And so remember, my good students, it is not the reflection that you should seek.

Consider studying the discourse given to you so long ago upon reflection. Let yourself view life through your heart. Let your eyes be the shining light of awareness and not deceive by the reflections from within. All eyes view life in a reflective level of consciousness. And so man must choose wisely what he reflects.

You see, my good students, as you view what you call life, you are looking into a mirror that has been created by what is known as your self. Now, this mirror that you look into, that you call life, is not life at all. It is a culmination of a multitude of so-called experiences.

Experience, my good students, is not life. Life is a stream of consciousness upon which you sail, ever onward, ever upward, returning to the source from whence you have voyaged so very far. That is true life. Life is the awakening within that knows beyond a shadow of any doubt. These mirrors that reflect your attitudes to past experiences are not life, for each thing that you see, touch, taste, and sense is the mirror. And the mirror is controlled by the judgments you have made so long ago.

And so, my good students, take a new perspective about life. It is not what you think it is. It never was, and never will be, what you think it is. For what you call life is created substance. You must go beyond the mirror that you view.

Good night.

JUNE 30, 1977

CONSCIOUSNESS CLASS 149

Greetings, students. This evening for our class I should like to speak to each of you personally. And so, beginning on my right, I would like the students to take their turn in speaking forth their identity or name.

[*A student speaks her name.*]

In keeping with your soul journey, the patterns of long standing, though bowing with great struggle, are beginning to do so. And it is the direct effect of your efforts in the soul faculty of gratitude. As you continue to place your consciousness, or attention, in those faculties, your horizons will continue to broaden and the abundant good that you have long sought will begin to reap its harvest in these coming years.

[*A student speaks her name.*]

Along your path has been much effort to awaken within yourself the real or true purpose for your journey on Earth. The greatest struggle, so to speak, in your earthly journey is the struggle of acceptance. The awakening within to the light of reason, which will free you from reliance upon creation, although a painful process for any soul in its journey, the years will pass in numbers of five, but the healing balm of reason will be in constant attendance.

[*A student speaks her name.*]

The willingness to try is a faculty—the faculty of willingness—that you have, for many centuries, been working with. And so it is that you often find yourself willing to do, willing to make the effort, but your feet trod newly upon the planes of consciousness known as continuity. Though you are willing, continuity, the ability to remain with anything until victory is at last at hand, is the struggle. And so patience is the faculty that must awaken and express itself. And in the awakening of that faculty, the faculty of patience, shall you experience the fullness of your journey.

[*A student speaks her name.*]

Many, many times your soul has risen—many, many times. But it is the throne of judgment that so quickly sends it back—your soul—into the realms of mental creation. But you will continue to rise and fall. And as you continue to do so, this rising and falling of the dual law of mental realms will slowly, but surely, begin to lessen. For it is your dependence upon creation that has robbed you of the peace that passeth all understanding. But that dependence, in the years ahead—and seven to be—is lessening each and every day, in each and every way. You have the blessing of the soul faculty of continuity, for many are the centuries that you have already spent in experiencing and expressing through that faculty. And so reason is rising, slowly and patiently, to transfigure your life. And the horizons that are ahead are brighter than your last two incarnations.

[*A student speaks his name.*]

Temptation is the function through which you must swim against the tide. It is known as the temptations of distraction. Though your soul views clearly the path and goal that lies ahead for you, temptation rises as a great magnet in the universe and pulls you to and fro. And so in earthly time, twelve years will pass, but, in truth, for you, they will pass rather quickly. And the healing balm of peace, rising spasmodically, when the function of temptation has worn itself thin, will increase that great peace in the years to come. Duty is the faculty that rises within your consciousness, for you know what is right, but it is the distractions of temptation of the worlds of creation that cause your mind to be pulled in so many different areas. But that shall pass and the peace you've sought so long shall come to be.

[*A student speaks her name.*]

The difficulty and struggle is due to a lack of understanding, which is the effect of wisdom, which is born from patience. And so patience, in all things in all life, is what your soul, in its journey, is learning—the great lesson. For as the lessons and the faculty of patience are learned, you are freed, step by step, from the bondage of form, the bondage of creation. And so each and every difficulty and struggle, from the moment that you entered the earthly realm, has been an effect of a lack of patience. But all of the lessons necessary to grant to you the fullness of that soul faculty are taking place. And as the faculty of patience opens for you, reliance is transformed and a universal consciousness, like the dawn, is awakening.

And so it is that in these latter months, there is a change taking place within you. And sometimes, in quick, seeming-short moments, this, strange to your mind, this strange consciousness is moving, is growing and unfolding. And so a universality is being born for you. And that universality will grant unto you a great understanding. And from that understanding will awaken the soul faculties of tolerance, of duty, of patience, of peace and harmony and responsibility. Though the lessons may seem to be strong, they are in keeping with the benefit and the blessing to your eternal soul.

Thank you.

[*A student speaks her name.*]

Duty, duty, duty. And so it is the soul faculty of duty, the mind has struggled to interpret. And so the mind constantly has questioned: "What is my duty? Where is my responsibility?" That is the effect, when the mind looks at what is known as the soul faculties. The mind is not designed to be an awakened instrument to judge or to decide what soul faculties truly are. But duty brings to you an awakening to personal responsibility. But the question is the activity of the mind. It attempts to gather and to garner, to make all decisions over your eternal being. It has done it before, for so many, many centuries. But it is, in truth, losing ground, so to speak. For it is in this, your earthly life, that you shall indeed be freed.

You shall indeed separate truth from creation and you shall be freed from the greatest plague known to the eternal soul: the plague of mental judgment. For they are passing slowly and painfully from your universe. And, in their passing, God's will, the divine will—the acceptance and right of all—is starting to take place. You must, in your endeavors, encourage your soul.

Encourage the simple, little child that is the true you. Regardless of all the activity of your mind, speak softly and encourage the part of you that is the true you. And it shall come to pass. For your soul is sufficiently awakened, and you shall, you shall remain upon the path of light. And that humble light will bring you your heaven on Earth.

Thank you.

[*A student speaks her name.*]

It is the sadness of the function of concern that robs you of the happiness that you know, in truth, is your birthright. And so it will take a few years, and more, to smooth over the edges, the sharpness of the activity of mental thought. But on the brighter side of evolution is the beautiful faculty of faith. For once it was fully in bloom in your consciousness. And once again, it is rising, through the weeds, as a beautiful flower. It is sufficiently strong this time to rise above the jungle and reach the eternal Light.

And so think, and think more deeply. It is the quickness of emotion that causes you your greatest struggle in life. And so it is the spiritual attribute of pause that will lift your soul. Pause before you act. Take the moment to pause. For in that moment of pause, your soul has the opportunity to rise. And as it rises, reason melts away all the seeming disturbances.

Thank you.

[*A student speaks his name.*]

Once again, you must rise. You must rise once again and walk through the doors of care. For God cares or you would not be here. And so it is from experiences and many disappointments the joy of care has almost died. But it shall not be annihilated, for care is a faculty of the eternal soul. And it shall, it shall rise again. And when it does—and it is in process of doing so—it will rise free of judgment; it will rise uncontaminated by the human mind. And then you will see the true purpose of life.

The fullness of the soul faculty of care is struggling, once again, in your evolution to rise supreme. To care and be free from concern, to care and be free from attachment, to care, because that is the way of God. To care and be freed from judgment, that is your journey in this life. And it is a journey that will be more pleasant with brighter horizons. So often in our rising through the soul faculty of care, we make judgments, for concern views care and tries to control it. But concern is a mental function and it cannot take what is not rightfully its own. So care, as it awakens more, once again, in your consciousness, will grant to you the freedom of communication and the fullness of understanding.

[*A student speaks his name.*]

How often, my friend, in your short life on Earth, you've been so disappointed. How often the function of disappointment has plagued you. But you came to Earth that you may find what is known to man as joy. And though you have had moments of joy, disappointment has often plagued you. And so it is that an awakening in the soul faculty of duty is leading you forward and onward, and joy—but not the joy of the dictates of the human mind, but true joy, spiritual joy—you are rising in consciousness to. The years are few before the fullness of that understanding takes place within you and only three in number.

[*A student speaks her name.*]

Oh, in how many, how very many, many ways of life your soul has wend its way, ever in its efforts to return back home once again. Harmony is the faculty of the fullness of your life and so harmony is ever rising in your consciousness. There is a greater peace, there is a greater happiness and harmony—that, you will be victorious and within a short two years, that harmony will pervade every fiber of your being. And there will no longer be questions of heaven, for heaven, within you, you shall awaken to. And so it is with great encouragement that we speak to you to continue on with efforts in your way, for harmony is the way of health, of goodness, abundance, and a joyful life. We are indeed very pleased, for this state of consciousness that your soul has risen to. And the shores of eternal beauty await your view.

[*A student speaks her name.*]

Oh man, how sad we make our life, how sad we make our life. However, in the sadness is the fullness of gratitude, for that is one thing that you have awakened. Indeed, the gratitude is deep within your consciousness, but it is the struggle between gratitude, your soul, and the quickness of judgment. The only thing that stands between you and the eternal Light is the throne of judgment. Let it pass, by a greater acceptance. Work on the soul faculty of acceptance and the gratitude of your soul, flowing through divine will, known as total acceptance, will bring you, indeed, the abundant good, as these five years ahead pass, sometimes so slowly for you.

[*A student speaks her name.*]

As the separation in consciousness, the separating of truth from the illusion called creation, is ever broadening within you, duty—duty to the divine Spirit that sustains you—must rise in equal strength. For without the fullness of spiritual duty, the separation, the awakening to the separation of truth from the illusion called creation, will take its toll on your faculty of enthusiasm. And to be enthused is to be in God. And you must remain in conscious awareness of God, for it is through your prayer and your effort to serve the very Intelligence that sustains your life that you will have the wholeness and the goodness that awaits, for you, just over the horizon.

[*A student speaks his name.*]

You know the value, the value to pause, for in your life's experiences before your earthly realm, you learned the benefit to pause. But to pause without reason is a cause of procrastination. And it is in the design of the divine plan that each form shall serve its purpose for which it has been designed. And so it is you will, slowly but surely, quicken your step, for you will awaken within you the spiritual attribute of security—not the function, not the mental aspect of security, but a security within yourself. That security is awakening within you, as your acceptance is broadening. As your eyes view and your ears hear, there is a greater acceptance that, "There must be something beyond my limited mind that is working in the universe." And so it is, your soul is ready. But you must not forget: you have a responsibility to the Light that has awakened within you. And that responsibility will remind you as a still, small voice as you go on in your soul's journey.

[*A student speaks her name.*]

Much time has been spent in the playground of creation and the time has come for energy, attention, to be directed to your eternal goal. Acceptance is the will of the Divine. And in truth, you are truly searching for that spark of Divinity to brighten within your universe. And so it is that life is offering to you, in keeping with the rigidity established by your mind, all of the lessons necessary to broaden your horizon, to accept the impartial, divine justice of God's law, to accept that there is divine grace, that divine grace, the mercy of the Divinity, is ever in keeping with divine law, that it does not transgress divine law, but is the handmaiden of divine law. And as you look at these lessons in life and as you see the struggles and suffering, though a universal motherhood strongly rises within you, acceptance, the will of God, will view it more objectively. And in that objective view shall you begin to free yourself from the little shell known as the human mind.

And now, my good students, we shall continue on with this phase of our class at our next meeting.

Good night.

JULY 7, 1977

CONSCIOUSNESS CLASS 150

Greetings, students. This evening, we shall speak to you on the expanding consciousness and shall continue on, at a later time, with our personal talk to you.

The Law of Evolution *is* the expanding consciousness. And the creative principle, which has already been given to you, *is* the Law of Identity. And so it is that the expanding, universal consciousness, which you truly are, is evolving through the principle of expansion by the creative principle of identity. As man, in his evolution, in his expansion, has become more aware of his surroundings, he identifies through this expanding consciousness. And so it is the first teaching that we brought to your world: be ever ready and willing to change.

It is the resistance to this evolving consciousness, it is the resistance to its expansion that is the problems created by man. In many ways we have spoken that you will, in time, accept this ever changing stream of consciousness, that you may go deep within your being and find the true you, the true security. And as this process of evolving continues to take place, regardless of the thoughts of man, there are the experiences of suffering and disturbance. It is the insistence of the mind upon holding whatever it identifies with. The human mind, the effect of the creative principle, ever strives to hold. For in its own illusion, it believes whatever it identifies with. But it is through that creative principle that the evolving, expanding consciousness is destined, in time, to illumine these many worlds in which the consciousness is moving.

You find in your daily thoughts and acts and activities, you find the so-called highs and the so-called lows: the direct effect of this Law of Identity. Some time ago we spoke to you on the Law of Ignore: to ignore and not to identify. Man, only in the flooding of his consciousness with the power of God, with the peace and the will of God—the readiness of acceptance to this Law of Evolution—only in that shall man find his true freedom. Whatever man views, man holds in consciousness, whatever he senses, whatever he feels, whatever he hears, for those are the functions. And it is those experiences in consciousness that cause man all of his difficulties. Freedom, the effect of the control of that principle, is where man is working his way to.

Let yourself freely move, for whether or not you accept or reject, the expanding consciousness cannot be stopped by the will of man. Everything that is necessary for your eternal good is, in truth, taking place. Though the many experiences are not often pleasant, they are, in truth, expanding.

And so man stands on the earth realm, the fifth planet in your solar system. He stands at the very demarcation line between principle and personality, between faith and fear. He stands on that dual line, ever moving back and forth. And, as he is the highest evolved being on the earth realm, he has earned a great responsibility: a responsibility to all of the forms on the earth realm—forms that he sees and forms that he sees not.

It is the true purpose of this philosophy to assist you in expanding your consciousness. It has been brought to your world that you may, through the divine will, through the Law of Total Acceptance, become aware of the world as it truly is— not the limited created world, that shall come and go, but beyond the world of identity is the world of reality. All of these things that fill your mind from day to day—they come, they go, they move. But you, the true you, is forever and forever and forever. Yesterday is not, in its fullness, your today. It is the shadows of yesterday that tug at your consciousness. And it is those shadows of yesterday, those disintegrating forms that call you ever backward. And though they call you back, ever backward, you still are moving, slowly but surely, ever onward and ever upward.

The lessons, so-called, in life, they repeat themselves again and again and again, until you awaken to take the essence from those experiences and from those lessons. To place the attention, the consciousness, through the Law of Identity, upon the question, is, in truth, to deny the eternal answer. For the mind that questions, also the mind shall answer.

It is when you accept, when you accept all of the lessons, when you truly accept all of life, that you are freed from the destiny of the human mind. For the destiny of the human mind is a constant repetition—a repetition of the things that you hold. It is only the things that you hold that hound you. It is only the things that you hold that bind you. It is what you hold in mental substance.

So few people seem to realize that it is not the things of form outside. It is the forms that are inside. It is your unwillingness to give them up, for that is the revelation of what is commonly known as the will of the mind or self-will. That is the will that must bend. It shall never break, for it is not designed to break. But it must bend. And when that will of the mind bends to the soul faculty of reason, that is when you begin to broaden and truly expand your consciousness.

We all know, as students, that the spoken word is life-giving energy. But we do not pause to think what we are building in these mental realms. We have a thought and we express it, without consideration or interest in the form that we are feeding. It is those forms that we are feeding, through our vehicle of thought and through the power of our spoken word, that rob us of that goodness, of that joy of living. Because we are so quick to judge another is the revelation and the demonstration that we, in truth, are quickly judging ourselves.

So let us pause in our mental activity. Let us pause that we may realize and, in the realization, expand our own consciousness. Because of the fear, which is, in truth, the expression of mental substance, which is the instrument, in truth, of preservation, that is where the problems truly lie.

Instead of moving freely in life, we move guided and controlled by the king of fear. He has become the king of our universe because we have relied upon our thoughts, upon our mental zone and sphere of action. It is our purpose to help you to help yourself to still the human mind. That does not come easily, for those many forms that have been created by the mind will not bow easily. They will haunt you until, through constant prayer, you are freed from them.

Some time ago I spoke to you of some of the experiences that I have had in centuries past in this other realm. And if you will recall, my guiding angel spoke to me in those days and instructed me, in kindness, to do whatever they ordered me to do. In so doing, I was freed from their control. For, you see, my good friends, you must understand the Law of Control. When man strives to control anything and that which he strives to control does not resist, then man loses control. You see, we gave to you some time ago that simple truth: that challenge stimulates the human ego. It is the challenge that the mind reacts to. And so, my friends, in your efforts to control, remember, you only control what resists.

And so my guardian angel gave me sound advice: not to resist; to do whatever I was ordered to do. Therefore, my good students, I was freed. Had I permitted my mind to rise to control me—and I could only be controlled by it by my own resistance to it. So you see, my friends, it is through acceptance, through the divine principle of acceptance, that you are truly freed.

We also spoke to you on a simple truth: that that you give thought to, you give power over you. And so this great peace that truly exists and is moving through your consciousness is constantly being robbed from your awareness of it. Do not resist the inevitable. Move with it and you shall be freed from it. The experiences that are without number exist for you because of your resistance to them.

It was also given to you that our denials are our destinies. You see, my good students, denial and resistance are inseparably born from the same principle. The day, in time, does come that we no longer resist and we no longer deny. And then, we move into the heaven, which is a state of consciousness awaiting all souls, to return home.

But if you are in the mind, the mind does not appreciate the word *nonresistance*. The mind does not appreciate the words *no denials*. For the mind to accept that, is to dethrone its great authority over your eternal being.

Many philosophies before us have taught the divine principle of nonresistance, but it has been little understood by the minds of men. And because it has been little understood, man continues on with his wars within.

That book given to you but a few centuries ago clearly stated: turn the other cheek. But the minds of men refuse to understand what it truly means. It simply states: do not give the mental realms power over your eternal life. Accept the divine authority and you shall see that great truth: that every dog shall have his day in court. For justice to be divine, man must first accept.

And in keeping with that principle, let us move onward and let us view these links in the chain of evolution. As you, in your evolution upon your planet, have earned charge over all other forms, so those who have advanced and evolved before you have earned charge over you. And so it is that there are the angels of light and the so-called angels of the lesser light.

There are those who strive and work without ceasing to help you, to inspire you, to ever encourage you to move and to do what you know, deep in your heart, is right to do. And there are those who have spent untold centuries in what is known as the gray realms of consciousness, the astral realms, who do all within their power to keep you where you are.

It is the purpose of the angels of light and your guardian angel to show you, to the best of their ability, the path of peace, the path of nonresistance to the divine Law of Expanding Consciousness. And it is the purpose of the angels of the realms of gray to hold to form. And so the centuries have already passed.

You know the path that is in front of you. And you know the path that is to the side of you. Many times the mind will distract you with all of its forms. Many times it will call you to step aside. And one sure way of knowing, in truth, how you are growing is when the forms of the gray realms, when they call the loudest for you to step aside.

Whoever walks upon the path of Light shall forever and forever view it. They shall always know that it is there and their day shall always come again. But you know not, in time consciousness, how long those days are apart.

Some of my students were a bit, perhaps the word is, surprised that it took me so many centuries to grow through the gray realms. But if you would but pause to think and ask yourself the honest question: How many years has it taken you, in your earthly journey, to make a microscopic change in consciousness?

The greatest growth and the greatest value of growth is when we finally become freed from what is known as judgment. And, my good students, it has indeed taken me many, many, many centuries. And I do not claim to be totally freed from judgment, for if I permitted that claim to exist within my consciousness, then that indeed would be the living demonstration that I am not yet freed from it.

So let us work to be freed from the little judgments. Work at the small ones and chip away at the mountain of obstruction. Work at the little ones. Do not try to take on more than you are capable of doing at any moment. But, in so doing, do not judge, for that only builds another mountain before you.

In the continuing of these classes and this philosophy, much, much will be spoken on divine will, on acceptance. For as that word, *acceptance,* floods into your consciousness, the expanding principle, which is inevitable, is sustained. And as you, in your endeavors, whenever you experience what is known as intolerance, flood your consciousness with the divine right of God, with the divine will of God, and you accept their right of expression, as you accept the right of expression of the individual, you will expand in consciousness and accept the right of expression of the whole.

You see, my students, a man is poor or a man is sick because he has accepted. He has accepted in mental consciousness and has identified with that acceptance, and therefore believes. In acceptance, man accepts the right of the level of consciousness, but he accepts that right from his own soul-awakened level of consciousness and does not identify and, therefore, believe and establish the law unto himself. It is through this Law of Identity that man struggles in the mental realms.

You have all had the experiences of a thought plaguing your mind, a thought that you did not want to be in your mind. And you have all had the experiences with the difficulties in trying to root it out. Whenever a thought repeats and repeats and plagues you in your mind, it is revealing to you that it is not being fed sufficient energy by you. The length of time that it takes to remove that thought—for it is only moved in consciousness. What truly takes place is that you, your true being, moves to another level of consciousness where that form or thought was not created.

Now, remember, my good students, you can only be affected by a level of consciousness that you personally choose to entertain. This is the great value and the great benefit of the flooding of your consciousness with the power of God, known as peace. In time, the day will dawn within you that when a thought that you do not appreciate in your mind insists upon you feeding it energy, you will be able to speak forth the word, the word "Peace, peace, peace" and the power of God, that intelligent energy that sustains all things, shall move you upward to another level of consciousness. For you have been granted in your evolution that great power: to speak forth the word knowing that it shall not come back to you void, but accomplish that which you send it to do. My good students, that is your birthright.

Speak forth your word. But if you speak forth your word from the level of consciousness known as identity, if you speak forth your word from those mental realms, then you establish all of the laws necessary to return to you to free you from the control of those forms. And those experiences are rarely, rarely pleasant to the mind.

Speak forth your word from your true home, the home of your soul. You will be freed from all concern. You will be freed from all need, all want. Speak forth your word. It shall not return unto you void, if you speak it from the depths of your soul and you speak through the instrument of your soul, known as the human heart.

Many indeed are the centuries that pass before my view. And untold numbers have I spoken to, in many realms of consciousness, to speak forth the word. And I have found in these untold numbers that it is indeed a rare person that can entertain the thought of acceptance, that can truly flood their consciousness with the right of God: to accept and to feel the fullness of the Divine Intelligence.

My channel has years yet to go in your earthly realm and many teachings are yet to be brought forth to those who are expanding in their consciousness. I have this very day spoken to my channel in reference to the continuity of these classes.

We have often taught that our interest is not in numbers, that it is the quality, not the quantity. And so it is that quality, a soul faculty, and quantity, a sense function, must be brought into balance. And in keeping with these teachings, we grant unto you according to the law that you, as a group, are demonstrating. And as the Law of Evolution is the very principle upon which this philosophy is founded, the numbers will be fewer. And in your world of form and mental substance, the rules and regulations shall increase. For in the mental realms, without rules and regulations, there is no control. And without control in mental realms, there is total license. And in license, there is darkness, and in license, there is bondage.

And so, as these few days ahead come into your world, my channel shall be instructed when to speak to you in reference to the seeming new rules and regulations governing these awareness classes. We are not concerned with the continuity of the philosophy, for that is in the hands of an intelligent Power that knows exactly what to do and has no need to be told. But our interest is in your expanding consciousness and in your evolution. And so, many shall leave and a few shall stay, but that is in keeping with the divine Law of Total Acceptance.

Good night.

JULY 14, 1977

CONSCIOUSNESS CLASS 151

Greetings, students. In completing this, the final class of this semester, we wish to speak on identity and the Law of Evolution.

The most important and valuable words that you will learn in your eternal journey are the words "I accept." They are the most valuable in your journey in keeping with the Law of Evolution, for it is the "I" which takes form with every thought that you entertain in mental substance. And through this form called "I" (identity), you become attached, in mental substance, to the form created as it exists in mind stuff.

Now, this identity or forms, with each thought that the mind entertains, stands in front of your eternal soul as it passes along this evolutionary path. And so the affirmation given to you—"I accept"—is an affirmation that has been designed to help free you from these created forms. Each time that the mind, in its creative ability, refuses to accept the created forms, it directs energy through the Law of Adversity and, in truth, becomes the victim of the created forms. However, in this process there is, over the many centuries, a refinement and evolving.

Let your mind drift in this moment. Let it drift in consciousness that you may, for a few moments, view the multitude of experiences which, in truth, are existing forms on mental levels, that you and you alone, in truth, are living with.

The separation of truth from creation takes place through the soul faculty of acceptance. It is the limitation of acceptance that creates a wall of obstruction for the eternal being. We speak often of this divine will, for as you continue to progress, you will see more clearly the value of acceptance. To accept is an experience that broadens the scope and the horizon of the viewer. Because you are, in truth, an inseparable part of Divine Intelligence, your eternal destiny is an acceptance of your whole being.

Your whole being is not the limited forms that you are presently serving. Your whole being is a consciousness that encompasses everything everywhere. This limited path, created by the Law of I, the form of identity, is a prison house that you are, in truth, slowly but surely, breaking through.

We have also spoken on the great ruler of the human mind: the ruler called fear or negative faith. For in order to sustain and to protect a pattern or attitude of mind, which is, in truth, created forms, the experience known as fear rises in defense. We have also stated many times that truth needs no defense. The only things that need defense are the things of creation, for their existence is dependent upon a continuity of energy, divine energy, directed by you to support and to sustain them.

And so this war of mental worlds is constantly taking place. And you, the true you, is ever in the battle, until the moment comes, for you, that you bow and accept. Most people, when they hear the words "I accept", are emotionally disturbed. Fear rises within their being. And the fear, the degree thereof, is ever in keeping with the forms who are striving to survive.

To speak to a person and give them the word *acceptance* does not create, usually, such great trauma. It is when you speak the words "I accept," for in the moment that you say "I," you are identified with all these mental forms that you have created. It is not you, the true being, that goes through this emotional trauma and battle when the word "I" is spoken. It is the mental identity with these patterns of mind, with these attitudes, it is those forms of creation that cause you the experience of fear and disturbance within you.

And so, in this, the final class of this semester, it will behoove you, as students, to spend some time with yourself in stating "I accept." For in speaking forth those words, you will have most interesting experiences take place within your zone of action.

You have also been given a simple truth which states: challenge stimulates the ego. Now, we know that the human ego is the house in which these many forms reside. And so, in thinking about this simple truth—challenge stimulates the ego—we must ask ourselves the honest question, "Do I, the true being—not the thought of I—but does my true being desire to continue to feed these many forms that are not bringing to me the harmony, the peace, and the happiness that I truly seek?" So, my good students, spend a few moments each day, speak forth the truth, "I accept." Become aware, each time you speak those words, of how you feel. And your feelings will reveal to you where your energy, in truth, has been directed in your lives.

You have heard so much in the philosophies of your day concerning positive attitudes of mind. When we first brought to your world this philosophy, we stated very clearly that life is the mirror of reflection, that man, not God, is the creator. Accepting the responsibility of being a creator is not necessarily an easy path. But accepting or rejecting that truth does not change that truth. We all are in a constant process of creating something. The sadness in our evolutionary path is that we do not make the effort to become more aware consciously of what we are creating.

You forever have been and you shall ever be. The expansion or broadening of your consciousness will always be, for it has always been. The expansion principle is something that no man can stop. For regardless of the efforts of the human mind to hold to the forms it has created, they are, slowly but surely, in a process of refinement and in a process of change. You, the creator, cannot stop creating, but you, the creator, can choose wisely what you shall create.

Religions, for untold centuries in your earthly realm, have spoken about the angels of light and the angels of darkness. This philosophy has spoken to you about the functions of the human mind and the faculties of the eternal soul. We have also spoken to you about how your spiritual body is garnered up from spiritual substance in keeping with the expression or energy passing through your soul faculties.

When you leave your physical body—and you leave your physical body more often than you consciously realize—you express through other bodies, bodies which are, in truth, created from the substance of the planes of consciousness. We have spoken to you a bit about these nine bodies through which you, in truth, express, if each of those bodies have, in truth, been yet created.

The functions and the faculties shall, in time, be brought into balance. Now, if you are interested in this path of evolution, which is, in truth, the path for all, then your interest concerning the functions and the faculties is, in truth, revealed to you in a multitude of different ways. Whenever you have a thought that is controlling you—and no one on earth is totally freed from the control of their own thought while still expressing through your mental earthly realm—then, in that experience, is the demonstration and the revelation of the function that has control of you.

It is all a matter of energy. Everything, everywhere is an effect of energy. Your health, your wealth, your peace, your joy, or your sadness, your misery and your grief is an effect, my good students, an effect of divine energy directed by your personal choice.

All of the good is waiting for your acceptance. We spoke to you in many different ways on viewing the good in all things, for good is God. And God, in truth, is that divine energy, sustaining all things. The mind is creating the forms of experience, but the Divine is sustaining them.

It is choice that you must become aware of. And the choice is so simple, so very simple. The acceptance of the right of the eternal Divine Energy to sustain the forms created by mental substance is, in truth, your freedom. I know, my students, for that acceptance came to me in a very painful and slow process. It is taking place, in truth, each and every moment of your lives, for each moment you are, in truth, accepting. But it is a broadening of your acceptance, it is the expanding of consciousness, the refinement of the Law of Evolution, that, through acceptance, you may harmoniously and graciously move.

We also stated that the power of the mind—and please note, not the power of the eternal soul—but the power of the mind to question presupposes and guarantees, no less, its power to answer. For what the mind knows as power is, in truth, a force. And so, when you question, you know you are not in your soul. When you question you are controlled by mental patterns, for, you see, my good students, your soul, a part of the Allsoul, your infinite spirit, it knows. It knows. It does not have to question. Should it question what it already knows? And so you find in your evolution that he who questions much, demands much. But it is not the true you that is so demanding. It is not the true you that is questioning. It is those things you have created. They question because they fear. They fear because they know their existence is dependent upon your directing infinite energy for their sustenance.

The statement that challenge stimulates the ego is a simple truth of great revelation. There is a certain feeling that takes place in the human mind whenever you challenge anything or anyone. But do you really know what causes that feeling? My good students, I assure you, it is the excitement of those entities of mind stuff that you have created. They are excited, which is a sense function, because they are at a great feast. It is like a person who has entertained the thought of being taken advantage of. What is it that causes that type of feeling? The thought entertained in mind and feeling in mental substance of being taken advantage of is a moment of awakening that the forms created by the individual have suddenly declared war within your own being. For they have suddenly become aware that they will not receive their normal sustenance of energy.

The separation of truth from creation, of principle from personality, is a slow and gradual process. But be rest assured, my friends, it is taking place all the time. So when we have these thoughts of blame and the thought of blame is directed to a cause that exists outside of our sphere of action, outside of our immediate control, be rest assured we are entertaining the king of deception.

We are here, in this academy, to open our sight to see how life truly is. To see these things and become, through awareness, a little step further along the path to control them. When you communicate with people—and sometimes you seem to have rapport and other times you do not—become aware inside of yourself of the level that you are expressing through. And remember that all creation cries out for its sustenance, that its cry never ends until you choose to end it for them. For they are your children and they can only cry to you. But ofttimes along the path, we hear the cry of the children we have created until we begin to cry for them. Now, my friends, when we begin to cry for the forms we have created, then the ship that carries our eternal soul to the heavenly shores of consciousness is no longer serving the purpose for which it was designed.

And in keeping with that stepping stone along the path, remember, when the tools no longer serve the worker, the worker begins to serve the tools. So when you begin to cry for the children of your creation, you, the worker, are now serving the tools.

The mind—and its creative principle—is designed by the infinite Architect to be a tool. And so these forms created are to be the servants of your eternal being. And when they no longer serve, it's time they no longer exist. For all things in creation are designed to serve a purpose. It is when your created entities, created through the intelligence of your human mind, begin to dictate to your eternal being what you shall do and they rise so great in authority that they control you, then it is time to pause, to think, to pray for the acceptance of the divine healing Power that will flow through you and remove any and all obstructions.

The eternal you has no need to fight for survival, for it *is* eternity and it knows it is eternal. The things that fight, the things that challenge, those are the things of creation. They are not your home, but they are your hell.

The moment you flood your consciousness with that great truth, "I accept," in that moment that you truly accept, you will no longer be controlled by the things of creation. You will no longer be their victim. You will experience your heavenly home in your earthly temple. You will not turn your back on creation, but you will face creation for what it was designed for: a tool and not a master; a servant and not a king.

Separate the illusion that covers the simple truth. Separate it and you will accept the goodness of life, for the goodness of life is all around and about you. It is not something you must chase anywhere to catch. It is wherever you are. It is never absent or away. You will personally experience the abundance of that goodness in the very moment of your acceptance. But when you say from the depths of your heart, "I accept," those tools that have been created by your mind must bow. And it is the bowing of those tools that is the trauma of emotional disturbance. But that is not you, my good friends: that is creation.

And so, in speaking to your soul, you know, and you know beyond a shadow of any doubt, that you are not those things. You are the peace that passeth all understanding. You are the goodness of which we all are an inseparable part. And so what affects your soul, in truth, affects my soul.

So many times I've heard the spirits speak—the spirits on the earth realm—I've heard them speak, "Peace, O God, grant peace, the healing balm, over their world of creation." Let harmony flow as an abundance as never before and, I assure you, my good students, through all the struggle of creation, your soul, in truth, is rising supreme.

If you find difficulty, if you find discouragement, remember that you and God *are* a majority. Never forget, when you open your eyes in the morning, to encourage yourself, for the soul faculty of encouragement is a great boon to lifting your soul. Look at the dawn and thank God for the moment of peace. Put your house in order when you consciously awaken, for you have the armies of creation to face. Stand still and face the dawn. Experience your true being. Do that each dawn and never forget, "I accept." And as the I of identity bows to the truth of God, who sustains it, your soul will rise and the heaven that you seek, you will awaken to. Find your heaven while yet on Earth. It is easier to find your heaven while yet on Earth, as it is easier for the blind man to walk in the dark than the man who sees. It is easier for you to find your heaven while yet on Earth.

Good night.

JULY 21, 1977

CONSCIOUSNESS CLASS 152

Good evening, class.

And before we get into our regular class this evening and because we do have a few new students to this semester, I would like to take a few moments to explain to you how these classes unfold. First off, you have, including tonight's class, 152 classes to study. We all know that we get out of anything in life whatever it is that we put into it. And so it behooves the students to make the effort to study what has already been given. Whereas this philosophy reveals these laws in a multitude of different ways, it is very important to the sincere student to make the effort to study and to apply. So that they may see, beyond a shadow of any doubt, that the revealed laws do work; that they work for one and therefore they work for everyone.

Now, much has been given in this philosophy in these past several years in reference to soul faculties and sense functions. And in the advancing of this philosophy and its expansion, you will find the relationship between the functions and the faculties—how to balance them and how to free oneself from the constant bombardment of so-called tapes of the mind, which is nothing more, nor less, than patterns that have long ago been established. Now, those of you who have stayed with the classes over these several years are already aware that the soul, in its evolution, establishes certain laws and, therefore, merits certain experiences in order to free itself from the entrapment of certain levels of consciousness.

You cannot, in any expanding philosophy, read a book or listen to one or two tapes and get the true essence of what is being given.

I know that most of you are already aware that, during the class, it is of vital importance, not only to yourselves, but to myself, that we remain as peaceful, without movement, as possible. Whereas it takes a thought of the human mind in order to move the physical body, when the physical body is in movement, our attention is not where it should be. In order to move the physical body, we are directing, through the process of thought, energy to what is known as self. Now, if this takes place during your class, it has its detrimental effects not only upon you, as a student, who have come here and paid the tuition fee to gain some understanding concerning this philosophy, but also to the basic vibrations that are in the room. So your efforts in remaining peaceful and still are greatly appreciated. And it reveals your ability to control the thoughts of the mind. Man cannot experience freedom without an effort of controlling the human mind. So it is the control of our mind that we must first make the effort to attain. Through control of the mind, the soul rises and expresses itself.

Now, so often a person will say they had such a wonderful spiritual experience when they were not even thinking at all—perhaps they were out in the woods or looking at the seashore or the sunset or the dawn or something. But that is the revelation: their mind was not bombarding their consciousness and their soul rose. And in that moment, indeed, they had a spiritual experience.

Now, our classes start, as they always have, by a reading of one of the discourses from the book [*The Living Light* and *The Living Light Dialogue*, Volume 1], followed by the "Healing Prayer" affirmation [*See the appendix for the text of the "Healing Prayer."*], and a few moments of concentration and meditation. The "Healing Prayer" affirmation that has been given to us, when it is sincerely used, will help you in gaining control of the mind and, in so doing, permit you to experience life as life was meant to be experienced.

[*At this point, Mr. Goodwin goes into a trance.*]

Greetings, students, and welcome to these continuing classes. We shall discuss, at this time, levels of consciousness.

As many of you are already aware, that there are nine spheres of consciousness and nine planes to each sphere, giving forth the eighty-one levels of consciousness, and that there are forty soul faculties, triune in nature, and forty sense functions, responding to the one divine principle which represents the totality of man.

As the figure eight is, in truth, the symbol of infinity and the number one, the symbol of truth and God, so man, the infinite, eternal spirit expresses through an infinite variety of expression. And so it is that on Earth, man is indeed well qualified in the functions and is striving along his evolutionary path to become aware of the corresponding soul faculty.

So often in these classes, students have requested to know the faculty that corresponds to a function in which they find themselves bound. Sometimes it is in the best interest of the student to have the faculty revealed. Usually, it is not. The reason that it usually is not beneficial to the student is because it remains as an entertainment on the mental levels of consciousness in which they find themselves. My good students, all of life is not dark, as all of life is not bright. It is necessary, this dual law, in order that you, the true being, may continue to expand in consciousness.

We have often emphasized the importance of thought, for thought, my good students, a vehicle through which God moves in a plane of consciousness, is the creative principle that man, in his evolution, has earned. And, having earned this process known as thought, he bears such a great responsibility:

the responsibility for that creative principle. As thought is the instrument through which God moves in those realms, man must make greater effort to become aware of the form which his thought takes. These forms, created by this principle, being the children of their creator, demand their sustenance. And it is the demand of these forms created that rob the eternal soul of its peace, its joy, and its divine right of happiness.

And so, as we continue on with these classes, we must make greater effort to become aware. We must learn to pause more often in our activities. To pause, that we may view and know, beyond a shadow of any doubt, the work we truly have to do.

I know that, at times, some have been amazed at the many centuries that it has taken me to grow through certain levels of consciousness. Do not be amazed, my good students, but view your short span of life and then you will understand the value and the benefit of simple and sincere prayer. Do not pray for things, for they are forms and, being forms, they're born to die. For birth and death, being but a change in consciousness, is an ever moving experience. And birth and death, because we are so much aware of form, of self, is, for us, a constant suffering process.

For to be aware is the first step in evolution. To move through awareness to objectivity or detachment is the second step of evolution. And from objectivity, detachment, and awareness, we move to universal consciousness. And in that universality of consciousness we breathe the fresh air of freedom.

And this process is not something that is going to take place. It is something that *is* taking place this moment and each moment of your lives. For we are constantly, in some area of endeavor, becoming aware, painfully becoming objective, painfully becoming detached, and joyously becoming free. And in the act of becoming, we lose the old to gain the new, for that is, in truth, the experience of Life herself.

So indeed does it behoove us to let go graciously, that that which is destined to come may arrive graciously. If you find difficulty and struggle in the things that you believe will fulfill your life, then the demonstration, being the revelation, is that you will not let go graciously and freely. For the doors upon which we knock cannot open until the doors that we have closed are reopened. And this is something that we must work on in the light of reason. And when you find yourself in want, in need, and desire, then you can be rest assured, in that level of consciousness, you have closed doors and refused to open them that the light of reason may shine upon them, so you can move freely and peacefully along the path.

Our path of evolution is beautiful in truth. It is filled with the light of reason, with the spirit of joy. And those who are ready and willing and able have found it that way. Oh, many things will distract you along the path—things, forms, the creative principle. Remember, my students, that birth and death, being merely a change, is taking place with all your thoughts, all your feelings.

Let your heart, the vehicle of your true being, open wide to the sunlight of truth. Know—as you open your heart, you *will* know—that you, indeed, have a very important job to do in the realm that you find yourself. Judge not what it is and the necessary energy will go to doing it. For there is a part of all of us, inseparable and free, that knows the vast tomorrows, for it remembers the distant yesteryears. And there are moments when you feel the ages of eternity, for you are, in truth, those ages.

Your earth realm will view within the next century the intelligent forms that inhabit the universes. And when it does, it will step back in awe that there are intelligent beings so far advanced beyond the earthly realm. There is a part of you that communicates with all of life, irrespective of distance or so-called time. And that part of you that has always been ever calls to your mind to speak. It ever whispers that you may still your mind and know.

But it must pass through the barriers of identity, for as man identifies, he builds these walls of limitation. And these walls of limitation do not permit his conscious awareness of this vast intelligence of which he is an inseparable part. Through the efforts of peace, the power that is, these barriers slowly, but surely, melt away. Learn to be with the forms of creation. Learn to be with them, knowing that they are, in truth, temporal, changing forms. For it is your identification with creation that is the bondage of your true being.

It is the divine eternal plan that man, formless and free, shall use the forms of creation as vehicles through which he may express and, in so doing, be an instrument of the Light for the refinement or evolution of those many, varied forms. But man, forgetting that he is formless and free, identifies and becomes the vehicle and the tool. Therefore, the true purpose of his evolution becomes contaminated.

We have spoken to you many times in reference to auric pollution. We first pollute our aura through what is known as negative or self-related thoughts. Now, there are many definitions of negative and positive. And in the use of the word *negative* at this time and in this way, I mean to say that negative or destructive energy is neutral, divine energy identified by the self to the self. When man identifies with the self, he begins a process of delusion and, in that delusion, believes that he is self-sustaining and, in that belief, denies the source of his sustenance. And in so denying the source of his sustenance, he rejects, by denial, the good that is waiting to flow through his consciousness.

Now, many philosophies teach the value and the importance of what they call positive thinking. My good students, all the goodness, all the happiness, all the joy of life is yours in the moment that you give the only gift you truly have to give to God:

the gift of self. The very thing that has caused you so much grief already. I know, for I know the centuries of grief that it caused me. Each and every time we direct energy to self, we deny what is waiting to uplift us.

Some time ago we stated a very simple little truth: the workers win. Work, my students, for the great Architect has designed you to do so. You have merited a form, advanced for your planet, designed to serve a great and good and just purpose: work. For work is the manifestation of the Divine Intelligence, called Love. Work, for the harvest is ready. Gather that, before it rots and returns to its elements. Use what you have wisely, for you have indeed a great, great deal. You have earned much. It is simply the common sense to use it wisely. Use what you have that your cup may be forever filled. Use it, for you are already overflowing with an abundance and, unless you give forth, you shall drown under it.

And if you ask the question, "How shall I use what I have?" then you have not placed the soul faculty of reason over all that God, in his infinite mercy, has already granted, in keeping with natural law, to you. Let us use what we have. Let us refrain from gathering and garnering. Let us take stock. And move out into the universe the hoards of things that are in our lives.

You know that forgiveness is the true blessing that brings unto us, from within our consciousness, that which we are truly seeking, called freedom. And forgive means, very simply, what it says: to give forth. Give forth, my students, all that you hold. Give it forth from the attachment of your mind. Give it forth to the Divine and you will be freed. It is not a matter of giving of physical objects, for to give a physical object without giving forth the thought attachment is to give not at all. That is known as loaning. And indeed we find ourselves loaning many, many things.

And we spoke before about loaning and giving, and we shall speak for a few moments, at this time, upon it. We find ourselves giving this and giving that. And then we find ourselves thinking about what we have given. And that, my good students, is the demonstration and the revelation, for we gave not at all. For if we had given, there would be no thought of what we had given. But because we never gave in the first place, we still have the thought about what we have done. And because that establishes the law of a loan, we find ourselves ever in need, trying to collect. But what is it, in truth, we're trying to collect? We, having not given in the first place, are still attached to what we thought we had done. And those are the things that pull us and tug at us as we try to move forward, which is our eternal destiny.

We have journeyed far, far, far, indeed, have we journeyed from home. But no matter how great the distance, we can go home in the moment of our choice, for home, our home, is our soul. And through our heart—the vehicle through which our soul speaks—through our heart, we go back home. And when the mind is still and the only thought is peace, we become that peace and we go back home.

Let us, my good students, let us go back home a little more often. Let us make it a daily practice to go home, for indeed it is not only refreshing, but indeed rejuvenating. It makes life worthwhile. For when we go home in those moments and we are refreshened and rejuvenated, we rise once again with a spirit of joy and enthusiasm, for we have once again become aware of being with God, without the distractions of creation, without the demands of creation. And we are healed, body, mind, and soul. And once again we face the world of creation with a new view, with a new attitude, with a new acceptance, with a new enthusiasm. And we do what is to be done and we do what is right, for we know what is right.

This philosophy teaches that total acceptance is the will of God, the divine will; that total consideration is the love of God, is divine love. We all have the will of God. We all have the love of God. It is the limits that we have placed on God's will, it is the limits that we have placed on God's love that cause us so many problems. For God loves all his children. And God's will is the evolution of all his children. And when the mind denies and the mind rejects, it must pay the price of standing in the way of God's will, of standing in the way of God's love.

Let us begin to step aside, but that will take the expanding of the soul faculty of humility. Let us be humble and accept the right of God. Let us be humble and accept the will of God. And in so doing, we'll be freed from concern. And in so doing, we will be freed from worry. And in so doing, we shall experience the fullness and the abundance and the goodness of perfect health, of perfect wealth, and perfect happiness. And let us remember the greatest wealth that God has given us: the wealth of good health.

Good night.

SEPTEMBER 1, 1977

CONSCIOUSNESS CLASS 153

Greetings, students. This evening we shall spend some time on the questions that you have prepared. And you may ask those questions at this time.

Thank you. It appears that great strides are being made to bring about the concept of holistic health, healing for the whole person—body, mind, and spirit. Would you please comment upon this?

In speaking on your question of complete healing, body, mind, and soul, we should first consider that the eternal soul is not what is in need of healing. Whereas the soul and its relationship to the Allsoul or Divine Spirit is uncontaminated and in full rapport with its true being or home, healing, so to speak, is necessary for the vehicles through which the true being is striving to express. And this is the reason that much time and energy is directed in this philosophy to the mental body. For the mental body is the true cause or lack of rapport between the soul and the fullness of the soul's expression.

So it is that as man, in his efforts and endeavors, slowly, but surely, begins to awaken, he corrects, so to speak, the errors and patterns of mental substance, which, in truth, build the discord or disease of the temple of God, which is the human body. Therefore, we should, in our consideration, never forget that we are, in truth, the formless, free spirit and the process of awakening or educating is necessary for the vehicles and not the true being.

Thank you. Although women appear to be more intuitive and more attracted to spiritual matters than men, why is it that the prophets and the great religious figures in history are men?

My good students, your history in these thousands of years has been dictated and controlled by the male species of your race. And so it is that it has been slanted ever in favor of those who have written it. It is not that women have not been illumined or are not illumined, but it is a rare occasion that you hear of a woman prophetess of old. In the many, many, many centuries prior to your limited recorded history, women took their full position and rightful place in spiritual matters and endeavors. And so the question asked is based upon the slanted and limited recorded history that you presently have.

Thank you. Is the women's liberation movement a step forward or a step backward spiritually for women and for society?

As all movements and organizations are designed to serve a specific purpose, and whereas they are in your world of creation, governed by dual opposing law, they will serve the purpose of goodness for those who go beyond this dual law and see the principle from whence it has been born.

Thank you. In dreams, does the soul express itself or is the source of the dream solely the subconscious?

The source of dreams is not solely the mind of the so-called subconscious. Ofttimes in dreams, the mind, in its efforts to interpret the impressions that it is receiving from the internal soul, and the mind being a limited vehicle with limited accepted experiences and patterns of your earthly life, it is indeed ofttimes much colored in the interpretation given to it by the human mind. So-called dreams are of two causes: the cause known as the external cause and the cause known as the internal cause. The external cause being the instruments or vehicles through which the soul is expressing. The internal and true cause being the eternal being in its efforts and endeavors to impinge direction and guidance to the human mind.

Thank you. What is the significance of dreams in our lives?

They are as significant as we permit them to be. And as I spoke a moment before, whenever the human mind questions, the human mind receives its own limited answer. And so it is that we have tried, over these many centuries, to share our understanding, that man may awaken to the great truth that it is your spirit and your endeavors and efforts in forming, from spiritual substance, your spiritual body. Man cannot experience what he does not have a vehicle through which that experience may be received. And so it is, my good friends, spiritual matters are perceived by the spiritual being.

Now, the vehicle of our eternal soul is a spiritual body created from spiritual substance. Man is aware of his mental body. Some men are aware of their astral body. Some are aware of their vital body. Some are aware of their universal body. And so it is that there is a body for each level of consciousness. Now, we have spoken many times on these triune functions and these triune soul faculties: that they must be brought into balance through the direction of the infinite, neutral, intelligent energy.

To truly awaken to spiritual matters is necessary to have the vehicle of your spiritual body sufficiently formed that you may see, that you may hear, that you may know, that you may feel spiritually. We have, over these years, often instructed our students to feel the presence, to feel the life-giving force of your planet, to feel the ocean, to feel the water. My good students, that feeling is an accurate sensing. And so it is, to awaken within your being this sense of feeling by a broader acceptance. It isn't that you do not already feel. It is that the feeling is limited in your consciousness. And so in all of your experiences, in the moment of your experiences, there is a still small voice that whispers within your consciousness, revealing to you the imbalance of the sense function and the soul faculty. It is that imbalance between the faculties and the functions that robs you of your joy, of your goodness, of your abundant life.

And so, my students, learn to feel and to listen in a much broader sense, for in so doing, you will have no need to ask. For deep within you, you will know. The prophets have spoken that in all your getting, to get understanding. And we have stated to you before, yes, in all your getting, get understanding. And in all your giving, give wisdom. For to get, without giving, is to build a prison for your eternal soul.

You see, my students, there must ever be a continuous flow through your consciousness. And that which is not in the vibratory wave of flow becomes an obstruction that shall, in time, pass on. For it is the very divine principle that all things shall be in constant movement, in a constant process of evolution, which is a guarantee of the Law of Constant Change. So wherever you have form, you have limitation. And therefore it is that limitation, known as form, that is in the constant process of evolution, of refinement, and of change.

In one of our earlier classes, we spoke to you on the gift of self, on giving the gift of self, on removing from your consciousness not the I, the principle of truth, but the thought of I. For, you see, my students, principle is formless and free, for it is the essence of truth. Personality is form or creation. And it is false in the sense that it is in a constant process of change. The true you has always been and will always be. Because it is formless, it is changeless. But that which is formed, being the thought, not the I, but the thought of I—for it is the process of thought in which the creative principle is working. And so, my students, remember, it is not the principle, but the form, which is personality. It is your identification with form that builds the obstructions.

Go beyond and get understanding. But let us also, in the getting of understanding, become aware of what that word truly means. To understand is to find the principle upon which all creation rests. And it is that essence of truth, that principle, once having awakened within your consciousness, that is the true you. As long as you permit the human mind to dictate what it is, then you cannot find it. It is when the mind is still that your true being is expressing. And so let us work more diligently upon the thought of I, that we may find the I that never sleeps.

Thank you. Would you please offer some suggestions on how we may best prepare ourselves for a peaceful night's sleep?

When the questioner asks for suggestions, back through the centuries I travel, and am always a bit hesitant to suggest anything. For there is a great difference between suggesting and recommending. So I do have some sharing and recommendation concerning the question, but I have no suggestions, for when we recommend anything, by the Law of Recommendation have we, to some degree, qualified ourselves by experience.

And so in reference to that question, I recommend an effort be made in an upright position to flood the mind with the great power of God, known as peace, to take control of this vehicle that has run rampant and wild. And the human mind runs wild when it forgets what sustains it. And so we must make that effort to place our attention upon this great peace. And in placing our attention upon it shall we, in truth, become absorbed by it. And in that process of absorption, the thought of I disintegrates and we, in truth, become one with the whole.

Your planet, Earth, on which you presently reside, as we have spoken before, offers you, as the fifth planet in your solar system, offers you the lessons of faith. And indeed are the experiences many, ever revealing to us—as the demonstration of each moment is the revelation of truth to us—offering to us each moment that great truth of where we have directed our faith. We spoke to you many times upon the functions of money, ego, and sex. And time and time again, as we view your world, we see this great power called faith directed to pieces of green paper. Each and every time that the human mind is permitted to direct this great power of God, known as faith, to a piece of paper, then that soul suffers his own denial of God.

So, my good students, in any area of your experience, remember, when you view the effect—when you desire the effect and you no longer desire the awakening of the cause within your consciousness, then you must pay the great price of building your false gods. And it is your false gods, created by your own beliefs, that imprison your being. But as each soul, in its evolution, has established, by the laws that it has itself, through its vehicles, created, those lessons, they come, they serve their purpose, and they go.

In your continued lessons in life, permit yourself to seek the good in each experience that you encounter, for in each experience God is there. For God is the power that sustains the form known as experience.

And we have spoken on taking the essence from the experience, which is the indispensable ingredient for the reeducation of the senses. The essence of experience is the very principle. That, my good students, is where you find God. Make some effort each moment to view that underlying principle. And there, in so doing, will you place God, or good, in all thought and in all endeavor. Each of us, in truth, knows what we have in life to do. We know, our true being does know. The seeming difficulty is in reeducating the human mind that it may accept what we already know.

Thank you. What is meant by the statement that we are in charge of all creation?

Indeed, we are. We are indeed in charge of all creation, for he who is the creator of creation is responsible. He has the ability to respond to his creations. And so it is in this understanding we have taught, and continue to teach, that God is the impartial, intelligent, divine Energy that sustains all things. It is this mental process that is the creative principle. In many ways and in many days we teach the same eternal, simple truth: as you believeth, you becometh.

Try to understand, my good students, when your mind asks the question, "Then, who created the stars in the heavens and who created the trees in the field and who created the rivers and the oceans"? Pause and think, my students, who, who established the Law of Identity? Or was the Law of Identity something that always was? You must pause and think, and think more deeply. Consider this intelligent power that will flow wherever there is an opening or vehicle through which to flow. It is not the concern of this divine power where it shall flow. Its nature or principle *is* flow or expression.

Then consider, permeating the atmosphere everywhere, a substance known as belief, and that this substance is governed by the very nature of multiplication. And so it is that the beliefs of man are ever in keeping with the effects of multiplication, known as complexity, and that the very destiny of complexity is confusion, that its inevitable path is regret. View this in the light of reason, as the form is ever refined and evolved—to return to the source of a much higher rate of vibration—and that this process is taking place constantly throughout all eternity.

It is, to say the least, difficult for any mind, limited by its own choice of identity, to accept the possibility of a universal consciousness that is communing with forms everywhere, though distant by many light years from the earth realm. You have often been taught that as a man believeth in his heart shall he be. My students, you know that the heart is the vehicle through which your eternal true being, called soul, expresses, uncensored, uncontaminated, unrestricted by mental substance. And so your prophets have taught for centuries, as you believeth in your heart, so shall you becometh.

Now, this vehicle called the heart, through which the soul expresses in its fullness and in its freedom, becomes restricted and limited the moment that the experience is recorded by the mental body. And so we see that belief is, in truth, identification. We are what we believe, which is, in truth, what we identify with. And so in order to bring about a more harmonious change in life's experiences, we must identify with the good. The moment that man starts to believe or identify with goodness, or God, the identification forms of the human mind begin to wage their war within. Now, these patterns, forms, entities, which are the effects of belief or identity, are what, in truth, is presently controlling the being. And because they have, in their growth—these identities—forgotten the source from whence they were given birth, they become the rulers of our realm.

But, my students, I assure you that you have the power within you to believe—as you know you must—to believe in the fullness of life. For the effect of that belief is the demonstration and the revelation. As long as your soul is expressing through a mental body, as long as your formless free spirit is expressing through form, you are governed by the Law of Identity. For without identity, that law, you would not be in form.

But when man begins to make the effort to change his identity or beliefs, the other identities, waging their war, present to your mind the justifications of why things are the way they are. And the justifications presented by the human mind are the first guard of defense—to defend the patterns of old. And so he who frequently justifies is in great fear of change.

My good students, this philosophy teaches the simple truth: there are no accidents. There is no truth in excuses. Life is simple and easily revealed. There is a cause for all things and the cause of things is the principle of things. But we must bow the temporal being, the human mind, and accept, through the Law of Identity, the right of peace, of abundance, of goodness, of health, wealth, and happiness. But to experience that birthright, that divine birthright, we must bow the pride, we must broaden the acceptance, for that is the fullness of God. That is the goodness of life. Look at all of life and see the good, for the good, or God, is there.

Yes, man, in his evolution has charge—the ability to respond or responsibility to all creation. For man's mental body is the refined, perfected body of the mental realms. And being the most perfected, in the sense of evolution and refinement, he is, in truth, in charge of those realms.

Look, my good students, at all of nature. Will you find an animal as cunning, as devious, and as clever as the human animal? Will you, in all your study and in all of your experience, find an animal as destructive, as discordant with nature and its surroundings? You cannot find an animal upon your planet or any planet in the universes as destructive, as cunning, as deceiving, as the human animal. You cannot find an animal with such total disregard of the other creatures of the planet. You cannot find an animal that has so willingly polluted the Earth planet. And the human animal has done so because it has forgotten the Source that sustains it. In its evolution and in its refinement, it has gained the function of pride, totally out of balance with the faculty of humility.

I recommend, my good students, that you study in your study book [*The Living Light* and *The Living Light Dialogue*, Volume 1], the meaning of the soul faculty of humility, that you may, in your study and application, gain the awareness of your responsibility and, in so doing, stem the tide of so-called scientific advancement upon your planet, that the spiritual awakening may bring a balance to your planet. And in bringing that balance, clear the atmosphere, the air that you breathe, the water you drink, and the food that you eat. For your scientific advancement has already far exceeded your spiritual awakening. And as planets before you have risen to fall, as great civilizations upon your Earth planet—far greater intellectually and in scientific advancement than you have yet reached—as those civilizations, they, too, polluted the atmosphere, not in the ways of your present pollution, but in pollution of spiritual truth, they rose and fell.

Take care of your universe and, in so doing, shall ye become the instruments of changing that around and about you. As a light in the dark shall gather the moths who are seeking to go home, so let your light shine in the darkness of your earthly realm. Be not concerned with how bright or dim it may be, for light is light. And it is the light of your soul, when you permit it to shine by opening your soul faculties. You need not speak, for truth is known by truth: it is that which is.

Thank you. What is meant by sterling character?

Sterling character is when the faculties of the soul and the functions of the senses are in balance. Then, man expresses what is known as a sterling character, a character of right and goodness. It is not necessary for man to study any religion or philosophy to have a sterling character. Many souls enter your earthly realm and, in keeping with their efforts of centuries, have merited a vehicle known as a sterling character. Bring your faculties and functions into balance and you will know the beauty, the goodness, and the justice of a sterling character: a character that stands upon the rock of principle, that bows not to temptation, for temptation is the voice that calls us to creation.

And creation was designed by a great architect to serve a good purpose. But in temptation man blinds his faculty of reason. He forgets the Source of his being and, in so doing, rises in pride for his accomplishments in life. He who is not easily tempted has awakened, to some extent, his soul faculty of humility. We all know whether or not we are easily tempted. And we all know if humility has sufficient value within us and is leading us through, that we may stand and face the light of truth, that we need not hide in the dark corners of deception, that we may be an open book in the library of truth.

My students, our book of life is written each moment. It is a very large book, for many life experiences are already recorded. You may benefit yourself by keeping your record where you can easily read it with your physical eyes. You only need make two columns. They're very simple. Mark one column "Motive" and mark the other column "Temptation." And you will know where you are at any given moment, for so often our motive gets twisted and turned as our mind views temptation. And when our motive is twisted by temptation, we lose the strength and the great essence of truth called principle.

My dear friends, principle will not fail you. It is the very essence of God that is sustaining you. Be not concerned about all these things. Let your heart not only speak, for speak it does, but let your mind, through your own efforts of controlling it, let your mind listen to what your heart is whispering. Regardless of all the thoughts of all the universes, listen and act upon what your heart is speaking. In so doing, shall you be freed from fear, for you, in those moments that you listen and act upon the simple guidance of your heart, in those moments you are home. Your soul is in the home of peace, which is, in truth, the power of God. And remember that you and God are a majority. And the majority shall not only endure, they shall win out for truth.

Do not let your soul, by the temptations of your created mind, do not let it be sold. Do not sell out. Do not sell out for anything your earth realm has to offer, for it is centuries on the other sides of life. I assure you, that one second of demonstrable principle, established by your own efforts, is equal to one hundred years in the realms that await your experience.

Good night.

SEPTEMBER 8, 1977

CONSCIOUSNESS CLASS 154

Greetings, students. This evening we are discussing the Law of Life, expression and experience.

As the Law of Life is, in truth, the divine, neutral, infinite energy and expresses through what is known as the eternal soul, which, in turn, expresses through the varied vehicles or forms in its evolutionary path, we find then, as our soul, ever unfolding in the sense of its freedom of expression through the form, the experiences recorded by the form are the necessary ingredient for the evolutionary Law of Change.

And so it is that some time ago we stated to you, "O God, I am grateful for all life's experiences, for I know that they are, in truth, my greatest blessings." And so, my good students, let us view our souls' expression and let us view our sense functions of experience.

As you know this, the eternal being, expressing through this eternal soul, wears many, many, many garments on its evolutionary path. And so today you find yourselves wearing the earthly garments, experiencing constantly a multitude of different things. These experiences are ever the effects to remove from your path the obstructions that have been garnered up from many, many years of error. And these obstructions are slowly, but surely, removed through the evolutionary process of refinement.

As the forms are slowly and often painfully refined, transmuted, and reformed, the soul expresses an ever-expanding consciousness through what is known as the forty triune soul faculties The faculties and functions are gradually brought into a perfect balance. This perfect balance, which is the awakening of the faculty of reason, brings about this transfiguration of the forms.

In these years of discussion of forms, we have not yet discussed the experiences taking place in other realms of consciousness in your daily activities. So often man views life as a school where lessons are to be learned, to be passed, and to ever move onward to a hopeful, final day of graduation. My good students, each moment we are graduating from something. And so it is in your study and awakening of the faculties and functions that you will find that each triune faculty and each triune function is, in truth, a vehicle of expression through which divine intelligent energy is being expressed in this your moment of awareness. These many bodies are something that are activated by the imbalance—the in balance between the functions and the faculties.

Now, I should like to spend some time in this particular matter, that you may fully understand what I am endeavoring to express. For example, if a person is expressing through the soul faculty of duty, gratitude, and tolerance, a form is created representing that soul faculty. Now, my good students, let us perhaps first view Nature herself. The tree does not automatically grow, nor does the blade of grass, nor does the human form, or any form in any dimension. The form, or vehicle of the energy, is created by the laws of creation, which the mental realms are responsible for. And so we find that when energy, neutral, impartial, intelligent energy enters into what is known as a mental realm, the mental realm is what creates the shape and the form of the vehicle.

You have often heard that the spiritual body is not yet complete or fully formed. You have also heard that the spiritual body is created through an expression of the soul faculties. You have also heard that the mental body, astral body is created as an effect of energy directed through the functions.

Man experiences in the realm of consciousness in which the divine energy is predominately being expressed. Man awakens to spiritual levels of consciousness through a conscious effort of directing this energy through the soul faculties. Without an effort being made to bring about a balance between the mental and spiritual realms, man finds life imbalanced within, as he is the one directing this intelligent infinite energy.

Each and every experience, though necessary for the evolving soul that it may fully express its beauty and splendor, each and every experience slowly, but surely, and ofttimes painfully removing the obstructions in front of the soul, can be brought easily and quickly into balance by bringing into one's consciousness the corresponding faculty that will bring the balance in[to] the experience.

When we leave in consciousness the mental realm—and it is within our power to leave the mental realm at any moment of our choice—we become aware of our true purpose in life. It is in that awareness that we accept, without reservation, the responsibility that we have in evolution incurred. In our accepting the responsibility—the ability to respond to the laws that we have established in mental spheres—in that acceptance, we are not only freed, but rise to the heights of spiritual joy. It is, and has been, our purpose to help you to help yourselves in bringing about this balance while yet in your earthly forms. The beauty of life, like anything in life, is ever dependent upon your acceptance.

So many feel that it is easier to go the way downward than it is to struggle on the climb upward. My good children, whatever your patterns of mind may be that you find difficulty in changing, you can be assured that it is a battle between what you have created and what you truly are. Man, through direction of energy, has given creation, or forms, the power to control him. Because man has given creation that power, only man—his eternal soul—can rise and bring about the balance: to place creation in its proper place. And its proper place being the tool to serve the eternal life. For that which is built, by the Law of Building, shall come to its end. And all of nature reveals to you constantly and demonstrates repeatedly this Law of Constant Change of all forms.

Let us in this moment begin upon the path of reliance—to rely upon that which is lasting and enduring. Let us be reasonable and place our attention, the infinite energy, upon the Source and not upon its limitless diversity of forms through which it is expressing. So often man says, "It is difficult. It is difficult to pray to that which is formless and free. It is difficult to rely upon that which the mind cannot, *cannot* grasp or control." It is not within the realms of possibility for the created forms to control the very power that sustains them. And each and every time that we attempt to learn about spiritual matters for the motive of controlling them, we place an obstruction between our soul and that which is its rightful home.

Let us, in our endeavors, learn to accept without reservation our right to the fullness of life. For he who accepts without reservation is free from the control of the throne of judgment. And being free from the throne of the control of judgment, the fullness of life, its goodness and abundance, is made manifest in that moment.

But pause in your thinking and see what truly takes place the very moment that you declare the truth, "I accept."

It is the thought of I that is in need of education, that through the process of education it may be refined and evolved that it may broaden the limits that it has created. Man says that he seeks the goodness of life. He seeks the abundance and the fullness of life. But that is where we stop. That is where we stop thinking and then we start reacting. For the moment that we have a desire for abundance and goodness in life, it moves through the mental realms of consciousness and the obstructions and the dictates from eons of past experiences in mental realms declare what we must do.

The thought of I, through the divine mercy, is not yet able to dictate what we must do in order to breathe. If it had control of some of those basic realms in nature, there would be chaos and upheaval.

My students, I strongly recommend, as a daily, daily effort, that you speak the words that free you and say, "I accept." Become aware in your daily activities of what happens in your mind, in your mental realms when you have experiences that you judge to be distasteful. Speak the word of truth, "I accept." You see, my good students, you have already accepted or you could not experience. So is it not foolhardy to have an experience and not declare the truth, which is, "I accept"? For, as I said, in order to have the experience the law that "I accept" has already been established.

But there is another part of the mind and it says, "I am not responsible for this experience." It says it is not responsible because, you see, my good students, there are eighty-one levels of consciousness and if, through prayer, you come into a state of peace, in a state of peace you will clearly see, "Oh yes, indeed that is the law that I set into motion. And this is the experience of that law returning to me. I do not find the effect of that law pleasing, nor beneficial. I do not find it beneficial because I do not yet see clearly the good that is contained therein."

My good students, there is no experience in all eternity that does not have God in it, for God is the power that sustains it. The form taken has been created from mental substance, but that which sustains it is good. It is always good, for it is God. Instead of battling—a house divided—unite in consciousness through the power of peace. And through that great power, you shall see God in all things. You shall view God in the most distasteful of experiences, for you shall know that God is there.

Remember that which comes is destined to go. There is nothing in the realms of experience that is not born to die. And so birth and death—links in an eternal chain—they come and they go, each moment, every moment. When you awaken within, you will find the joy of death as you find the joy of birth, for as you experience death, through the power of peace you will, in that moment, experience birth. It is ever dependent upon our view.

So let us view the horizon that we may see its beauty and its fullness. Let us not be sad of that which is passing, that we may not be saddened by that which is coming. For to be sad in the coming or going is to establish the Law of Sadness and guarantee the experience thereof.

We have been given everything. If we do not yet believe that we have it, it is but an error of ignorance that is blinding us. For it is in the very atmosphere that you move and breathe: All the goodness you are, in truth, a part. The experience of that goodness is dependent upon your total acceptance. Be not divided in consciousness, my students. See life as life is. It has given us everything good. It is our thought—the thought of I—that makes it seem, sometimes, to be bad.

You may ask your questions at this time.

Thank you. Please give us your understanding of the importance of work.

This intelligent Energy, known as God, is in a constant process of movement. It is never still. It is ever active. It has ever been and it shall ever be. This energy in a constant process of vibration moves all things, be it the thought of man, the sun, the stars, or Earth itself. And for man to go contrary to divine, demonstrable, natural Law of Vibration is to establish an obstruction to divine flow.

So often man seems to experience a shortage of something. The experience of man's lack and limitation, the experience of man's shortages is a revelation, by the demonstration of lack, that he is not moving in divine flow.

Now, work, the principle of work, is the very essence of divine flow. We are designed, as forms, to move. And the energy flowing through us is in a constant process of movement. And so, as man works, man moves. And as he moves, there is an evolutionary refining process that takes place. Let man view his endeavors. Let man view those endeavors objectively that he may see. If they are not moving, then the divine energy is not flowing unobstructed through them.

We said to you some time ago in reference to the business of success that it was, in principle, the lack of concern. For when man gets out, God gets in. And when you are seeking the divine flow, then there is one word that you must flood your consciousness with and that is known as *work*. Work is love made manifest, because it is the instrument through which God moves. Let us awaken the joy within us—the joy for the opportunity of work. For he who does not work is in a process of self-destruction. For the energy shall flow, and it does flow. And in reference to work, it is inseparable from selfless service, for through the removal of the thought of I is work truly the love of God.

Thank you. Please share your understanding of why people sometimes insist upon being naive.

In keeping with the evolution of the eternal being, there have been so many, many experiences that man has chosen to forget. And in so choosing, he establishes the law of their return. And as he slowly, but surely, becomes aware of the return, he builds up, in his consciousness, what is known as a defense: not to view that which he has already judged, from experience, to be distasteful. To be naive is a demonstration of a unwillingness to accept, to communicate, and to be reasonable.

We have all created within our minds an illusion called a self-image. And we spend much time and much energy on protecting the image and on defending the image and on expressing the image. But it is only an image, subject to the laws of creation. And because it is an image and because, being an image, it is subject to the laws of creation, it is in a constant process of change. But man, being the creator of the image, does not want that which he has created to change. And so man builds up this cloud of being naive, unaware. He attempts to blot out the inevitable, known as the Law of Change.

And so it is many factors are involved in what you call being naive. However, through a sincere effort and a pure motive to find the truth which frees you, this cloud of being naive shall disappear and the sunlight of reason shall shine. And in so doing, the soul faculties shall open, understanding shall expand the consciousness, and the freedom that is rightfully the home of the soul shall come to pass.

Thank you. Please share your understanding of serenity and tranquility and how these differ from peace.

My good students, you may call it what you will, but peace is beyond the description offered by the human mind. When the questioner seeks to find distinction or difference between tranquility, serenity, and peace, it is the seeking of the mind which ever questions, which ever sees duality. For that which is dual can only experience the dual. But that which is one is truth. So let us not tempt to control peace, for it is not the peace of the mind, but it is the peace of the soul which *is*. You may find tranquility for a moment in mental consciousness. You may even find serenity in consciousness. But peace is that which is. It is not that which you find.

Thank you. Please share your understanding of prayer. Are there unrecognized so-called tests that one must pass in advance of receiving what one has prayed for?

All tests are ever in keeping with the judgments established by the human mind. As the soul aspires, the form perspires. That is the simple so-called rule of thumb. When you find yourself perspiring from love made manifest, called work, you may be rest assured, the aspiration of your soul is in full bloom.

Thank you. We are taught that you cannot grant to another what you have not granted to yourself. Is the converse also true, that when you grant to another you are then able to grant to yourself?

My students, the statement given some time ago is that you cannot grant to another what you have not first granted unto yourself, for you cannot become qualified without first granting it to yourself. And so it is that what you do not grant to yourself, you cannot, in truth, grant to another. For you cannot be an instrument of granting unless you first qualify yourself for the position of doing so.

Let us then put our attention upon accepting that which is ours. Let us refrain from denial, for God denies no one. And surely we all know that we and God are, in truth, a majority. We are a majority by our acceptance thereof. Let us place our energy and our efforts upon acceptance, that our horizons maybe broadened. And in so doing, all of life shall rise up and rejoice. Let us make that effort for the Light to shine within us. But remember, friends, we must not judge the Light, for in so doing we lose the Light. God is not the judge. God is the witness. And the witness never judges.

Thank you. Please explain further how we can give a desire back to God.

By recognizing, from first accepting, that from God it came and to God it shall rightfully return. Desire is the divine expression.

Some time ago we spoke to you on desire, the divine expression, the expression of God. We spoke to you this evening that the soul expresses and the senses experience. Now, my students, you ask about giving a desire back to God. When you have the experience of desire in your mind, you must ask the question, "Does it come from God?" We all know that, in truth, the very principle of desire is the expression of God. But man's mind, ever in keeping with what it thinks it knows, has made many, many judgments. And man has judged that some desires come from God and some desires do not.

I assure you that the principle known as desire *is* the divine expression. The form that desire takes is ever dependent upon the human mind, which has the experience. The soul, your soul has the expression. Your mind has the experience. And so desire, emanating from the divine Source, flowing through the soul in expression, recorded in the mind as experience, brings to man, instead of the goodness of life, a multitude of problems.

We must look at life as life truly is. We have decided what is good. Therefore, supposedly we know what is bad, for that that we have decided is good fits into a sphere of limitation that we alone have created in mental consciousness. And anything that does not fit into that little realm has to be bad. And yet, in your short lives on Earth, you have already, *already* viewed, "What I thought was good has now proven to be not so good. And what I thought was bad has now proven to be good." So what is good or bad but the judgment man makes by his own errors of ignorance?

We see the day and we see the night. We say that one is light and the other is dark. I assure you, my good students, it is all light. It is but a lesser light. And so it is the degree of light, as it is the degree of acceptance that we are experiencing in life. But remember, above and beyond all of that is the peace that is.

The wars of Earth shall end in time not too far distant. They shall end because, in keeping with the evolution of the

Earth planet, the Earth is entering a greater acceptance. And as that greater acceptance takes hold of your earthly sphere, wars shall come to an ending and peace shall reign supreme. Without judgment, there is no war, for there is no war within. And with divine will, which is total acceptance, judgment cannot survive. Wars are the effect of judgment. They are the effects of limited acceptance.

And so it is that our school brings to your world the divine demonstrable truth: that God rejects nothing, that God is the epitome of total acceptance, and that love—not the love of your mind, but the love of your soul—shall reign supreme, that as you make your daily efforts to keep yourselves in the peace that is, you become an instrument of the Divine. And the light, though not visible to your physical eyes, goes out into the world wherever you walk, wherever you move, wherever you speak. And in so doing, it attracts, from the realms of light, angels of light that you may not stumble in the darkness. So be not concerned with your minds. And in being not concerned with your minds, the light shines more brightly in your earthly realm and untold thousands of joyous souls enter into your realm of consciousness and peace reigns on Earth and heaven has come at last.

Good night.

SEPTEMBER 15, 1977

CONSCIOUSNESS CLASS 155

Greetings, students. This evening we shall journey to the realms of idea.

As man is the effect of an idea, so it is in your realm, through the process known as the thought of I, that idea is made manifest and man, as you know man, is in your earth realm. We have spoken to you ofttimes on the problems that man has being directly related to the thought of I. By a removal of this mental thought of I, man is freed from the entrapment of mental and physical realms and freed in consciousness to once again return home to the allness, to the unity of all of life. Because man, in truth, is an idea, individuality is an effect of this principle known as idea. So man, in his journey ever onward and ever upward, slowly and ofttimes painfully, is freeing himself from this manifestation in mental realms, this mental thought of I.

As this awakening and refining process continues on, there is a broadening of the thoughts of man. There is an expansion of the acceptances and the divine right of all of life.

It has been said by some that it is not that man needs more of anything. It is that man's needs are the acceptances of the rights of all. Let us, my good students, in our efforts and in our application of our daily activities, let us truly pause. Let us pause in our thought that we may, in so doing, become, slowly but surely, aware—aware of this unity, aware of this oneness of which we are, in truth, inseparably a part of. For it is in those moments that we pause that the soul faculty of courage is given an opportunity within us to rise up and stand firm on principle. And in so doing, we see more clearly. Let us, in that process, never, ever forget that what affects one, in truth, affects all.

We have indeed earned a great responsibility, a great responsibility in our evolution that by a simple change in our thought, the universe, as a whole, is being affected. For when we truly consider that grave responsibility, the universe in which we have been moving seemingly suddenly expands, our view broadens tremendously, and then we truly know: we know what we must do. And in that awakening, we begin to do what is right. We indeed know in those moments of pause. We know what is right for us to do.

We are freed, by the soul faculty of courage, we are freed from fear. Fear which is, as we already know, the mind's control over our true being. We must, in our efforts, we must be courageous. We must learn the wisdom of patience and we must know beyond the shadow of any doubt that that which is good, that which is divine, is rising supreme in our consciousness. Let us not look so often at our struggles that we may enjoy those moments of peace that are ever waiting for us to enjoy. Let us truly look for the good in all of life's experiences, for the good is the essence, the God which sustains the experience, not the experience in and of itself.

But as we view the good in all of the experiences of life—which, in truth, is taking place within our own mind—by making that simple effort each moment of life, we direct the divine energy to the goodness within us. And the goodness within us strengthens moment by moment and, in time, our lives reflect that blessing.

Man, as he makes that effort and through that very process of directing the thought, the form, to view the goodness, what man, in truth, is really doing is sending the created forms of mental substance to stand and bask before the light of reason. This, my good friends, is, in truth, the transmutation process of mental substance. As each thought that you entertain in mind is directed by your thought of goodness, it must go before the eternal light of reason. There, the substance of this thought form is transmuted, is transfigured by this light of reason and returns to you, the creator or father of it. We spoke to you in one of our other classes about directing the thought upward and this, in other words, is what we're speaking about again.

Man has brought with him, in his eternal evolution, man has brought with him the throne of judgment. It is a very old throne. It is the effect of the thought of I, for in this the thought of I is the denial of the oneness of God. It is the thought of I that is the judge. It is the thought of I that is the maker of the laws of our mental universe. And this, this judge that we have brought with us in our evolution, has had a multitude of experiences and is ever alert and ever conscious of each feeling and thought that rises within what he has judged is his domain.

And so this judge, which we, in our errors of ignorance, have been serving for centuries, continues his demands upon our efforts and upon our life. Pause, my students. We spoke a moment ago to pause and in the pause shall your soul faculty of courage rise, for it takes great courage, great courage to face the judge who is so old, who is so limited and so definite in his dictates. But he must—and he is being dethroned. And as that dethronement process is inevitable, for all form rises and all form falls. The judge of which many religionists have spoken, he sits on his throne in your realm of consciousness. When you leave your physical bodies, fear not, for fear is the weapon that controls you. Be freed from fear by the faith in the eternal Light, called God.

And think, my good students, this great judge does not want you to think unless it is a thought that he directs to your mind. This great judge does not want you to pause, for he knows when you pause, your strength of your soul rises. Try to consider, to be compassionate with this created entity. Be patient, for patience is the very thing this judge cannot endure. For each time you are patient, the judge is immobile in the moment that you are patient. He cannot dictate. He cannot express. In whatever area of life that you choose to use the soul faculty of patience, the mind cannot control.

Some time ago we spoke to you on the pain of patience. Patience is very painful to the judge that controls the mind, for he must look at, each moment of your patience, he must look at the light that shines, the light of reason.

For some time in these past semesters, we have spoken about these varied forms. Now it is time, my good students, to consider these simple applications. There is never a moment that the mind is not active until your soul rises and controls it. And each time that you control your mind, you must be willing to pay the price. Think how it is when your mind has desire and the light of reason has risen and simply spoken, "The Law of Patience." Your soul does not suffer. It is only the forms created in the mental worlds that make you think you're suffering. Remember, you are not the forms of life. They are the tools designed for your use. Place them in their proper perspective. They are not you, my students, and they never were. They never can be. Use these tools of form wisely, by not being deluded by them that you are them or that they are you.

Many times have we asked that you separate truth from creation. That separation takes place in the moment that you pause. But do not confuse that faculty of pause with the function of procrastination and justification, for there is indeed a vast, a very vast difference.

Of all creation and of all of the refinement of it that is taking place, there is good in all things. Because we have indeed forgotten to use it wisely has it brought to us difficulties and struggle.

The journey of your soul on the earthly realm is indeed very, very short. But it offers to you the opportunity to grow, the opportunity to expand, for that, in truth, is what growth really is. That which grows expands. And it is an expanding consciousness that is really taking place. Those of you who have been with us for a time have already demonstrated, in many areas of your life, your growth, for many things that you would not permit to expand in your consciousness have indeed expanded. Perhaps you think sometimes that you have not grown, but you only think that way because you are viewing one small, minute area of your life. You have made changes and changes are expansion, and expansion is growth or evolution. It may not be taking place as rapidly as perhaps you would like, but your desire for increased rapidity, for things to move faster, is certainly not a demonstration of your soul faculty of patience. But it is a revelation of a sense function that wishes another sense function to be annihilated in order that it may grow.

Think, my students, think about the beauty of change. Think how much you have already changed and you're changing every moment. Every moment something new is being introduced into your mind. Every moment it's taking place. That is what life truly is. Graciously accept the new. Be not so concerned about the old. The fountain of youth is ever dependent upon the broadening of your acceptance. You will always be young, you will always be youthful, if you will always graciously accept the new. It is in your graciousness of acceptance of things that have not yet been accepted by your mind, it is your graciousness of acceptance that your youth—that fountain of reason—is dependent in your life.

As each thought entertained in the human mind affects the physical body, either in peace and harmonious affect or in discord and disease, your health and youthfulness is dependent upon harmonious thought. Now, when you permit the human mind to have the rigidity of thought that is already in it—it is this rigidity, it is this holding on to thoughts which have, in truth, worn themselves from lack of rejuvenation of new thought, new activity, that is, in truth, wearing out your mental and physical bodies. Man was not designed by this architect to stay on Earth for a limited number of years. And we have discussed that somewhat in one of our other classes.

Because there is a constant process ever taking place that grants unto man what is known as the right of choice, the laws that you have already established may be reversed. You have this 10 percent so-called free will to direct, through the vehicle of thought, positive harmonious energy to any area of your life.

Many students have asked why they have had certain experiences. And sometimes the answer has been forthcoming. Sometimes it is not in the best interest of the questioner to receive the answer from without at that time. I say to you, my students, that you may find the cause of all experience, that you may find the cause of your health, your wealth, and your happiness—or its opposite—by simply taking stock of the patterns and thoughts of your mind: finding which ones are discordant and therefore diseased; finding which ones are harmonious and therefore healthy. Take stock of how the mind works.

Through your efforts to pause and think more deeply, you will become aware of how quick the human mind is to judge. But that is not you. You are not the human mind. You are that wonderful, beautiful spirit that is expressing through a vehicle known as the human mind. You are the life, the light, and the love of God. That is what you truly are. And when you remember what you truly are, you will, slowly but surely, remove the energy that is being directed to these forms so that you, the light, the life, and the love of God, will express more fully, will express more freely, and live more abundantly.

Let not those forms dictate to you. They were not designed by God to do so. It is our error of mind that has made it so. Place your attention upon what you really are, for in so doing do you not only benefit yourself, but in so doing you are then in a level of consciousness to see that in another. For, my students, whatever we see in another is the level of consciousness through which our soul is viewing.

We also stated that hate was simply love distorted. That's what it really is. Distorted by the errors of ignorance, by these varied forms of creation. Pause and think more deeply, that you may be flooded with the faculty of gratitude, for it is through gratitude that God's love flows unceasingly. If you feel that you are short, if you feel that you are in need, if you feel you are limited, then in those moments of feeling so, ask yourself the simple truth, "O God, am I grateful? Am I grateful or am I, through an error of ignorance of my mind, dictating to you? Am I dictating and, in so doing, unable to receive?"

When we give up the thought of denial, we will receive the principle of acceptance. In other words, my good students, when we give the self-will, we gain the divine will. It's a simple, so simple transaction.

But it is not the giving of things. It is the giving of the cause of things. But that is a great gift to the judge who sits on the throne of self. It is a great gift. Give, my students, that which is inside. You have heard it stated many times that the gift without the giver is worthless. But who is the giver? Who is it that makes the gift worthy? What is it? When you give something—no matter what it is you give—unless you give your relationship, your mental attachment, to that which you give, then you have not given at all. And the gift, therefore, is not worthy of proper or good use. My students, when you give the self related to the gift, the soul moves in all its beauty and goodness with your effort. It multiplies the goodness around and about it and the showers from heaven come like golden rain. And the most difficult gift of all to give is the gift of self.

And now you are free to ask your questions.

Thank you. Please explain why it is that wishing will not make it so?

If wishing made anything so, then man would not be able to live a life at all, for wishes are the fantasies of the fantasy realm. They are created in realms of fantasy. They live in realms of fantasy and they lack the principle substance to bring them into mental and physical realms. Man wishes for so many things. But that is a realm of fantasy. And in that realm, only the foolhardy spend time and energy.

Thank you. We have been taught that both sex and pride are counterbalancing functions of humility. Would you please elaborate on this?

In reference to your question concerning pride and procreation or sex and the soul faculty of humility, you must also—the questioner—ask, "What are they? Is pride, my pride, unique to me?" And you must answer honestly that indeed it is. Not that others do not have pride, but their pride is different. You must ask yourself also the question in reference to sex, "Am I, in that respect, in my thought and in my mind unique?" And your answer comes, "Oh yes, indeed, indeed I am. Not that it is not with others, but it is unique to me." It is this thought, this thought of I, that controls not only pride, but sex; that puts the totality of self into action. And it is this totality of self that is man's great problem. Though the self says, "Oh yes, others have those things, but not identical with me. Not exactly the same."

My students, when this faculty of humility floods our mind, there is no longer, there is no longer separation from principle. We have no longer this uniqueness. We are, in our mind, no longer special incarnations of the Divine. It is through our efforts to detach ourselves from this mental illusion of uniqueness— my students, think. Stop, pause, and think. God's manifestation is variety. But you are more than the manifestation. You are, in truth, the very essence that sustains the manifestation, for God, the true you, is moving all creation.

Whenever you permit the throne of self to dictate, through the function of pride or sex, your uniqueness, you are so filled with the manifestation of the function that you can no longer view the principle, which you truly are. Therefore you become, in that moment, a house divided. There is no principle to balance out your personality. That, my students, is where the problem truly lies. However, if, in your efforts, you pause to give your soul the opportunity to rise, the faculty of humility will speak within you. And then you will once again be reunited with the principle, and harmony, balance, and reason will bring you peace.

Thank you. How can we overcome our attachments, such as a mother's attachment to her children and fear for their harm?

We have explained before that fear is the control over the eternal soul exercised by the human mind or self. Whenever we permit the mind to express, to experience what we call fear, we have, in those moments, denied God. And a mother's attachment to her children is the demonstration, depending upon the degree of attachment, of the denial of God. For that that we love—that we truly love—we do not bind or attach, for to attach is to limit, to attach is to bind. And if we love—whatever or whoever we love—if we truly love them, we could not, in our heart, possibly bind them. We could not, in our heart, possibly limit them.

But beware, my good students, for the mind that receives that simple truth quickly blinks its eyes to license, for it does not view principle. We must use reason in all things. But a mother who believes she is attached to her child is not flooding her consciousness with God, for if she was, the light of reason would clearly show, "My attachments are binding the soul. Though I accepted this soul from God, I have claimed it for my own and, therefore, denied its right of expression."

Though God, the divine Principle, is flowing through us, we must not permit our minds to dictate that we are God, for in the word *we* is limit and personality. And if we permit the mind to say that *we* are God, then we have limited God. So when we say, "We are attached," what, in truth, we are saying is, we have controlled and bound, enslaved and ruled another soul which, in truth, is God's. And because we have done that in our errors of ignorance, we shall pay the price. And price is ever just and ever in keeping with the laws divine that have been transgressed.

And so in our efforts to be free from those errors, opportunity has knocked. The questioner must open the door. And remember that yesterday has gone, tomorrow has not yet come, but this moment you can be free, for in this moment you can give your child to God.

Good night.

SEPTEMBER 22, 1977

CONSCIOUSNESS CLASS 156

Greetings, students. This evening we are discussing the law most frequently expressed in your earthly journey. That law is the Law of Application.

As we view our lives we see that each moment we are, in truth, directing energy through one of the many levels of consciousness. And in the directing of this energy, we are demonstrating, in those moments, the Law of Application. And so it is that all of us, in truth, are well, indeed, well qualified in this particular law. However, as man, by his choice, directs this energy to any particular level of consciousness, through that direction and the repetition thereof, the level of consciousness, in time, becomes superior to all the other levels through which the divine Intelligence is flowing. And in its error, from lack of consideration of other levels—through that great error, it begins to control. And in its control, we become not only the victim, but we become the slave to created substance—created substance meaning temporal. And that is where man sees such difficulty and such struggle in life.

Life, the expression of the divine Principle, was not designed for struggle and strife, was not designed for conflict and turmoil, but is, in truth, a harmonious and beautiful flow of infinite, intelligent energy. It is easier, to many, to pluck the tooth from a chicken than to change a thought in the human mind. Now, we all know that a chicken does not have teeth, as we know them. And so we see by that analogy that there is, by our own beliefs, difficulties and struggles in life.

In these many, many classes we have often repeated simple, demonstrable truth. And in that repetition there has been, and continues to be, a seemingly slow and gradual, but sure, change in the consciousness of the students. We alone are directing this energy. It is not only our divine birthright to direct it, but it is our destiny. For we are, in truth, the instruments of creation.

It is through our personal choice that these many things that we experience are created. If we permit our minds to dictate the struggle and the difficulties, then struggles and difficulties will reflect in our consciousness, that we may prove unto ourselves that we are right. It is the very need of the human mind to continue to prove to itself in order to support its authority of so-called individuality. It is the very need to prove that it is right. And so we go about, in life's experiences, entertaining a multitude of different thoughts. And we work like little beavers in order that we may prove what we said it would be. Unfortunately, it does seem sometimes that we spend more time and energy on proving that we are right in negative areas rather than in positive ones. But remember, my good friends, law, being impartial, works for the negative as well as for the positive.

Above and beyond the worlds of conflict and turmoil are the worlds of peace and the worlds of harmony, the worlds of abundance, of goodness. That is the true home for all of us. And so when our minds consider that there is a home that is better, that there just has to be something better, in that type of thinking the door begins to open. It is through our acceptance of the possibility of change that we grow and grow more graciously. So let us consider more frequently the possibility of something better. We need not dictate. We need only to accept what is true. Accept the possibility, for that opens horizons that the soul has sought for many centuries.

So often I hear on your earthly realm the question of what is it really like beyond this physical, material realm. My friends, learn to direct the energy that is flowing through you. Many, many times have we asked you to pause and to think more deeply. What does that statement truly mean, "To think and think and think more deeply"? To go beyond the thoughts, the feelings, and the attitudes that you are consciously aware of.

To make that effort to go beyond those conscious thoughts is to direct energy into areas of consciousness that you have not yet, through personal experience, been consciously aware of.

Think, think what is available to you at any moment of your choice. When you believe that it is a great struggle and difficulty to put the harness of reason upon the wild horses of thoughts that flow through your mind, you direct energy to the obstruction, to the difficulty. I say to you again, as I have spoken to you before, it is judgment that establishes the laws of the mind. But you are the one who has the power over the throne of judgment. You are not the judgments. You are not the struggle. You are not the strife. You are, in truth, above and beyond all of that.

If you do not make the effort to direct this intelligent energy to the thoughts, which are forms, of goodness, of the abundance of life, then you are, in truth, the instruments through which energy is directed to the opposite. When we think good, we feel good. But we must think with the soul faculty of reason.

There are many schools of thought in your world of positive thinking. They appear to work for some, but not for all. Positive thought must be united with the soul faculty of reason, for it is the soul faculty of reason that transfigures the form. It is the positive thought which permits the awakening in the conscious mind of the transfiguration that has taken place.

We are aware of what we choose to be aware, and we are not aware of what we choose not to be aware, in the sense that we do indeed have control over our conscious thought when we so choose. There is no magic key to open any door. But the truth, my students, is that doors are opening all the time. Throughout your days, opportunity is knocking. It continues to knock in many, many different ways. We ofttimes do not see opportunity for what it really is. The years pass by and we look back in what is called hindsight and say, "Oh yes, oh yes, indeed that was a golden opportunity."

Let us see now the opportunities that are knocking at our door. We can do that by accepting the possibility. My students, the path of possibility is the path of joy, the path of abundance, the path of goodness, the path of peace. Think, whenever you say it can't be done, think, whenever you say you have not, that's where you place possibility.

Long ago we asked that you think well of yourself—humble, yet well of yourself. For that "humble" is a soul faculty and "well" is a sense function. The balance of thinking well is the faculty of humbleness. Through the faculty of humbleness, recognition of a greater authority enters our consciousness and we are flooded with the divine will, called acceptance. The divine will is flowing through all of us. It is only in need of being broadened.

Possibility, my students, to you all things are possible. But first, you must believe that it is. Take stock of the things you think are not possible, you will indeed awaken to a great number of things. But as you think about the possibility of abundance, the possibility of happiness, the possibility of goodness, listen carefully to what your mind says, for it will speak to you filled with judgment of why it cannot be.

All of these experiences that you have are in a process of passing through your consciousness. Some, you let pass freely and unattached. And some, you hold on to with a great tenacity. Yet, those, too, are passing. We are all changing, my students. But change is the joy of life. I would not want to be the experiences that I once thought that I was. And so I am indeed grateful and ever willing and hopefully ready to change. Let us welcome change, for it holds for us the golden key of opportunity, the path of possibility.

Think of the things that you presently believe are obstructing what you desire. Put possibility in their place and do not dictate how things are possible. To God all things are possible. And if you truly want this greater unfoldment and abundance of good in your life, then do not stand in the way of your own light.

Do not take the foolhardy path of dictating the ways of possibility, for, in so dictating, God cannot work, except through the limited channels that you have granted to the Intelligence of all. The Intelligence is never absent or away. The Intelligence works in ways the mind cannot conceive. Let the Intelligence work unobstructed in your life by entertaining the goodness and the greatness of possibility.

The mind wants so many things. It wants to be rich and it wants to be poor. It wants to be healthy and it wants to be sick. It wants to be lonely and it wants to be happy. The mind wants all things. This may seem to be, to some, a little difficult to understand. But when you study the laws of creation of which the mind is, in truth, composed and you truly accept the demonstrable truth of the duality of the created substance, then you will see that the mind, in truth, ever seeks to gather, ever seeks to garner all things unto itself. And so at moments you may say you do not want to be poor. There are other moments when you establish all the necessary laws to be poor, for the mind is a part of all creation and so it seeks all creation. The mind is never satisfied. It only seems to be temporarily.

My students, peace, joy, and happiness and the goodness of life are above and beyond creative substance. And when I say that you seek to be poor and when I say you also seek to be rich, I am speaking of that vehicle of duality in which the grief in life is to those who depend and rely upon it. We may ask the question, "Why should such a vehicle, known as the human mind, offering contradiction and duality, be the instrument through which the eternal soul must express on Earth?" That we may learn the greatest lesson of all lessons: to be with it and not a part of it.

As we drive our cars and the years pass on and we view them in their slow, but sure, disintegrating process, are we saddened by that process? Are we overjoyed by that process? Or are we unaffected by that process? To be free from birth and death is to be free from creation. To be in it and free from it is the great lesson that is being offered to you. To separate that true you from all of the changes taking place in the mind—that separation is a gradual process that has been taking place with you for many centuries untold. And the steps that are so simple are to ever remember the possibility of something better.

The willingness to change is inseparable from the possibility of something better. We must offer to the human mind a way. That way is called possibility. For by its very nature, it must garner, it must gather. But when it comes to giving, its struggle truly begins. Think of the many feelings and thoughts that lie within the universe of the human mind. Think of all those things and your willingness to move onward will increase greatly.

There are, available for all, the realms of beauty. As I sit here with you this evening, I view them and enjoy them and know that your soul is working its way, moment by moment, to them. For they are indeed yours, as much as they are indeed mine.

And work is not what your minds have dictated that it is. Work is not a chore. In these realms of joy, work is a pleasure, an upliftment of conscious direction of infinite intelligent energy.

To watch the souls unfold as you watch the unfolding of a beautiful rose is an experience that, once having had, there is no question left that you are, in truth, all people and all things—a united inseparable whole. Look at life from a different level. Look at it above and beyond the gray areas of the human mind. Do not look down and do not look up at the human mind. Do not look up and do not look down at any created form. For, in so doing, you are blinded and cannot see that that which sustains it is the real you, the true you.

Through your conscious choice of direction, you may enter the realms of heavenly peace while yet in your earthly realm. It is available for you now. Think not of the tomorrows. Work on the todays. But not work as you have dictated work is: a drudgery and a chore. Work is love made manifest. But it cannot be love made manifest if you have judged it otherwise. All of the horizon that you are facing is filled with the light of reason and wisdom. You may see it if you will pause in your thought.

Long ago we asked that you think of a word, that you repeat it thrice, for that is a simple so-called task to do. Don't you understand, my students? You cannot think without becoming. So choose wisely your thought that you may become what you truly desire. Think more of the good. See the way and not that which stands in front of it. Let not your view of life be obstructed by errors in thought. Let it not be obstructed, for there is no need for it to be so.

Look at life with the great abundance that it has. Do not judge how goodness shall come to you, but become the goodness and you will not have to be concerned about seeking it. Become that that you desire. And so we go backwards in your earthly time. How does man become? It was given to you long ago, long ago: awareness belief become. Do not chase the universe and dictate all the paths that are necessary, for it is foolhardy and, in truth, wasteful of energy and so-called time.

Become aware and you will believe. And in your belief, you will become. You need not move in anyway except in consciousness. Learn, my students, to move within. Become aware of those movements, moving from level to level, when you have—and you all do—these moments of feeling what you call good. Become aware of why you believe, for in that believing have you become. So many times we speak of, "Oh, how I wish I could feel the way I did the other week." But, don't you see, we can feel anyway we choose to feel at any time we choose to do so. Be the captain of your ship and not the ship itself. Become the captain of your destiny. Awareness brings belief and then indeed shall you become the thing that you have sought for so very long.

Believe, my students, believe in the possibility of goodness and abundance and joy in life. For if you, in your present thinking, feel that you do not have it, then you know you believe it and indeed your belief has established and sustains that very law.

And so, in truth, we are all believing, for we are, in truth, all becoming. Let us believe on that that we believe we truly want. A house divided cannot stand. You cannot, in truth, believe that you want abundant good and at the same time believe you do not have it, for that is division and something has to go. And in this class we dedicate our effort and our energy that you may, in truth, believe in your right to the fullness and the goodness of life.

Good night.

SEPTEMBER 29, 1977

CONSCIOUSNESS CLASS 157

Greetings, friends. Speaking this evening on repetition, the Law of Change, and repetition, the Law of Form.

As we view creation, we see so many varied forms and, in our viewing, do not stop to consider what it is that is sustaining the forms that we view. Whereas man has been given, by the Law of Merit of his own evolution, charge over all forms on the planet on which he resides, we must go beyond, in our thoughts and understanding, and view this energy that we are directing, by the Law of Repetition, to sustain these many, many forms. As all form is an effect of directed energy, so man's personal responsibility for being creator—by being an instrument through which energy is directed—man's responsibility indeed weighs heavily.

We have spoken to you before and asked that you consider flooding your minds or consciousness with certain healing affirmations that have been given you. For as you journey on through so-called time and space, you will become aware that the human mind is in a constant process of recording thought, that the human mind can be likened unto a target that is being constantly bombarded with directed energy through what is known as thoughts. In time, through this awareness that slowly, but surely, takes place, man begins to consciously choose the type of thought forms that he will permit to enter his own mind. As you begin on the path of constantly and consciously flooding your mind of the thoughts of your choice, you will become more aware of the ones that are already there. They will battle for their survival, for they, through many years of growth, have become the rulers of your mental realms.

In time, we move above and beyond these realms of duality. We move beyond these realms of thought and find a peace, a quietude, a neutrality. And there we pause. It's in those moments of pause that we are free and experience the joy that is truly life. The path of nonresistance is the path of peace, for that that we resist controls us, that that we battle we become the victims of. Wise is he who learns that simple truth. And that simple truth is easily learned when we separate truth from creation, when we truly become the observer and not the observed, when we become the captain of our ship of destiny and not the ship itself.

For we have stated to you some time ago that that—whatever it be—you give thought to, you give power over you. This is the reason that we have, over these years, tried to encourage you to give thought to peace. For in the power of peace, which is known as God, there is no control, for there is no desire; there is no self-interest. There is only divine neutrality. As you give your thought—and it is a constant process—give it to peace, for there is your true being.

The path of nonresistance is the path that will free you. But you must first, through your own evolution, gain the wisdom, through understanding, that you are not all the things of the created mind. And being not those things, you have nothing, no thing, to defend. Truth needs no defense. And so, my good students, when you are in the light of truth, there is no resistance, for there's nothing to defend. In that level of consciousness, you speak your word forth into the universe, knowing that it shall not come back to you void, but accomplish that which you send it to do.

It is the very purpose of this philosophy to help you, in helping yourselves, to awaken that level of consciousness within you that you may stand on principle, peacefully and joyfully, knowing that whatever the mind is registering at any moment is in the very process of passing.

What is it that we permit our minds to fight so hard and so difficult for? Because we are yet to separate ourselves from our minds. We must step outside of the vehicle. And we do that in the moment that we pause. That's when we stop for a moment and that is when we awaken.

In one of our other classes, I spoke to you a bit about my personal life in the centuries long gone. And in so speaking, you will recall that I discussed some of the realms that I had visited and the many orders that I had received from those who believed they had charge over me. I was indeed fortunate and grateful for the guardian angel that guided me through those realms that advised and counseled me not to resist, not to struggle, not to battle, for, in so doing, I freed myself. For through nonresistance—don't you see, my students?—you disassociate.

You have, at any moment, the choice of identification. And whatever you identify with, you become a part of. When you identify with the struggle, you become the struggle, for we are what we believe and we believe ever in keeping with our conscious choice of identification. Identify with the good that you may become the fullness thereof. Identify with the abundance of life that you may truly demonstrate your birthright. Identify with health, wealth, and happiness, for it is, in truth, much easier to identify with health, wealth, and happiness than it is to identify with its opposite. For to identify with the opposite, you must create a discordant form in consciousness. And discord is contrary to the Law of Refining Evolution.

Think, my students, and once again think more deeply. Identify. Identify with that which is the goodness of the universe, for that, in truth, is what you really are. Become more aware in your conversations, become more aware in your thoughts and activities. Identify in the very depths of your being, that the fullness and abundant good of life may be your moment-by-moment experience.

You may ask your questions at this time.

Thank you. Will a simplified version of the philosophy be available on tape for the children in the near future?

As near, my good students, as your value and the demonstration of your appreciation, through your personal and united efforts, yes.

Thank you. Various insects and animals represent different soul faculties and sense functions. As there is no separateness, would you please explain what significance this has for us?

In reference to your question, please repeat it that we may have a broader or more fuller understanding of what is being proposed by the questioner.

Various insects and animals represent different soul faculties and sense functions. For example, spiders are said to bring prosperity and butterflies bring disappointment. As there is no separateness, we are all one in the universe. Would you please explain what significance this has for us?

First, we wish to clarify that butterflies are an ancient symbol of doubts, that wilted flowers are ancient symbols of disappointments, and that spiders are ancient symbols of supply. Now, my good students, it is not someone, somewhere at some ancient time that, at random, chose to make a statement that a spider is a symbol of supply. But it is the demonstration of that particular insect. It is the demonstration that the insect is doing that represents supply.

And now we must question, Did you ever see a spider that did not have sufficient substance to weave a web? You never did and you never will. And so the spider represents the divine Law of Abundant Supply and the spider demonstrates that this supply is ever within. It is not something that the spider is gathering from without through which he is weaving his web. And so it demonstrates and teaches to all who wish to view it that the supply, the goodness, the abundance, that you seek lies within you, that it is ever waiting for *you* to go to work, to work within, as the spider demonstrates in weaving its web.

Now, my students, when you speak of this philosophy, speak with the efforts of thinking more deeply. Do not accept things on face value. The spider represents supply because of its demonstration. The butterfly represents doubts because of the butterfly's demonstrations. And so on throughout all creation. As the coiled serpent represents wisdom by its demonstration, so the uncoiled snake is representative of so-called evil by its demonstration. That is the living truth that you, through your personal efforts of investigation and study, may view. Truth is truth, when through our efforts we have perceived it. And so this philosophy gives to you the many guidelines of study and application, but that light of truth must rise from within your own being through your own efforts.

Thank you. Would you please clarify what our duty is concerning serving on a jury and being placed in a position of being legally asked to judge another soul?

He who has judged shall be judged. And so it is, if, in keeping with the laws that we have established, we are to serve on a jury, then we have called that forth from the universe for a lesson for ourselves. We have earned that opportunity, as all opportunity is earned. It is what we do with what we earn that reveals to us how awakened we are at that moment.

As opportunity constantly is before us, we are in a constant process of choice. And when we make choice, as we do each moment, we may make choice in a balanced universe, known as the faculties and the functions, or in an imbalanced universe of the functions only. When we make these choices in an imbalanced universe of the functions only, then we are controlled by what is known as the throne of judgment. To be free from judgment, it is necessary to have the fullness of total consideration and that requires a perfect balance between the soul faculties and the sense functions.

Now, my good students, with so many experiences bombarding the mind each and every moment, it certainly does behoove us to make the effort to flood those mental realms with the power of peace. Though you may not, at this moment, feel your question is answered, it is sufficient unto the need of the questioner.

Thank you. One of the sayings in the Serenity Game is "A death wish is an intense desire of the educated conscience to eliminate guilt in order that the soul may be free." Would you please elaborate upon this understanding?

The educated conscience, as I am sure most of you are already aware, is that which we have earned in our present life experience. We have earned it as an effect of centuries, of course, of evolution. The educated conscience is aware of the duality, of course, of creation. And within that awareness is an inner knowing, an inner knowing of a higher state of consciousness that *is* the true home that it desires to reach.

This death wish, which everyone is experiencing, not spasmodically now and then—but the death wish is something that is ever within the human mind. The human mind is a dual instrument and is in a constant process of desire and the need to fulfill its desire and, being a dual instrument, constantly views what it dictates is the obstruction to the fulfillment of its desires. As it views the obstruction, it wishes for the removal, elimination, or death of what it has judged to be its obstruction.

Now, an old teaching clearly states that a house divided cannot stand. And so it is that we stumble along the path of life: one part of us constantly wishing for another part to die because we permit ourselves to view life from realms of consciousness that see only form or creation. We will, however, and we do—more often than we realize—we do rise to higher levels. And we do look and see that in order to bring about a neutrality, there must be opposing forces of creation. Be not overly concerned that a part of the mind is in a constant process of wishing something to die, for as it directs this energy to that wish, the law of the mind is brought into balance.

The mind is not something that should be viewed with distaste, for it has been wisely designed to serve the purpose for which it was designed. When, in time, we weary of moving back and forth in the realms of mind, we set into motion a law of something better. And by entertaining the thought and entertaining the possibility, we begin to move through those realms. Although it may seem a long time before we get through them, we do, we do indeed get through them. So let us not view the vehicles through which we are expressing as something distasteful or not truly useful.

As we go on in life, the mind becomes more refined and so does the body that it moves. And these other bodies, they become more and more and more refined. As the bodies through which the soul is expressing become more refined, in the refinement they become more universal until they become a part of the whole of which, in truth, they are. And you move beyond time and space. There are no limits, for you are limitless. And the acceptance of that limitlessness is indeed what many call the cosmic consciousness, the true inner awakening.

But that which is healthy is a slow, sure, and steady growth. You cannot move from limited identity to limitless being in one, short leap. All of this refinement is taking place and, in truth, serving a good purpose. My good students, in the years that you have been with us, the things of yesteryear, so many of them, seem so small, so petty. They no longer serve the purpose for which they were designed and they pass on. And we, through that process, become more and more refined.

What is necessary is taking place. And, in truth, we all—our forms, our thoughts, which are forms—are changing. We are changing constantly. Let the change be joyous. For regardless—and no matter what we do—we cannot stop evolution. We cannot stop changing.

If you are weary of change, the Law of Evolution, then you must make the effort to go beyond it. For it is only the forms that change. The true being, the essence, the principle, which you truly are, does not change, for it is above and beyond creation and, therefore, evolution. The soul, through which the divine spirit, which is the true you, the soul, a vehicle through which the essence expresses, *that* evolves. You never change. You never have changed and you never will change. Your identity changes because identity is form. All things that are form, being all thoughts, change.

And so the mind asks, "Who am I? What am I? And where am I? Where have I been and where am I going?" My students, you have been many places and you have been many, many things. Where are we going? We're going onward and onward and onward, awakening each and every step of the way, that we may finally accept we are not the form; we are not the thought. We are that great essence that moves it all. Accept that truth in the depths of your heart. You are the principle, the essence, the light, and the love of life. That *is* what we truly are.

And when that is fully awakened, you will sail on a sea of harmony and peace; you will still be in the world, but no longer a part of it. And it brings to mind that little saying, "Once I was an apple and then I was a tree and when I am an apple tree I'll no longer be just me." Think about that, my friends. That was given to you long ago and reveals truth, so pure and simple in reference to the Law of Repetition and identity. And remember that you cannot separate the Law of Repetition and the Law of Identity. They are inseparable. They are a united oneness, through which the river of life flows forever and ever and ever.

Good night.

OCTOBER 6, 1977

CONSCIOUSNESS CLASS 158

Greetings, students. This evening we should like to, once again, speak on the subject of viewing the form of the spoken word.

Some time ago we gave to you a simple exercise: to think of a word, to repeat it thrice in the mind, and speak it forth. When we awaken within and we view the form that our spoken word doth take, then we are better qualified to make the effort of establishing a vibratory wave of unity. For, as has been often stated, that concentration *is* the key to all power. And whereas it is ever in keeping with the divine law that it takes energy or power to fulfill any desire entertained in mind, so it is that it behooves man to view his spoken word.

So often we speak a word and experience the opposite results, for we have established within our minds those types of reactions. For example, we may speak the word "work." But when we speak the word "work," the mind creates the form of the direct opposite. As we speak that word, the mind, in its creative process, establishes visual imagines and feelings and forms of pleasure of relaxation, perhaps of the mountains, the seashore, or the beach. And so it is that speaking forth a word and having an opposite-created form does not accomplish what man speaks forth.

And so it is that in your endeavors and in your efforts to view the form of the word you speak, you will become more alert and more aware of what, in truth, is being created in your sphere of action. All of life, as we have often said, reacts to this creative principle, to this divine energy flowing through our own form. And it is within our power and indeed our divine eternal right to choose wisely: to speak forth words that contain the power and the energy to accomplish that which we are speaking forth, but we cannot do that, my friends, until we awaken within ourselves. It is in the stillness of the human mind that illumination slowly, but surely, floods a light before our path that we may no longer stumble along the dark ways of error and of ignorance. For this life, which is, in truth, all life, is laid before us to enjoy and to benefit.

These needs that rise from the depths of our being that continue to plague us, they are the signals that tell us to change: to make the change within that life without may be more abundant, more peaceful, and indeed more enjoyable.

And so these steps are necessary. They are necessary and indeed shall the time, this illusion of time, be shortened for us, if we make this effort to view these forms which our spoken words are, in truth, creating.

So often in life we say we have spent so much time and effort and energy and the result is not in keeping with the energy that has been expended. My good students, then we must ask the question within ourselves—If indeed so much time and effort has been spent in any endeavor and it has not yet born a fruitful result, then we must look to the contradiction that is taking place within our own mind.

The key to success is a key of reason. The door of success is on the hinges of effort. But we must awaken and use that key wisely. We must know beyond a shadow of any doubt, when we speak, what form goes out into the universe to call forth its like kind and to return unto us to bring us the barrenness of need or the fulfillment of life itself.

I see that many questions, you have presented. And we shall spend some time this evening to share our understanding on those questions with you. You may ask them at this time.

Thank you. How can we best express the neutrality of the Divine within us?

How can we best express the divine neutrality that flows through us? By no longer contaminating that neutrality or being an obstruction to it by the limited patterns and attitudes of the human mind.

This philosophy has spoken a great deal upon the divine will of total acceptance. How does man demonstrate this total acceptance, which must, indeed, include the limited tapes, attitudes, and patterns of the mind? By a recognition within oneself that these attitudes and various levels of consciousness are not the person themselves, that they are tools that have been designed and devised by the human mind to serve a specific purpose at a specific time in your evolution. We are no longer what we were. As far as the human mind is concerned, we are no longer what we were yesterday. And so these various attitudes, having served the purpose for what they were devised at the time of service, no longer serve well. They must be permitted to go back to the source from whence they have risen.

In order that we may express this divine neutrality, we must view life and its vast multitudes of experiences as tools that are temporarily being used. We must learn to separate this eternal being from these many created forms, attitudes, and levels of consciousness. These levels of consciousness exist by the creative principle of form.

We leave a physical body and will live in one of the forms, whichever form is the strongest. Now, the strongest form is the one that we have directed the most energy to. So let us pause and let us think where we want to live in consciousness. This is why we have asked you, a moment earlier, to speak your word and view its form. In many different ways, we have given that same lesson. When you speak the word "pure," does your mind create forms of purity? Or does your mind create forms of the direct opposite? To find our way through these realms of dual creation, we must, my good students, make the daily effort. When you speak the word "peace," does your mind create forms of peace or does it create forms of conflict, turmoil, and war within?

You can very quickly view for yourselves whether or not the soul faculty of reason is flowing and to what degree and extent that it is flowing by choosing any word and speaking it forth. For you will very quickly see what form that it is taking. And so when your mind, being under your control, speaks the word and you view the form of the word spoken, then you have not only gained a degree of control of your mind, but concentration, the power that is, is flowing through you. That is the power of the Divine Intelligence and you are no longer a dual, opposing form in its way.

This is the most important daily exercise that has ever been given to your world. And to you students it has been given in so many different ways. We gave to you an affirmation some time ago that clearly states, "I speak my word forth into the universe, knowing that it shall not come back to me void, but accomplish that which I send it to do."

The spoken word is designed to be a servant for your soul. The creating process of the human mind is designed to be a servant of your soul—and not the other way around. So as you make this daily effort to speak the word and view the form—and you very quickly shall see that the forms are not in harmony with your spoken word. It is known as a house divided. How do you make the change, my students? The change comes about not by a battle with the opposing forms, but by the power of peace, through the avenue of prayer.

Thank you. Would you please show the relationship between self, ego, and mind?

Well, my good students, without mind, there is no thought of I, which is the self or the ego. And so self, mind, and ego are inseparable. We have taught before, and continue to teach, you must not make the effort to annihilate what is called the ego, for it is an avenue of expression. It is through your efforts to educate it or to cast the light of reason upon it that it will serve you well, that it will serve you in the way that it has been designed to serve you. That, my students, through your efforts to separate yourself from this vehicle of mind, this vehicle of self and so-called ego—to ever remember that you, the true you, is in charge, that it is a tool, that it is, by its very nature, in a constant process of change. Accept the demonstrable Law of Evolution of form. Accept it for your mind, for yourself, for your ego. And when you truly accept this demonstrable Law of Change, this process of refinement, then you will no longer be troubled and plagued by it.

Thank You. What is the soul faculty that balances the sense function of hunger?

Well, the sense function of hunger is necessary in the present state of the form's evolution. It wasn't always necessary. And, once again, the day will return: it will no longer be necessary. And so you ask for the soul faculty of that sense function. I can tell you this, my students, that it is directly related to the soul faculty of patience. And so when you find yourself in an excessive, an excessive expression of the function of hunger, if you will make the effort to open the faculty of patience, then you will bring about the light of reason, which will transfigure you and free you from the control of that function.

So often in the expressing of a function and when we become aware of a corresponding soul faculty or a faculty that is related to the function, our mind immediately states, for example, "I am hungry, but also I am patient, for I was very patient before I fed my hunger." But, my good students, that looks at the personality or the form of the expression. It does not look at the principle involved. So often a person is hungry for affection. They are hungry for companionship. They are hungry for so many different things, besides food. And yet in their hunger for those many things, they have created an obstruction in their mind and their hunger is not fed. So the hunger turns to whatever avenue it can to feed itself and most often that is the hunger that turns to food.

Thank you. Am I correct in understanding that, in addition to brain tapes we have developed since childhood, we also have tapes from past evolutions and carry with us all our tapes to our next expression?

That is indeed correct. That is what self has to offer. For the moment we entertain the thought of self, we identify with self. And in that identification, it is not limited to this short Earth experience.

You see, my students, look at the good that it does indeed serve. As we continue in our daily experiences to entertain thoughts of self, we identify more with self. In time, we become so weary, so bored, and so sick, so to speak, of self, that we drive the self to something greater. And that something greater is the freedom from self. You see, self is a limited universe of one's personal experiences here on Earth and the many experiences prior to Earth. And when the attention is directed to the self, then this divine energy feeds the forms of self and, in time, the created forms of self become greater than the true eternal being.

Our teaching has always been that self*less* service—that is, the service of the true being, less the limited self—is the true and only path to spiritual illumination. We have also stated it in another way: when the mind is still, the light doth dawn within. Because the stillness of the mind is the sleep of the self. Now, when all of these forms, they lay down and they pause in what you call sleep—for that is the closest similarity that we can present to you at this time—then this light, which is you, it begins to shine inside of you. And as it does so, it goes out into the universe. It lights the path before you. The vibratory waves of harmony and the goodness of life are then experienced.

We've spoken to you so often on the throne of judgment. That is simply the effect of an over-directing of energy to the self. My students, it is indeed a miserable world when all we can do is entertain thoughts of self.

Thank you. Please explain what takes place when someone is placed on the healing list.

That is dependent upon the motive in the placement itself. Many people request and seek aid to free themselves from levels of consciousness that, through errors of ignorance, they find themselves trapped, so to speak, in. Through prayer and through the power of peace, God's ministering angels come to assist those who request that assistance. This vibratory wave of peace, which is the only eternal power, shines over the many forms that their minds have created that are now plaguing and disturbing them, robbing them of their good health, robbing them of their peace of mind and goodness of life. And this light is cast over those forms and those forms lie down. And they pause. And the individual who has been victimized by their own created forms experiences a sense of well-being, a sense of goodness, and that experience will last and will endure as long as they make the effort. All healing is temporary unless the one seeking the healing begins to make the daily effort.

Thank you. What is the meaning of the card in the Serenity Game, "The body cannot illumine for without attention, no sensation is possible"?

My good students, the body cannot illumine for without sensation—without attention, no sensation is possible. The very basis of our teaching of our classes. The body does not offer attention or energy. It is not within the power or the realm of the body or form to grant illumination, for it is, as we mentioned earlier, in the stillness in the silence that the light, in truth, doth shine. And so that statement that you just heard—"The body cannot illumine"—is a very deep philosophical truth. And if you will only remember: that that is form is not Light, but is sustained by Light, but in and of itself is not Light.

All form is in a constant process of movement. But the Light is the Light of perfect stillness. The Light is peace. Now, you all know that peace is the power of God. If you, in your seeking, desire anything, then let your mind be still and let the power of God, known as peace, do that which is to be done.

Now, how does God, this power of peace, do anything? My students, when you become what you truly are, when you become it by stopping all of the activity of the creative principle, then you truly awaken. And in that awakening, there is no concern; there is no activity. There is the great void. And that is when, once it is awakened within you, you will no longer chase the universe looking for things that come and go, for in that great void, there is no need. You are then your true being.

Thank you. Please explain how the faculty of tolerance is balanced by the function of friendship.

My good students, the faculty of tolerance is a faculty, once being awakened, that brings about a friendship with everything. For he who is tolerant has no enemies. And he who has no enemies has no battles. And he who has no battles has no wars and, therefore, *is* the peace, the power of God.

Thank you. Please clarify the difference between logic and reason and also how reason and intuition are related.

Well, my good students, we have indeed covered that ground, so to speak, long ago. We will speak again on logic and reason.

Logic is based upon whatever has been introduced into the human mind. And when man uses what he calls "logic," he is relying totally upon what is offered by the human mind. When man uses the soul faculty of reason, he is, at his disposal—at man's disposal is all of the universes, through the faculty of intuition. Everything that has ever been, that will ever be, and that is, is available for him to view. Because that is the way that it is in the fullness of the faculty of reason. That is where the power transfigures the form. So let us pray, in our prayers, to use reason, to be not so conceited with logic. You see, my students, the functions bring conceit; the faculties bring acceptance.

Thank you. Please explain the expansion and contraction principle.

In reference to the human form or the forms of all of life, as the form contracts or as energy is withdrawn from the form, the form returns to the substance from whence it was created. As that takes place, the true being expands in its awareness of life itself. Many philosophies, throughout the ages, have been aware, and are aware, of this expansion-contraction principle. For example, as you direct more energy to a particular desire that you may be entertaining, the form of that desire grows ever larger. The other forms that you have created, they begin to shrink, so to speak. And this is why it is so very difficult for anyone who is overbalanced in what is called self to make any changes. For to introduce a new idea into the human mind, it takes a great deal of repetition in order, number one: to get it introduced; and number two: to sustain it as a form that it may have life. Though it cannot have life eternal, for it is created form.

So when you make the effort to bring about any changes in your life, it means that you are directing some energy to these new forms, or form, of your choice. And in so doing, the forms of your mind, already created, and literally feeding off of your energy, become very upset. For, as you direct energy to this new form of your acceptance, that means less energy you are directing to the old forms.

Now, my students, we all know that change is the Law of Evolution and evolution is, for the form, inevitable. There is no denying that simple, demonstrable truth. And so we must look at our forms by speaking forth the words of our choice to see what the forms, that are united to them, really look like. Are they in harmony or in discord? And so, you see, my students, it is an educating of the human ego that is necessary. Do not try to annihilate it. You will not be successful. For there is a law, very clear and very demonstrable; and it is known as the Law of Responsibility—personal responsibility for all of the forms you have created. Cast the light of reason. Use the soul faculties in working with the sense functions. Use the wisdom of the ages, eternal, in casting the light over these created forms.

And now you know why, whenever you are in self, it is so very difficult to make changes: for those forms that you have been feeding for so very long, they are very selfish and very greedy and they are not about to permit you to direct that energy or food to any new forms. For they are controlled by the Law of Self-Preservation.

However, be not discouraged, for change is in process. Regardless of what the forms of the mind scream and do, you are evolving, for that is the law. And that law is superior to any other created law, for that is the law that is the law of evolving form. So they must go. They must be educated. They will respond to the soul faculties—to compassion, to reason, to love. They will respond if you use the soul faculties to educate them.

Good night.

OCTOBER 13, 1977

CONSCIOUSNESS CLASS 159

Greetings, students. This class we will spend some time with the questions you have prepared.

Thank you. Please explain the saying, "By their deeds not their creeds shall ye know them." Aren't our deeds determined by our creeds?

Indeed, they are not. Ofttimes our deeds, like our thoughts, are in contradiction with each other. So often in life's experiences we are aware of the laws, impartial, that apply, but we do not so very often demonstrate those laws in application. There is a vast difference between knowledge and application. There is the indispensable ingredient known as effort. Ofttimes we have good intentions, in reference to the endeavors of our choice. Because when we make a choice, we are controlled, unfortunately—though we need not be—we are controlled by the dictates of judgment. He who chooses anything and respects with equal respect that that he has not chosen is freed from what is known as the throne of judgment.

And so it is that our creeds and our deeds are rarely in harmony. And so we must ever look to the effect or to the result of any endeavor and use the wisdom known as common sense to help guide us to do what is right because it is right to do right.

Thank you. What is the meaning of the saying, "Freedom of the soul is pride's payment"?

Freedom of the soul is pride's payment for there is no pride without judgment. And so our eternal soul, which is an inseparable part of all, does not judge. It is a witness to all things throughout all eternity. It is the witness and never the judge. It is impartial, respecting the right of all of expression. And so, my friends, as we have often spoken, it is our judgments that build up our so-called pride. Whenever you encounter an individual with a great deal of pride, you may be rest assured there has been a multitude of steps of judgment to build the pride so great.

Thank you. It was previously stated that in cloning—asexual reproduction—the clone has the same soul as the original organism. If the original then dies, does the soul live on in the clone or does the clone also die?

Whenever this so-called essence of soul, of spirit is removed from any form, the form returns to the elements from which it was created. And so it is with a clone or whatever else it is, when this essence is removed from it, the form returns to the source of its own creation.

Thank you. When a body part is transplanted, does it retain the soul of the body it came from?

That is like saying when the tire of an automobile is changed, does it retain the other parts of the automobile that was left behind? Only to the extent, only to the extent of its vibratory attachment to the original. And so it is with any part of the human body. The intelligence of the human mind permeates each and every part of the human body. When a part of the human body is removed, that intelligence remains in the part that has been removed. Being a part of the original body, it has that inner knowing or awareness of its true home.

And so it is in so many transplants that have been rejected by the various forms, there is a lack of rapport of this intelligence that is permeating the very part. For example, each and every form garners unto itself what is called personality. In other words, it is the effect of the false belief of individualization or overidentification. Now, individualization is the effect of the imbalance between the functions of the form and the faculties of the soul.

So often in man's activities, he finds such great difficulty in freeing himself from a certain thought pattern, a certain emotion, or a certain attachment. It is because, in that particular area, of the overidentification or the imbalance of the functions with the soul faculties.

Thank you. Would you please clarify the difference between understanding and wisdom?

Understanding—man understands many things. It is when the understanding is brought into application or use that wisdom is born. For understanding without expression or use has no true value. It is the use of the understanding that has been earned that brings wisdom to man.

Thank you. If we want to make a commitment to give a monetary donation to a spiritual cause, but we do not have the cash on hand or sufficient in our budget according to our mind, how do we deal with this spiritually in order that God may manifest the funds?

By removing the judgment—through forgiveness, removing the judgment from the human mind. To remove anything from the human mind, it is necessary to give it forth or to forgive it. Now, to give forth or to forgive man must accept something to give it to. And so when we have these so-called problems—financial or money problems—and we try to give it forth and it returns unto our mind, it is simply revealing that our acceptance of something to give it to is not yet sufficient. And therefore it returns unto us. It takes faith, it takes belief, and, certainly, the divine will of acceptance to give forth or forgive these many judgments that our mind has made.

First, my good students, we must accept an authority greater than our mind that we may give these things of the mind to. That authority must be so indelibly registered within our consciousness that our faith guarantees that it shall not return unto us. And so, my students, if you, in your spiritual commitments, as the questioner has stated, have the faith and the acceptance of an intelligent authority greater than the dictate of your mind, the Divine shall never fail. It is man's mind that fails. It is not the Intelligence of the universe that fails.

Thank you. The angels from the realms of light come to guide and inspire us. Yet, we must solicit specific help on many things. They do not wish to make cripples of us. But how do we know when we should ask and when we should be trying to proceed without soliciting their help?

Reason, the soul faculty, brings the light that will balance. And when in reason, we have no need—no need to concern ourselves with whether or not we should ask.

You see, my good students, when we speak forth the word and ask, we have so many dictates. We must first accept that this Intelligence works through all forms, is not limited to any form. When we ask from a level of consciousness of acceptance of God, then we shall receive from God. But when we ask with preconceived thought, then we shall receive from the realm of preconceived thought, for like attracts like and indeed becomes the Law of Attachment. So when we speak our word forth, we must be aware from what level is the word being spoken. For the demonstration *is* the revelation.

My good students, often we have spoken on the faculty of tolerance. Everyone, in truth, in the mind seeks success. But there is no success without tolerance. The faculty of tolerance must be awakened and activated, for the faculty of tolerance is the first step in acceptance.

It is the will of the divine that holds all things in space. It is the will of the divine that sustains any thought that we choose to entertain in our mind. We are constantly making the choice. Our God is a great God, for our God sustains whatever we choose to think. Think of that, my students. How impartial! What a great servant is ever, ever with us, around us, and about us. No matter what we choose to think or to do, this intelligent energy sustains and supports our endeavors. Therefore, it is not God, this intelligence, that fails. It is not God that moves us. It is God that sustains whatever we choose to do.

If you choose to entertain negative and self-destructive thoughts, this God of the universes will sustain your right to that negative, self-destructive thought. Do not pray to God to be free from your negativity. Simply pause in your thinking and become aware of how negative and how often you entertain those thoughts.

We look around the world and we see, percentage-wise, that over 96 percent of all thoughts permeating from the earth realm are negative. And we must ask ourselves the question, Why are so many minds broadcasting negative thoughts? Think of that, my good students. Why, why does it seem to be easier to entertain a negative thought in reference to anything than to entertain a positive thought? Without judgment, there is no negative thought. And so you can trace this chain of events of negativity and you can see the more negative, the more judgment; the more judgment, the more pride; the more pride, the more overidentification with what is called self.

If we want to be free, then someday we shall have to give the greatest gift of all to the Divine: the gift of self. And when we stop and look at what we think self is, we see a form that's in a constant process of birth and death, we see thoughts rise and express and die, and we see patterns of mind fighting tooth and nail to hold onto their existence. That, my friends, is what the self looks like: a suffering entity, unwilling to change.

Time and time again, we have spoken to you, be ever ready and willing to change. How do we become ready to change? From whence cometh the willingness to change? To be ready to change is to be free from judgment. Think of that, my students. If you find yourself having difficulties in making changes in your life, then you have to look at what the cause is: the judgments sit firm and will not move. But they shall move, for the Law of Evolution is inevitable. They shall move and they shall change. But that is not you. Separate that true you from all of those created forms, from all of the rigidity. Separate your true being from that. The mind looks out and it questions and it wonders and it rises with its fear: "What shall tomorrow be? From whence cometh my sustenance?" If we have spent our lives and taken pride in what is known as self-reliance, then our fears are very great.

Look at each moment and each experience for the goodness that is being offered to you. Look at the kindness that is all around and about you. You are never alone. If you think you are, then you have closed the door on the multitude of souls ever waiting to help you to encourage you to inspire you to be a doer, to move in the world, to enjoy the world, for it is indeed your birthright to do so.

But, my students, it requires changes. And in order to be ready to make those necessary changes, the judgments of yesteryear, they must bow, they must bow. It will happen someday. So why not let it happen today, peacefully and harmoniously? How often, whenever we are given or have merited a job to do in life, that we are about the business of doing the job, when change comes about? Do we change happily or are we filled with dictates and emotion? Are we filled with trauma and resentment? Or do we move on to this and that and ever onward and onward and onward? I assure you, my good students, the wall that stands between your fullness of life and you is only the wall of self-judgment.

Thank you. We are taught that it takes understanding to unfold tolerance. Would you please discuss the importance of forgiveness in unfolding tolerance?

My good students, without forgiveness, the mind continues to direct energy to the things it finds intolerable. It continues to repeat itself within the human mind. And so it grows. Like a little child, it grows on and on. And someday becomes an adult form. And so it is necessary to express this giving forth or forgiveness in order that the soul faculty of tolerance may be expanded and, in turn, understanding awaken in its fullness within our consciousness.

Thank you. Would you please describe the process that takes place in the emotional body when one suffers the so-called anxiety attack?

These anxiety attacks that you speak of are something that is taking place whenever we are thinking about what we call self, for in this realm, known as self, are an untold number of unfulfilled desires and hopes and fears. And so if we stop for a moment and we direct our attention inward to our feelings, to our thoughts, we will become aware of a multitude of conflicting desires and hopes and fears. Now, that is one of the many things that self has to offer. It offers all of that trauma of yesterday. It offers all of that frustration. And so we find that people who have problems with what is known as anxieties are directing this energy, through attention, to what is called self.

My students, the world has so much to offer, so much wonderful goodness and beauty! It has so much waiting for you, but you must come out of self that you may first see that, for you, it is possible, and then move on and be free from these anxiety complexes, these time and money pressures. I never found a person who insisted they were under time-pressure who was not under the control of money-pressure.

You see, my students, this great delusion is that time is money. Well, we all, I am sure, will agree that time is an illusion. And therefore if time is money, therefore money, too, is an illusion. So should we spend our lives continuing to chase these illusions? Or should we stop for a moment and look at life as it really is? It's ever dependent upon our acceptance, and our acceptance is in a positive process of expansion. For today we accept more than we did yesterday and tomorrow we will accept, yea, even more than the day before. So why not choose, why not choose to accept more of the good in your life?

Don't look outside and say, "I wish I had this" or "I wish I had that." You have it. It is yours. It simply waits your acceptance. You see, my students, when you tell that to the mind, the mind says immediately, "Well, I've got to do this and that and that and that in order to have that." The mind makes those steps of judgment. Therefore, controlled by the mind, you must make the steps that you have set into motion as a law, for man indeed is a law unto himself. But I assure you that there is a level of consciousness above and beyond that. Yes, indeed, we must do our part, but our part is the acceptance, for the acceptance is the will—think of that, my good children—acceptance is the will of God. There is no greater power.

Thank you. When the mind registers resentment to rejection, what is the process that takes place in plotting its revenge? Please give us some how-tos on controlling the mind so revenge will not be carried out.

Well, my students, from rejection to retaliation to revenge. You wish not to be vengeful? Then make the effort to be free from self. And many words have been spoken on the ways to free yourself from yourself. The only obstruction is the so-called self. If you would only make the effort each day to look at what the so-called self is offering to you, I assure you, once having looked at it, you would make immediate effort to be free from it.

Thank you. What does frustration truly result from?

It results from the efforts of so-called self to have the way that it has dictated life shall be. And because it experiences obstructions in its path, it becomes what is known as frustrated. In other words, it keeps moving with its effort, but it gets nowhere. That that moves and gets nowhere is known as a frustrated human being.

Thank you. Would you discuss the qualities one must possess to truly be an effective counselor?

To counsel oneself. To be able to speak to oneself, to use reason, to accept changes in one's life, to accept the right of all life to unfold the faculties of duty, of gratitude, of tolerance, to understand that they, in truth, are an instrument of a divine Light, that they bear a great responsibility to permit, by their gracious acceptance, the divine Light to heal all with whom come in contact of the Light, that through their constant prayer, moment by moment by moment, that they flood their consciousness with the power of God, known as peace, that no matter what comes or goes, no matter whether they're on the heights or the depths, they are never too weary to do the work that they know they have to do. And so physician, heal thyself and ye shall be the demonstration of the healer of God.

Thank you. Would you please explain how things that seem contradictory are often the same in principle?

It is ever dependent upon the level of consciousness from which we are viewing the so-called contradiction. You see, my students, to one level, we see and view things contrary. To another level, we see a bit more clearly and we see the unity and the inseparableness of all of life. So it is ever dependent from which level we are viewing. And we can view from any level that we choose to view. We have, by the grace of the Divine, we do have that choice.

Thank you. If one frees oneself from the bondage of the ego during one's sojourn on the earth plane, does this mean one could become free at an earlier age on the plane of the next planet of their incarnation?

My good students, if you have reached, in your evolution, a state of freedom here on your earthly sojourn, then your entrance into your next form is that of freedom.

Thank you. Please discuss how we tune into the spirit of spontaneity.

By stilling the human mind.

Thank you. Please give your understanding of the difference between annoyance and irritation.

The mind is annoyed with anything that it has dictated is not in keeping with its own judgment. Now, irritation is a light cast upon the shadows of the human mind. And it is like a search light: nothing in the human mind escapes it. This philosophy has always taught, in truth, that exposure frees the soul, that irritation awakens us. And indeed it does. But, my students, stop and consider what really happens in what is known as exposure frees the soul. That that is exposed—the various forms and the attachments of the human mind—is not only irritated, but it rises up to defend itself. And that is known as emotional trauma. But the mind does not forget those various forms that we, over the years of directing energy to—they're very unhappy that the light of reason has been cast upon them. And so they go to work in our little mind to find ways of getting even, for they have been hurt. They have been attacked and they rise to defend themselves.

Now, do you see, my students, truth, truth needs no defense? For truth is not creation. Truth is not form, for truth does not change. Creation and all forms, they change. They're born and they die. But truth lives on forever and ever and ever. Truth has always been. It cannot change. It is beyond change, for truth is beyond evolution. You cannot evolve truth. You can only evolve your acceptance of it. Truth is timeless and changeless, for truth is the spirit of life itself.

Thank you. Would you please explain what is meant by the holy ghost as referred to in many religions?

The holy ghost you speak of—you speak of the father, the son, and the holy ghost. The holy ghost in our understanding—and a strange word have they given the infinite, divine Spirit, for there is nothing ghostly about the essence of life. It is very definite. It is a very clear principle from whence all things do spring. And so regardless what you call this infinite intelligent Spirit, it does not change the nature of it.

Thank you. Please explain the teaching in Discourse 30 which states that sexual desire is given birth in the faculties and expressed through functions.

Indeed, indeed, it is. It is the very nature of the eternal soul to express. It is its nature to expand. This is an ever expanding universe. And so it is that as we view our short life here on Earth, we see that, in truth, we are in a constant process of expansion, a constant process of new thought and new ideas and new experiences. And so it is that this eternal soul, its nature is to express, when it is in a vehicle, such as the human form, its expression—in the respect of which you are speaking—may be directed to the procreation function. It rises in the soul, not the thought of what you call sex, but the very essence of expression.

Thank you. When an actor acts out the roll of a fictional character, as in a play, is he setting laws into motion that will affect him in his personal life?

Yes, indeed, for he has, in truth, created that thought form.

Thank you. Can an actor, in truth, portray a character who is opposite in temperament and motive to himself?

Oh, yes. Oh, yes, indeed, a *good* actor can.

Thank you. Would you please give us a clearer understanding of how painting or playing a musical instrument lifts the soul?

Music and color is the very language of the soul, for music and color is vibration. When you look at a painting, when you look at any color, there is a musical note that is sounding in the universe from that color. If you would pause and be perfectly still, you would hear the musical sounds of all color. If you would pause and be perfectly still, you would view the color of all music. For there is color and sound or vibration all around and about you, permeating your very being. You may see it and you may hear it when you still the thoughts of self.

Still the mind, my students. Still it that you may perceive the great beauty of life itself. Still those thoughts of yesterday. Still those fears of tomorrow. Be in this, the moment—in the moment of your own heaven. It is a moment that is so precious, a moment that is so dear and valuable to the soul. Still your mind. Forget yesterday and do not judge tomorrow. Live the fullness of your life by being in the divine infinite moment of neutrality. For that's when you are neutral.

When your mind thinks no thought of yesterday and projects no thought of tomorrow, then you will rise above and beyond creation. And when you rise above and beyond creation, you will view the vast eternity. Like a great open book, you will see the many journeys that you have taken. You will not only see what you have already walked, but you will see what you are yet to walk. Be still.

You see, my students, when you no longer think of yesterday or tomorrow, you no longer identify with the limitations of creation. And when you no longer identify, then you rise to universal consciousness. There, you will see everything. And you will, in the moment of that view, wonder why you waited so long.

Good night.

OCTOBER 20, 1977

CONSCIOUSNESS CLASS 160

Greetings, students. This evening we shall speak on identity and the Law of Responsibility.

As each thought that is entertained by the human mind moves, by the vehicle of air, through the temple of God or human anatomy, man, in his awakening to these various centers—control centers within his body—soon learns how this energy has a direct effect upon his life within and his experiences without. The control center for the vehicle of thought is located in the area of the neck. As the vehicle of thought is the air element, so it is that man is enabled to control his thoughts by control of his breath.

Thoughts contain varying degrees of energy. And thoughts that are given birth in the functions of the human mind must be brought into balance with the corresponding soul faculty. For example, energy passing through an electrical wire may burn the wire if the energy is more than the wire is capable of carrying. And so it is with the thoughts of the human mind. Thoughts carrying a great deal of energy passing through the control center in the human body ever strike their mark, so to speak. And it is the neutralizing, balancing power of the corresponding soul faculty that brings harmony to the human being and the effect of perfect health.

We stated some time ago that the weight of responsibility must never exceed the love of God. And so this evening we speak on the Law of Responsibility and the Law of Identity. My good students, it is the thought of I that is the Law of Identity. And so man finds his responsibilities in life ever in keeping with his identification, for as we identify, or place the thought of I into any, any area of interest, we incur responsibility or the ability to respond to that which ever we have identified with.

We have also spoken to you in reference to the vibratory wave to ignore. You have heard it spoken in many philosophies—to rise above any particular situation that you find disturbing. My good students, whenever the thought of I is placed in any area, we must become aware, in that moment, of the many levels of consciousness that we, in truth, are moving through. For we, in our identification and through our errors of so-called ignorance, are not aware of these abilities that exist within us to respond. There are so many things we find in life that we sincerely wish we would not respond to, but that is contrary to the law we have established of identification.

Man's world, of course, is ever in keeping with his identity. And the weight of his responsibilities are ever in keeping with his so-called interests.

To free ourselves from so many distractions on this path that we all are treading, we must learn to breathe. We must learn to control this breath of life. We must learn to slow down the rapid process of our mind by first making the effort to control what is known as the air center, located in the neck. By a slow, but sure, process of control of our breath, our thoughts begin to slow down. As they slow down, we become more aware of what our minds are truly doing.

We spoke to you about rising the thought and releasing it upward. But it takes the soul faculty to do that, for, you see, my students, this process of neutralization, this process of balance, this light of reason, is the effect of control. And it is ever in keeping with your willingness to identify with that which will uplift you, which will bring unto you, in keeping with the Law of Return, bring unto you that which you are truly are seeking.

There are so many exercises given in your world to bring about some degree of control of the human mind. But no exercise is lasting and enduring without your daily effort. So, my students, apply these breathing techniques that have already been given to you. Use them. Be patient with their use and let so-called time pass, for they have worked for many before you and they shall work for you. Learn to inhale the vibratory wave of peace. Learn to release the vibratory wave of peace.

We have also stated that peace *is* the power of God. It is up to you to use it and to use it wisely, for it shall return unto you, for all things return to their source of origin. Thoughts return to the realms from whence they were given birth and so do aspirations return to the very soul of their source. Remember, all experience is an effect. You are viewing the return of all things to their source of origin. You are viewing the birth of all things going out and coming back. You know that all things return. Be aware of what you send and you will never be surprised at what returns.

In your world and in your scientific age of material growth, many things are waiting on the horizon. Scientists have studied for many years to find the so-called missing link of the human being. We stated long ago that you would not find the so-called missing link on your planet, for on your planet it was not given birth. And so in the years that lie ahead of you, you will awaken to these intelligences in the universes, for they have been, and continue to be, the witnesses of what came here—namely, the human being—so many, many ages ago. Just on the horizon are these so-called experiments and demonstrations of so-called cloning or duplicating of forms. And the religions of your earth world, though they have changed much, shall go through the greatest change ever known in the history of the planet Earth.

My good students, some must be prepared. And the preparation is an acceptance of the universality of being. Your forms are what they are ever in keeping with the identification process. And as you identify, in your earthly experiences, with limited, small areas of life, then limited and small areas of life shall you continue to experience, for you shall continue to respond only to that which you identify with. But you can indeed change your identifications, for you can control your thoughts and you can control your life, for that, in truth, is not only your divine right, but it is your eternal destiny. Slow that it may seem to be, it is taking place.

Look at your daily thoughts. Become more aware of what you are identifying with. Does it bring you the abundant good, which is, in truth, your right? If it does not, then change the identity. Redirect the energy. It is within your power to do so. Become more alert to what you expose yourself to. Be not so interested in being liked. Be interested in being free. For that that is free has no lack and no discord, for it is free to move in the realms of peace and harmony. And abundant good is its constant watchword. Let abundant good flood your consciousness by identifying with it. View not these obstructions created by the human mind. View that which is, in truth, your right.

And so, my students, though many are the words that are spoken to you, some of those words will register in levels of consciousness that are ready, willing, and able to move, for it is in movement that we grow and expand. All things must move, whether they move ever onward and upward in a greater fullness of life's experiences or they move in the decaying processes of the return to their origin.

Think, my good students. All things return. All things, all thoughts, all identities, all abilities return to their source of origin. And so it is as you willingly accept the new, the painful experience of returning to the original sources is no longer experienced by your human mind. What is going from you is destined by the law to do so. Let it go graciously and freely. For as you permit it to do so, the new will come in keeping with that attitude of mind, with that level of consciousness and the birth of the new will not be as painful if you will not permit the dying of the old to be painful.

How many times have we spoken, Hold not to form, for form shall pass? Hold not to thought, for thought is passing. Hold not to things, for things are passing. And so it means a control of identity, that there may be a flexibility in your life, that you may enjoy life. For life is intended, by its very design, to be enjoyed.

And think, my students, if we only held onto the things that we now have, surely we would soon be bored and life would lose its spirit of joy. Creation is a playpen and only children should play therein. But children are ever seeking the new experiences of life. There is a spirit of enthusiasm within the child. There is a spirit of joy for what the next moment shall bring. And as long as man is in creation, he must sustain and maintain that spirit of joy, that spirit of enthusiasm, to see and to enjoy a passing panorama.

For what awaits all people is in keeping with this moment. It is in keeping with the moment and what they are identifying with. As these thoughts pass into the control center, these vehicles formed by the etheric waves, or air, carry this energy. And this energy moves through your physical body. If this energy is not in keeping with the very nerves on which it passes, if there is an overabundance of this energy, then it slowly, but surely, burns out those various areas of the nerves. If the energy is insufficient to carry this thought form through these various nerves of the body, then that at the very end of the nerve is not sufficiently energized and, therefore, is no longer what you would call healthy.

And so it is, my students, that each and every part of your anatomy has been charted by the divine Architect to reveal unto you what you are doing with your house of clay. You can change any disturbance within your house of clay by first being honest with yourself. And through the faculty of honesty, it will awaken within you the disturbance in your mind that is out of balance. And you will awaken to the corresponding soul faculty and restore your health, your wealth, and your happiness.

My good students, health, wealth, and happiness is an inseparable triune faculty. For without health, there is no true wealth. And without health and wealth, there is no happiness. And so health, being the very apex of that faculty, is the thing to work on. To restore your house of clay, your being, to its rightful place of perfect health. That is within your power by restoring balance to your being.

And as we said earlier, slow down your breathing process. And as you slow it down, you will indeed be amazed at the thoughts within your mind that you were not hitherto aware of. But in becoming aware, fear not, for the power of the Divine is greater than the thought.

And keep God in all thought, for that is your opportunity to bring balance in your life. Your soul faculties are the very light of the Divine. And when you put God in your thought, you are turning a key in the door of understanding, which will permit the corresponding soul faculty to the sense function to enter. As it enters, there is a restoration of goodness, abundance, and joy in your life. I assure you that it does take some degree of conscious awareness, some degree of effort, but the benefits are beyond description. Start this moment with each thought that you are consciously aware of by putting God in it. You will very quickly become aware of the difference in your life.

Application, a soul faculty that is the very instrument through which the Divine Being moves, ever responds to you. In your endeavors in life, through the faculty of application, the energy flows unobstructed. Whatever it is that your interests are in, apply. Application means "total expression of the being." Put the totality of your being in your efforts and you will never be concerned over the results. But before you can put the totality of being in your efforts, you must become aware of the levels of consciousness within you, that you may assure yourself that the totality of your being—meaning all levels of consciousness—will cooperate, will unite, and then success is absolutely assured.

And so, you see, my good students, without tolerance, there is no success. For these various levels of consciousness all want to maintain their varying degrees of authority within you. And so tolerance, the soul faculty, must rise supreme that they shall all bow in humbleness to that authority and you move on to ever increasing and expanding success in life.

United, man stands united when he becomes aware. And to some along the path, it is disturbing to them to awaken to this contradiction that exists within them. But remember that forgiveness frees. But before you can have forgiveness, you must have tolerance. And before tolerance comes gratitude. And before gratitude, duty. And before duty, we must look and see responsibility. And before responsibility, we view identity. And so in the final analysis, all of these multitudes of forms and experiences are all given birth by the thought of I.

How beautiful life truly is, when you give up the thought of I. Your limited, restricted universe opens up and expands and encompasses the totality and the allness everywhere. Declare your right. Accept the broader horizons that are before you this moment.

But man often asks, "How do I change my identity?" My good students, your identity is in a constant process of change. And so the question should be, "How do I control my identity?" And so it is become aware, for you cannot control what you are not aware of. Become aware. And when you feel good, become aware of what you are identifying with. And when you feel the opposite, become aware of what you are identifying with. And so you know you change your identity often. It's all a matter of choice. But choice is an effect of control. You cannot choose what you do not control. And you cannot control what you're not aware of.

Awaken, my students, yea, even more, for you have awakened indeed a great deal. More than most of you realize, you have awakened. For you have awakened to areas of consciousness that the masses would not yet consider. But do not stop now on the birth of your awakening. Think and think and think more deeply, for in that thinking is your awareness given birth and in that awareness, you view the Law of Identity.

Good night.

OCTOBER 27, 1977

CONSCIOUSNESS CLASS 161

Greetings, students.

It is indeed most encouraging to view the slow and ofttimes painful growth of the students of this class. We must ever bear in mind that the obstructions we seem to encounter are only effects, effects that we have made necessary for our own evolution.

And so this evening I wish to speak to you on a most personal and indeed important level of consciousness in your material world. And so we shall spend this evening's class on discussion of the thought of the lack of money. And it is indeed our hopes that you will, from this discussion, take the essence of the lessons that are given, view them with an objective mind, that the light of reason may heal your very being and restore peace to your body, your mind, and your soul.

It is interesting to note that the thought of the lack of money first must be viewed as denial. For to entertain the thought of lack—whatever the thought of lack may be—is to deny the abundance which is ever waiting and willing to manifest itself.

You were given long ago a saying that states our denials become our destinies. And so as man in his creative thinking mind establishes these laws of denial, he destines himself to experience them. Now, a person may well say, "My mind is experiencing these lacks and I have these thoughts constantly plaguing me." This teaching and this philosophy is most demonstrable: to accept the right of the thought is the first step in freeing it from the mind, for to deny the right of the thought is to establish the Law of Denial.

Now, these laws established are mental laws and they govern your mental world. But you are more than a mental world. You already know you are a physical world and some of you are aware that you are indeed an inseparable part of what is known as a spiritual world. Now, your soul and your infinite divine spirit, inseparable from the wholeness of the Infinite Intelligence, can manifest in your life only to the extent and the degree that you accept it. This acceptance, known as the will of God, is ever dependent in its expression upon the choice of man. And so your experiences in your earthly life and your destinies are ever in keeping with your denials.

My good students, a person may say, "Well, I have a cold, but I deny that I have it." To do that is to battle in a mental world with the authority of that mental world. And that is not the way to be freed from the experience. When we entertain these denials, these thoughts of the lack of money, we experience a great deal of emotional trauma, a great deal of fear. This fear is directly dependent upon experiences in our life—the experiences of yesterday. And so it is that to accept the right of that experience is to free it from your mind. So that from denial, you will not have to destine yourself to the constant repetition of those experiences.

My good students, you can speak forth a thousand affirmations and you can use every positive affirmation that you have ever heard, but if your heart is not in it, then it cannot work for you. For your heart is the vehicle through which the authority of your soul expresses. And it is the authority of your soul that is necessary to free you from these mental experiences. How does man permit his heart to express? Only by stilling the human mind, for these echoes of yesteryear, they are constantly speaking in our mind. But we are not constantly aware of them, for we have yet to make the sincere effort to still our mind. All of life is the effect of directed energy and we alone, we alone are directing the energy in our life.

We stand at a crossroads on the earth realm. It is the planet, the fifth planet, known as the planet of faith. Each and every moment of your earthly experiences you stand at that crossroad. You constantly make choices. Now, ofttimes those choices are not the conscious choice of the moment, but they are choices that have been made sometime in your earthly experience and, through the direction of energy, have become the masters of your soul. It is these masters of our soul that we all must face. You are indeed blessed to have the awareness of their existence. And so it is encouraging that there are some who have had sufficient demonstration to become aware of their existence, for their greatest weapon, their greatest weapon is the error of ignorance.

But you are aware of these forms to some degree. You are aware of these thoughts to some extent that are in your mind. You are aware of how they plague you. You are aware of the fears that rise within your mind. And so, my students, you stand at the golden gates of reason. There, to look straight ahead, in faith, in humbleness, and bow the supremacy of the mental world to the divine eternal Light of truth. And you must honestly ask yourself the question, "What will you do?"

All of the experiences of life are within. They began within us, they exist within us, and they can pass only within us. Let us, then, indeed be grateful to have the awareness that they do exist within us, that they are self-created, that they are self-sustained, and that they are changing.

What does the world have to offer—the world of creation—in comparison to your eternal life? We must take honest stock of our priorities. What has value to us? To say that we will think about eternity when eternity comes is to deny the very moment in which we are aware. For it is this moment that is the eternity. And so think, my students. This moment you can change. This moment you can choose the path of reason. This moment you can rise your eternal spirit over the temporary disturbances of your creating mind. Look at the good of the principal of creation.

We spoke to you about outer manifestations are revelations of inner attitudes of mind. If you are not pleased with outward manifestations, do not entertain the displeasure outward, but use the feeling of displeasure to awaken inward to see what the attitudes of mind are that you are entertaining that is causing your displeasure. Of what benefit is this philosophy if it is not applied? But be encouraged, for there *is* some application. There *is*. And the students—all of you—are making that application in many, many different areas of your life.

But when you face the great masters of the sense world—the master of money, number one; the master of the human ego, number two; and the master of the function of procreation—then you face the battle of battles. Look at life, your life, and ask yourself the honest question, "When, when do I experience a lack of peace and goodness in my life?" Ask yourself that question honestly. And I assure you, my good students, it is only when you are serving the master of *m-e-s*.

When you are freed, through effort, of serving that master, your soul rises. You enjoy this wonderful world that's around and about you. Your health and your harmony are expressed to its fullest. So that is the choice, my good students, that all people must make someday: to choose the path of light or to stay in the shadows of the night.

Let us, in our endeavors and in our efforts, this moment become more aware of our responsibility to ourselves, to the divine Source of which we are an inseparable part. Let us become more aware of what we emanate out into the universe. There are only the masters of creation of the functions—only those three masters stand between you and the eternal Light. And the eternal Light that awakens our soul has a greater value and a greater priority than those temporary functions.

I am aware that many, in communicating with our world, communicate with many varying dimensions. But let me speak for a few moments on communication—not only of communicating with our world, but communicating with all worlds. We can only communicate with that which is receptive to our communication. We can speak, but if there is not a receptive ear, then there is no communication, for there is no response. And so it is, my friends, that there are those who communicate with the astral world and they view the expression of those masters of the functions, for those souls are still in those bodies. But there are also those who communicate with other dimensions and those functions have long ago served their purpose.

And so whatever you, on Earth, predominately entertain in your mind, those are the levels of consciousness that you are receptive to, that you can communicate with. If you wish to communicate with levels of peace and harmony, with levels of reason and common sense, then you must awaken within yourself those levels of consciousness. For it's like turning a dial on the radio: you can only hear what you turn your dial to. And so it is in your power to tune in this dial on the radio and to be receptive to the healing balm, to be receptive to abundant good, to be receptive to the fullness of life.

Can you not yet see, my good students, it is the created forms of the human mind that stand like a wall between you and the realms of spiritual light and happiness? But because it is a created wall that your minds, through errors of ignorance, have created, that wall shall fall. For it began and it shall end. Let it not be when you leave your physical body. Begin the crumbling of that wall this moment. Begin it today. It is indeed most difficult, I know, for anyone who relies upon the human mind as the total source of their supply and information in life to push that all aside and to try to rely upon something that they cannot experience with their limited senses. But some day that must be, for the day comes that the senses, having served their purpose, shall go.

It is like a person who asks, "When I leave my physical body, will I continue to eat food?" My good students, of course, you will continue to eat food as long as that desire is the higher priority in your consciousness. And that desire for food will keep you on those realms where it exists. But in time, you will move from those realms and those needs will no longer be experienced within you.

You see, my students, you can only experience need as long as you insist upon denial, for need is denial and denial is destiny. So when you permit your minds to tell you of its many needs, you continue to establish that law of denial and you destine yourself to those continuing experiences.

In many different ways we have spoken to you on belief and why you experience so many different things. And as long as you permit your soul to be totally controlled by the thought of self, you will have denial, for the very thought of self is the Law of Denial. It is the thought of I that denies your very source of life.

Now think about that, my students, when you are not happy, you know you're in the thought of I and the house of self. You have established the Law of Denial and are experiencing the destiny of it. But when you free yourself from the thought of I and you move above and beyond the little house of self, you feel the goodness of life. That is the moment that you go home, the home of your soul.

So many people misunderstand the home of the soul and they misunderstand the spiritual realms of consciousness. You are moving in and out of varying realms of consciousness. You don't all wait until you leave the physical body. When you move out of the house of self, you enter the universal home of light and goodness. And when you do that, you are receptive to all of the abundant good that can be offered. When you entertain the thought of I and live in the house of self, you emanate that wherever you move or breathe. And everyone in form is receptive, within themselves, to their own thought of I and to their little house of self. And so we find discord and disturbance when the thought of I and the house of self is in control. Now, the thought of I and the house of self offers to you the limitations and fears that have built it.

You see, my students, the thought of I is created by mental substance, by negative faith: that is, faith in dual expression. Mental substance is a dual or opposing law and, by the very opposition of that law, creates friction and through that friction flows the creative principle. So each time that you direct your faith to the mental world, you experience what is known as fear from this very opposition or friction.

Now, you all know that God or infinite divine Intelligence is this neutrality. It is not positive and it is not negative, for there is no friction. And that's why it's called neutral. When you are in that neutral state of consciousness, you experience peace, the very power of God. And it is the power of God that can, and does, free you from that friction or fear. And, my good students, as you continue to unfold, you will awaken to the great value of control of the mind. For without that control of the mind, you lose your health, your wealth, and your happiness.

It is not easy for any mind to rely on a neutral principle because it is contrary to the nature of the human mind. Mental substance thrives on friction. I know that many of you have asked the question, Why do people rush to accidents and disasters? Because there is friction. Because there is the experience of fear and they call that excitement. The senses are activated and express themselves.

The path of peace is a neutral path, but it is freed from judgment because it is freed from friction. You cannot have judgment without a dual expression.

And so, my good students, if it comes, it comes and if it goes, it goes. That is the wise counsel of your soul. For each moment is different and each thought in your mind is different. Only a fool relies upon a constant-changing substance. There is nothing in your mind that you can rely upon, for today it is here and tomorrow it is gone. How foolhardy to rely upon a vehicle known as the mind, which is in a constant process of change. And he who relies upon the mind shall suffer the consequences of his own judgments. The mind dictates; the soul counsels. There is a vast, vast difference.

The suffering of life is ever equal to the thought that we have judged. Think of that, my good students. Think of your destinies, review your denials, and move to acceptance. You cannot, you cannot change the laws of evolution. You cannot hold back the laws of change. You may fear them and you may entertain many thoughts about them, but you cannot change the divine laws that sustain the right of all things. Accept the right of all thought that you may free it.

You see, my students, if you do not accept the right of the thought, then you deny the right of the thought. And that denial becomes your destiny. But if you accept the right of the thought, you place yourself in a position to control it. But you cannot control what you do not accept. And if you do not control the thought, then you cannot give the thought to God. I do hope and pray that you understand that simple law of the mental world.

I shared with you some time ago some of my personal experiences in these centuries. And it was a beautiful angel, my guardian angel, that counseled me to accept. And when I accepted what I judged at the moment to be an intolerable situation, I was freed from it. And though many centuries, since that day, has passed—many centuries have passed, all that I have viewed and experienced, I have accepted. And in that acceptance, I have been freed.

Hopefully, in those many years of experience, some light has dawned within my consciousness, for I know, beyond a shadow of any doubt, I know that it works. I know that God moves in when the minds of men move out. And I know that it takes acceptance for God to get in and the mind to get out. Free yourself and change your destiny that you may enjoy the beauty and the goodness that God has brought to you. For I assure you, there is nothing in the worlds of form that can compare to the freedom of your eternal being. And surely, my good students, you have been given sufficient unto your present seeming needs in your evolution that you may apply this demonstrable truth and set yourselves free.

Now is the time, when the need is the greatest, for, as I spoke earlier, the need is the denial. Stop denying, my good students, and start accepting the right of all thought and experience. Accept it. That moment you will control it, that you may give it to the only source, the only power, that can transform your life.

And, in keeping with that truth, let us once again speak on keeping faith with reason, she will transfigure thee. For it is the power of God uncontaminated by the dual law of the mind that flows unobstructed through the soul faculties.

And remember, when you say, "I don't understand," you establish the law of supremacy of the human mind. And as long as you entertain that mental thought, my students, you cannot understand. And when you give what you have to give and are freed from the attachment of what is done with it, then shall you see the Light. For he who gives, with his own attachments and dictates, his own judgments and establishes his own laws of denial has given not but unto himself.

Let us not deceive ourselves with our doing. Let us face ourselves with our constant coming and going. Let us look clearly at these eighty-one levels of consciousness and let us choose wisely which ones we care to live in. For that which energy is directed to is destined to grow. And energy is directed through the vehicle of thought. But you cannot control a thought that you deny.

There's a better way to live. And it is our purpose in bringing to you this Living Light philosophy that the Light may live ever brighter within your universe, that you may, through your own awakening, direct more energy to its application, that you may receive the benefits of its demonstration. We can only assure you that it works, and it works to the degree and the extent of the energy that you direct in it. Let it work more fully in your life. Do not be discouraged by the seeming mountains of obstruction that your minds, through the errors of fear, have created.

We all are destined to move onward. And onward are we moving. But our minds do not like the change, for these minds—all minds, created form—they want to live. Whatever thought you entertain has your intelligence in it. And that intelligence not only wants to express itself, it wants to continue on and on and on. The mind abhors the thought of death and, therefore, does not readily, nor easily, discuss it. But all things of form are born and all things of form shall die. It is the true you, the formless free spirit, that is the home of your eternal soul. But when you speak to the mind and you tell the mind that its very essence and being, that which sustains it, is formless and free, above and beyond the laws of identification, it is not pleased with that truth, for it lives in the limit of its form.

It is our purpose to free you from the limits of form that you may find your true being. The mind lives within a casement, so to speak, created by itself. And living within this casement or shell, it judges its security. And so when you, that true being, begins to rise above and beyond that limited shell, there are experiences of fear and pain and suffering. But as the egg must hatch, so shall you. You cannot change that. We call it, in this philosophy, a broadening of your horizons. As you make the constant effort to demonstrate the will of God, known as total acceptance, shall you experience more harmonious and joyous effects.

I know that some of you have felt that we spend much time in the mental realms and you would like to move on to the varying other dimensions of the worlds of spirit. My students, you cannot move out of anything that you don't understand, for that which you don't understand, you don't control. And control we must. We must control all vehicles of expression that our soul is moving through. And therefore in all our getting, we must get understanding, that we may use these varying forms of creation, that we may use them wisely, that they may serve the purpose for which we have designed them. For it is our mind that is designing these thoughts and forms. Let them, as the tools that they truly are, let them serve us wisely.

When you have faced the greatest fear of your life, you will know how great God really is.

Good night.

NOVEMBER 3, 1977

CONSCIOUSNESS CLASS 162

Greetings, students. This evening we will speak for a moment on life.

As man follows his own thought and calls the experience thereof life, so man's life, his experiences, vary in keeping with his willingness to accept. We have spoken to you in these many classes a great deal on the divine Law of Acceptance, for all of experience is dependent upon your willingness to accept. We have spoken to you on the bondage of rejection: how we are controlled by that which we reject and how we are, in truth, freed by that which we accept. And so it is that this divine will, called acceptance, is the very thing that will bring unto you the goodness of life. Whether or not, in following your own thought, the experience is something you are, in truth, adverse to, by this very Law of Acceptance you gain control over it. And by gaining control over it, it is then within your power to give it up. But you cannot give what you do not have. And that which you reject is that which binds you and controls you.

And so, my students, as we view this divine Law of Acceptance, we can easily see the great benefit in using it wisely. No matter what the experiences of life are, if you wish to change them, you must accept them in order that you can contain the power within you and gain control over those experiences.

And at this time, we wish to spend some of this class in the many questions that you have submitted.

Thank you. What is the Spirit's recommendation to improve oneself as a writing channel?

To forget oneself. For example, the questioner has made a judgment and in the judgment has limited their own potential. To forget the self is to free oneself from these multitudes of judgment that limit the divine expression.

Thank you. What is meant by a screen of mind, which acts as a barrier to interdimensional communication?

As each thought, fed energy by the Divine—each thought that man chooses is governed and controlled by the Law of Creation. Whenever a thought is entertained in mind in the mental world, it creates a form. The form that it creates is dependent upon the laws established—laws established eons ago. These forms, once created, must receive energy in order to continue to exist. Now, it is the very nature of the human mind, once having created, by this thought process, a form, for this form to continue its existence. For example, you can stop and think about your own mind. You do not entertain the possibility of its total extinction, not in truth, because that is contrary to the very nature of mental substance.

And so these forms, which are being fed by this direction of energy to them—there are a multitude of them. They stand between you—in a mental world—and your view of the Light of eternal truth. Whenever you permit your mind to think of itself, then you direct energy to an untold number of thought forms. Because there are, in each person's life, so many varied forms and because they are so gigantic, so to speak, in keeping with the energy that has been directed to them, you cannot see beyond that mental realm.

So, my good students, this philosophy has taught a process of breathing and proper meditation in order for you to slowly, but surely, gain control of your mind. So that you will not spend so much of this divine energy on those multitude of forms. When you gain control of your mind, then you can choose, in the light of reason, to free yourself from the mental realms and view the spiritual or eternal realms. Without this effort, you, as individualized evolving souls, continue to build a barrier of mental forms that encircle you and build your own prison.

How many times have you already experienced a thought repeating itself in your mind, plaguing you, moving wherever you go, like a shadow, and robbing you from your peace and your happiness? That is the revelation that the created thought form is not only hungry, but has gained indeed great control over you. In your early efforts to gain this control in the mental realms, you will become very aware of how many thoughts plague you when you try to be at peace.

Now, we have stated before, that peace, peace is the power of God. God is the allness, the wholeness of Life herself. When you are in a state of peace—a true state of peace—you are freed, in that moment, from all mental created forms. It is that experience of freedom, which is the effect of what is called the peace or power of God, that all souls, in truth, are seeking. To separate that peace, that freedom, that truth, from creation is within the power of all people.

So many times we pray to God for so many things. And we demonstrate, following our prayers, the direct opposite. If we accept within us this simple truth, if we truly accept that total acceptance is the will of God, the will of the Divine, and then we spend our days in rejection, then we are indeed a house divided. And we can only experience what a divided house offers to us.

My good students, as we speak forth the word and, through our own demonstrations, our own applications, demonstrate the opposite, this philosophy—or no philosophy—can benefit us. We must take a more honest view of our efforts. We must take a more honest view of what we are doing.

We all know that we follow, in truth, our own thoughts and we experience what those thoughts have to offer. But that, my students, is not life. That is what the mind has done with life that we experience. There is so much more to life than the mental world and following these multitudes of thoughts—to feed and to care for those forms. There is so much more to life. It is the peace that is offered to you by the control of your mind that is the home of your eternal being. That home is in the moment of your effort, is in the moment of your acceptance.

Whenever you reject, in those moments that you do reject, you deny God. And in your denial of God, you are destined to what rejection has to offer. I am sure that all of you will agree that rejection offers no pleasure, no joy, no fullness of life, no peace, and no happiness. So whatever it is that you do not like, accept the right of its expression. And by your acceptance of the divine right of its expression, you, in that moment, have the power and the control over that form. For that rejection is a form that only you have created. It is a form that you have created by a judgment that your mind has made and, by accepting its right of expression, by accepting its right of existence, you then, having accepted, can give it to God. When you do that, you raise your consciousness. You lift up your soul to realms of peace and harmony. There, in those realms within you, you experience the goodness and the fullness of life.

It is not easy for anyone in evolution to free themselves from judgment. I spent many years, many years of my life as a judge and I do know the struggle to be freed from judgment. To be freed from judgment, one must stand guardian at the portal of their thoughts, for thoughts rise quickly and continuously in the human consciousness.

And so, my students, give it a try. Accept. Accept the things you don't like as well as you accept the things you do like, for what you don't like and what you do like is an effect of your own judgment. And so why live in deprivation when you can live in the fullness of life? The God of our acceptance is not a god of limit. The God that is the true God sustains everything, whatever you choose to think. For any thought you entertain in your mind is sustained by the divine energy directed through you and by you. Direct that energy through the law of the divine will. Direct it that you may experience the effects of more harmonious, peaceful, and abundant thoughts.

Let your thoughts be of abundant good, of your right of that experience, and do not deny, for denial is rejection. Do not deny what the mind offers. Accept what the mind offers that you may give it to something greater than the mind. That way, my students, you will not be plagued with lack and limitation. You will not be plagued with denial. You will not be plagued with rejection and bondage. Your health, your wealth, and your happiness will reach a fullness never before experienced in your evolution. Truth is so simple, so very simple, my students. But it takes a constant effort to change the patterns so long endured.

Thank you. Please give us some understanding of how our spirit guides and teachers work with us.

Ever in keeping with the laws that we establish. My good students, angels from the realms of Light come to all souls on Earth to help, to inspire, and to encourage them. But as the minds of men insist upon the dictates of limit, those souls who are beyond limit cannot long stay in our universes. It is like a person that wants to stay dry and they jump in the ocean. You can't jump in the ocean without getting wet, no matter how dry you want to be.

And so it is as you expose yourself to helping anyone—whether they are in the physical body or the ethereal body, it matters not—you can work with them, but there comes a moment when either they swim with you or you sink with them. You, in that moment, must make a wise choice, for it is your duty and your responsibility to save yourself. And so it is with the angels who come to inspire us, to guide us, and to encourage us, if we do not make the effort to help ourselves, they do not long stay with us.

Thank you. Would you please give us your understanding of why some ethnic groups, such as Jews and etc., have been persecuted through the centuries, when they seem to be peace-loving people who value freedom, culture, and education?

In reference to your question of why is a person persecuted—a person or a group of persons, it matters not—what matters is the question, Do we, in our understanding, deny the demonstrable Law of Personal Responsibility? If we deny the very basis of this philosophy, the Law of Personal Responsibility, then, my students, we have indeed far to go. In keeping with that law, which is the foundation stone of the Living Light philosophy, is the law that states like attracts like and becomes the Law of Attachment. If you accept that persecution is your destiny, if you accept that things have always been a certain way and, always having been a certain way, shall always be a certain way, then you establish, rigidly in consciousness, the authority of self-will over divine will. And that is established by what is called judgment.

So often in life we look at others and we make our judgments—whether they are happy or miserable, whether they are successes in life or failures. But how little do we, in truth, see. The law that man can only, in truth, experience what he has, in truth, accepted and demonstrated in his life applies to one person or many people.

And so when you, as individuals, entertain thoughts of self, you experience what self has to offer. It offers persecution. It offers all of lack and limit. It offers suffering, because self, self is the very height of denial. When we rise in self, we deny the allness of the Divine. When we rise in self, we deny God. And it is in our denial—an effect of self—that we suffer and persecute ourselves. I can assure you, my good students, anyone who entertains frequently the thought of self and self-related thoughts is not a person that is experiencing the goodness and fullness and joy that life has to offer.

Because, in our error of ignorance, we have done that to our eternal being, we must pay the price of that error. And so it is that there are no divine eternal laws that choose a person or group of people to be persecuted. The persecution is the experience of errors of ignorance.

Self is a very expensive illusion to entertain. It separates us from the great joy of life. It not only separates us, but it is the very thing that is the cause of our experiencing need. Without the thought of self, there is no need. As the thoughts of self increase within us, so our needs grow and grow and grow. No one, in truth, wishes to live in deprivation—to be deprived of the things that they desire. But face the eternal truth, my children. Face the demonstration that life offers. It is only the self that deprives us. It is only the self that offers the suffering, for it is only the self that rejects.

Your true being, your soul, does not reject, for the soul does not judge. It is only a witness of time passing on. Your soul is the witness of things that have come and things that have gone. Your soul is not the judge and your soul is not the jury. It is your mind, the self, that is the judge. That judge you face each moment. That judge is the form that orders you to do the things you do.

But you can be free from that judge because you created that judge. And you created the jury that helps rule his throne. And because he is, in truth, your child and the jury are your children, you can remove the energy that is their sustenance and they shall return unto the essence from whence they were given birth. You can do that any moment you choose. And when that happens—that takes place within you—then you experience the peace that is yours. You become one with all things, for you are, in truth, all things.

And when you rise to that level of consciousness—being one with all things—there is no need. There are no unfulfilled desires. That is the great benefit of applying this simple truth: you are one with all and being one with all, you cannot need; you cannot question, for the answers you are therefore a part of. That moment shall dawn within all people in time.

You have earned, through your evolution, you have earned the opportunity and been shown the way for that moment to be in this eternity known as now. It is within your hands. It is within your power to do it. No one can do it for you. They may encourage you. They may prompt you, but you must do it, someday, for yourself.

It is when we are in that prison house called self that our needs are so great. The more we entertain those thoughts of self, the greater our needs become and life seems to shrink around and about us, when there is such a beautiful way to go. Surely, my friends, it is foolhardy to choose the downward path of self.

Thank you. Please expand on the statement, Use wisely what you have and you'll never be in want.

Use wisely what you have and you'll never be in want. All things are designed to serve a purpose. When they are used wisely, they serve the purpose for which they have been designed. When you demonstrate the principle of that law—to use the things you have to use for the purpose for which they have been designed—then you move into the unobstructed divine flow of principle. For example, a spoon has been designed to serve a purpose of placing food in the mouth. He who uses it for a shovel to dig in the earth is not only foolhardy, but is not using the tool for what it is was designed.

Now, man has all of the tools necessary to serve him. He has those tools within him. These tools are so often, so very often badly abused, for they are used not for what they have been designed, but for what man has judged that he may use them for. Now, the mind may question, "Well, how do I know for sure what this or that was designed for?" All you need do, my students, is pray for peace in that moment, and within you shall awaken to you, clearly and simply, the purpose for each tool that you have within you. And you know. No one needs to tell you whether you are using it wisely or you are abusing it.

We all know the simple law that the lack of use is abuse, for each thing is designed to fulfill a just and rightful purpose. But the judgment of the human mind, in its great error of ignorance, abuses the tools of life. Look at your body and see if in all parts of your anatomy—all those areas and all those parts are tools to be used, not abused. If you have used them wisely, then they are serving the purpose for which they have been designed. If you are not, then they are not serving that purpose.

So, my good students, when you rise in principle, you free yourself not only from personality, but you free yourself from yourself. You free yourself from judgment and rejection and you move into peace and acceptance.

Thank you. Would you please elaborate on the process by which a sense function becomes a soul faculty?

A sense function, all sense functions, all functions have been designed to be in balance, a perfect balance, with a corresponding soul faculty. As the seed planted in the ground grows to become a tree or a plant, depending on the seed that is planted, so functions evolve by this perfect balancing with the corresponding soul faculty. It is not, it is not the annihilation of functions that a wise man seeks. It is the balance.

You see, my students, the functions are under the control of the mind and the faculties are under the control of the soul. We don't try to eliminate the mind, for it is a tool. We must make the effort to use it wisely that it may serve its purpose of design. And so it is that these expressions of the mind, called functions, and these expressions of the soul, called faculties, must amalgamate, must unite through a perfect balancing. When this takes place, there is an exchange, in that perfect balancing, there is an exchange of energy that moves across a so-called invisible bridge and that energy moves and mixes between those functions and faculties. It is casting light upon the shadows. And so when the faculty rises in balance with the function, the light of reason eliminates the shadows and then the functions serve the purpose and man uses the tools wisely and is never again in want.

Thank you. Please speak a bit about courage and how faith bolsters it.

Courage is a soul faculty. And man is constantly moving, following his thought into many areas of life. So often man has a desire, a thought. It seems good, until he starts following it where it leads him. For when you have a thought, that thought is related to a function. And unless you have a balance with the corresponding faculty, then you do not know where that thought is really going to lead you. This is another of the great benefits of bringing about this balance between the faculties and the functions.

And so it ofttimes takes courage, it takes courage to continue to follow the thought. It takes faith to know that the final outcome is going to be good, for it can be good if you have the courage and the faith to make it so.

My good students, your destiny is in your keeping. There is no one in any heaven or hell that has power over you. Your destiny is in your hands. The law is impartial. The law of the Divine is infallible. It is not that you are not aware of these divine laws, for you are. It is when it comes to applying them that the struggle seems so great. You do know many of these divine laws, for they have been given to you. But we must learn to listen. We all hear, but few of us listen. It takes effort to listen.

Thank you. Please explain what God's promise is.

God's promise is the fullness of life. That is the promise of God. The fulfillment of those divine laws is the promise of God. And so divine laws are unchanging and inevitable. All souls shall go home. Some go home while yet on Earth. They have those moments. But the laws of God are being fulfilled every moment of your life.

Though it is ofttimes perhaps difficult to view an adverse situation and say, "Thank you, God, for demonstrating the infallibility of your divine law. Thank you for demonstrating your eternal promise: the fullness of life." My students, the truth is we are all experiencing the fullness of life, for we are experiencing the fullness of where our own thoughts have taken us and are taking us. And so whatever we choose, we experience, in truth, the fullness of our choice.

And once before it was stated, we always get what we really want. Think about that beautiful truth, my friends. We always get what we really want. But it is those wrappings that come with the package that we don't like ofttimes. But we always get what we really want. But because they come with different wrappings, we don't often recognize that we are getting what we really want.

Now, where does this excess wrapping come from? We send out a thought and a desire. It seems simple enough. But we have the desire and all kinds of thoughts rise up and cover up the desire. And it goes out into the world covered with many wrappings. And so we go through life and we say, "That's not what I wanted. And that's not what I wanted." We're looking at the wrappings. We're looking at the covering. For we are getting—and we always get—what we really want. We've just got to learn to recognize what is beyond the appearances, for they are deceiving. Yes, my students, yes indeed, when we are honest with ourselves, then we know, yes, God, we are getting what we really wanted.

Thank you. You have frequently referred to the eternal moment of now, the eternity of consciousness. Would you expand a bit on this, please?

If we stop this moment and be in this moment with the fullness of our being, then we are receptive to the fullness of the power of the divine intelligent Energy. In this moment, we can accomplish much, but we must make great effort to be in the moment of now. For now is a moving stream of consciousness. It is a constant moving and we cannot move consciously with this eternal moment until we free ourselves from ourselves, for self offers the rigidity and inflexibility of judgment.

To experience the eternal moment is to place oneself in a position to use this infinite intelligent Energy wisely and constructively for the goodness of our own lives. But you cannot experience eternity as long as you tenaciously hold to the thought of I, which gives you and grants you the house of self. Pause in this eternal moment and experience this great peace.

Thank you. Please expand on the teaching, Fascination is the demonstration of the Law of Greed, which leaves the soul in void.

Fascination is the demonstration of the Law of Greed. Think, my good students, about what you experience when you fascinate. You create a form and forms. And they change and they move and you create more forms. And you're never satisfied with the forms you create. You always find a flaw and there's always a constant, constant insatiable need for more and more and more. And so the mind continues on and on and on and on and on. It's never filled. And so it fascinates and it fascinates and it fascinates. And the soul never gets in, because the mind is in total control. And the mind is constantly utilizing the energy to create more forms and different forms. And so the soul is void, for the soul is not expressing. The soul is not in balance. There are no faculties expressed. And so fascination and greed go hand in hand. And it's never enough. There is no gratitude, for there is nothing to be grateful for. For there is constant, constant more and more and more.

When a person has a desire and the desire is being fulfilled, there should be a moment of pause. For in the pause does man experience the soul faculty of gratitude, in that moment of pause. But in fascination, there is no pause. There is just the constant, constant utilizing of energy to create so many mental forms. And you know it's never enough. It's never enough.

Think, my students. Think what self offers. It's never enough. No matter what you have or have not, it's never enough. And so let us pause more often. Let us enjoy the moment to pause. Let us be grateful for the ability to pause, for in the pause, you experience your true being. You're freed from the processes of fascination. You're freed from need and need and need that grows and grows and grows and grows.

Pause, my students. Pause more often. Stop the wheels in your mind from turning. Learn to pause a few moments every hour. Pause as often as you can, for when you pause, you enter the life eternal. In that stillness, in that pause, you experience all of life. Nothing is left out when you truly pause.

Good night.

NOVEMBER 10, 1977

CONSCIOUSNESS CLASS 163

Greetings, students. In concluding this semester, we should like to spend some time in the discussion of how we came to be.

As you know, the illusion known as time is indispensable to what is known as experience, for all that has been, or is yet to be, in truth, is. As long as our minds entertain thoughts of time, then we shall continue to experience, for the illusion, through our own identity, becomes.

Out of the so-called void rose a light, a light of intelligent energy—its very purpose "being." And the purpose of "being" is expression. And so it is that all things came to be and continue to be in keeping with the expression of the Light or so-called God, known as intelligent Energy.

We must not view this as some event that happened eons ago. For it is a continuum: It continues to take place each and every moment. And so it is that we are encircled in this intelligent energy field. Its very nature, "being." And as we permit ourselves an opening or broadening of our horizons, so this energy flows through us, around us, and about us. The death and birth of people, places, and things is ever dependent upon what is known as the illusion of time. As man, in his evolution, evolves above and beyond time and space, he awakens to the reality and the totality of Life herself. Out of this great sea of light, form began to take shape. It took shape in keeping with the Law of Resistance.

Now, you have heard much spoken about denial and rejection. You have also heard us speak on destiny, the effect of man's denial.

As resistance is indispensable to the shaping of so-called form, so it is that each thought is resisted. So it is that each feeling is resisted. For without this Law of Resistance, there would be no creation. And so for each step forward, something is making a step backward. For each movement ahead, something is returning to its source. That is the law. And when you awaken to the simplicity of that truth, then you will move more graciously through this great illusion called creation.

When the loss is experienced equal to the gain, in that balance shall you rise to the neutrality which is your true being and, in so doing, be beyond the laws of duality. As all things must divide in order to conquer, so it is that our thoughts divide. And so it is that all form divides. For division is the Law of Form.

It is our purpose to help you to help yourselves. For he who helps another and, in so doing, makes the one helped dependent upon them, has helped no one but himself. So in our efforts to study and to apply, let us ever remember the simple Law of Solicitation. Let us remember that presence is that law, that presence is the Law of Solicitation.

And let us view this intelligent infinite Light of which, in truth, we are. We are that Light. We are that wholeness. We are, in truth, that goodness. But it is the world of creation, this world of division, that blinds our view. Go beyond the screen of time, for it is a screen between you and your eternal home that is this moment. There is no past and there is no future. There is only the moment of your awareness. That *is*. For truth *is*. Truth, my good students, needs no defense. For truth is beyond the illusion of need.

How does man free himself from these created illusions? By total acceptance, he rises beyond the Law of Creation. He no longer resists. It is our resistance that creates the obstructions in our path. And the days in eternity, the moments of now, are filled with so many, so many forms, so many obstructions. Look, my students, at what you do not resist. And see how freely it flows through your consciousness. So whatever, whatever it may be, go home—home to the Light which you are—for there is not only your divinity, but there is your fullness of life. For there, in truth, is your allness.

Many philosophies have spoken on soul mates and have spoken on guardian angels. Be rest assured, for every form there is a mate. For you are only a part in form. And there is another part. And when that is amalgamated, then you have that totality in level that of consciousness. But above, above form, above creation, there is where all of the joy of life expresses. Do not continue to limit your lives. And remember, only through resistance is limitation possible. For only through resistance can the barriers, formed from mental substance, be created for you.

Many have said that man is the effect of his thoughts. That is indeed the man of form. How does man, limited by his thoughts, become universal in consciousness? Through the slow, but sure, effort of withdrawal. To withdraw the mental activity from a world filled with variety, that is what is, in truth, taking place. Many of your endeavors, many of your interests no longer serve you well. And you have withdrawn from them. Some of them by conscious choice and some of them from so-called necessity. But remember, our necessities were choices. Because we will not permit our minds to view circumstances or necessities as an effect of laws that we have established, in no way frees us from the laws that we have established.

Beyond all of that is that light that is the true you. Beyond the many forms of your earthly experience and the many forms that you brought with you to Earth, beyond all of that is you. Uncluttered, uncontaminated, that so-called "pinhead" [Discourse 12] known as the eternal being.

Whatever and whenever you find that light is the right place for you. For be it the true light, it shines in many places and it is. And so the paths of my students are indeed varied. Sometimes they pass on by having barely touched the light. But the light is awakened within. Though the changes do not *seem* to have taken place, the law has been established and the changes are taking place on levels that the conscious mind cannot view. For what you have already, in your efforts, established has been set into motion, though you frequently rest by the well, you will rise again and move onward on your journey through this so-called time and space.

To go beyond that illusion, one must first accept that it is illusion. And one can easily, in the light of reason, accept the illusion of time and space, for they can view through their own experiences how quickly time passes when their attention is upon anything that truly interests them. And how slowly time passes when they find, from so-called circumstances, the necessity to endure that which they find little or no interest in. So we already have the necessary experiences in life to teach us the simple truth: that time indeed is dependent upon many things.

And so it is that space is dependent, as an illusion, upon many things. As these barriers of things or forms, begin to disintegrate before the light of truth, man will find himself limitless and free. But to find yourself limitless and free you must first accept in your thoughts the possibility. And so how does this apply to this moment of your struggle? My students, it is the very foundation upon which you build a successful and full life. For then, in those moments beyond creation, in those moments that you easily can rise to, you know in that moment that all things are in a process of passing. They will pass quickly or slowly, dependent upon you. For it is from you that the law is being established.

We identify and through that law become so many things, my students. We experience so much. And then the day comes when we ask ourselves the question, "Why am I here? Where am I going? Oh, where have I been?" I assure you that you have been everywhere, that you have been all things. For you cannot separate the intelligent light of energy which you are. When you accept what you really are, you will no longer experience these struggles, these difficulties, these wants, these needs, and these desires. For you cannot need what you already are.

You cannot want, nor, yea, desire, that which you are. Slowly, but surely, do we rise in consciousness to that truth.

And it is moments of great peace when we go home. Let us, through our acceptance, go home more often. For there, basking in that intelligent energy, freed from all forms of so-called life, there, my students, is the great fountain of rejuvenation. There, you, once again, are born. That is the so-called rebirth. Only to go out to wander again. But in your wanderings again a conscious awareness of that light, of that energy, guides you through the jungles of creation.

So often in the jungle we view what we think we have lost. Rarely do we see what we are gaining. But it's all a process of movement. It is all coming and going at all times. If it takes us days, weeks, years to realize that it is passing, then, for us, it shall take those years. Hold not to form is our basic teaching, for form shall pass. Hold not to the form of your thoughts. Hold not to those things. Use them, don't abuse them. Let all form freely go from your life. And then all shall freely enter your life. But that does take some effort on your part: to be aware and to stay awake. Sleep not in the sea of satisfaction. For in so doing, the pain is great when you awaken and awaken, all souls are destined to do.

Some of you are working diligently in levels of consciousness that you yourselves are not consciously aware of. But you are working, because there is a part of you deep inside that knows. And so, in truth, God's greatest work is done in silence. But remember that silence wears many garments.

In concluding this semester, we once again view the many areas of your interest. We view your struggle with compassion. But we know that for you it is necessary. We also know that it is not eternal and we know that you are freeing yourself from yourself. Though your minds ofttimes convince you that you have lost much and have gained little or nothing, I assure you it is the limited view of the mind. And the mind's view is limited by its own experiences of yesteryear.

You are moving ahead, for you are moving on an upward path. And many experiences you have already had and many more shall you encounter. Accept them all and be free. When they tear at the very foundation of your emotions, remember, it is necessary for you that you may have a better life, a brighter day, a greater way. For it is the payment, my good students, of attainment. It is indeed serving its purpose and you, in truth, are benefiting. Not in the ways perhaps that your minds insist upon dictating—but remember, your minds brought you here. It brought you where you are and it has already made many so-called concessions.

But you are better, regardless what you think or think not. For you know a better way and it is within your power to apply it. And you must not permit yourselves to be discouraged, for you are applying it in your way on your day. Perhaps you are not applying as much as you would like to apply, but the growth is slow, but it is sure.

Some of you will return for the continuing of these classes and some of you will go. I have never been concerned with numbers, for I know that those who come, the intelligent divine Light, known as God, has brought them. And I know they will be with us as long as it is in the divine plan. I am not sad over the coming, nor am I sad over the going. That is my earnest prayer—that you, too, may have that wonderful freedom and be not saddened over the coming and going. For all things that come must go. Someday I, too, shall go from these earthly classes. I know that. I am not saddened, nor should you be saddened. For when our duty is done, we must move on and on and on. I will meet with you again many times in your earthly life. And some of you will continue on with this school in our world when you come over.

It is indeed interesting to many, I am sure, that the mind looks and wonders, "When will it end?" Well, when will we graduate? My students, each day is graduation, each day is birth, each day is death. Truth, having no beginning, has no ending. And the Light, the very nature of the Light, is expression.

And so our school is like a circle: without beginning and without ending. We move on and on and on and on and on. And if you feel you need a rest, then ask yourself the honest question, "O God, with what am I bored?" For those who seek to rest by the well have permitted themselves to be bored. Reawaken your enthusiasm, for life has so much to offer. And why do we get bored with life and then say we need to rest? My good students, repetition is law through which change is made possible. And when we tenaciously hold to things and refuse to change, the repetition which is the indispensable ingredient to bring about the change, meets the wall of boredom. When we are close to victory, we ofttimes become bored, distracted on the path of success. Victory and success are for the courageous of heart. It is not for the weak ones. So you must be strong willed to be courageous. The will of the Divine—that is the path of light.

Look around and about your world. Is there any denial of the Divine? All forms receive the energy in keeping with their receptivity. Everyone receives the goodness that they will permit themselves to receive. I assure you, my students, the only thing that stands between you and the abundant greatness and goodness of life is the dictates of the human mind. Accept, my students, accept this abundance that is your true being. Accept your true being. Stop the activity of the mind for a moment and in that moment feel the greatness of life. You are as great as you will permit yourselves to be. You are as healthy and wealthy as you alone will allow. Stop, my students, denying your abundant good.

Each time you give power to man, you deny your divinity. Each time you give power to creation, you build the walls of obstruction and must suffer the consequences. I urge you earnestly and from the depths of my soul to accept the abundant goodness of life. It is waiting for you. It is with you this moment, my friends. It is not something you must chase throughout all creation to find. Let your ears listen. Enjoy the goodness your life has to offer. For I know if you will truly make that effort while yet in earthly flesh, you will be freed from so many dimensions after you leave your earthly bodies.

The dictates of the mind are strong and potent forces of creation, but you need not forever be their victims. Whenever you feel in need and want and desire, just accept the fullness thereof. Accept it, my students, for then you will experience the will of God.

Good night.

NOVEMBER 17, 1977

CONSCIOUSNESS CLASS 164

Good evening, class.

As I am sure you have all observed, our classes appear to get smaller, as our church and organization grows stronger. So that, of course, is in keeping with the law that quality, not quantity, and unity, not dissension, is, in truth, the key and the path to success.

Now, that that applies to anyone can, and does, apply to everyone. And so the business of the common sense of living is demonstrated by the philosophy that you are here to study. Once this philosophy is applied—and is applied from the levels of reason and consideration of all—then man finds the success in life that he is truly seeking.

I know that many of you are aware of what was spoken, I believe, at the forecast [Annual World Forecast 14] in reference to this material world: that when you stop chasing what you desire, whatever it is you desire will start chasing you. And so let us pause more frequently in our daily activities and let us begin to think as we have been taught: to think more deeply. Let us be aware, when we're in class, if all of us is in class or if just a part of us—only one or possibly two of our eighty-one levels of consciousness—is present.

Now, we all know that untold thousands of words have already been given in these classes and many thousands yet shall be given. The same simple truth presented in untold thousands of different ways—because the human mind is designed to preserve and to protect what it has already accepted. And when we do not make the effort to accept what is not already in the human mind, then we are bucking against the inevitable tides of evolution. For in spite of our tenacity of protecting what we think we have, the day always dawns for us that we lose what we think we have in order that we may gain what we think we desire. All of life, in creation, is the effect of desire. And all of us, I am sure, are aware of that. So often we chase these desires and they seem to pass like sand through our fingers. But we have not, in those experiences, honestly asked ourselves the question, What is it we really want?

Everything in life is sustained and supported by energy. And when we feel this lack of energy, then we do whatever our mind dictates to receive the energy that we need to sustain us. This philosophy teaches, and continues to teach, that there is an infinite abundant supply of energy, that it is dependent upon us to remove the restrictions that exist within our mind, that we may be more receptive to this energy. The effect of energy is ever, of course, dependent upon the direction that we send the energy. So when, in our lives, we find that things are not going the way that we wish them to go, then we must make the effort to control, to control our mind, for our mind is the vehicle that is doing the directing. Whatever the experiences are, they are directly the result of where we are directing the infinite, impartial, intelligent energy.

And so in these coming twelve weeks, we will spend some time in trying to help you to help yourself in the control of the thoughts that are in your mind—the ones you are conscious of and the ones you are not yet conscious of.

We spoke once before about the illusion of accidents, that they are nothing more or nothing less than experiences. And this success that all of our minds are seeking in life is, in truth, available for all of us. And the truth of the matter is that we are successful in many areas of life. It's just that when we view our desires that are strong within us and they are not yet fulfilled, then we feel that we are not successful. But that is not an honest or an objective appraisal of our lives, because we are not viewing, at those times, the areas in our lives in which we are indeed successful. So what we are really asking for is a change within our consciousness in order that we may direct this intelligent energy to our present desires.

[*At this point, Mr. Goodwin goes into a trance.*]

Greetings, students. Indeed it is a pleasure for me to be with you once again, for without service, there is no meaning, nor purpose, to life itself.

And so it is that we continue on in sharing with you what is, in truth, shared with us. In keeping with the basic principle of these classes, we shall continue to review and to expand, for without expansion there is no growth, nor evolution.

Some time ago we spoke to you on the freedom of forgiveness and mentioned at that time that to forgive is to give forth. But man cannot give forth what he has not first accepted. The great value of acceptance is the freedom from judgment and the path of denial. For the expression of God, the divine Intelligence, is known as desire. And no matter what you do, you do not, in form and in creation, free yourselves from desire. But through the will of God, the path of total acceptance, you can, and do, free yourself from the dual Law of Creation, known as judgment. For to accept desire, to accept its right of expression, to accept the possibility of its fulfillment, is to free yourself from judgment and the dual path of creation. This is something that will take a conscious awareness each moment on your part, but I assure you that it is not only the path to freedom, but it is, in truth, the path of fulfillment. For all things desired are fulfilled in keeping with the Law of Directed Energy. And in keeping with that law, man need not be bound by the dual Law of Creation or judgment.

Many philosophies in your world have taught that truth, many in allegorical form. For as we view the books of the centuries past and we enter into that scene of allegory in the Christian Bible known as the Garden of Eden. And so, according to that story, God created Adam—whole, complete, and perfect. And Adam had everything the mind could desire with one exception: Adam had the awareness of self. And the awareness of self recorded in his consciousness what is commonly known as loneliness. For Adam, becoming aware of self, experienced the pity of self, a judgment of the human mind. And so, according to the story, God brought about Eve. And now there were two.

And Eve was tempted by the serpent of knowledge, for knowledge knows much. Knowledge knows the Law of Duality, for knowledge is the throne on which the king of judgment sits. We spoke to you in one of our other classes about knowledge—that knowledge knew much, but wisdom knows better. And so the serpent, the judge on his throne, beguiled her. What does that mean? The serpent of knowledge beguiled Eve. It meant that within her consciousness she registered and recorded what is known as temptation. Being faced with choice, the mind is tempted, the mind is fascinated and knows and, in its knowing, judges and, in its judgment, establishes the path of destiny, known as denial.

And so Adam, tempted by Eve, who was tempted by knowledge, controlled by judgment, descended into the mental realms with Adam and from that day forth knew so-called good and so-called evil. The teaching of this philosophy is the divine neutral intelligence—neither good, nor evil, but above and beyond the realms of creation, above and beyond the throne of judgment. And so it is, my good students, what I have come here to Earth to share with you always brings into my consciousness the untold centuries of experiences in the realms of creation controlled by the king of judgment.

That book teaches that we judge not, yea, we shall be judged. But we judge because we choose. We see opposites. Our eye is not single. Let us make our eye single and, in so doing, experience, while yet in your earthly forms, the beauty, the greatness, the goodness, the allness, the wholeness of what life truly offers to us.

In our moving through life—for life, in truth, is movement or motion and expression—let us ever remember that we are, in truth, a living light, for that is, in truth, what we really are. We are the soul expressed, a living light in the universes, inseparable from all living light. And the essence of all things, which is, in truth, the soul of all things, is living light or intelligent energy. We are using this intelligent energy constantly, directing it in what we know as thought, which is, in truth, form. Let us direct it in the path that will bring unto us the true fullness of life. And that, I assure you, my friends, is the divine path of acceptance.

For what you resist, you create. And what you create, you must face. So let us, in this higher vibratory wave of simple truth, flooded with the multitudes of desires that we are flooded with, accept all of them. Just speak forth the words, "I accept." Whatever thought enters your mind, speak forth that truth, "I accept." And soon you will find that this king, seated on the throne of judgment, will soon bow down. For, my good students, through acceptance, you no longer direct living light or intelligent energy to sustain those forms.

In many ways we have tried to get you to see. And here again we speak to you on the great benefit of freeing this energy—being freed from the duality of creation and experiencing the truth of life itself. Many, my good students, are the centuries that are being removed from your path from the efforts that you are making in your earthly realm. And, viewing that, my heart is filled with the spirit of gratitude, for no one, having experienced those centuries past, would wish or desire it for anyone.

Patience is the path of wisdom. All of your desires shall be fulfilled in keeping with that Law of Patience. Free yourself, my good people, from this dual law. Free yourself from the judgments that plague you. Your life is as beautiful and as good, so to speak, as you alone permit yourself to accept it. I know that it takes so-called time and directed energy known as effort to make the changes in consciousness that are necessary, but, don't you see, my friends, we are revealing to you one simple way: accept and you will not judge and you will not experience the opposing laws of creation.

Do it with the small things in your life first, the things that you have not yet placed such great value upon. Do it first with those things, for it will be easier for you to do. And once having demonstrated that simple truth unto yourselves, move on to the bigger things in life. Move on. Just move on, for that—moving on—is your soul and those realms of consciousness are so beautiful, so harmonious. There is where inspiration reigns supreme. There is where the angels truly sing.

We cannot spend too much time, for too much time cannot be spent on bringing to you the simple truth. Over these many centuries, having viewed and experienced what is offered in the mental realms of creation, there is nothing that that world has to offer that can compare in any way with the realms of spiritual light and peace. You need not be concerned that you will not have all that is in your best interest. The only thing is, my students, you will not make that judgment, for you cannot enter those spiritual realms of joy until all judgment has bowed. In my personal experiences, I listened—and thank God, again I thank God—to that angel that guided me. And I did not resist the masters I had earned. I bowed and I learned the great value of acceptance. I learned beyond a shadow of any doubt that indeed acceptance is the will of God. It frees the soul. It frees the soul. It frees the soul. For it permits it to experience its true home, the home of harmony.

Think of the force that controls the mental world. It is known to you as fear. For the very nature of the mental world—to preserve and protect—is the force known as fear. But, my good students, you cannot experience fear without judgment. I show you in simple words the path of light and reason. Freeing yourselves from all fear is an effect of your efforts to accept and not to judge. Man walks upon the waters, upon the coals of fire, man rises like a bird in the heavens in his physical, earthly form the moment that he frees himself from judgment, for he, in that moment, is freed from fear, the force of the mental world.

So many minds ask how this works and how that works. It is the mind that wants to know. You, the true you, already know. But the mind questions, for the mind ever seeks to control. And in this experience that you have within your minds, of this great need to control, remember, it is the need to control the very thing that is dictating you to control. You control it that it may stop controlling you.

I assure you that to God all things are possible. And you experience God by the will of God. And the will of God is acceptance. It is a demonstrable truth that no mind can deny. For all things are sustained by intelligent energy. That is the living demonstration that you have to view. That is the demonstration of God's will: acceptance.

Flood your minds with the acceptance of the possibility of something better, the possibility of fulfillment, the possibility of something greater. But do not forget that word *possibility*, for, you see, my good friends, when you accept the possibility, you do not dictate the results. And when you do not dictate, you do not judge and it is freed in God's will. It is God's will that you have all that you desire. It is God's will that sustains all of you and every thought that you choose. Stop choosing and you will stop judging. But do not attempt to stop desiring. Choice and judgment is your will of your mental world. Desire is God's will of God's world.

We are, of course, an instrument through which God flows, but we, our minds, our vehicles, are not God. That Essence, that Living Light, is God. When you identify, through total acceptance, with that infinite Light, then, in that moment, are ye Gods. For in that moment you are freed from creation. You are in creation, but no longer a part of creation. You are with people, but no longer a part of people, for "people" is form and you are formless and, therefore, free.

In this semester we shall make great effort to help you see the value of flooding your consciousness with the will of God, for we know that through that effort shall your lives experience the joy that is your infinite and divine birthright.

And remember, as you go out in your new year of '78, the vibrations of the fullness of God are everywhere. There is so much in this year of '78. There is so much fullness. The vibrations are the best. But you must, within your minds, accept that possibility, for all of your experiences to this moment are in keeping with the Law of Acceptance, limited by choice, controlled by judgment, and doomed to disaster just prior to their fulfillment. And you ask, Why they are doomed to disaster? Because, my friends, there is no unity. There is only division. Unite. Unite within.

The sun is rising o'er the horizon for those of you who have demonstrated their interest, for though it may, at times, have been difficult for your minds, you have continued on.

As a teacher, I am always grateful for a student. I have not, nor am I concerned with how many, for the blessing of return is ever in keeping with the original motivation. And I assure you, my friends, I am motivated to share that you may be free from the centuries that my mind demanded I experience in yesteryear. I do not view them in regret, though they still remain, in memory par excellence, painful to me. But it was in keeping with my evolution that it should take me so long to learn my lessons in life. No greater blessing could return to any teacher, once having learned a lesson or two, than to share it with a student that they may, through their efforts, be freed from those particular lessons. My greatest failing was my judgments. And such a failing it was that I chose that profession. And the centuries helped to awaken within me my reason for my choice.

All of these things that you view in creation are in that constant process of birth and death. But, as you know, you are not birth and you are not death. Only your thoughts, which are form, are birth and death. Hold not to thoughts and forms, for it is the path of pain and pleasure. My good friends, joy is far greater than pleasure. Reason is far brighter than pain.

Move onward in this your new year. Move above and beyond pain and pleasure. Move into realms of reason and realms of joy.

I sometimes consider working in a more consistent way with each of you who are demonstrating your efforts to apply. And perhaps in your rather not too distant future that possibility shall come to be, for I well remember, in my past experiences, when I had merited a teacher. And I know the great value of daily effort. I know the great value of constant exposure to the light of reason. I also know that it's so very easy to slip, so to speak, unless there's someone that cares enough to make the daily effort to help us. And so it has been now my sincere prayer for some time that that possibility may come for the few who really care about the possibility of a better life.

Good night.

JANUARY 5, 1978

CONSCIOUSNESS CLASS 165

Greetings, students. Before speaking to the questions that you have prepared, I should like to take a few moments, this evening, to speak especially to my students who have been experiencing the planes of consciousness known as discouragement.

When we understand the true cause of discouragement, then we are well on our way, through application, to freedom from that realm. And so it is in any study or endeavor that we must experience these different planes of consciousness. And discouragement is one, indeed, of the most interesting and complex. Whenever the mind makes effort to study any subject, in its efforts, it makes decisions and judgments concerning the completion or victory, so to speak, of the study. Ofttimes this is not, for the student, a conscious knowledge. However, it is instrumental in breeding the level of consciousness known as discouragement.

Especially in the study of life and of spiritual principles, the mind is quick to garner and to gather for the sole purpose of use and control. And so it is in spiritual studies that laws are revealed that are demonstrable, that work, to those who apply them, in keeping with the principle under which those laws have been established. Now, spiritual or so-called divine laws cannot be controlled by mental zones, for they are laws that exist and work in spiritual realms of consciousness. Though the mind experiences the effects of these laws, the mind cannot establish that which is above and beyond its domain.

And so it is, my good students, that the endeavors to study and to gather and garner unto the mental realms, until they are so filled that they finally bow their interest of control, is a good sign—discouragement—for it is not a spiritual experience, but it is, in truth, a resignation by the human mind that it cannot control what is not within its domain.

In these many classes it has been revealed to you again and again and again how these laws work. All of my students have had experience with some of these laws working in their lives. But the mind, not being able to control what is not its right to control, becomes discouraged: the first step in bowing its great need to control that which it cannot control. So many times have we spoken on giving up that which disturbs you, on bowing to an authority that will bring you the goodness and greatness of life. But the steps that you are trodding are necessary for you to attain that which you so dearly are seeking. Though patience is, to the mind, a painful experience, to the soul, to the true you, it is an open door with a light of reason that never goes out.

When man views from higher realms of consciousness the eons of time, the experiences beyond number that he has already had, he will begin to gain in the wisdom of patience. My good friends, what is a year in this great sea of eternity? If you say you do not see this great sea of eternity, then it is because you have yet to choose to view it, for all of these spheres and zones and planes of consciousness you are moving and breathing in this moment.

This moment, value this moment, for it is this moment, moment by moment, that is your health, your wealth, and your goodness of life. Tomorrow, the mind fears. For it is the way of the mind to fear, for that is how the mind controls the true you. Long ago we stated to you that faith, this great power that is available to all, directed in a positive way, moves all mountains of obstruction for you. Directed in a negative way, used by the human mind, it creates. And it creates, for it is the nature of fear to create. Man fears whatever he has chosen not to experience. And so man has chosen many things and he has made many decisions about what he will not experience. And so man, his mind, where fear exists, fears many, many, many things, for many are the things he has rejected in his error of ignorance. And because he fears, he directs energy. Divine authority is directed by his mind and that intelligent energy creates the very things that he fears.

But here, if you will listen, you can use that same energy to create the things that are desirable and beneficial for your life. As fear works for the mind, so faith works for the soul. It is an infallible intelligence that is at your command each moment of your eternity.

We have spoken on freedom, the effect of self-control. We have spoken much on divine will and self-will. And now it is time, in our ever-broadening horizons, to share with you our understanding of what self is and what divine is. You are divine and identify with form. And through your identification with form, you fear. For identification is a mental process. And so you cannot help but see the benefit of staying free from self, for self is fear and divine is faith.

Now, fear or faith brings you whatever your mind images. And every time you entertain a thought of self, you identify and are controlled by what is known as fear. Every time you disassociate, you no longer identify with self. You become a part of the whole, of the intelligence that sustains everything. And so the benefit to you is beyond the limited consideration of the human mind.

Think, for a few moments, of all of the things in your life that you consider to be problems. If you will think about that for a moment, you will quickly view the fear that has created them and brought them to you. And so when man, in self, separates himself—because he has identified with limitation, he shall experience limitation, for he is under the Law of Fear. He is under the Law of Separation and is no longer united in consciousness with the whole and, so to speak, is left out in the cold.

How does man make this transformation from being controlled by the force of fear to being freed by the power of faith? When man makes effort each moment of his day to broaden his horizons, to free himself from himself, to demonstrate, to apply the Law of Disassociation—for we cannot experience in those mental realms what we are not associated with. We can only experience in those mental worlds what the force of fear has created, as we have planted the seeds of thought in the fertile soil of creation. This great power works for everyone that is willing to accept the possibility in their heart.

The many centuries of viewing what the great force of fear had returned to me was not all distasteful, for not all things in creation in mental realms are distasteful. For being in form, we use the vehicle of form that offers the forty functions. And being in soul, the vehicle of divine Spirit, we have those forty faculties. And the force of fear, which controls the mental worlds, returns to us these thoughts, these seeds that we have planted. Some of them are pleasant seeds. All of them, all of them have the basic instinct of self-preservation.

The moment you entertain a thought, we stated years ago to you, you feed, by directed energy, a form. That birth is determined to preserve itself. And its way of preservation is by the natural force of creation called fear. As determined as you alone—the creators—are, so are your thoughts. Remember, they have the intelligence that you have. The intelligence of your entire mind is available to them—to use or abuse, depending upon their need to preserve themselves.

Now, my good students, in viewing all of this creation, that is known to our minds as our world, we must never forget to view it with the power of faith and never the fear of force. In these many experiences over these centuries, through the peace and the stillness of the human mind, the great power of faith disintegrates these multitudes of forms in these mental worlds. Through the Law of Disassociation, we no longer fear. And when we no longer fear—being doers, we are doing something. And I assure you that something is known as the power of faith. The greatest good you can possibly experience in any sphere is the good which is the result of what is known as faith. But to be freed from fear means you must give that which you hold, that stands between you and the fullness of your life.

And we discussed in our last meeting the great benefit of giving up that throne, that judge that so deludes the human mind that the soul waits ofttimes for centuries to serve. Step down, my children, from that throne that blinds you. Walk across the bridge of understanding and enter the beautiful realms of wisdom. For that is the home that all of us return to. Don't think about stepping down at some future time, for that establishes a law that is controlled by fear and the struggles become even greater. Step down that you may enjoy your earthly life today.

Free yourself from those shackles of fear. You cannot die, for there is no death. And so you must ask yourselves the question, "O Lord, my God, what do I fear?" And the answer, if you ask in honesty and sincerity, will quickly come. My child, it is not you who fears. It is those forms created in your hours of darkness that fear. For without that force, they can no longer have you to be their slave. Free yourself, my children. You have been given the way.

You will not go in want if you make the effort to stay free from that force. It is such a simple way. The child—they quickly learn. It is possible for you, for all things are possible for you. There is nothing in any universe that is beyond the potential. There is nothing that can be beyond your touch, when you free yourself from fear. The greatest illusion created by that force is to convince you that you don't have fear in the very areas of life where fear, that force, is the strongest. You know what happens when you feel smug and content about anything that your mind judges you have accomplished. You quickly find that it fizzles, so to speak, like your Alka-Seltzers. So ask yourself, my children, "What, in truth, does that reveal?"

And now, we shall spend a few moments in sharing with you our understanding of the questions you have presented.

Thank you. Please give your understanding of the function of humiliation. Is the ego without a defense when this emotional reaction occurs?

Yes, my good student, the uneducated ego is without defense, for the educated ego knows that truth needs no defense. And so it is that we experience in our mind what we call humiliation as the soul faculty of humility is being expressed.

Thank you. Please give us your understanding of the faculty of joy.

The soul faculty of joy does not mean what you refer to in your world as pleasure or enjoyment. The soul faculty of joy is an expression of harmony in all levels of consciousness. When this takes place, the functions and the faculties are in a perfect balance and the experience of the fulfillment of all good takes place on all levels of being.

Thank you. Please explain the saying, A man in desire is like a runaway horse—afraid of looking back.

A man in desire is like a runaway horse—afraid of looking back. You see, my students, a man in desire, not a man experiencing desire, but a man in desire—and indeed there is a vast, vast difference. To experience desire is to be the recipient of the divine expression, for desire is the divine expression. To be *in* desire is to delude oneself that they are the cause and the completion of the desire. And so that little saying is referring to a man in desire, like a runaway horse, fears to look back. For he fears to be reminded that he has had that same experience before again and again and again and again. And so he fears to look back at yesterday to see that each time he moves in that delusion of being in desire that it always ends without his total control.

Thank you. What connection, if any, is there between a weight problem, either under- or overweight, and the attitude of mind known in this philosophy as universal motherhood?

The attitude of mind referred to as universal motherhood is a need within a person to gather, to garner, and to control all things of its interest. Now, it would not be in keeping with truth to say that a weight problem—overweight or underweight is a judgment made by the human mind—it would not be in keeping with truth to say that that is a direct result of an attitude of mind known as universal motherhood But one may well consider that the attitude of mind of self-interest keeps directing energy to the self. And the self continues to react.

Now, you have many things in your earthly world. You have all of these weight clinics and etc., to direct your energy to self. But I assure you, my friends, when you forgive or give forth— for indeed is it human to forgive or give forth—you are moving in consciousness to the divine experience of forgetting it. To forget something is to free yourself from the constant self-interest that is disturbing you. And until the effort is made to forgive or give forth, you cannot move to forgetting it and being free from it.

Thank you. In The Living Light, *Discourse 51, [and in* The Living Light Dialogue] *you speak about levels of mind. Would you please explain the solar conscious, the celestial, the terrestrial, and the others, if we are ready to learn about them?*

I will be happy, at this time, to share with you a bit more on the solar conscious. Much has been spoken in this philosophy on soul and soul evolution. Some time ago we gave you an indication of your souls' journey and spoke to you on mathematics, the key of the universe. You see, my good students, everything is numbered. Everything is counted by an Intelligence that the limited mind cannot comprehend. Everything has a pulse. Everything has a certain number or beat. Whether it is a human, a tree, a plant, an animal, or a mineral, it is all in motion; it is all pulsating.

Now, the human species has a counted so-called average beat or pulse and it fluctuates in keeping with the individual's moving from the vibratory wave of the whole, known as the human race or being. Your number responds to all numbers of your species, for there is that number or beat. Whenever, through the Law of Disassociation, you no longer identify with being what you call a human being, then you become receptive to the number or beat of other species. So many people have asked in my experiences, "How does one communicate, for example, with an animal or a plant or a tree or other forms of life?" You communicate by disassociation. By the efforts you make to no longer identify with self, with your species, you start to become receptive to a different beat, to a different number. This exercise, given in its essence, is within your study book [*The Living Light* and in *The Living Light Dialogue,* Volume 1]. You can establish rapport with any and all things.

And the most interesting thing, in speaking of numbers and rapport, the most interesting thing, my students, is that all of creation is awakened and receptive to the beat of the so-called human being. Nature, you understand, has a broader horizon in that respect than man. The animal is receptive to your feelings, to your emotions, to your thoughts, to your motives, and to your drives. The plant and the tree are receptive. And it knows, as the animal knows, not what you say, but what your real motive is. Oh yes, nature, not being limited, not being limited in its identification—you see, my friends, all form, having identity, has what you a call an ego. A tree has an ego and a dog has an ego and an ant has an ego. But their ego is more educated than the human being. And because it is more educated, it is not overidentified with self. And because it is not overidentified with self, it is more receptive to the other forms of life around and about it.

We shall speak more on this subject at a future time.

Good night.

JANUARY 12, 1978

CONSCIOUSNESS CLASS 166

Greetings, students.

This evening I should like to spend some time with each of you personally in reference to your earthly journey and the causes of your experiences on Earth. And so I would appreciate the group on my right speaking forth their first name only and presenting their question in reference to their journey.

[A student speaks her name.] *How can I better allow the power of God to work through me?*

In your soul's evolution long ago, you were awakened to how that was possible for you. And because of the great curiosity and inquisitiveness of your mental body, ever seeking to gain control over that which it is interested in, you lost sight of the simplicity of truth and, on your earthly path, are once again striving to reawaken that great peace and fulfillment that you had so very long ago.

You will note that in your earthly experiences that it has always been difficult for you to concentrate upon any particular object of your choice, that your mind has always been quickly and easily distracted. And so it is, my good student, by a great effort daily on your part to flood your consciousness with peace, to flood your consciousness with acceptance, will you, yes, in this earthly journey of yours, once again awaken that simple truth that will free you from the dual laws of creation.

[Another student speaks her name.] *What is the lesson or lessons that I came back to this Earth life to learn and that I learned?*

My good student, I have great compassion for your journey, for it is, in many respects, similar to my own, so long ago. Because you are quick to judge, because you fear that which you do not make the effort to understand, the struggle is great. However, before you leave your earthly path, reason, the light that will transfigure all souls, will rise in your consciousness. It is the forgetting of the sustenance and source of your being, it is the forgetting of that source and sustenance that causes the power of the mind, the force of the mind, to bring into your life and your earthly experiences so very much fear.

Those lessons you shall learn on Earth. It shall not be within the coming month or year or two, but years. You shall pass through those lessons and be strengthened with greater fortitude, with even greater character, and greater determination to do what you know you have to do. In keeping with the law of your destiny, you shall remain in the light of reason and truth, but it will not be without the battle between the authority of the throne of judgment and the humbleness of your eternal soul.

You, my good student, have not returned to Earth. You are evolving through Earth. There are so many planets that you have already experienced, as all souls have, and there are indeed many more to go. When your mind rises so quickly in all things to judge, in those moments, make great effort to pause and to be at peace. For in so doing that which has control of you shall, in time, bow to a greater light and you will fulfill the purpose for which you have entered Earth. You need not be concerned in returning to Earth, for you have always had the inner sight to know that you must move on. That which has served its purpose must go. And new experiences and new endeavors are ever moving you along the path.

Thank you.

[A student speaks her name.] *What is the purpose of my journey on Earth?*

As you, I know, are well aware, that ever since you entered the earthly realm there has been a strange, but persistent, inner feeling of loneliness. That, of course, you brought with you. Because you want to be a part of everything, but in so wanting and desiring to always to be a part of all things, you have dictated how they—all things—shall be. That is the lesson that you have on Earth to learn: that, in truth, there are many ways to accomplish the good in life. And you have, in this past few months on your Earth experience, began to truly broaden your horizons. And in so doing, those deep inner feelings of loneliness do not plague you as often as they used to.

And so it is that you will continue on being freer from the past, though it tries to call you to return in consciousness to it. There is new strength, spiritual strength and vitality, that is entering your consciousness and your universe is being strengthened as never before in your past five incarnations.

[Another student speaks her name.] *How can I put God first in all aspects of my life?*

My good student, by removing pity, a mental function, from your universe. The sadness that you have encountered on Earth is the effect of much energy, thought being directed to what is known as the self. To accept something greater is the eternal destiny of all man. And so your journey, though very slow, is moving you step by step from the depths of pity, for we only pity what we do not understand. And so a greater awakening, an opening up of your consciousness to the truth that God's love moves through all, that you are no longer separated from humanity, that your wrongs or mistakes in life are not exclusive to you, that God in his great compassion is the epitome of forgiveness. And so, my good student, as you make greater effort to forgive, shall you be forgiven, freed, and filled with the goodness that life, in truth, has to offer.

[A student speaks her name.] *Why do I seem to have such a strong bond with rejection?*

The great need brought with you on the last six journeys through eternity, the great need for attention, has been dictated by your mind—how to attain it. And so as long as you permit your mind to feel need, as long as you permit that, shall you experience, in keeping with the decision made by your mind, so you shall continue these feelings of rejection. There is a great need within you, within your mind, to have things in life be smooth and harmonious to you. That seeking for harmony serves a good purpose if it is respected by the faculty of total consideration for all of God's children. Your soul, in its destiny of rejection, entered life on Earth under the vibratory waves of rejection. Be of good cheer, my student, for long before you leave your earthly experience, you shall be freed from that great need.

[A student speaks her name.] *Would you please tell me what my lessons are that are to be learned on the earth plane?*

Yes, my good friend, the greatest lesson of the many lessons that Earth is offering to you is to accept, as you experience, and have experienced, this insatiable need to control is a need to organize or control that which is within your mental sphere of action. You, I am sure, are well aware of this great need to mother or to control all things with which you come in contact. Those, my good student, who are easily fascinated have great needs to control. And so it is that as you entered your earthly life, you found yourself in a family where there was great need, great need for control. And so as you journey on, slowly, very slowly, but surely, shall there come the balance of common sense, shall there come the great acceptance of the power of prayer through the vehicle of soul known as the human heart. Take moments each day to flood your mind with encouragement with the spirit of positive action and you shall free yourself from the fret and the fury of distracting fascination.

[Another student speaks her name.] *What is the purpose of my life?*

My good friend, the purpose of all life, and your life, is to serve. For without service, there is no purpose to life. But in serving, one must ask the question, "O Lord, my God, am I aware of what, in truth, I am serving?" Awareness, awareness—the awareness of what, in truth, is taking place within. And from the awareness, a broadening acceptance of the true cause of all experiences.

My good student, you have, in many ways, made much growth in accepting the causes of some things. And we view that growth in an ever expanding process. You can, as all souls can, change all things by directing the energy, through the Law of Attention, to the realms of mind that create and control them. To cast this light upon those levels of consciousness, though painful at first, is the truth and the freedom that you have sought for so very long.

Stop in all experience and ask the question whether or not you are giving power and control over your eternal being to something or someone outside your sphere of action. Whenever you desire to accomplish anything, stop and think. Within you is the power. The illusion in life is that someone else has what you are seeking. Someone else, my good friend, only has what you are seeking as long as you sustain the illusion created by your judgment. Withdraw the energy from the illusion and declare the truth within you: that you are whole, complete, and perfect; that your happiness, joy, and goodness of life is not dependent upon any illusion that is dependent upon anything outside of you. That is the lesson, the great lesson, that you have to learn in your journey. And that lesson, in many ways, each day, is being learned.

Thank you.

[A student speaks his name.] *What is the lesson needed in my journey?*

Yes, the world, the universe, and all things begin to shrink when we no longer consider their importance to the whole. It is the little things in life that are ofttimes instrumental in freeing us from the dictates of our mind. The heart, we know, is the vehicle of our true being, the soul. But its expression must ever be under the guiding light of reason, for reason brings the balance between the functions and the faculties. Your lesson on Earth is a greater awakening of the soul faculty of care, to awaken to the importance of the little things of life to those who care for the little things of life.

Love is the energy known as the Infinite Intelligence. He who limits it shall pay the price of his own obstruction. Care is an expression, through the soul faculties, of this infinite Love, known as God. To love is to be all inclusive, is to be considerate of things our mind may dictate have no value, nor importance. It is our mind that restricts God or limits the expression thereof.

In order to accomplish the transfiguration of our life, we must bring all things into balance. And that is what is truly meant by keeping faith with reason, she will transfigure thee. Now we cannot truly express reason unless we are considering all things. For we cannot bring balance into our lives when we leave out the many little things which will, in truth, establish that balance. Reason, my good friend, is the path on which you struggle in your earthly journey. Look up and take hold of the hand of care. Your horizon will broaden, the faculty of gratitude shall open wider, and you shall experience, through the Law of Continuity of effort, a more productive and successful life.

And now, my good friends, we shall continue, at our next class, these discussions.

Good night.

JANUARY 19, 1978

CONSCIOUSNESS CLASS 167

Greetings, students. This evening we shall discuss application of what has already been given and shall continue on at a later time with personal discussions with you.

All that has been given can, and is, to some extent, demonstrated by the students. The question must rise in our consciousness, "What is working and how is it working?" And if it is not working in our lives, then we must pause and think much more deeply than we have already thought.

In the mental world of creation are the tears of limitation. And so as we have often stated to you, it behooves all souls to make that daily effort to rise above these mental realms, where you may view life, the principle of life, and use these mental worlds as the tools that they were designed, in truth, to be.

I know that much has been spoken on use, not abuse, on objectivity, on the faculty of reason. Exercises, affirmations, and many laws have been shared with you. But without the application of these laws, man cannot reap the benefit and the harvest that is waiting for him. One of the most valuable statements revealed to you some time ago was flooding the consciousness. That is, flooding your mind with peace, with acceptance of greater possibilities in your life. For the experiences in life, in your mental life, in your mental world, you all know are effects.

There is no reason to continue on with experiences, which are effects, that are not pleasant and harmonious and good in your life. The mind is an instrument, broadcasting out into mental worlds that which exists already in it. To bring about a change within your life, you must be willing, you must be ready to make that effort of flooding the mind, your mental world, with the positive and the goodness which is truly yours. The changes do not come about in a matter of a day or two, for the energy released into those mental worlds in a positive and constructive way must come into balance with that which has already been emanating for so very long.

For each time in your daily activity, each moment that you pause and affirm a positive good in your life, each moment that you live in the acceptance of a better way, of a greater way, you are establishing that in those realms. But ofttimes the student rises for a moment or a short while and makes that application and experiences, though perhaps in a microscopic way, some good in their life and then forgets the way that they know.

We all go on and on and on and on. The beginnings and endings are mental factors. They exist only in a mental world. And so let us, in our mental world, begin with this thought: "In my mind exists the beginning of things and in my mind exists the end of things. Therefore, it is my mind. I begin them and I alone can end them. I begin them in a mental form of creation. I can end them in the same way." For that which is begun in a mental world can only end in a mental world. For that is where it was given birth and only there shall it know death.

So whatever your struggle of the moment may be, remember, you know the way to end them. For you know, in truth, how you began them. It's known in this teaching as direction and redirection. When the thought is not filling you with the spirit of happiness, end the thought. If the thought is bringing you the goodness and the fullness that you are truly seeking, support and sustain the thought.

Much is discussed in these classes, much on the mental worlds and yet more shall be discussed. For it is foolhardy to try to move from one world to the next when we do not yet understand the world that we are experiencing.

Application of the revealed laws strengthen you in your efforts to begin and to end, for that is what is, in truth, taking place within your mind each moment. The value of this teaching is through your efforts to become aware consciously, that you may consciously choose your beginnings and your endings.

The soul faculties are expressed through the conscious mind. The sense functions flow through the subconscious mind. And so it is with your conscious effort that balance is brought about between the functions and the faculties. It is through your conscious effort. For effort made by the subconscious is not under your control of the moment.

And so it is that we gave you long ago these many exercises. We explained to you the great value of what you were putting into your mind as you went off to sleep, the great value of what was in your mind as you awoke. Work, my good students, and apply more frequently. And your efforts, be they of pure motive, shall reap you the harvest that is justly yours. Be not so discouraged. Be not so disappointed with this great wonder of life. For it is, in truth, a great and glorious life. It is the way, that way when you open up your heart. For, you see, my good students, rejection does not exist in your heart. Denial does not exist in your heart, for your heart, the vehicle of expression of your eternal true being, is open to the eternity, to the unity which you truly are.

Apply, apply, my students, that which is demonstrably true, that which works for anyone that makes the effort. Do not permit your mind to dictate to you that you have made the effort and it is not working the way that you judge that it should. For those are the echoes, my good students, of the patterns of long ago, rising up from the depths of your own mind. They are so devious and so clever, that the old patterns may endure. You cannot compare the effort made on a positive path to the many years of darkness that have already been experienced.

Become more aware of the echoes of the mind. Become more aware of what they dictate. Bridge the gap that you may hear clearly what they say. Those are the voices within. Those are known as the voices of the subconscious. They call up and they emanate vibrations in your mental world that bring you experiences that you do not consciously want.

I know if you start this moment and you make the practice in your life of flooding your consciousness and you truly make that effort and, each moment that you are consciously aware, you flood your consciousness with divine truth, I know within a short nine days of totality, you will have the demonstrable experience of what God can do, through what is called the power of faith.

Now, we all have faith and we all have it in equal amounts, so to speak. But we direct it in different ways. It is not easy for many to declare the truth of accepting the possibility of all the goodness of life, because those patterns rise up and tell you how foolhardy it is. And they justify their judgments by telling you how bad things are going and how miserable and what a struggle that life is. Those voices from within are the living demonstration of man's faith in his own mind.

I show you a path of direction: to direct that great power, that great intelligent energy into flooding your mind constantly with goodness, with the greatness of life, with the abundance of life. And life, if you truly make that effort, life will respond to that broadcast from your mind. It will respond. Perhaps in a small way at first, because, after all, my friends, in truth, it's a small beginning effort.

It is time for all my students to stand up and make that great effort to become aware of what is being broadcast from their mind. Because I know when they truly accept the responsibility of their life, they will—you will awaken and, in that awakening, stand firm on the rock of principle, seeing clearly that all experience is a return of a level of consciousness.

Redirect your faith, my good students. Redirect this great power. For that which brings you the things you desire not is the same intelligent Energy that can just as easily bring you the things you desire to experience. That is your choice. But that choice cannot be fully demonstrated until you apply the law that works.

Fear directed to the human mind becomes the force. Faith directed to the human mind becomes the force known as fear. Now, many, many philosophers have taught your world that whatever you fear shall befall you. So the experiences that you do not like are the effects of your fears. And fear, of course, is an effect of judgment. Judge not, my students. Fear not, my students, and live the abundant full life that is your right. But to fear not means to judge not, and to judge not means to become, once again, a unit of the whole. For he who makes the effort to become a unit of the whole is freed from judgment, for he is then freed from separatism, freed from the need.

You see, my friends, when we experience need, we have moved from universal consciousness to limited consciousness by the Law of Identity. Now, we cannot—and this is a most important demonstrable truth—we cannot experience need without first descending in consciousness from the universal whole. So when we make this move downward, we first experience what is known to our mind as a need or lack. And from this experience of need, the Law of Identity is given birth and we identify in order to fulfill this vacuum or need that we have created. But the filling of that vacuum or that need is very temporary and shall always be fleeting and temporary.

As we make this effort, through flooding of our consciousness, we rise up and once again reunite to the universal whole. As we reunite, the judgments, which follow the Law of Identity, and the fears, which follow the judgments, they melt away. They melt away. When we descended in what we call creation or these mental worlds, in order to identify with what our mind chooses to call individuality, we must constantly, constantly judge, constantly fear in order that we may sustain and maintain the illusion of individuality.

And so when we first came to your world, years ago, we asked that you broaden your horizons. For in the broadening of your horizons do the judgments, the identities, and the fears melt away.

The path of identity, the glory of individuality, the throne of the kingdom of judgment offers to all souls what is called a living hell. Make the effort each moment. Accept the right of all and be freed from the identity, which is, in truth, the pit that all souls are trying to crawl out of.

You know, all my students know, that when the pain is so intense it is indeed a blessing to think of something else. It's called redirecting. The choice is ever yours. When you think less of self, then you are less identified. Then you are less separated from the universal wholeness of which, in truth, you are a unit inseparable. The separation between you and the universal wholeness is an illusion created by the Law of Identity. But you, my friends, through the error, chose the path down and, through the light of reason, can, this moment, choose the path up.

Now, now is the hour. Break the back of procrastination. And do it now, for all that is good is waiting for you. When your mind judges that the life experience has become so intolerable, speak to your mind. Put the reins on that thought form and let it know who's the ruler and the captain of your ship. Speak kindly, but firmly. But do not battle with your children. Do not fight them, for they have been created by mental form of tenacity equal to you, for they are your children. Speak kindly, but firmly, and redirect that intelligent energy.

Cast the light of reason over the Law of Identity. Begin to use *it*. Stop it from using you. In another way, we gave this same teaching to you years ago when we stated "O dreamer, dream a life of beauty before your dream starts dreaming you." It's the same truth: the Law of Identity.

Think how many times, my good students—stop this moment and think—how many times in the course of a day does your mind dictate need? That's how many times a day that you descend. Stop and think: How many times a day do you speak forth need? How many times and in how many ways? And each time you think need and each time you speak need, you descend, yea, even farther. Down farther, by the Law of Identity, into judgment and fear. Stop and think how the human mind truly works. You think need, you speak need, you experience need, and fear rises and judgment rules. That's what truly happens.

Good night.

JANUARY 26, 1978

CONSCIOUSNESS CLASS 168

Greetings, friends.

Indeed are we grateful to see that some of you are making the effort to demonstrate, at least for a short nine-day period, the truth revealed to you at our other meeting. As you come closer to that ninth day, set the law into motion to continue for another cycle of nine short days. Though, in your efforts, there have been a few moments where you have had to struggle, be rest assured the results shall clearly show that, through those efforts you are now making, the light is getting brighter and the path will get clearer. Victory over any level of consciousness is something that takes constant vigilance by the faculty of reason.

My dear students, the growth that you have made should be your constant companion and encouragement. And when you think growth has been little, it is only because you have finally become aware of how much growing there really is. As you, in this nine-day program, continue to make the effort, you strengthen the levels of mind that bring about the necessary changes in your life that you are seeking.

For some time now, we have witnessed, with this student body, an ever growing and increasing, expanding spirit of unity. And in speaking on this vibratory wave of unity, that we are so pleased to view, do not think for a moment that it means in any way you are becoming like someone else. Do not fear that you are losing your so-called individuality or personality, though some day you will. And then the fullness of life shall you experience. But this spirit of unity has brought unto you many of the students from our side of life. And you will note slowly, but surely, new thoughts and inspiration entering your consciousness.

So be of good cheer, for though you may think your struggles are great and you may view your past as being better than your present, it's only a change of direction that is reaping more goodness for you than your past has ever offered. There is, spiritually, this great change taking place amongst the students in my earthly class. And it shall continue and go on and on and on.

At our last meeting, we gave to you what could readily be understood as the key that opens the door of understanding and lets in the fresh air of wisdom. Continue with your efforts in applying what was given to you. And I want to greatly encourage the ones who have not yet started on that nine-day program, for I assure you, my students, through your effort, through your application, the abundant good of life is guaranteed as the effect. Use—use it wisely, use it well, and do it now, those who are yet to begin.

As I view the horizons of your spiritual worlds, I pause, for the wonder of life and the perfect balance of life, in the final analysis, is indeed something to behold.

I want to assure you, as students, that we shall continue on, though not at this time, this evening, but we shall continue on with the personal discussions with each of you.

But there are greater things you are yet to know. The great purpose that you have to serve, for each of you, having come to the earth realm, have come with a responsibility to serve realms of consciousness to awaken within yourselves that great, eternal journey.

I know you all have heard that so-called history repeats itself. And some of you have wondered and some of you have questioned how long has this philosophy, known as the Living Light philosophy, been brought to the world. To your world on Earth, but a few short years. But you are here, in this Living Light class, in keeping with the Law of Evolution brought about by the cycle of repetition.

There are moments when some of you are aware of what is yet to come, in reference to your classes. Though those moments are rare, pay attention, my students, for long before you went to Earth, you were in class. What may seem new to your earthly minds is only new to earthly mind. And your journey, your graduation, took you to the earth realm. And so you bear great responsibility to the school, to the truth, to the philosophy that you have studied for so very, very long.

I told you some time ago that you were not new to me, nor, in truth, was I new to you. And now it is time that we consider our great spiritual duty. My good students, the nursery school of your earthly realm is very young, very tender, and very ignorant. And so for untold centuries the intelligent beings from far, far distant solar systems have visited, are visiting, continue to visit, to prepare your planet to help to awaken it to the inhabitants upon it. For as your technology advances and as you send these earthly forms out into the distant space, there are grave responsibilities that your Earth has not awakened to and, therefore, has not considered. Changes must come about to raise the level of consciousness to spiritual realms, for the imbalance of material, scientific advancement far out shadows the spiritual growth of the planet Earth.

And so you are here and must begin your duties in considering the universes. You must expand beyond your limited Earth existence, for no matter how microscopic your effort, it is needed for the centuries that lie ahead. Because of the lack of spiritual awakening upon your planet, because of the scientific material advancement, the imbalance with the nature spirits is very great. That imbalance not only affects the planet Earth, but it has an effect out into the universes. For if Earth, the fifth planet in the fifth solar system, does not stem the tide of discord and bring about a greater harmony, it shall affect and be detrimental to untold billions of beings.

Face your true purpose. Be a clear instrument, as you were designed to be. You have the opportunity to do your work well. All you need to be is the light that you truly are. To bring about the balance in nature, become balanced within and then that light, invisible to your physical eyes, will become the healing balm wherever you walk, whatever you touch, whatever you sense, whatever you view.

As you still creation in your universe—and you still creation by the great power of peace—that light, called the Light of the Divine, shines brightly in the darkened world of discord. Become a balanced being. Let not the thought forms of creation rule you any longer. Declare that truth in your mental universe. Declare it each time those forms dictate their discord, for so much is at stake. And do not permit your minds to judge that someone else will do the job, for that someone else shall always be your conscience.

There is so very much to be aware of. And so much we all have to do. It must be done within the coming twenty years. What to many today on Earth think are fantasies of the mind shall prove to be reality. For there is great need in your creation for balance, for the planet Earth has overidentified as a mass planet. And because of its overidentification with self, the planet Earth, it has denied even the possibility of its brothers and sisters in the universes. Therefore, the mass of its inhabitants are deluded by self-interest and self-identification and face not their universal responsibility.

As you face your responsibilities in the small things of life, you will begin to awaken the universal consciousness within you and, as you do that, become aware of those amongst you that you hear not and see not and sad, but true, care not.

Good night.

FEBRUARY 2, 1978

CONSCIOUSNESS CLASS 169

Greetings, students. We shall spend some time this evening in discussing the process of awakening.

Repetition, the law through which change becomes possible, is also the Law of Irritation. In our experiences in life and in creation, we are in a constant process of change, for we are ever in the stream of evolving. And so it is, this school of the Living Light is founded on that very principle of evolution. As you will well recall, there has been, and continues to be, much repetition and slowly, but surely, a revelation of change taking place within your personal lives. He who understands the very principle of evolving is then freed from the experiences of so-called irritation, for through an understanding of evolution, through an acceptance of that which is inevitable, man no longer tries to fight against the tides of life.

Now, we have spoken to you in many ways in order to help you to see clearly this basic principle of evolution. Whenever you are working with anyone and you, for any reason, find it necessary to repeat, you will notice a reaction of irritation by the person that the lesson is being repeated to. My good students, when you encounter experiences in your life that insist upon repeating themselves in your consciousness, you can be rest assured that the defenses of the human mind are still successful in their resistance to change.

It is indeed foolhardy to fight that which is inevitable. It is foolhardy to go against the ever moving stream of consciousness. We stated to you some time ago, "Hold not to form, for form shall pass" [CC 1]. It is your efforts in holding to that which is necessary to be removed from your life, in order that you may evolve to yet even higher levels of consciousness, that is causing the seeming difficulties and problems that you are experiencing. When these lessons in life continue to repeat themselves in your life, it is revealing to you that a change of attitude within you is the only thing that will free you from the repetition of the experiences.

In all of these universes, there are untold numbers of intelligent forms expressing. Because you are not yet aware of these many intelligent beings, you will, someday, become aware. We stated to you that the Law of Destiny is the effect of your own denials. And so man, fighting against the evolving stream of life, establishes these limited laws of experiences.

Whatever you permit to freely leave your life, you also permit higher levels and grades of experiences to enter. The poor receiver reveals himself to be a poor giver. To permit these experiences of life to enter, to be objective in your viewing thereof, and to leave—this is the time to make that effort, for, then, with that effort will come into your lives an awakening in consciousness, a broader and wider and greater world than you have yet, in your earthly experiences, encountered. Of what value, in truth, is the constant effort of battling the inevitable, when you know already that beyond a shadow of any doubt you are changing, for you are evolving? Why not enjoy that which is to be enjoyed? And that, my friends, is known as life itself.

After all the study has been set aside, you find that you still are. For, in truth, you have always been. Now that which has always been—and that is you—not only shall ever be, but it is what you permit it to be. It is a matter, in truth, of a reeducation of the human mind, for it is not serving you well if it is not serving you in the vibratory wave of peace and harmony. Let be what is to be. Through the divine will, know that you are, in truth, an ever moving, ever expanding consciousness. For that, my friends, in truth, is what you really are.

This identity that keeps you from awakening is in a slow, but sure, process of change and expansion. As this consciousness expands, as this limited identity becomes, in time, the limitless, then you not only awaken and free your true being, but you, in truth, experience the fullness of life, which is your true destiny.

Over these horizons that are ever before you waits the counterpart. It waits over the horizon of your consciousness. It waits for the broadening of your acceptance. It waits for the expansion of your being.

Indeed, much has been spoken about the forms of all creation, but what of the formless and the free? How can we speak of that which is formless when we are limited by the form of the spoken word? It is your imagination that is the gateway to heaven. It is your imagination that has no limits and knows no boundaries. And so, in truth, through this great gateway known as imagination, this great gateway of image, do you enter the realms of freedom. To awaken to that process—for you have always used it, that process of image and imagination. But you have used it, and use it, in such a limited way.

As all of life and all experience we know, beyond any doubt, is the effect of energy, each form and each experience is created by directed energy. You, my students, and you alone, direct the energy for your life's experiences. And because, in truth, you are the directors and because, in truth, you are the captains of your ships of destiny, you, indeed, have the world, your world, in your hands. The purity of your motive is the right of your action. The experiences in your life are the revelation of that truth.

When we resist the Law of Evolution, when we resist change, we do it in seeming strange and mysterious ways. The reason that man so frequently on Earth blames outside for what, in truth, is going on inside of himself is because he is resisting change. And he hopes by putting the blame out, on others and on life itself, that he can somehow, with that deception, resist the inevitable laws of God. And so we find on Earth few souls facing the Law of Personal Responsibility, for the energy is still directed to resisting change and evolution. But in time we start to grow up. We begin to accept our responsibilities for our life. And when we do that, the changes that have been knocking at our door of understanding start to move and we begin, again, evolving into the next level of consciousness to new experiences and new endeavors, to new attitudes and broader horizons than we have already had.

It's time to face ourselves by accepting ourselves, for we cannot face what we do not yet accept. But we do not accept ourselves because we know, in so doing, we must accept change. We have accepted and identified with an image, a self-image, of our choice. But that image is not our true being. And those images that we have accepted as ourselves were created as the effects of fear and insecurity.

Those are the forms that cry out for survival. And because we have so identified with those images, we believe that it is us, our true being that is crying. But in time you will see that is not you.

All that you accept in life, you free yourself from. Now, let us, in our discussion, present to you on Earth some earthly, so to speak, examples. In your material world, perhaps you have decided—as so many seem to have done—that things are not going for you too well. Perhaps they have not been going for you materially well for some time. And so your mind, in its study of this philosophy, becomes a bit confused. It knows that you have accepted that things are not well for you, because without an identity with that judgment, you could not have the experience.

Now, we have spoken often on acceptance, the will of God, total acceptance, the will of God. And the minds of the student rise up and say, "I cannot accept that! I will not accept that! I can accept this." And so they're back under the realms of judgment. We stated to you to accept the right of all life, to accept the right of all experiences. In accepting, you do not experience unless you identify. Because you can only experience what you identify with.

And so man, in his earthly struggles, he accepts. That is the law of God. But when man identifies with what he has accepted, then man establishes the Law of Destiny. For in his identifying with his acceptance does he deny and, therefore, descends from universal consciousness to limited consciousness. And so in his struggles, he need only redirect. To identify with a thing is to become the thing, for the Law of Destiny, through identification, has become established. And so destiny, the handmaiden of denial, grants what is known as limited consciousness.

To accept the possibility of something greater and to refrain from changing the identity of what you presently have is not to experience that possibility at all. You must identify with what you desire to become. Now, a man that identifies with poverty does not experience wealth. And he who identifies with abundance, through the Law of Acceptance, becomes that abundance that he has identified with. But, my good friends, you cannot identify one moment and then change your identity the next moment and have what you truly seek in life.

Choice is that which is ever your eternal divine right. And in time, you will view the path of neutrality: not moving to the left, nor moving to the right, but seeing both for what they really are: one and the same. For the only difference there ever was, the only difference there ever can be is that which the realms of mental judgment make so.

And in time you'll move beyond that duality, for without judgment, there is no duality. Above and beyond the mental worlds—that's where neutrality truly is. And when you, through your own efforts, see no difference between the ant and the angel, you will have found your eternal home and, in so doing, no longer wander and, in so doing, no longer wonder. For there, in your true home, there are no whys. There are no questions, for there are no answers, for everything is.

The moments of silence, the few moments that are needed to keep you on a path of reason and balance, must be rigidly adhered to for your own good. When you take those moments each day to pause and to meditate, if you enter that silent sanctorium freed from judgment, then you will leave that silent sanctorium free from mental experience. For that daily time is a time in which the mind should be still that the soul may rise. But that, of course, is up to you.

In sharing with you some of my personal history, I wish to review again when I served as a slave to the masters of those realms. My heart, centuries and centuries later, is still grateful to the guardian angel who guided me to resist not, to deny not, to totally accept the orders, for in so doing I was the one that was freed. The path of nonresistance is the path of spiritual awakening and illumination, for it is the true path of selfless service.

My good friends, your soul does not resist, for your soul is an inseparable unit of the whole. Your soul is the total acceptance. It is your mind, it is the so-called self that resists. And that resistance, following the Law of Identity, brings the denials and destinies of your life.

In your material world, your minds may think it impossible to follow the path of selfless service, the path of nonresistance. But it is not impossible and it is the path of wisdom. But you must separate truth from creation in order to follow that path. For you must know in the very depths of your being that there is an intelligent power that has never failed you, when you accepted it, and, therefore, never will. And when that day comes, your soul will reign supreme. Regardless of the experiences of creation, you will be not moved, for you have separated truth and, in so doing, found the way.

The path of nonresistance is a very ancient, ancient teaching. It is the true teaching of all religion, of all philosophy. But it is not understood and, therefore, is yet to be practiced. I assure you, it brings all that I say, but not in the way the mind may dictate.

Look out across the worlds, for that's where, in truth, you are going. Your earthly journeys, indeed, are very short. And what you are doing on Earth is preparing you for your next step. So think, my students, and think in a broader sense of the word. Think beyond the limited identity of the moment. Go beyond it. And once having done so, you will return with greater understanding, for you will have gained a greater tolerance.

Yesterday has gone. Do not mourn the passing. Do not mourn the changes of life. Stand still and look ahead. Become aware of the hundreds of thousands of times you look back, that you may make a greater effort in looking ahead.

At our last meeting, we spoke a bit on universal consciousness and your responsibilities. And for many of you, the class seemed a bit difficult. But I assure you, it was only difficult to the level of limited identification. Consider more than the limited self and you will experience a much happier life than you have already had. Pause more often, my good friends. Pause that you may think and, in so doing, gain the lion's strength. You cannot turn back, for you know the Light is ahead. And you'll only have to rise another day to start again. If the struggle is great, then it shall not long endure. If the struggle is not so great, then indeed can you endure it.

Good night.

FEBRUARY 9, 1978

CONSCIOUSNESS CLASS 170

Greetings, students. This evening we shall spend some time with the questions you have prepared.

Thank you. Please explain this quotation from Discourse 49, "Cherish your beginnings. Guard them well. Protect them and feed them on the levels where it really counts."

Protect them and feed them or direct energy to them on the levels of consciousness where it really counts. Each moment the mind is in a process of creating or beginning many, many things. And the levels of consciousness that really count are the levels of consciousness that man, through his own efforts of prayer, have united for the purpose of accomplishing some good in his life.

And so it is that we find, from our experiences in life, that we begin many things, but few things do we accomplish, in keeping with that Law of Beginnings. Through an effort to place the God consciousness upon the level that is experiencing the desire of beginning, we make that effort to harmonize these levels of consciousness that they may be united for the common good in our lives. And so when you, as you do each moment, have so many thoughts of beginning a new, of trying a different way than you have tried before, ever in the hope, which is eternal, that this time it will be successful and rewarding, then you must remember that without the cherishing of the level where it really counts, without putting God, the acceptance of a greater authority, into the level of consciousness and making the effort and doing your part in uniting these levels, then it cannot reap a good, nor beneficial, result for you.

Thank you. In Discourse 63, we are taught, "The heel represents the door to understanding and one should keep it closed: otherwise it mixes with the understanding of others and man does not know himself." Does this suggest that we are not to share our understanding with others, with students?

No, that is not what that is referring to. But it is referring to the demonstrable truth that the secrets of the universe are never given to the blabbermouth. And so it is that you must consider what it is inside of you that prompts you, under the guise of sharing, to express your understanding. For example, so often under the guise of sharing one's understanding is the true motive of control. And we must become aware of that motivation of the human mind that we do not deceive ourselves between sharing, which is a givingness, and the mind's control over whatever it judges to be the right way for itself and everyone else.

When we gain understanding, we lose the need for support for our understanding. There is no need to convert the world, our friends, and relatives and everyone we meet, for in true understanding is the security of wisdom.

Those lines, in that discourse, are referring to your awakening to your motive for sharing. For all sharing and all givingness—behind it is the prompting of motivation. Now, if your motive is sincere and pure, then the results will be beneficial and good, not only for yourself, but for those to whom you share your understanding. But remember that truth is individually perceived. And from what level of consciousness are you believing that you are sharing? Do you look, in this so-called sharing, for results? For if you look for results, then it reveals to you that you are attached. Therefore, having attachment, you do not have the freedom of true understanding. When you give what you have to give and you truly care less what is done with it, then you are free from the level of control known as attachment. For we attach ourselves to things and people in order that we may feed or direct energy to our need for control outside of our own sphere of action.

We have spoken before on this great need of control. It is a need recorded within the human mind and it can, and does, serve a beneficial purpose when it remains inside. For there is—and the mind knows—a need for the light of reason to keep it under control.

There's an old saying in your world that an idle mind is the devil's playground. An idle mind is a mind that is not under the control of balance and reason and the light of wisdom. And so it offers, like any jungle offers, an enclosure in which man, sooner or later, cannot see the light above.

So let us consider, in our needs for sharing our understanding, let us pause and weigh out our true motive. Let us not, however, in weighing out our true motive, let us not block the light of reason. Let us move on in a world in which we are here to serve, for that is truly the only purpose for life expression. For without service, life does not express. But we must always be on guard in consciousness. We must be awakened to what we are serving. That we will find through an honest and sincere effort to prayer.

We have spoken to you many, many times on the great need of constant prayer, on the need to flood the consciousness with the peace, which is the power of the Divine Intelligence. And sooner or later, we know that all souls shall awaken. For the expression of the soul is truly through the heart and the heart is the open door to the Divine Intelligence, known as God.

But we so misunderstand the word *prayer*. We misunderstand it because we have judged in our minds what it really is. But if we will pause more often in our activities and we will really make the effort of constant prayer, which is a recognition, an acceptance that the Intelligence that sustains all of your thoughts, that that Intelligence knows the right way for you—for recorded within, indelibly, in that intelligence that exists within you is all of the paths that you have ever trod. That intelligence knows why you are on Earth. It knows the lessons that you have failed and it knows the lessons that you have yet to learn. Therefore, it is a reliable, intelligent, an infinite guidance for your life.

But you cannot have two authorities in life and walk a single path. For two authorities are the path of duality and creation. The purpose of the soul is the service of the light of reason to bring balance into all things that it expresses in. And so it is that with your efforts of accepting that Intelligence, which permits your soul to rise and cast the soul faculties over the experiences that you are encountering, then you will know that is a lesson that you have faced in life before, that you turned your back upon that lesson who knows how many thousands of times. But that lesson, like a great shadow, will not leave you until the light of reason has been cast upon it.

Our effort, wisely directed, to accepting the responsibility for our life's experiences is the first step in opening the door to the soul faculties. When you truly accept that you and you alone are the alpha and the omega, that you and you alone are the beginning and the ending of all experiences that are recorded within your consciousness, when you truly accept that responsibility, your soul will rise, through that acceptance, and then you will know the experience—why it has come to you, which laws you set into motion to guarantee it, how long the experience will be within your consciousness, and then you will have a new attitude concerning your life experiences.

No matter what your struggle may seem to be, you are never left without choice in all of eternity, for choice is your eternal, divine birthright in each and every incarnation. You entered the world of experience by the Law of Choice and by the Law of Choice do you leave the world of experience. And so you and choice are one and the same. And because you and choice are one and the same, the scales of balance are, indeed and in truth, your guiding light. It is when you forget that you have choice that the light of reason goes out in your universe. And so as these experiences rob you from your peace and serenity, they do so only when you forget God gave you choice.

You may choose a new experience than the one you have. You may have that new experience by your choice. And you establish that choice by a change in consciousness by changing your attitude. For when you change your attitude, you change your level of consciousness. You exercise your infinite, divine right of choice. So whatever it is that you wish to be changed in your life, simply choose your change. For that, my friends, is your right.

Now, no one likes to hear "Change your attitude" when they are having—or what they have judged they are having—a great struggle. The level that is in control is the level that becomes irritated whenever it is told to change its attitude. For the level knows if you, the true being, change your expression, the level will no longer receive the energy that it is receiving.

What is it within us that seems to take so long to choose a better way? I am sure that we will all agree it is not us. For I am sure we all will agree that we want something better, for everyone can see there *is* something better. So why should you be left out from the something better that some seem to have? We're left out by choice, our choice. And the first step in establishing, which is, in truth, our eternal right, that right of choice is accepting that life is reacting to our attitude of mind. That is the nature of mental substance. It reacts, but you, you are the driver. You are the captain. It's only when you forget that you are the captain of your ship of destiny that other levels of consciousness rise up to keep you in the bondage to that level.

We gave to you a simple, little exercise to go nine days at a time. For we know if you can go nine, you certainly can go ninety plus. You see, my friends, with all of the laws that have been revealed, with all of the teachings that have been given to you, without your exercise of your birthright, they cannot be personally demonstrated in your personal life. You must exercise your divine right: your right of choice. You must not permit your minds—those levels that have you in control for a time—to dictate to you. I know that it will take some effort on your part to once again reclaim your birthright. But I know that you will, for that is the destiny of your soul.

As you make that effort to reclaim your divine birthright, that right of choice, you will become increasingly aware of how much of your life and your daily experience is being controlled by levels of consciousness that you know are not bringing you the good that you seek. As you become aware of that truth inside of you—and some of you are aware of that truth at times—you will find that most all minds on your Earth planet are under the control of these various levels. That there are few who speak forth the word of truth, because there are few who apply the truth.

Many times we have mentioned to you about the spoken word. It cannot work if the demonstration is not made inside first. Now, let us, for a few moments, discuss that great truth of the spoken word. "I"—the Law of Identity—"I speak my word forth"—The Law of Identity gives into the universe, not limited to this world, nor the next—"knowing that it shall not come back to me void"—a declaration of the authority of the human mind, for the mind knows. "I speak my word forth into the universe knowing that it shall not come back to me void, but accomplish that which I send it to do." Now, that is the mind speaking forth to the universe, to this great mental substance. But man must first experience within his own consciousness that he alone is responsible for all his spoken words, that no matter what word he speaks, it does not return to him void. Each spoken word returns in an experience.

And so, in truth, all minds are demonstrating that authority in a mental world. In some of the ancient philosophies in your world, there were many students who demonstrated, through their constant silent prayer, something greater than a mental world. They knew the force of the spoken word, but they also knew the power of silence. And so they spent their lives in your Earth in total silence, where God does his greatest work.

Now, speaking your word establishes the mental law and returns unto you the experience in accordance with that word. If you are united within—and you can only be united by accepting the truth of personal responsibility—then your spoken word will return to you united and accomplish what you have sent it to do. But if you are not in harmony within—united in consciousness—then your spoken word will come back to you in the fragments of experiences: so-called good and so-called bad. The discord that you may experience without is only the discord that is within.

But God did not leave you without choice. It's time to make that effort to change our attitude. Surely we have spent enough years on Earth and untold centuries before Earth to learn that wonderful lesson of demonstrating our birthright. You have a right to health, to wealth, and to happiness. But the experiencing of that right is dependent upon your change of attitude by accepting your right of choice.

We spoke to you before on what is called auric pollution. But auric pollution is not to be used as a device to deny the Law of Personal Responsibility. For in the midst of the Philistines, the God of Gods shall deliver you. If in the midst of auric pollution, you demonstrate your birthright of choice and, in the midst of pollution, through constant prayer, you raise your levels of consciousness—for that, my good students, *is* your right of choice. Let us, from this moment forth, let us demonstrate that which is truly ours: the right of choice. For we all know what thoughts we feel good in entertaining in our mind and we all know which thoughts we don't feel so good or comfortable with.

I have always tried in these many centuries, and continue to try, to make that effort: never to leave a soul worse than I have found them. For to leave a person worse in consciousness than you found them is to establish the Law of Debt. For out in the universe their soul cries and you are an inseparable part of their soul and you have a grave responsibility. Though often people may not like what you say, if your motive is pure, they shall always return for the Light knows the Light. It needs not to be told.

To be a friend of God is to be hand in hand with the greatest guidance you could possibly have in your life's journey. And so, my friends, it is time, indeed, it is time to stop denying and to start applying, for the school cannot benefit you until you start benefiting the school. You see, we only get out of anything what we put into it. If we put in denial, then only denial shall return. If we put in our effort to apply, then the results will show what our effort is.

When you find yourself denying the demonstrable truth—and that, for some, seems to be a daily experience. Each time you dictate, you deny. And a house divided cannot long endure. Let us become more aware of our denials that we may see clearly our path of destiny. When we deny the abundant good by insisting upon the authority of the level that speaks, then we are not exercising our divine birthright to choose something better. Let us not cry over the experiences or lessons of life, for the crying is denying the right of something better.

In making our choices in life, which we have already done—but that's not the place, my students, to stop. The right of choice is not a stagnant law: it is a moving divine principle. Let us not forget that we are evolving. But let us truly make that effort. Let us become more fully the demonstration of this divine truth.

We cannot move in the divine abundant flow of God unless we choose to do so. But choosing the divine abundant fullness of life means what is already in control must be dethroned by a change in our attitude. And now the question must arise, Are you truly ready? Are you ready and willing? For I know you are able. Are you ready and willing to give up the things that stand in your way? Are you ready to give them up that, through the Law of Choice, you may have something better?

I would rather have—if I decided I needed—energy or attention on a full stomach rather than an empty one. Think about that, my students. Think about your acceptance and your life.

And in thinking about it, choose to be constructive. There is no God that is a true God that lives in denial and lives in judgment. So choose a God that will care for you in a more full and abundant way. Choose that God for that is a good God.

Good night.

FEBRUARY 16, 1978

CONSCIOUSNESS CLASS 171

Good evening, class. We're going to have a little change from our regular routine this evening.

And before getting into our classes, as some of you, I know, are already aware, we had a front-page headline Tuesday [February 21, 1978] in reference to our church, to myself, to our religion, and concerning the house that we, as members, are the sole owners, under the chartership of our national association. The article that appeared immediately recorded in the minds of most, I'm sure, a degree of emotional trauma and upset. And as you are all aware, I'm sure, that I do not particularly appreciate being referred to as an "oil-rich shah" or anything of that nature.

However, in these experiences we must always ask ourselves the question, "Is there good in this experience? If so, then help me to find the good that my mind cannot yet see."

And so I spoke to several of you Tuesday—who were present—to look for the good that is in this experience, because if you will look for the good, then the good will appear for you. But it cannot appear as long as you fall into the pits of judgment and create the obstruction to the good that is trying to manifest itself.

And so today, Thursday, I had a call from Channel 2. And they asked if they could come over to do some photographing and an interview. Well, my mind immediately reacted and I told them no. If all they were interested in was what the *Independent Journal* was interested in—from their demonstration in the paper of the material aspect of the Serenity Church—then I was not interested. And the man said to me that no, that they reported the news accurately, impartially, and neutrally. And I asked who did they want to send over for this interview today. And he said Andy Parks. Well, that registered in my mind because I happen to periodically watch the Ten O'clock News and I have always felt that Andy Parks is basically a spiritually-minded, impartial—as much as possible—type of a newscaster. And with a little further assistance from my mother who said to tell him to come over, I immediately thought, "That's what you said about the *Independent Journal*." [*The Teacher laughs.*] But I said, "Well, what day did you want to come over?" And they said within the hour. And so they came. Now, that is going on tonight's newscast at ten o'clock—or definitely tomorrow—according to Mr. Parks.

But what is important for the class—very important—when you read the headlines of the *Independent Journal* which states, "Church keeps leader in hilltop luxury," then you have to try to become objective. You have to try to understand that newspapers, in order to sell their papers, are controlled by sensationalism. And so their stories are always colored with that that appears to be sensational.

However, if you'll recall, several weeks ago, we discussed with you that our church building would come into this material world. In so speaking, a law is established. The law is very clear: that it shall come to pass, for you have spoken the word and the word shall manifest itself for you ever in keeping with your faith and belief.

So we must look at these experiences for what they truly are: stepping stones to the attainments that we alone desire. You see, so often we desire so many things and when the steps necessary to attain the fulfillment of the desire that we entertain begin to manifest themselves in our lives, we suddenly and surely change our desires. And so in looking at the steps ahead, not only for myself, but for this church, for this organization, and for its members and its students, we must never forget what our goal truly is. Our goal is not building buildings. That has never been our goal.

I told our contractor, before we ever broke ground upon the hill, that this house [*the church office*] would serve the purpose of bringing many, many, many souls to the Light, that many, many people would come. Now, if a physical structure can be instrumental in serving that purpose, then a good spiritual purpose is being served.

And so it is in all of your desires, you must ask yourselves what it really is that you, yourself, are looking for and not be detoured from your path by the seeming obstructions that come your way. You see, when you receive adverse publicity—first, we must face the Law of Personal Responsibility. And in facing these adversities, you can turn them around in your consciousness to serve a very good purpose.

The first thing that rises up in the mind—and I know what the mind offers because I have a mind that tries to be as active as possible. In fact, the newscaster asked me today, he said, "Well, Mr. Goodwin," he says, "Do you ever disagree with those eighty-one spirits that guide your church?" And I said, "Oh, yes, quite frequently." "Well," he says, "Do you ever win out?" And I said, "No, I'm not quite that foolhardy." I said, "First of all, I made an agreement." I didn't want to open a church. I agreed to open a church under one condition: that I would not have to make the decisions governing it. And I have remained free from that. Even though ofttimes I do not agree—my mind does not agree with the Spirit—I have learned, over the years, to at least give them a chance to see what is going to come out of the situation and not rise up, with my mind, to block the way.

And so with all of your experiences and your seeming adversities, you have two ways of looking at them. The mind offers, in the experience that we encountered Tuesday, the mind offers fear, for that is the mind's control. And so the first thing that rises in the mind: this newspaper goes and reaches many people in this community. And many people believe what they read, unfortunately. And that could affect not only the support of the Church, that could affect its attendance, that could affect its bake sales. It could affect so many different things. This is what the mind offers. The mind immediately judges from fear. And so I recognize that, of course, those kind of thoughts to be my mind and I go to work on that before they establish laws and experiences for me.

I can assure you that there are many changes coming in the Serenity Association. It was only six weeks ago that I spoke to the vice president of your church and told him that there are many great changes coming for this church and that those changes are right upon us.

Now, when you receive publicity—which, fortunately, I have been freed from for most of the years of serving in this work—you have to stand firm in facing the duality of creation. For there will be those who are for you and there will be those who are against you. And so we must prepare ourselves for our public service here on Sunday mornings. And we must prepare ourselves for all of these floods of people that will be coming to this light in Serenity and to pray that we may be guided in such a way as to never lose the spirit of dignity, never to lose our character and our respect for our religion and our philosophy.

Our basic teaching is that truth needs no defense. And so to those especially who will be up at the house answering the telephone—I have already instructed the vice president: if you receive phone calls that are adverse and detrimental, do not involve yourself in those levels of consciousness. Be very polite and simply hang up the telephone, because that is part of growth and success. When he read that article on Tuesday, the vice president did say one thing: "It spells undeniable success." And that is true. And so to have success and to sustain success, you must be willing to stand on principle.

You see, you have, coming to you very quickly, the opportunity to demonstrate what you have already learned: that no one sleeps for you and no one eats for you. Then, you would be so foolhardy to let them think for you. So no matter what they think or what they say, if you permit [*The Teacher loses his voice.*] that to affect you, then you are controlled by those levels of consciousness. And obviously, it had some affect upon me or I wouldn't have lost my voice for a split second. [*The Teacher coughs.*]

So in order for us to move harmoniously with the growth of our own church and our own school here, we must not forget our responsibility.

I know that some of my students were deeply hurt in the knocks that we received in the newspaper. But it wasn't all knocks. There was some boost. When a paper says that thirty-four people are able to bring about almost a half-million-dollar house, that thirty-four people were able to raise $80,000 to $90,000 in twelve short months and goes on to say that established religions are not even able to accomplish that, then you must look at those things in a positive way.

And you must try to understand, when the paper, the newspaper reporter stated that the house was filled with "copper and pewter artifacts" and "specimen plants"—I really didn't know what the word *specimen* meant, used in that contents—in that context. And so I asked one of my students and he said, "Well, it means rare." Then you must understand that the reporter, when they saw the copper and the pewter, made the statement that she always wanted those things, but she had to settle for brass because she couldn't afford them. She doesn't understand that she is paying for her own judgments.

You see, that's the truth about life. You can have whatever it is that your heart desires, but you must give up the judge that stands between you and your heart's desire. And if you will give up that mental judge, then you will have the fulfillment in life that is really yours. You see, we have to give to gain, but we cannot judge what it is we're going to give that we may gain what it is we desire, because if we judge what it is we must give, then we're still controlled by that same realm in consciousness, that same realm of judgment.

I had a call today from a lady and she said, "I read the article about your church in the newspaper and it's exactly what I'm looking for." And I said, "Well, what's that?" And she said, "I want to get into your classes right away." And I said to her, "Well, I would suggest that you come to the church so that you may see if what we are offering is really what you are truly interested in." And she said, "No, no," she said, "I'm interested in the classes. I know it's exactly what I need. I'm a trance medium and I want to get exactly what you got." Well, that's very sad. And she wanted to register and I told her, "You can't register for the classes. You have to come to church to register. And besides, it is a limited class."

So that's only one of many experiences that you, as students and members, must prepare yourselves for, because that's what's coming. But along with that is also the good that is coming for the church. A lot of good is coming. A lot of growth is coming. And whether we like it or not, the church—and ourselves, as a body of the church—continues to evolve. There's one thing about change: it's totally impartial. It doesn't care whether you like it or you don't like it, because change is what we're doing all the time. We're constantly changing. So, in truth, we constantly have to let go because we are constantly moving ever forward, ever onward, and ever upward. And it's the things, the thought forms, that we hold to that are standing in our way.

And so I did want to speak to you about those things. It's very important, because in the material growth of your church, we must never lose sight of the spiritual growth. As the newscaster said to me today, asking about the philosophy, the religion, and the house—I said to him, "You know, I've always tried to teach a God of abundant good." And I said, "For me to demonstrate the opposite of what I am striving to teach these many years is to indeed be a hypocrite." And he agreed with me wholeheartedly, because to teach one thing and to demonstrate its opposite is an absolute guarantee of failure. Now, I don't teach a God of limitless gold or money. I teach a God of abundant good. And if gold or money, copper or pewter is a part of that abundant good in our life, then that is our God and that is our right.

You see, we are never left without choice. And we've spoken about that many times in these classes. You can choose the possibility of something better in your life or you can choose the judgment that you have already created. But if you're not happy with the judgment that you have already created, then reason dictates—and common sense agrees—it's time to make a change. So it is obvious, of course, that the student body—over 51 percent—are making changes in a positive direction or the church would not be moving in a positive direction, as it is.

So let us take a few moments each day to consider something beyond and something greater than these limited daily experiences that we have. Let's go beyond and find the cause of all these things. And if we will do that, then we can make all the changes that are necessary.

I know that it is difficult, being exposed to the jungle out there, listening constantly to the hue and cry and the limitation. It's amazing sometimes to go out into the jungle and to hear so many things. The people are so filled with desire and they're also so filled with suppression. They'd like to have this, but they can't afford that. They'd like to do this, but that can't afford to do that. Because each time desire rises in their consciousness, just hand in hand rises the king judge. And so they live a life of frustration, a life of lack, and a life of limitation. But we all know that that is not God's fault. We all know that we are directing energy through our thought to constantly creating those obstructions.

I have said many times, and our teacher has said many times, that until the philosophy is applied, it has no value. I've always tried to be a very practical person. I've never minded spending money. In fact, I think I enjoy keeping it in circulation. But I've tried to be practical that whatever has come into my life that I would have consideration for how it came into my life and, in considering how it came into my life, that I would care enough to take care of it. Because I look at this material world as an effect—because that's all that it is, is an effect. It's not a cause, but it is an effect. It's an effect of a mental world and that mental world is an effect of a spiritual world. So whatever you have or think you have in life, if you do not cherish and take care of it, then you are demonstrating a disregard for the effort and the energy that was necessary to bring it into your life in the first place.

I know the *Independent Journal* called me a "spit-and-polish stickler," that I demanded absolute perfection in a house and a garden. But, you see, that's an effect. If you care enough of how things come into your life—the good—if you really care, then you will take care of them. And by so doing, you will demonstrate your appreciation and your value of the infinite, intelligent Energy that moves through your being. That's what's so important about the faculty of care. If you care for your eternal life, then you will give some thought to it in the course of a day. If you care about you, the real you, then you will make the effort to separate truth from creation, to separate these various levels of your mind from your eternal soul.

Now, that's what this philosophy is all about: to recognize what are the levels that, through errors of ignorance, have been created by your mind—not that you are not responsible for them, for indeed are we responsible for all our experience. But make that effort to separate truth from creation. And, also, to make the effort not to be so quick to judge experiences, but to accept the possibility of something better. That, I can assure you, *that* is what really works.

In speaking to our attorney yesterday—because someone has judged that we have no right to a tax exemption for our church property. I said to our attorney, "He [*referring to the individual who challenged Serenity's tax exemption*] is not God. There is something greater than his judgments concerning this church and concerning its property." And I said, "I hope that you'll never forget that." Because, you see, if we permit ourselves to work on the mental levels of consciousness, then we will react, for we will respond to fear.

I am a firm believer in the divine scales of balance: that no one can sincerely make effort to try to do good in their lives with a pure motive that sooner or later that good must return. For that law is infallible. And if you are experiencing the opposite, never forget: it is only the stepping stones that you are viewing. You have lost sight of your true goal. Don't lose sight of your goal in life, for your goal in life is your lifeline. But we must take stock of what we believe is our goal in life. If it is happiness and peace and joy and abundant good, then we must sacrifice, if that's the word you care to use, or give up all of the judges that stand between us and that good we're seeking.

The mind is so quick to dictate, but that is its very nature. It's very quick to garner. It's very quick to judge. It's very quick to establish the laws in our life. But you all know the way to be free from your mind. It doesn't mean that you should look at your mind as not serving a useful purpose. Your mind serves a very useful and good purpose when it is under the direction of your eternal soul that knows all of the lessons and all of the tests that it has ever had. It knows what is best for you. The mind is not a reliable instrument in knowing what is best for you. But the mind is a vehicle that was designed for you to direct. And it is only through your efforts of taking control of that mind—that was designed for you to be the driver—that you can free yourselves and enjoy the life that you came here to enjoy.

Now, in reference to the word *enjoy,* don't permit your mind to dictate what enjoyment is. If you will do that—take control of your mind and let it not dictate what enjoyment is—then you will have enjoyment and it will be lasting and it will be enduring. It is when our mind rises up with its authority to dictate to this Divine Intelligence. You will not lose your individuality, for your identity is well anchored in this Earth experience. So you need not concern yourself about the loss of identity or the seeming loss of individuality. If you'll make efforts to free yourselves from the mind, then you will have moments of universal consciousness. And those moments you will never forget. For it is like being freed from a very heavy, burdensome weight, because the mind is a very heavy weight upon the soul. It's that because we gave it too much control over our lives. We did that in an error, of course, of our own ignorance. But that does not mean that we have to live that way forever. We can change this moment if we really want to.

So look out at life and get a new attitude. Many, many times I've spoken to the students about attitude—just to change your attitude, that's all it takes. Whatever it is that disturbs you, remember, it is controlling you. And if you change your attitude concerning it, it will no longer control you. I know you are all intelligent people. I know that consciously you certainly do not want anything controlling you that is not beneficial to your life. It is only through error that these mental forms are controlling us. And it is one of the purposes of these classes to awaken your consciousness that you may see clearly the various patterns of mind that are your obstructions and that are making the difficulties in your life. I assure you whatever you give up here, you gain over here. And that gain is lasting forever and ever and ever. Your thoughts, they come and your thoughts, they go, but your character, your being goes on forever and ever and ever.

Earth offers you a great opportunity. It is the planet of faith, and faith is what all of us are demonstrating each moment. And we stand at that crossroad: our faith either goes on to our soul or it goes to the vehicle known as the mind that we are using. It is because so much faith has been directed to our mind that we live in so much fear. I don't believe the students are really aware of how strong and how potent fear is in their lives. You look around and you see there's a fear of "Where I'm going to live, the fear of my health, the fear of my wealth." Stop and think how much fear there is in your life. Each time desire rises—and desire is God's expression—fear comes up with all of its judges. Think about that. Think about how many times you justify and give excuses why you don't have what you really desire. That shows you how much fear is in your life.

This philosophy gives to you the simple, unadulterated truth. And when it means enough to you, you will demonstrate it in its fullness. But do not be discouraged over the stepping stones. Do not be discouraged that you still experience fear in your life. Become more aware of how much fear *is* expressing in your life, because you can't do anything about anything that you're not aware of. Think, when you go to sleep, what fears are in your mind. And think about the fears when you wake up. And think about how many times you justify why you do this and why you do that. Become aware of why you do things. Be honest with yourself.

There is a part of everyone's mind that's very tenacious, that's very determined. And that part we see in everyone. But it can be used for a good purpose. And as I said to the students in reference to this knock that we received, I said, "Well, there's one thing about persecution—it unites the people." And I'm happy, in that respect, to see there is an ever increasing and growing unity within the organization. And please don't misunderstand the word *unity*. My students are still as individualistic as they were the day they came to the church. Oh, they're very individual, very definite, and very positive about what they want and what they don't want. And I'm sure that I must be a bit stubborn myself to have attracted so many stubborn students. However, as life is a miracle of existence, Serenity continues to exist.

Now, I've taken quite a bit of time discussing how you may react to experience. That you may look at it and say, "Thank you, God. There is great good in this experience." No matter how adverse or how difficult the experience may seem to your mind, always remember, it is a stepping stone to something better. Remember that. Remember that it is moving you ever closer to your goal in life. Don't ever forget that truth in your experiences: that you are moving along the steps that are necessary for you to attain what you truly desire to attain. And if you will always remember that, the experiences, they won't stop coming and they won't stop going, but you will feel a lot better about facing them.

Remember, my friends, when the law is established and experience is on its way, you can run from the North pole to the South, it will chase you like a great shadow. How many times I have told people in reference to marriages and divorces and things of that nature! Well, you know what you've got—hopefully you know. You're not too sure about what you may get. Because, you see, my friends, the philosophy never to leave a person worse than you found him is a very practical philosophy. For a person is attracted into your life in keeping with a law that you established. Now, if you do not face that experience for what that experience has to offer you—for you're the one that set the law into motion—if you turn your back and walk away from it, you may be rest assured the experience will chase you all over the universe. And you will face it again, again, and again and again.

It's just like having a job. If you go to work and you have a job and you make the judgment, "It's a terrible job. It's just awful," don't know how you merited such a thing and you say, "Well, that's it. I quit," you may be rest assured, you'll get another job someplace, somewhere, and the same lesson will look you square in the eye. You don't face it and you quit again. You will have another and another and another and another. For repetition is the law through which change is made possible. And if you are experiencing a repetition of certain experiences and you wonder when they're going to stop, you may be assured they are going to stop when you have had enough. For then, you will have learned the lesson that is being offered to you. That is the moment that those experiences will stop and you will move on to greater things.

Now, a person may say, "Well, these experiences have been repeating themselves for years and years and years and years. In fact, they keep getting worse. They don't get better." But that, my friends, is a very good sign: it means they're getting stronger and our tenacity is getting weaker. That's when the rainbow begins to appear—the symbol of the promise of something better.

And so I do have compassion for my students, for I have a little bit of understanding of what it's like to be stubborn and to be tenacious. But, you see, you can use that stubbornness and tenacity to serve a good purpose. Don't think I wasn't stubborn and tenacious in my decision that there was something good in the experience of Tuesday's newspaper. And don't think I haven't worked on my own mind to remember that truth.

We are in the driver's seat when we stop and we pause to think and declare our right. And more important than that, that we declare our right to our right. It is our right to be free and it is our right to be happy. It is our right to experience the good that this life has to offer. That is our right. And if we do not declare and demonstrate that right, then it's time to take stock.

Because, you see, my friends, we're all going over. And for some of us, it will be sooner than we realize. So let us do what is to be done here and now so we don't have to come back to do it. You know, many times—especially in this type of religion—people wonder and are concerned about earth-bound spirits. If you have faced the experience that Earth has to offer you, then you don't have to be concerned about being earth-bound. But if you keep running away from the lessons that you alone have earned, then you'd best give some thought to that so-called earth-bound realm, because you came here to experience and to grow and to pass the lessons, the tests that this Earth life offers to you. If you turn your back on those lessons, you will have to meet them someday and you cannot leave the sphere of the planet that is offering you those lessons. So, friends, whatever you have to do, get it done now. And so you can move on in consciousness and have a much better life.

Thank you.

FEBRUARY 23, 1978

CONSCIOUSNESS CLASS 172 ✤

Greetings, students. Once again it is our pleasure to speak with you in this way. But remember, my good friends, I am always with you through universal consciousness.

And in speaking this evening on universal consciousness, we must consider the strength and the benefit not only to ourselves, but to all of those with whom we come in contact. As you rise in your own levels of consciousness, through an ever increasing and broadening acceptance, do you attain this universal consciousness and, from that attainment, become the strength of a united whole.

And so it is that the time, indeed, has come for the Light that has been brought to you to spread farther and broader across the land.

I especially want to speak to those of my students who sometimes feel discouraged in their efforts. As part of a united body of Light, you must accept the demonstrable truth, as a unit of the whole, you must view the whole. And in so viewing, you cannot deny that the body of Light is moving forward, is evolving, is strengthening, and is growing. It is indeed difficult to see the tree for the forest. It is difficult to view the single purpose that is moving ahead when we are distracted by so many thoughts and attitudes that are in the process of leaving our universe.

Do not cry, my good students, for that that is passing, for in so doing you do not clearly view the good that is growing in your lives. Do not look at the steps of attainment, for the energy passing through your being should be directed to the attainment and not the way of its accomplishment. For in directing the energy to the way of accomplishment, you build obstructions, through error of ignorance, through lack of understanding.

Some time ago we stated to you, when the student is ready, the teacher will appear, and when the teacher is ready, the students will appear. Let us not, in our evolution, put the cart before the horse, so to speak, for it reveals, in so doing, that we yet lack the wisdom of patience. It reveals the impurities of our motive. And those impurities are obstructions in consciousness. Because, my good friends, all things exist in consciousness. And without consciousness, there would be no existence. Can you now not see the work must ever be done within?

The acceptance of all things does not, as we stated before, guarantee the experiencing in consciousness of all things, for we only experience through the Law of Identity. Let us, in viewing that which is before us, face the responsibility of our true being, of our eternal being.

So many steps have gone before you and you are facing the work that has been postponed for so very, very long. Let us never forget that that work is within our consciousness. Working within is the law of building without. And I know that many of you are not particularly pleased that your efforts in building without have yet to prove to your minds the worth of the effort. But only a fool is discouraged by viewing a short few years and not viewing them in comparison to the many centuries that it has already taken them to reach the point in evolution at which they stand. You have indeed come very far, seemingly in a short time. But it is an effect and a realization that doesn't yet view the many years that have preceded it.

To become qualified in any endeavor requires the personal experiences to qualify oneself. If you wish to help another, then you must first help yourself in the area in which you desire to help another. You must first pass the test within yourself. And this is what you have been offered. It is the opportunity you have earned in this little organization. The crumbs of life are the essence upon which the loaves of life are built.

And I want to speak on that Law of Supply which flows through the open door of gratitude. All of you have the opportunity each day of demonstrating gratitude for the crumbs of life. And I would like to share with you this evening what happens when you don't demonstrate gratitude for the crumbs of life. Whenever you have an experience and you permit your mind to dictate that it was a good experience, but there should be more, you direct energy to the throne of judgment. And the energy necessary for the little crumb, the essence, to grow and become a loaf is dissipated by your choice of the mental superiority over your spiritual being. It is sad, but true, that through errors of ignorance the masses of your planet continue to live in unfulfilled desires because of that one, simple transgression of the

Law of Supply. I do hope that you will take to heart this evening, that the faculty of reason may rise within your being supreme, that you may see, clearly and fully, how, by denying the crumb by the judgment of more, that law truly works.

My students, yes, make more effort on the little things of life, for it is those little things that build the abundant good that is your right. Tell the mind to be still and when, by your own efforts, you receive the crumbs of life, remember, in those moments if you permit your mind to dictate more, that essence disintegrates, the crumb leaves your universe, and your loaves never come to be.

And so it is not only in your material world, but in your spiritual world. For you are this moment, and every moment, you are building your spiritual abode. For each time your mind dictates, you deny the Divine Intelligence, called God. And your denials continue to be your destinies. Let us demonstrate more fully the crumb of gratitude, for there is indeed not only for you, as earthly individuals, but for the body of Light that has been brought to your world—and that body of Light shall strengthen through unity, yea, even more.

The greatest teaching that could pass through your universe is your personal effort to demonstrate what has been revealed to you. It is within your power and the time is now. There is no escape from that which is distasteful in your lives. There is only growth through it. You are growing and you will—most of you—continue to do so.

The effort of constant prayer is a demonstration of the Law of Gratitude: a recognition of an intelligent Power greater than your mind. And as you become more open and more receptive, by your recognition and your gratitude for that infinite intelligent Power, that infinite intelligent Power will flow more freely and more clearly through your universe. And any obstructions that you see today, redirect your view. For in so redirecting do you become a more open channel.

I know that some of you have a bit of an obstruction in your minds to being a channel of anything. But I assure you, my students, it is better to be a channel of one intelligent infinite Power that never faileth than to be a channel of a multitude of forms that have interest only in their own survival.

And so look more reasonably at your attitudes of mind. Remember, in so doing, to separate yourself from them, for only in separating yourself in consciousness from them can you be, in time, freed from them.

Let us demonstrate what we have earned. Let us, this moment on, demonstrate the abundant goodness of our God. Let us do that by our spoken word and act of gratitude for the crumbs of life. For I assure you, my good friends, if you truly make that effort for those little crumbs, you will live on Earth to see the day of the greatness, the goodness, and the infallibility of your God.

Good night.

MARCH 2, 1978

CONSCIOUSNESS CLASS 173

Good evening, class.

Whereas current events involving Serenity Church clearly demonstrate teachings given in these classes, this evening we shall discuss some of those events and how they relate to inner attitudes of mind.

Now, all of you present are aware that over a year ago we started to build a house for our church in order that we may have a building of our own in which the activities and functions of this church may be held. Now, in bringing this about, there were many different feelings and thoughts of the members and the supporters of the church. Some agreed that it was a wise and practical step: to build a house in order that we may do our printing, may do the baking for our monthly bake sales, may prepare the various brunches for our church, and may record the tapes of these classes and the many activities that are done at the house. In being a practical person, it was the only sensible and logical step. For to attempt to build a church building and to continue to pay rent to house your minister and many of the supplies of the church was not a practical move to make.

And so with $120 in the church checking account, you all know that we purchased a lot. We raised the funds—$16,000—raised the $2,000 to pay for the closing costs on the land. Got a mortgage for $60,000—a construction loan. Got a completion loan for $50,000. And then got a second mortgage for $25,000.

Now, the house has been built. That is an effect that reveals the majority of the members of the church—that means over 51 percent—entertained a positive attitude of mind, a vibration, in order for that to be accomplished. When that house was in construction, I spoke to some of my students and I told them that that house—a demonstration—would attract many souls into the Light. How they were to be attracted was not discussed.

And so we have moved on and, here, in these past few weeks, have been experiencing what I am sure most of you will agree is publicity that does not appear to be constructive or to be accomplishing any good for Serenity Church. But we must ask ourselves, What laws have we, as a group, as a unit, as an organization, set into motion?

Our philosophy clearly states that there is good in all experience, that a wise man, through prayer and through peace, will, in time, view that good and, by placing his attention upon that good, that good shall become the predominate vibration that he shall experience.

In the construction of your church house, there was much discussion and thought of who it was being built for. Whenever we entertain these thoughts of doubt, whenever we entertain these negative thoughts, we establish—we become instruments through which laws are established. And because we, as a group, are personally responsible, as a group, for this church and this organization, we must not turn our sight from our own responsibilities.

Our philosophy teaches that we get out of a thing whatever we put into a thing. And so we are getting out of our church and our organization ever in keeping with that law. During the building of our church house, some of our people, through errors of ignorance in their own mind, believed and discussed that it was being built for their church minister. Those souls do not yet know, somehow, that I have no need for a house of 7,000 square feet. I have no need for a house of 1,700 square feet. I lived, and did my work very well, in a one-room apartment in Forest Knolls. And the truth of the matter is that this organization was founded in a one-room apartment.

I did ask for a room with my own bath, considering that I have lived in a house for years in which this entire church operation and all of its work is done. To many of you, I am sure, you would not find that pleasing or something that you personally would desire, for it's more like living in a hotel lobby. And therefore to desire what you might think someone else has is not seeing very clearly. I have not—and I do not object to living in a house with so much activity each day. I have tried, and do try, to demonstrate the Law of Gratitude.

I was well aware that we were paying $283 a month in a rented house and I was very much aware, in the building of your church house, that we would have to move to a much more considerable monthly payment. And so we have moved from $283 a month to $1,200 a month just as a monthly payment, not including, of course, increased cost of utilities and everything else that it takes, financially and spiritually, to operate such a large asset.

Many of my students have asked why we have, and are receiving, this so-called adverse publicity. But we must ask ourselves, What is, and what has been, our attitude concerning the building of the house and concerning the operation of our own church? Have we been in harmony with the Council and the authority of the organization? Or have we clearly demonstrated by our thought, by our act, and by our deed that we are not in harmony with the authority of our own church?

Some of the students felt that the publicity received was lacking in presenting the philosophy that the church truly represents. But that is not a true statement. The very foundation and the very basis of our philosophy was brought about, and is brought about, by spirit communication. And so the basis of our philosophy was clearly demonstrated on the television newscast and anyone who viewed that newscast could not help but see that the very basis of our philosophy was presented: namely, communication with the world of spirit. The way it was presented was indeed most interesting, for each time that communication with a spirit world was mentioned, a television set was shown or a video recorder was shown; whenever a discussion of voices from a spirit world, stereo equipment was shown. The message, my good friends, was very clear.

Now, we must ask ourselves, What is our attitude and what have we demonstrated in respect to the very basis of our philosophy? Have we accepted spirit communication when that communication is not in accord or in harmony with our personal desires of our mind? If we have demonstrated that we have not accepted spirit communication, the very basis of our philosophy, when that communication is contrary to our personal desires, then we must look at the demonstration of the publicity that blatantly and clearly ridiculed even the possibility of communication with a world of spirit.

So let us, in looking at ourselves, let us ask ourselves those questions very clearly. Let us see what the news media has demonstrated in reference to presenting our philosophy, for if our philosophy is to be presented as it has been presented—the very foundation of it—then it is certainly and clearly not in our best interest to have publicity concerning it, not until we, as students and members and supporters of the organization—the Serenity Spiritualist organization—make changes in our own attitudes. Have we harmoniously, fully, wholly, and completely, accepted a greater authority in our lives than what our mind dictates? Have we, as members and students, demonstrated that truth? That is the question that we must ask ourselves. Do we, in all honesty, look at our own church assets with envy, with jealously, with greed? We must ask that question of ourselves, for the demonstration of publicity reveals that over 51 percent of us have demonstrated that very level of consciousness.

You cannot expect the world to view you any differently than you, as an individual, are viewing the world. If you are viewing the world with a lack of understanding, if you are viewing the world without thorough investigation of anything you are interested in, then that is what will return unto you.

One of my students asked why the spirit people did not reveal what type of publicity we would be receiving. How sad that our faith is yet to be demonstrated. Do you think for one minute that a spirit world, who can clearly predict the rain that shall fall and when it shall fall, that can help you through your trials and tribulations, is not aware of what is to come concerning the very church that they have founded? My good friends, if you think my life is so soft—for that must be the thought of a predominance of my own students in order to have received that in publicity—if you think my life is so soft, then your understanding of the word *soft* is quite different than my own.

Many times I do things at the request of the founders of this church. My mind does not agree with them, but I do it because I made an honest agreement in the founding of this very church and because I made that honest agreement, I do what is necessary in order to keep that agreement. Because I do not tell everyone everything that I may or may not know does not mean that I am not aware of many things.

In keeping with the laws demonstrated by over 51 percent of the church membership, we have the experiences that we have today. My personal choice—that I spoke to one of my students just the other day—is that this publicity may, by the very power and peace of God, pass into the nothingness, that it may have served the purpose—the good that is to come. But that is not the personal choice of many of my students. And so the choices of my students I respect and I will do what is necessary and what the authority of your church requests in order to keep this church together.

Now I will assure you, beyond a shadow of any doubt, that the Serenity Association will continue to survive. It will continue to prosper. It will continue to grow and serve the very purpose for which it has been organized. The work that I have to do for my God shall continue to be done.

But we must really take stock of where, as they say in today's language, our head really is. We must give more consideration to what type of thoughts we are entertaining as a group. An organization is composed of people. An organization has what is known as a predominate vibration. That predominate vibration may, at any moment, be negative or positive. The teaching of this philosophy is that peace is the power of God. And it is sad to witness when this philosophy is used, at times, by the very students of it to support and to sustain levels of consciousness known as fear. It is a sad day to witness. Because your philosophy teaches that peace is the power of God in no way implies that you are to lay down and be trampled upon and not stand for what you believe is your right, your right to worship God in the way that you choose to do.

It is very easy to say that you don't want to be bothered with the hassle, that you don't want to get yourself involved.

That's a very easy thing to say. But what does it, in truth, reveal? It reveals that there are personal priorities in front of your responsibility to what you have already involved yourself in. You cannot go into any organization—no matter what it is—and take from it without facing the personal responsibility of putting something back into it.

My good friends, we shall move on and the Light shall go out, yea, even more to the world. We must look at the good that has been accomplished, that *is* being accomplished, and we must face those feelings and attitudes inside of ourselves when we desire what we judge another has.

It should be interesting for you to note that the publicity was attracted by a physical demonstration, called a house. It was not attracted by the spiritual truths of which the house is an effect. And so we must look clearly to see not only where we are, but where we intend to go in our lives. Each and every time that this church makes a step forward, we always seem to lose a few members, ever in keeping with the very foundation of the church, which is, to grow or to go. And each time we lose a few, God brings us a few more. And the work continues on.

Some of you have stood up for your right, guaranteed by the constitution of the United States of America. You have stood up for your right of religious worship. Some of you have obviously decided, by your demonstration, not to bother with what you consider to be the hassle. I have spoken to some of you to do what you feel is right for you to do, for that's the type of church this really is. If you don't feel that it's right for you to stand up for what you believe, then this philosophy and this church respects your right to believe that way. But, by demonstration, you are not in accord with the majority of the organization or the principles upon which the organization is founded. Therefore you cannot reap the benefit, nor the harvest, that it has to offer you.

What seems to have disturbed most of the students is that the publicity received was not in keeping with their judgments. And so where do we go from this eternal moment, in which we have, by our own acceptance, the power of God? Through your efforts of prayer, through your true acceptance that there is something greater than your mind, peace shall reign supreme. I am well aware that it is my mind that desires that the publicity die, as it was born, for my mind says then peace shall reign. But that is not the peace that we should pray for. We must pray for peace and accept God's way. We must not permit our mind to dictate how peace shall come, for in so doing we establish, through our error of ignorance, mental, dual laws.

So you can do your part through your prayers for peace and you can do your part by standing up for what you believe is right. This philosophy has never taught to turn the other cheek: If someone hits you on one side, then turn the other to be hit again. What that teaching really means is far misunderstood. When that Nazarene spoke about turning the other cheek, he was speaking allegorically. He was clearly telling his students when you receive an adversity, do not react from the levels of your adversity, for two wrongs never made a right. To go inside in peace to ask for guidance and the light of reason that you may stand up on the rock of principle, for in the midst of the Philistines is when God delivers us.

Let us now view the positive and the good from these experiences. There is nothing in the world that unites a people greater than persecution and prosecution, for then they unite for the common good. And the great benefit to all of you, including myself, is that you have to take a stand with what you consider your friends and your acquaintances, for perhaps they never heard of Serenity or only heard what you had to tell them and now they have heard what others believe. This is a golden opportunity for you, a golden opportunity. For you will either stand on principle—what you believe is right—or you will sell out. It is never our soul that sells out. It's only our mind that sells out, for you cannot sell what you do not have. And it is only your mind that has. It's not your soul. And so there's the choice you have to make: to move from your mind into your soul and stand on your right or to remain in your mind and to sell out what you think that you have.

There is a vast difference between the mind and the soul. It is the mind that attaches to its own attitudes, to its own patterns, to its own thoughts. And it is the mind that offers you fear. It is your soul that offers you faith. And so in the midst of this golden opportunity, you have your friends, your acquaintances to face. Will you remain in your mind and sell out your soul? If you do, you will do it from fear, from a fear of losing what, in truth, you never had.

In the Christian Bible, when the Nazarene was asked who were his brothers and his sisters, he very clearly stated, "Those who follow me in the Light are my brothers, my sisters, my mothers, and my fathers." Those who follow the Light. And so you, my good students, are facing that choice. Some of you will face it very quickly. Some of you it will take months and years. But that decision between your mind, which is temporal, and your soul, which is eternal, you and you alone will have to make that decision.

I know to the mind, to any mind, it is not pleasing to be involved or associated with any movement that the majority consider not to be good or wholesome. You have to make those decisions yourself. You see, my friends, for over a hundred years the Spiritualists have spoken of the front door Spiritualists and the back door Spiritualists. And it brings to mind an experience at the church in the city that I was a member of many years ago when a lady who lived in an apartment house received a letter from the church with the name of the church stamped on the back of the envelope. And someone in that apartment building saw the name of that church and her persecution started. At a membership meeting one year, she said that if she was going to be a member of that church, then a regulation would have to be passed that no letters or any printed matter could be sent to her address listing the name of the church on it. Now, this church has come a long way since those days. I was at that membership meeting. After all, at that time I was the chairman of the public relations committee. It was the first time they had ever had a public relations committee and I happened to have been the one responsible for having envelopes printed with the name of the church on the back of the envelope. I wanted it on the front, but I wasn't allowed to do it at that time. So I, and the committee that I was chairman of, was responsible for sending out those letters and therefore I had much to say during that membership meeting well over ten years ago.

And it was indeed interesting to me, for the sign on that beautiful church deletes the name Spiritualist or Spiritualism. All of their stationary simply listed their address and never mentioned the word *Spiritualist*. But by a majority vote, I was out voted, because of fear, because of the fear of Spiritualists and what their friends would say. And in the founding of this church, I have made very sure to list the full name of the church, as your sign each Sunday morning clearly shows. For I know, and all of you know, if you have something to be ashamed about concerning your religion, then your religion is filled with holes and you're not in a religion for you that is wholesome, that is good, that is worth being involved in, let alone worth standing up for. That is not the kind of Spiritualist that I am and I have no intention of becoming that type of Spiritualist. But I do understand those Spiritualists who, by fear, are that way.

We look at history and we see that untold hundreds of thousands of people, millions to be exact, were persecuted for centuries because of their race. Many changed their name that, hopefully, they may be known as Christians, for they feared being known as Jews. But times have changed. And it is very clear to see the changing of those names is nowhere near as frequent as they used to be, for there is less fear for them today than there used to be.

If you have some type of martyr complex and you enjoy being persecuted and prosecuted, then all you have to do is to entertain fear, and the world will mow you under. But your philosophy shows you a way. It shows you how to take control of your mind. It shows you the thing you fear befalls you. And it clearly demonstrates that truth. In reference to the news media presenting our philosophy, until we ourselves merit them doing something different with our philosophy than they have already demonstrated—in reference to spirit communication, the very basis of the philosophy—then it is certainly not in our best interest.

It is not the numbers, nor quantity, that has brought this church to its present growth state. It is quality that did that. It's not a hundred people that built a beautiful home for your church. It's not even the total membership that did it, for it was far less than thirty-four people. Now, that's the real story of a house on the hill.

And if I have any members or friends of this Association—or students—who truly want to live where they think I live, I am more than happy to step down. All they need to do is to make that simple request and to demonstrate, by their thoughts, their acts, and their deeds the very laws necessary to put them in a house on a hill. For I am not attached, with God's help, to any physical substance or mental substance. For I know that it comes and I also know that, by that Law of Coming, that it shall go.

Now, let us think, my good students. Think of the wonderful opportunity that each of you has merited. Stop and think of this great opportunity to talk with your friends and relatives, when they open the door and they say, "You see, it's just the way I judged it to be." Either you can look them in the eye and pray for their soul to be freed from the errors of ignorance—to try to have compassion for their eternal soul that their minds are so quick to judge what they clearly demonstrate they have no interest in, for those who are interested in anything make the effort to investigate it before they make the judgment to condemn it.

Now, with God's help this philosophy, this light will go out. Not the way that our minds want to dictate it to go out, but may it go out God's way: in the spirit of peace and harmony to those who are seeking it. For unsolicited help is ever to no avail. And so I sincerely pray that each of you may continue with your experiences and the opportunities of speaking up, when you feel it's right to do so, that you may not hide in the closet and be fearful of the world, for fear only exists in your mind and your fear is ever in keeping with your judgments. If you, in your mind, judge that your friends are not going to be your friends anymore because they will not agree with you, having found out suddenly that you're a Spiritualist in the Serenity Church, then you are denying the very philosophy that you are making the effort to understand. For more than once it has been stated that true friendship, being use and not abuse, respects the rights of difference and will weather any storm.

I know that some of you are not strong enough to continue on with the growth of this philosophy and the growth of this organization. But I also know that what you have put in, you have received. I know that it is recorded in your memory par excellence. I know it will serve you well in years and centuries yet to come. And for that I am very grateful, for many souls come through these doors. Some stay for a while and then they face the crossroads of life. They face their crises and either their mind, in fear, becomes their master in those moments of crises or that humble servant, known as God, brings to them—the greatest servant of all brings them peace, happiness, and prosperity.

To entertain any thought is to direct God's energy to creating the form thereof. And so all experience reveals the thoughts we entertain. That's how we change experiences, by becoming aware of what we alone are doing. You may direct that God energy to good in your life or you may direct it to the opposite. You and your life are revealing what you're doing with that energy. This philosophy clearly shows you—and demonstrates—that it is ever your choice, that all of your experiences can serve good in your life, no matter what your mind may say. But in serving good in your life, you must make the effort to direct that energy to good, for everything returns to us.

Though these experiences of these past few weeks are most distasteful to certain levels of my mind, I see the good that is in process. For thirty-seven years of my life, with rare exception, have I stayed free from what you call publicity. But, you see, we all must face anything we judge to be distasteful. But if it was my personal choice of my mind, you may be rest assured the door would never have opened. But then, many souls would not have grown, for you have now the opportunity to stand face-to-face with your friends and your relatives, without emotion, in the spirit of peace and harmony and simply declare your right to worship God. As you grant those relatives and friends of yours their right to worship God, then you have the opportunity to help them to respect others. For if they are not respecting the rights of others, then they are clearly demonstrating a lack of respect for their own rights and, therefore, cannot have the peace and the good in their lives.

Some of you, I know, feel that you don't want to get involved in all this so-called hassle. But, my friends, by the Law of Association, you are already involved. Therefore you must make your choice. We cannot be involved in anything and say, "I'm involved with this part of it. The rest of it, I want nothing to do with." For that is not true involvement. That is looking for something for nothing. We want what it has to offer in a certain way, but we do not want to pay for what we want to take. Now, friends, I'm not speaking of what some of you are thinking—a green piece of paper. I am speaking about character, for you are a part of a unit—a unit of a whole. And that whole has a character. Your church has worked very hard to establish a reputation in this community. You are a part of that reputation whether you like it or not. That's the demonstrable truth.

Now, your church grants unto its people as much freedom as is possible in order to sustain and maintain a semblance of organization. Some think the discipline is a bit strict and some think the work is too much. But I ask you, If the discipline is too strict and the work is too much, then who is going to keep it all together?

You should be grateful. Your heart should be filled with gratitude that such a small group of people could accomplish so much in such a short time. But having accomplished it does not free us from the responsibility to sustain it. Now let us think about that. We must face our responsibilities. Whether we agree with our responsibilities or not is really immaterial. We are the ones who have incurred the responsibilities and therefore we are responsible for them. Let us face them in a spirit of joy and let us face them like adults. Let us look at the world and stand firm on principle. And let those who we think are friends express their right. But let us not, in that very process, deny ourselves our own rights. For if we do, we have far to grow spiritually.

Any organization or person that works to bring any good to the world that is not in keeping with the established patterns of the world at the time must face the adversities that come their way. I do sincerely hope that you, as students of Serenity, will face those adversities the way they really are and never forget that you are greater than them if you choose to be.

Spiritualism has come a long way since 1848. It's come a long way since it was incorporated in 1893. But it's still got a long way to go, a long way to go. Today, we send out our magazine. We send letters to our members and supporters. We are not ashamed of our organization, for if we are, we're in the wrong church, my friends. We must face that honestly. If there is anything in this church that you are ashamed of, then you are in error for not bringing it to the attention of the only authority of the church. So if there is nothing in this church that you are ashamed of, then you cannot be ashamed when you speak to your friends, if they open the door, concerning your church. For if you are ashamed, then it is a sad day indeed. For I can assure you, I would not associate myself in any way with any church that I felt ashamed of. I am not ashamed of this church. I do not often agree with the authority that runs it, but I made my agreement in its founding and I will stick to that principle regardless.

I would much prefer to assess the membership of this church on an annual basis, based upon their income, rather than personally listen to the constant cry of lack and limitation. And I am sure that you, as members, if you were in my position, would personally choose a fair share assessment based upon your income. But then that would deprive you of facing that level within you as frequently as you must face it. And when we do not face a level frequently, then we do not place the light of reason upon it and we cannot grow through it. You cannot change what you never face or rarely face. Attitudes of mind have received much energy. They are not born overnight. Fear did not rise within our minds from some dream we had the night before. It's energy that we have directed to the authority of our mind.

Now, we all know the way. So let us encourage ourselves. Let us encourage ourselves and get the work of this church done, for this is a working church. Even the news media had to agree with that. We are not under the trees laying around experiencing

God, because if we can't experience God in our work, then don't think it's God you are experiencing under the tree. If you judge the only place you can get God is in the woods, then that's the kind of God you have: the one who serves your judgments. But this church is trying to show you a God that will lift your soul to heavenly heights while you are yet in earthly flesh, not a God that you have to wait until you get to some other dimension in realms of glory. My friends, if there's any glory, it's the glory of work, for the glory of work is clearly demonstrated as love made manifest.

So often I see so much hard work done by some minds to keep out of work. They run around in total fascination, which utilizes a great deal of energy, rather than do the simple job that they're asked to do.

You know, I am aware of the people who have come and the people who have gone. I'm also aware of how they think. They've certainly made it very clear by their spoken word. And usually, as some of you know, they say, "Well, the philosophy is beautiful. There is nothing like it. And that Richard Goodwin, as a person, he's very nice. But the organization itself—I cannot go along with." And so they leave. Now, in that type of thinking we must ask the question, "Is the organization an effect of the philosophy?" And we have to agree, of course, it is. So how can we go along with the philosophy and be against the organization? For one is the effect of the other. But I assure you, my friends, when those statements come, it's always from a level of the functions being clearly demonstrated. And we all know what the functions are. They're known in this philosophy as *m-e-s*. And it's the first of those functions, called money, that seems to create, in our head, all of our problems.

You see, this organization is designed to help you to face those so-called money tapes as frequently as possible. There is no law and no regulation that says you have to give so much, but you are given the opportunity, for you, your soul, knows what you can do and your soul also knows what you should do. Now, that's where the problem really lies. We all know how much we think we have and we all know what we think we want to do with it. And so when we're given the opportunity to replace a tea towel at the house because we, as members and students, have destroyed them, we don't like facing that level. And it's always interesting to me, whenever that happens—as it did last week—nobody seems to know how come all those wet tea towels got thrown into a basket and got mildewed. No one seems to know. And you all—most of you—contributed and spent $30 for a rack upon which the tea towels can be dried. So these are the levels that seem to upset us. Like little children, we get caught with our transgressions and we don't appreciate it.

I spend much of my time trying to help students to see the light of reason and make some changes with their attitudes of mind. Those attitudes, they don't appreciate the light of reason, for those levels have been used to leaving lights on, those levels have been used to leaving doors and windows open while the heat is on. And it's part of my job to correct those levels. But instead of my students being grateful for that effort being made, they seem to be upset. Yet I am instrumental in helping you, as individuals, to stop throwing away your money. If you have to pay $200 for utilities rather than $125, that means you have to pour in an extra $75. So I ask you, Where is the gratitude? When you take tea towels and you throw them—wet—into a basket so they can mildew and then you have to dig in your pockets to replace them because you are the ones who destroyed them, why do you get upset? And everyone says, "I can't imagine who would do such a thing!" There is no spirit that I am associated with that materializes and pulls them off the rack wet and throws them in the basket! No, only those spirits who are yet in physical form are doing those type of things. There are no poltergeist at Serenity house, thank God. Only the ones who are yet in clay.

So friends, let's think about all these things. Let us make the effort to pray for peace and perhaps this divine power, with God's help, will descend over Serenity and greater good, much greater than our minds can imagine, we shall live on Earth to experience.

Thank you.

MARCH 9, 1978

CONSCIOUSNESS CLASS 174

Greetings, students.

This evening, as we near the completion of this semester, I have a few questions that I should like to ask you, as students. And so I shall begin with the group on my right. If you will kindly—each student—rise, I should like to speak to each of you individually.

[*A student rises and speaks her name.*]

In what way are you applying the philosophy that you are studying and are you so doing daily?

I can't say honestly that I'm applying it in, in the way that I would hope to in the future—wholly. I meditate daily, as of late. I do attempt to say my affirmations daily. And sometimes I, sometimes I slip. And I attempt to become aware of my thoughts more frequently than I have in the past.

Do you believe that there has been changes for the better brought about in your life through whatever effort you have made to apply the philosophy that you are studying?

Most definitely. There have been changes in my mind.

Thank you very much.

[*Another student rises and speaks her name.*]

Do you believe that the philosophy that you are studying can bring about, through your own efforts, a transformation in your life for the better?

Yes.

Would you be so kind as to give examples of that?

The personal responsibility law, I have found that I've had experiences where I absolutely know that I am responsible for setting laws into motion. And I know that it's my judgments that are my obstructions.

Then you are aware, through your efforts, that changes for the better are dependent upon your own personal attitudes of mind?

Yes.

Thank you very much.

[*A student rises and speaks her name.*]

Do you feel that your effort in studying and applying this philosophy has brought fuller and more abundant experiences into your life?

Most definitely.

Would you kindly give an example?

Well, I used to be very lonely. And I'm not lonely at all anymore. I find—I listen to the tapes on the way to work every single day. And I find the most difficult parts of work, in the past, have—I've grown through many of them. I'm still working with something this week, as a matter of fact, that I feel real better about today. But as I apply what we're—it's as if each week I was being taught my own next step. And as I apply it, I seem to grow through certain areas of the problem with certain office jobs and procedures. And I feel much better about it.

To what effort on your part do you credit the absence of loneliness?

The awareness that I'm not alone at all. The spirit is all around me. And God is there. And I just don't feel it any more.

Thank you very much.

[Another student rises and speaks her name.]

Do you, in your study and your efforts in this philosophy, believe that your life has and is making a change for you for the better?

Yes, I do.

Kindly give some examples.

I feel that I've had a great deal more peace in my life since I've come to Serenity. Serenity has also helped my . . . And I feel that it has helped me in some difficulties and situations where I don't feel that I've mastered . . .

In what way do you feel you have gained more peace in your life?

Well, as I say affirmations and think upon peace, I have felt that I have gained more and I can, in turn, help others.

Thank you very much.

[Another student rises and speaks her name.]

Do you believe that you have expanded your conscious awareness of the world around and about you and, if so, to what do you credit that change?

I certainly do feel that it has expanded. And it has been through the understanding of this philosophy, through understanding where judgments lead, of trying to apply greater acceptance of the divine right of others' expression, and just developing more tolerance for others.

Do you believe that you are more free today than the recent past in reference to judgments and your awareness of them?

Definitely. Definitely, I'm much more aware. Even though I may make a judgment, I do become more quickly aware that I have made it and it helps me the next time that I stop to make a judgment.

Thank you.

Thank you.

[*A student rises and speaks her name.*]

Do you believe that your understanding has expanded, that your faculty of reason has awakened in keeping with your efforts in applying what you have learned in these classes?

My understanding has expanded. My reasoning sometimes, due to my judgments, is still cloudy, because I do make judgments, which means I have no tolerance and patience. But, becoming aware of them, I can understand myself better today and the people around me than I could before I came to Serenity. And that they have a right to express themselves, as well as I do.

Thank you very much.

[*Another student rises and speaks his name.*]

Do you believe that more effort is made on your part today to trace the cause of all experiences to an attitude of mind that you alone have entertained?

Yes, sir.

To what do you attribute that awareness?

Well, if I may go back a few years and relate to the experiences that I had prior to coming to Serenity, before it was either just judgment on my part—and going back in my life, the faculty of care was completely, totally out of the picture at that particular time. But since coming to Serenity, I'm aware of something greater than just my mind, that the faculty of care has been rising. And I have been getting every necessary experience to face that particular level. And I know that it's just a direction of energy to something greater that will transform our lives.

Thank you.

[*A student rises and speaks her name.*]

In your efforts to understand the philosophy that you have been studying, do you believe that your efforts are daily? Do you believe that your sincere desire to be freed from experiences that you desire to change is taking place through an application of what you are studying?

I feel that there is effort being made, through the understanding of the philosophy. And I feel that when I pray for peace, I'm aware of the conflict within. There are some changes made. And I feel that the changes are being made pretty slowly.

Do you feel that your efforts are slow or quick?

I feel they're slow.

Then, you are able to see that the experience would, of course, be of like kind?

Right. But then, I'm responsible for the experience.

And so slow effort breeds slow results.

Right.

Thank you.

[*Another student rises and speaks her name.*]

Have you, in your efforts and in your study and application of what you are studying—do you believe that your life is growing and expanding in a positive and beneficial way?

Yes, it most certainly is.

Kindly give an example.

Primarily, I feel the most valuable thing is the understanding of the separation of truth from creation. This has helped me a great deal in understanding my own mind and understanding experiences that I draw forth. More specifically, if you like, this is in every area from my health, to my job, to my personal relationships with people.

Thank you.

[*A student rises and speaks his name.*]

In your efforts to understand what you are studying, have you at any time accepted beyond a shadow of any doubt that all experiences that you encounter are an effect of causes within you, that through effort on your part you may trace directly to a level of consciousness within you?

Yes, I have.

Example, please.

Well, it's generally when things are pointed out to me. I haven't been too successful doing it myself, but when it is traced back through the various steps, and I think about it for a couple of days, I can see what level I was on at that time and what it does breed.

Thank you.

Thank you.

[*A student rises and speaks his name.*]

In what way, if any, do you believe your application of this philosophy has benefited your life?

The most dramatic benefit has been the improvement of my health.

Kindly give the example.

I'm a much happier person. I try to speak forth gratitude, if only to myself, constantly. And as a result, this is probably the best springtime I've ever had.

Thank you.

My good students, we shall try, in the short time left to us in this semester, to speak with all of you. But as I have sat here listening to your testimony—for I've never been particularly fond of the word *testimonials*. There's a vast difference in presenting testimony and evidence, to testimonials. But as I sit here and listen to this evidence and testimony, you must understand that it takes me back untold centuries to a different time and a different era, to when I sat at a bench in a much different way than I do here today.

But it is important to you, as students, to bring into your conscious mind the awareness of what effort is being made by you, that you may gain, hopefully, a brighter light of reason of what can be done. To place your attention and your energy upon that which is growing and constructive for your greater good—as the last student stated, expressing their gratitude daily, if only to themselves. But you must understand that the expressing of gratitude, the opening up of that soul faculty, attracts unto the one making the effort all equal and like vibrations in the universes.

And it is so very important not only to become aware of what your thoughts are, but to make, and to continue to make, the effort to control any thought that does not bring into your life a feeling of goodness. For any thought that does not bring that feeling of goodness with it is not God ordained, for God, the neutral divine energy, is what we know as good.

In these several years of speaking with you, indeed have I spent much time in sharing with you our understanding of the human mind. Everything necessary to take you through your earthly journey and the many realms that still await you has indeed already been given. There is much more yet to be said. There is much more yet to be given, for the fountain of Living Light is endless. There is never a drought to the living waters of truth. But unless you, as students, make the effort daily to encourage yourselves, you cannot attract from the universe vibratory waves to support encouragement.

We must all be courageous, for we are designed by the great Architect to be so. To stand firm on your beliefs on the rock of principle, to be firm, but not tenacious, for all things evolve in life. And you, each of you, and I, are evolving. To be awakened by the small humble effort of a daily prayer, to be awakened to a world much broader than, yea, your minds have yet imagined, to face with a joyous heart the responsibilities in your life, not to push them aside that they may rise another day in another way ever calling you backwards—face all of them today that you may be free to go on to brighter horizons, to fuller lives, to greater good, to greater abundance.

The mind, a dual instrument, is in a constant process of broadcasting a message to you. You must take hold of that broadcasting station and choose—and be firm in your choice of—what you will permit it to broadcast into the ethereal waves, for that is where you should stand guardian each and every moment. To he who broadcasts abundance and who uses the soul faculty of patience and reason to sustain the broadcast, abundance shall manifest in his life. But when you permit the mind to broadcast the message of abundance, remember abundance is a principle. Put it in the hands of divine guidance that you not experience an abundance of what you desire not to experience.

And so, my good students, all of life, in your world and mine, is the effect of the release of energy on one of these many levels of consciousness. It is our purpose to help you to help yourselves to grow through these levels by accepting their divine right of existence and by identifying with something greater. Learn and apply the divine Law of Acceptance and the divine right of identification. Accept the rights of all things and all levels of consciousness, for they are within you. Express your divine right to identify with those of your choice of reason.

We cannot, in sharing with you this ancient philosophy, take control of your minds and do it for you. But we show you, again and again, how you can declare and apply your birthright. I know that in some ways you are doing that. And those little steps that you are making are important ones for you. I wish but to encourage you to make a little more daily effort that the frequency may increase, that the Law of Continuity may strengthen you through the unity in your own consciousness.

The experiences of the moment are passing as you accept their right of existence and identify with something greater. The mind, when it experiences, makes the judgment and sends the vibratory wave outside of itself for the blame. And so the wheel of illusion continues to revolve. Take hold of that wheel by accepting that you are, in truth, the captain, that you alone can change the experience by granting its right of existence and identifying with something that is greater than it.

Because experience is a created form in mental substance and has the intelligence of its creator, it returns as a child, or an adult, and it knocks at the door of your consciousness and it asks to enter. If you permit your mind to tell the experience that its home is elsewhere, by blaming another for your experience in life, then what you do, in truth, is send that intelligent form, that you alone have created, out into the universe to wander. And so it wanders out into the universe and it gathers up substance of like kind and it returns unto you and knocks on the door of your consciousness louder. And it shall continue to return until you accept the simple truth that you gave it birth. And because you gave it birth, by acceptance of the birth that you gave it, it can die. For it was born and all birth, in truth, is death.

We have told you this simple truth in a multitude of ways. Perhaps, in telling you once again this truth and in this way, a level within you will be able to accept it. And in so doing you shall be able, by application of that truth, to be freed from these multitude of experiences that you do not seem to enjoy. The divine Law of Acceptance and the divine Law of Choice—identification. When we stated to you to be in the world and not a part of the world, to be with a thing and not a part of the thing, we gave to you the same law.

Stop fighting the children you have created. Start accepting the truth that you alone have created them. To say that you accept that truth and then to place blame outside of your own sphere (to another) is to deny the truth you claim to accept.

The changes in your life shall take place, and are taking place, in keeping with your acceptance and your personal responsibility. You have learned many things in these past few years and there is much yet to learn. But the changes in your life are taking place. You are evolving and you will continue to do so.

The faculties are opening. Though we stumble many times, there is something within us that always picks us up. And so remember—for all minds remember what they choose to remember—remember the good in your life. For to entertain your mind with thoughts of the bad is to create a continuous wheel of experiences that your mind may prove that it is right. But your mind, as you know, is many levels of consciousness. Let reason flood over these levels of mind that balance may be brought into your life. Balance in life is a triune expression, for you are body, mind, and soul. You are soul with a dual covering, called mind and body. You must separate those coverings from who you really are.

You have attracted unto you, as students, students from the classes on our side of life. They work to help you, as you, in truth, are helping them. For each time you stumble, they work to pick you up. They are on levels of consciousness in keeping with your soul aspiration and your own efforts. So let them find you not wanting in effort.

Throughout the multitude of experiences in life, the soul ever works to rise supreme, for that *is* the soul's divine right. To be supreme over the forms of its creation, for creation is ever in a process of return.

Before you lies dimensions unlimited. They are here and now. Open your eyes through the faculty of effort, directing God energy, this Divine energy, to the faculty of reason. Reason brings a light and rises up opposing creation to a perfect balance. Your life, when you experience harmony, health, and wealth and the abundance of what is, in divine right, yours, reveals that you are making some effort to bring balance or reason into your life. I know that some of you—that all of you are making some effort, that some of you are making greater effort. But let us remember, friends, the greater the need, the greater the effort. And when you find yourselves at the bottom of what you call the barrel of life, be grateful, for there is no bottom without a top. And if you are truly at the bottom, then you are, beyond a shadow of any doubt, on the way up.

If your mind says it's not quick enough, then it simply reveals that wisdom is not being expressed, for patience is not being demonstrated.

You did not get where you are in the blinking of an eye. And you will not move on to what you desire in the blinking of a eye. It takes time to get to the bottom and it also takes time to get to the top. But there is something, my good students, much greater than the top and the bottom. There is that which holds them apart and makes them top and bottom. There is that that is indispensable for this Law of Duality or creation to exist at all. That is the something that you are moving towards. Called, in this philosophy, the Divine Neutrality, that is where your home is. That's the home of your soul. That is where your soul is ever working to return to. Beyond the day and beyond the night, beyond the bottom and beyond the top, beyond the north and beyond the south, beyond the east and beyond the west, your soul is wandering, wandering homeward. Not after you leave your physical body, but now in this moment.

And when you flood your consciousness with the power of God, known in this philosophy as peace, your soul goes home. Then you experience this greatness, this simple truth. There you are free from all concern, for you are free from all thought. You are home. That, my students, is the place to be. Separated from your vehicle, yet using your vehicle. No longer identifying with the vehicles that you use, using them by the light of reason, you are with them and never again a part of them. You are in the worlds and not of the worlds, for that is all form. You are no longer tempted. You are no longer trapped. The mountaintop to which you go is the mountaintop of reason. That *is* your home.

Practice what has been given [to] you. Practice that you may demonstrate unto yourself the Law of Disassociation. Then, in your home of homes, you will look out at all creation.

You will see it from all sides and be blinded by none. No greater experience can you ever have than the awareness of the home of your soul.

Good night.

MARCH 16, 1978

CONSCIOUSNESS CLASS 175

Good evening, students. As we all know this is the last class of this semester. We will have a semester break and we will renew our classes in May—yes, the first Thursday evening of the month of May.

Now, so appropriate is this the last class, in reference to the philosophy you have been studying, in reference to the experiences your church is growing through. And so I want to take some time here and talk with you about these experiences—what they can mean to you, if you permit them to, and your wonderful opportunity, through prayer and meditation—you may turn your chairs, if you wish—through prayer and meditation, to rise above and beyond the mental realms of fear and demonstrate your faith in something that's greater than what this old mind of ours has to offer.

I spent, today, two and a half hours with an investigator contracted by Channel 2, the Cox Broadcasting company. When I was contacted by Channel 2, in reference to would I give another interview, I said yes, at the request of the Spirit Council, because your church had sent a letter to Channel 2 in reference to their inaccurate statements on the broadcast on Serenity Church. To refuse to give that second interview would deny us of the opportunity to speak up the truth as we know truth, which, I'm sure we all agree, in keeping with our own philosophy that we are studying, is individually perceived.

I want you all to be aware, as members, students, and supporters of this church, that the investigation underway is not a surface investigation of the Serenity Church. It is an in depth investigation in order that the television channel may get at what they call the facts. Mr. Jim Clancy is a professional investigator, hired by various television channels. And so he has been hired by Channel 2 on the Serenity investigation. Many of you will be contacted by this investigator. You have the opportunity to deny an interview to him or to accept it. That, in keeping with the philosophy of this church, is your divine right.

Whenever a person faces an investigation, usually the mind rises up with its fears—"Oh God, what skeletons might I have in my closet?" I do not have that fear. Not that I think that I am so saintly that someone could not find skeletons, if that's what they're looking for, but I do not have fear of skeletons because I know there is no one on this Earth planet that is perfect, let alone saintly.

I can assure you from today's experiences that Mr. Clancy is not only well qualified for the job he has been hired to do, but he will dig very, very deep. One of the most interesting things to me today, in the interview, was the questions in reference to my selling spiritual favors. Now the Catholic Church was accused of that by Martin Luther and you had the birth of Protestantism. Well, I asked for a clarification on that type of questioning. We have it recorded for our own use, of course, if any of you wish to hear it. And it seems that some people, for some unknown reason, believe that they will be given great spirits by me, somehow, to help them get what they want in life, if they give enough money. I found it not only interesting, but, to be perfectly honest with you, I found it very humorous.

And so we had much discussion on this philosophy and we had discussion on this, which he called "revelation." Now it seems that this investigator, who had already talked to many people before he came to me today, had been informed by many people that, why, I could just look into their house and tell them where the furniture was, what was on the wall, if they got a letter last week, who it was from, and what it was all about.

But the spirits that I am in contact with, and have been for all these years, are interested in bringing to you a philosophy that cannot only be demonstrated but, through your application, can bring about goodness in your life. That philosophy that is being brought to you does not have a price tag on it, because the gold that this Earth has to offer is not sufficient to purchase it.

And when you are contacted, some of you, by this investigator, you alone, and hopefully with prayer and meditation, must ask yourself the question whether or not you, as a human being, wish to involve yourself with the church that you are attending with the philosophy that you are receiving. Neither I, nor the Council of this church expects from you that you have to do anything. But should you decide to grant an interview to this person, I hope it may be in my divine merit system that you will be representatives of a philosophy that is not only demonstrable, but one that works.

I honestly do not know of anyone who could truly believe, in these many years of my life to bring this, this teaching to Earth—I do not know of anyone that could believe in their heart that I sell what some people call favors. For in the midst of my financial struggles, tempted by the human mind, as all people that have a mind are tempted, never once did I sell, in any way, shape, or form, anything such as spiritual favors to anyone. I have tried these many years to treat each soul in keeping with the law demonstrated. And by that I mean their efforts spiritually to try to free themselves from the entrapments of judgments of their own mind, regardless whether they gave this church $1,000 or they gave this church $5.

For many years, as many of you will recall, and we still do keep the tuition of this class as low as possible and still keep the organization together. You all know that we are faced with a $1,400 tax to the county before April the 9th, because we can't wait until the last gun is fired. I have great faith and I know beyond a shadow of any doubt that God, not man, is the source of my supply. But I am only one member. I am only one student of this church. You must know and have that faith in God, for the debt incurred is not mine alone. It is the debt of all of us, for our church belongs to all of us. I do not permit my mind to dictate through which channel or person that this shall flow. I know that it is already on its way and therefore I am not concerned in that respect. I try to do my part to speak it forth into the universe, knowing that it shall not come back to me void, but manifest that whichever is in keeping with the law that we alone demonstrate.

So, my good students, in this the final class of this semester, we all have indeed very much to consider.

When I was informed that it was time to get a lot and build your house—for it is the church house—I had my own mixed feelings. Because I know for every step ahead, for every attainment in life, there is a payment. And the mind so often gets bogged down with looking at the payments in life that it loses the beauty of life. And I didn't want to get myself in that kind of a position. But I listened to the spirit and I went ahead. And I will still go ahead.

I have assured you before that your church and my church, it will carry on. The experiences that we are having have a great essence of good in them. And as my mind thought the other day, "Well, how many churches merit front page headlines? How many churches' homes get placed on the six o'clock news and the ten o'clock news?" And so my mind thought, "Well, good or bad is what the mind judges, but out of every knock shall come a great boost."

And when Mr. Clancy finished his interview with me today, he said, "Mr. Goodwin all that flak you got from Channel 2, on your other interview, is going to do you a lot of good." And I said, "Well, I do believe, Mr. Clancy, that every knock is a boost." And then, of course, as he was leaving, he said, "You know, you're not really the ogre that everyone says that you are." And I immediately said, "I hope not." I honestly didn't know what the word meant. Fortunately, the directors were there and they said it means something about a mean man. Well, I went to look it up in the dictionary—we have a fine dictionary, given to me many years ago—and I couldn't find it: *o-g-e-r*. I couldn't find it. So I called the Civic Center library and I asked the girl if she knew how to spell it. And she said, "Well, I think it's *o-g-e-r*." And I said, "No, no," I said, "I have a big dictionary here and it's not that." And then I heard a little voice say, "Why don't you look farther and look for *o-g-r-e*." And while I was on the phone, I saw it, I thanked her and hung up. And I am glad I did, because when I read it, I wasn't too happy. The dictionary says, "a hideous monster." It's a Hungarian word, I guess. It says, "Hungarian; a hideous monster who lives off human beings; a king of terror; a cruel and mean man." And I thought, "Now, I don't recall ever being a terrorist." I didn't think I was really cruel, let alone mean. But then, of course, we all must have a fair image of our self or we would blow our brains out!

And then I began to think. When we fear, we create, by fear, these monsters in our own heads. And we can only be responsible for our own thoughts, our own acts, and our own deeds. And I guess that there are many people, not understanding spiritual communication or mediumship, who possibly, I am sure, entertain these great fears. And so each of us, we have our responsibilities. We know—all of us know what is right for us and all of us know what is wrong for us. And that's very individual to each and every person.

I spoke to our national president, Reverend Merrill, after the interview and he said to me that he had received much correspondence from California. And he said, "You know, Richard, one of the, it seems, biggest claims against you is that you have hypnotized your members and students and friends of your church. And that they are so hypnotized that they give you all of their money and everything." And I said, "Well, Mr. Merrill, if you could only come out and spend a few days with the potent, strong, independent egos that I have merited as members and students, you would never ever think that those people could be hypnotized by anyone." [*The students laugh.*] I am grateful I have merited strong egos. It's a reflection of my own and I never claimed to have a weak one, because if you're going to be successful in life, you have to be willing to pay whatever payments there are to be paid. And that's very individual to each person.

I never thought in my life of being successful in anything. I did think, "Well, if I have to do this mediumship work, I hope that I can do a good job." I don't like to do halfway jobs, no matter whatever it is I'm involved in. And those of you who have been around for a while, around the office, are well aware: if I get involved in something I pour all the energy I possibly can into it to its completion. It doesn't matter what the project may be.

It seems the difficulty with the news media is that they calculated the cost of God's home—they divided it by thirty-four members and came up with the amount of money that each member would have given, which would have been untold thousands of dollars. What they didn't consider, as I said to them today, was a $135,000 mortgage, was camp lands that we had sold, and the hundreds of supporters of the church. So we see clearly that these judgments of the mind are caused by errors of ignorance.

When Mr. Clancy said today that I spoke in trance in a feminine voice, the secretary of the church was rather upset. I told him honestly I didn't know whether I did or I didn't, because I was not aware. But anyway, he asked for a tape. But he was very specific: he wanted the forecast tape. I asked him if he would like a class tape, but he wasn't interested in that, he said. No, he wanted the forecast tape of last year, which is fine.

Now, what does all of these experiences have to do with our levels of consciousness? We must relate the outward manifestations in our lives to the inner attitudes that we entertain. I believe beyond a shadow of any doubt this philosophy. I believe that life is ever as great as we choose to make it. I believe that there is no moment in our experience that we cannot choose for it to be good. I so firmly believe that—I should. I spent untold thousands of hours in my life flooding my consciousness with that truth.

I will never forget when I started flooding my consciousness with that truth. When my earthly teacher, Mrs. Becker—Reverend Florence Becker, who has passed on. When I was at the bottom of the financial pit and I was living for months in the freezing cold in Woodacre—and if any of you know the San Geronimo Valley, it snowed that year. And you can imagine how cold it is in Woodacre. It's the coldest spot in Marin County. And I was taking those ice cold showers. And the only thing that I had hot was a cup of coffee. I was eating potatoes for my breakfast, lunch, and dinner and giving the peelings to my dog, because that's all that I had at the time because I had my lessons that I had set into motion.

And Reverend Florence Becker, one day she called me and said, "How are you doing, Richard?" And I said, "Terrible!" And I was in a terrible mood, number one: I was wrapped up in a blanket in my chair because it was so cold. You could see your breath in the house. And I had to get up out of the chair, walk over, and pick up the phone and my arm almost froze when I got out from under the blanket. So I was not feeling very good. And she said, "Well, Richard, *dear*, you're getting just what you merited." And she hung up. Of course, she was aware I had a little temper.

But that temper served me very well. I was furious. Of course, first, I blamed her. "How dare she say such a thing, when I was doing everything I could to get through this mess that I had gotten myself into!" But, of course, when you're in these messes and these ruts, you know, it's always some circumstance out there. The first thing that the mind entertains is because of so-and-so and so-and-so and so-and-so and because of such and such, well, you're financially broke. Well, that was the first thing that happened. And after spending about a minute and a half on that delusion, I got mad because I was entertaining that delusion and not facing personal responsibility. Then I got mad enough that I made some changes in consciousness.

Now you must understand, friends, that that took place before this book [*The Living Light*] was published, that took place before all of these discourses came—I only had the few from 1964—that took place before the Serenity Spiritualist Camp Association was founded [August 20, 1968]. Because it was founded after I moved out of that big, gigantic house that I was freezing to death in and into a little one-room apartment in Forest Knolls. And slowly, but surely—and I still say that temper can serve a good purpose. If it serves to help you to change a level of consciousness and get out of any rut you have dug yourself into, then it can serve a very good purpose, because that's the good purpose that it served for me. And I don't know of many people—and I don't mean to be egotistical—that are equal to my temper. I don't think that you people present have seen it expressed very much, but it used to be very great. In fact, the very first message I ever got, years ago at the Golden Gate Church from Reverend Becker in a billet, was, "You must learn to control your temper, your mother says." Well, that was her daily message to me. So it's understandable it would be the first thing that she would say to me when she came back.

But what I'm trying to show you, friends, no matter what experience your mind is entertaining, you can change it. And if you have to use your temper inside yourself to change it, then you use your temper and change it. Because all of these experiences that the mental world has to offer, it's only an effect, you see. The news media, the newspaper, the taxes, and all these things, they are an effect. They're not causes. So all of your experiences in life, they're only effects. They're effects of your mind. That's all that they are. They are no more, and they are no less.

Now, you can choose to ride through them, hopefully, graciously, with dignity and character, or you can choose the delusion that it's someone else's fault: that if only someone else would change, you would be fine and everything would be beautiful; that if somebody else would do what you have judged is what is necessary for them to do, so you can be happy, so you can have your desires fulfilled. That's the great delusion of the mind. That's not where it is. So use whatever is necessary, for the method is legal, if the motive is pure. Use the tools of this mind, whichever one you find will work for you, to get out of the rut that you judge, perhaps, that you might be in. Because you can get out. And if it takes temper to do it, then use it; don't abuse it. If you have tried prayer and you have judged that prayer doesn't work, you're not a lost soul. There are no lost souls in God's universe, for God's eye is on all of them. So use what will work for you to move you in consciousness that your experiences, that you desire to be changed, will change. For that that works, just works.

And I know what works for me. I know with the stubborn level of consciousness as I had in Woodacre and I know with my mind that took me down to the gutter, it took the use of that mind to establish new experiences. And then I started, really started to learn about the benefit, the real benefit, of prayer. Because, you see, if I really had known the great benefit of prayer at that time—because I was praying. Oh, I was praying all the time. But nothing seemed to change, you see? I kept on praying and praying and praying and praying. But, you see, what you must realize—we all can pray until hell freezes over, but that prayer is only as effective as the changes which are necessary in consciousness that are obstructing this flow of energy. We have to learn, one way or another, in life to get, as Emerson said, our "bloated nothingness," referring to the human ego, out of the way.

Now, we're all here—my students. I've merited very strong individuals and very potent egos. And I am trying to show you how you can use that instrument to bring about some changes in those planes of consciousness. If you don't like where you live, move. If you do like where you live, stay. If you don't like the job you're doing, change it. If you do like the job you're doing, try to do better at it. I mean that's really, my good friends, that is where it is. It's in your hands and it's always—forever and ever—up to you.

God, of course, the energy, the intelligence, works through us. The obstructions to this Divine Intelligence and goodness is something our minds alone have created. The church didn't create it. The philosophy didn't create it. The wives and husbands and brothers and sisters and girlfriends and boyfriends and all those, they didn't create it. And because our mind created it, our mind can change it. We can change our direction at any moment that we choose to do so. Like the investigator said today, "Well, what happens if they repossess this house?" And I said, "God forbid." Now, that is one thing I don't see—I can assure you of that—not as long as I am able to work. And I try to do my work seven days a week. Because I don't believe in retirement. That's when we start to dig that hole in the ground. We all need something to do! Because if we aren't doing something, then that energy is getting expressed with all these uncontrollable thoughts, and life, sooner or later, it seems not to be worth living at all.

But, my friends, remember, if you ever get tired of living, just remember, no matter what you think and no matter what you do, you'll never stop living. If you think you're tired of living, then all you have to do is say, "I'm tired of living the way I think I'm living. Therefore, it's my thinking that's got to be transformed. Let those thoughts that tell me life isn't worth living, let them die. I gave them birth. Then let me give them death. Because I am not greater than God, I cannot, I *cannot* die. I can change my thoughts. That is the only thing that will change my life." Whether we like it or not.

You may take off your coat (your physical body), but you cannot get rid of your mental body. You can only change your mental body through your own efforts. For, you see, my friends, your soul has identified with what you call your mental body; that is, by the Law of Identification, you. The effect of that mental body is what you call your physical body. You may remove the effect by an act against the physical body (by the mental body), but you cannot remove the mental body, where your thoughts live. You cannot remove that. Your mental body, a shell, like your earth body, will return to the elements of its creation. Your mental body can help the physical body to return as quickly as you choose, in the sense that you can free your mental body from your physical effect. But without a spiritual body, you cannot move your soul from the mental shell. You can move your mental body from the physical shell because your mental body is created. But you cannot move your soul from your mental body until your spiritual body is garnered up or created.

So they say that this philosophy—sometimes my students say—is a bit tough. And I assure you, for certain patterns of our minds, it's very tough. But I do want you to understand how these bodies return to their elements. When the body of finer vibrations is fully created, they return to their elements from which they were created by natural law.

And so in this philosophy and in these classes, you are given the soul faculties. You are taught to bring those faculties into balance with the sense functions, the functions of the mental body. It is when you, by directing energy or expressing through the soul faculties, that this spiritual essence is garnered up and begins to form your spiritual body. It is one of the very basic purposes of these classes: to show you, by demonstration and by your own application, how this spiritual body, by your expression through the faculties, is garnered up.

You see, my students, you cannot view a spiritual world unless you have spiritual sight. And you cannot have spiritual sight unless you have the spiritual eyes to see. You cannot express in a spiritual world, you cannot speak in a spiritual world, you cannot hear in a spiritual world unless that part of your anatomy has been garnered up.

I was asked today, in fact, I was *told* today, is a better way of putting it, that a person who has revelations, such as myself—although my mother wasn't particularly fond of that word and tried to clarify it several times—a person that has revelations, they said, such as myself, is therefore a spiritually illumined person. And I told the investigator that is absolutely no guarantee of spiritual illumination, because you may be able to see and hear in another dimension. After all, there is the astral world. We're very close to it. And we all have an astral body. There is the mental world and we are very, very deeply involved in that. We hear and see very clearly in that world. And then there is the spiritual world. So a person that is able to see someone's past or see what they call psychic, that, in and of itself, is absolutely no guarantee whatsoever that that person is spiritually illumined. You must look at the trees of life by the fruit that they bear.

So, as you take your semester break, you will find it in your best interest to make some effort to understand the soul faculties and the sense functions, to make some effort to direct, through application, some of this infinite energy passing through you into those soul faculties, for your spiritual body is dependent upon your own efforts, not the efforts of anyone else. It's up to you.

Let not your interest be to see or hear. Let your interest be motivated by a sincere desire to do the work here and now that your soul, in its untold thousands of years of journey, has come to Earth to do. For, you see, each soul has come here for a specific job to do. So that when your moment and your day comes, you will not live in regret in the astral-mental realms that you did not accomplish what your soul tried to whisper so softly to you to get done. No one wants to hover over this old Earth world for who knows how long doing a job that they knew deep inside of themselves they came to Earth to do. Get your job done. So that hopefully, when your moment comes, you won't have to stay around this old earth realm to finish it.

You see, my friends, no one has to tell you the job you came to Earth to do, for deep inside of you, you know. And you know very well the job that you have to do. Your mind may not like that job. Your mind may say, "Oh, that's a crummy job. I couldn't possibly, in my evolution, have merited that!" But you must remember, we are not, in this philosophy, reincarnationists who have descended from great and glorious positions in the universe. We are evolutionary incarnationists. And when we look at these steps that we think, perhaps, they're not only crummy steps, but they're literally crumbs, then we cannot see clearly that without the crumb of life, there's no loaf to experience.

To me, in these years, I find life very beautiful. I have found it that way for a very long, long time. That does not mean that I don't have a job to do and I don't have to speak strongly to some people sometimes. But if I speak strongly, you may be rest assured that's the only way that that particular level the person is expressing is going to respond. For I am sure we will all agree that, in some levels of consciousness, we are indeed tough as nails.

So, my good friends, think about your job. It's yours. It's unique to you, for you are an individual. It's the job that you earned. It's all yours. No one gave it to you and no one can take it from you. It's what you came to Earth to do. Now, a person may say, "Oh, good Lord, did I come to Earth just to play a piano? No, I don't like that job. Did I come to Earth just to be a housewife? I don't like that job. Did I come to Earth just to be a salesman? I don't like that job." My friends, that's your job. Make your job the beauty of life, because it is yours and as you make it the job that you know it should be—don't you see?—it is an extension of you. And in that respect, in that evolutionary respect in individualization, that is yours. That's your child. That's your baby. And it's in your hands—what you do with it.

So many times I know that we get ourselves so discouraged that we don't know what to do with ourselves. But we should never forget that is a tape in our head; that is a level we happen to be expressing at the moment. That is not really us unless we permit that tape in our mind to convince us that it is us. Now, I want you to think for a moment: What is it in our mind that works so hard to convince us that a level we are expressing at any moment is really us? Don't you understand, my friends, a level of consciousness, a tape of the mind, created forms, created by mental substance of past experiences, when they are able to convince us that they are us (that the level we express is really us), they receive from us much more energy than if we are awakened and we say, "Yes, that tape, I have expressed that before. That tape really upsets me. But I know that that's not the real me." Then you don't give anywhere near as much energy to those levels of consciousness that you are finding detrimental to yourselves.

And so we will move on. We will all move on. It may not be exactly the way that we think that it should be. But all of these wonderful experiences, we will get to grow through each and every one of them. They won't kill us off, you may be rest assured of that. The man today wanted me to be specific. Well, he got some specifics. No, they'll not kill us off. Serenity was not ordained by the minds of earthlings. And the work that it has to do has really yet to begin. We've only been, these last seven years, in the preparatory stages. We've just been, slowly but surely—sometimes it seems a little quick to me—getting things together to kind of build a little foundation upon which we could stand. Oh, no, my friends, we have yet to move. No, Serenity has a long, long, long life ahead.

And with God's help I will be able, be it in divine order, to finish the work I have to do. Because I can be rest assured after seeing so many souls for so many years hovering around Earth trying to finish jobs they didn't finish when they were in the physical flesh, it is just not particularly appealing to my mind to visualize myself—and I hope not to make it an adversity, like all this publicity—to visualize myself hovering close to Earth trying to get the job done that I didn't get finished. Because, you see, with my job, that means that I would have to work like who knows what to get through somebody's ego and I don't know how much of the words I'd have to say would come out accurate. So, you see, it's not really a pleasant job to look forward to. So I intend, to the best of my ability, to get the job done here and now.

I know to some, they wonder when I am going to get a rest. Well, of course, once in a while I entertain that thought myself, but it doesn't last long. My mother assures me to entertain those types of thoughts are not only detrimental, but they drain a lot of energy that I could be using to work. That's why I never asked the Friends for money, because they have one standard answer: "Well, just go to work." And if you tell them you're working, then I just get this answer: "Well, do more work. Get a second job, a third, a fourth, or a fifth." So, you see, I've learned a long time ago. I don't ask them for money—not that I'm afraid of work. But we perhaps can look at this year ahead as a prosperous year, that was prophesied last December—prosperous to those who are willing to accept that mass vibratory wave that is in our universe in this year of 1978. But it's up to us, you know, to get in step. There is nobody else that's going to push us there. We'll have to make that effort on our own.

Now, before we conclude this class, I would like to ask those who are interested in coming to our next semester to kindly raise their hands and make arrangements with the treasurer after the class tonight. Because, you know, our system is to sign up for the class for the next semester at the last class of the last semester. And this is the last class of this semester. So how many of you are choosing, or wish, to come to our next semester? All right. Then, would you kindly register with the treasurer? And I believe our system has usually been that it's—how much is it down?

Fifty dollars.

It's $50 down. Well, you see, there's always a way. So if you people will try to make that effort, we'll take that towards that $1,400 that's due.

And I thank you very much for being such fine students. Because, you see, it was like I was asked today, "Well, Mr. Goodwin, which of your students is the best in giving revelations?" I said, "Well, as a teacher, I think they're all the best," Because, you see, I know a little something about what it's like.

And if anyone thinks it's the easiest job in the world to stand on this podium and try to get that mind out of the way and just let something happen—it's not easy. You see, you just can't come up on Sunday morning and have it happen. You've got to make the effort seven days a week. And we call that, here, meditation.

So, I wish you all the very best. Some of you, I know, we'll see in our next semester. Some of you we won't. But that that you have put something in, by your attention and your study and your application of what is given, I know that goes with you. And I also know that it will serve you well in your times of need. Because it is in our great times of need that our minds bow the obstructions that are in the way—bows all the judgments. And we turn to whatever will work. And I know that this philosophy works for everyone who applies it. I know that it works beyond a shadow of any doubt, because I know it works for me. I see it working in many ways for many of my students. Perhaps it is not yet working in the ways that we judge that it should be working, but it is that judgment that is the obstruction. And when we move that judgment, we remove the obstruction and then it works.

Thank you all very, very much. Thank you.

MARCH 23, 1978

CONSCIOUSNESS CLASS 176

Good evening, class. Before we begin our new semester—we do have a few new students that are with us—and I would like to explain some of our procedure, if you're not already aware of it from the students who have recommended classes to you.

You all have the study book that we use in our classes [*The Living Light*] and, of course, it can only be as beneficial in your daily life as you allow it to be from your own efforts. Now, *The Living Light* (book) has the essence of this philosophy in it. It has been vastly expanded through almost 200 taped classes. To those of you who are studying this philosophy in order to bring about the changes in your life that you are seeking, it would behoove you—when you open your book each day and you read the passage that has been meant for you, ever in keeping, of course, with the level of consciousness that you are on at the time you open the book, the message that is there for you is very personal to you. And you should take the predominant message that you find that day and trace that, through the philosophy, that you may find the cause of the particular experience that you are having at that time.

Now, the Serenity Association has gone to great effort to catalogue this philosophy. So that when you open your book each day and you find the personal message for you, that you can trace that message through this philosophy, through almost 200 taped classes, that you may find the cause of your experience of that time. Because if you don't find the cause of your experience, you cannot understand wholly the experience. And when you find the cause of anything, it qualifies you, according to your acceptance of that cause, to make the necessary changes in your life, in your thinking, to bring about new experiences in your life that are more harmonious, that are more joyous, that are more in keeping with the peace and the harmony that everyone is seeking.

This philosophy teaches a basis of forty senses functions and forty soul faculties. It teaches that each experience is an effect of a level of consciousness that you are on and have established the law which is returning to you. The very basis of this philosophy is personal responsibility, which is the ability to respond to all experience in your life in the way that you personally choose to do so. To permit the mind to entertain the thought that the cause of anything in your life is outside of your control is an absolute delusion by the mind. Our purpose in presenting this philosophy to you is to help you help yourselves to bring about a more abundant fullness in your life, to attain the peace that all souls are seeking. But in order to do that, we must first learn about the levels of consciousness—how we are controlled by them from our own errors of ignorance and how we can bring about these changes by first becoming aware of those levels and making the constant effort to remain in levels of consciousness that are beneficial in our lives.

[*At this time, the Teacher goes into a trance.*]

Greetings, students, and welcome to class.

In beginning this semester, I should like to share a bit of my understanding on the biblical story of Adam and Eve, for there is, in that story, a great deal of truth to be understood about the so-called fall from grace: the descent of the soul from realms of peace, of so-called paradise, into the direct opposite.

And so it is, the story is told, that Adam was in a spirit of joy in a heavenly paradise until he recorded in his consciousness the thought of I. Whenever we permit our minds to experience the thought of I, we set into motion the mental Law of Identity. Having set into motion that mental Law of Identity, we guarantee the experiences of duality, for each pleasure shall be an equal pain, for each gain shall be an equal loss. And so it is that Adam, having registered in consciousness the thought of I, experienced what is known as loneliness or separation from the universal consciousness of which we are, in truth, an inseparable part.

It is through the Law of Identity, through the judgment of I, that the veil of illusion is created from mental substance. Whenever you experience the duality in life, you can be rest assured that you are in mental realms that are, in truth, an illusion which you have consciously chosen to be in. It is interesting to note that the experiences of the newborn child do not yet have firmly established the thought of I, but, by the very Law of Incarnation into form, the essence of that principle of I exists. How does this apply to our daily experiences? And how does this apply to freeing ourselves from the entrapment of illusion in the world in which you presently are? Whenever, my good friends, you become aware of your world and are not fully appreciative of the experiences that you are encountering, you can, in a moment, choose to free yourself from that illusion in one of two ways: make the effort to lift your true being to realms of consciousness that are not firmly established for you in the thought of I or redirect your attention to a level that you find more beneficial.

We have shared with you, for a number of years, the simple teaching that selfless service is the only path to spiritual illumination. For we cannot enter into spiritual realms until such time as we have freed ourselves from mental realms. And we cannot be freed from mental reams until we give forth, or forgive, this illusion known as the thought of I. For as the story of Adam clearly reveals, it is the thought of I that gives birth to pride, a function of the mind. It is the thought of I that gives birth to temptation, the illusions of the senses. The senses of the human mind have a purpose and, when kept in balance with their corresponding soul faculty, they neutralize and, in so doing, free you from their control.

Experience, the effect of directed energy, repeats itself in life eternal until such time as man gives forth this illusion to the realms from whence he has gathered it. For all of life is in keeping—our life is ever in keeping with our choice. It is in becoming aware of these choices that we begin to walk upon the path of light, the path of reason. Each and every step that you are taking is a step forward, though it may not seem to be that way at times. We all are moving, evolving, and expanding in consciousness.

To remember, and not forget, that each thought entertained in your mind is a created form, that you, being the mother or father of it, have the responsibility to care for it or forgive it and be free from it. For these created forms in these mental realms, they grow and strengthen, as we have often mentioned to you. And they come home—home to your world where they were born. For all things return to the source from whence they came. And so, my good friends, in all of your experiences, remember, they come to you, for you were their home of their creation. They cannot go home anywhere else. Be not discouraged by that truth. Be encouraged and face in life what you must, for it is a life of goodness if you will permit it to be so for you.

Because the mental realms and the mental body is the body that carries us on from your physical world, because in mental creation is the true and only obstruction to the abundant goodness of life, we spend much time in discussion of it. Only by becoming aware of that mental world can you move through it and awaken to your spiritual home that is waiting for you each and every moment. For your spiritual home is as much with you now as it will ever be, for you are spirit and you are home in spirit when you are freed from the discord and the distractions of mental substance.

My greatest struggles, through the centuries after I left your earthly realms, were struggles through the astral and mental worlds. And many, many times I stopped in despair and discouragement. It took me centuries to learn that the experience within my mind of despair, the experience within me of discouragement was a created form that I had created and that that created mental form, having received energy from me for so long by my consideration of that level of consciousness, that form, having the intelligence of my mind, being created and born by my mind, did not want to die.

Our thoughts know birth. Because our thoughts know birth, our thoughts also know death. For birth and death exist only in mental worlds of dual creation. Each and every moment we are born and we die in our mind, for our mind is in a constant process of receiving and giving.

It is the purpose of this philosophy to help you awaken to worlds within you that are light and clear, that you may not stumble through the centuries in darkness, that you may see, that you may know what is happening to your world, why it happens, and how to change it.

But only you, and you within, can adjust the priorities in your life. For it is, in truth, an adjustment of our priorities that first we become aware, beyond a shadow of any doubt, of what our priorities really are. Once having made that honest appraisal within ourselves, we can use the lighted path of reason, awakening to wisdom, knowing what we're doing, knowing why we're doing it, and knowing where it is leading us.

So often we permit the illusion within us to dictate that no one leads us but ourselves and, in the next breath, we despair for where we are leading ourselves. We are all lead in keeping with what we have set into motion. But here we pause to think, to consider that life indeed is beautiful, that the world in which we choose to live is a wonderful world. Our minds are programmed and it is the programming of our minds that we are not so happy with. And so either, through our own personal effort, through the demonstrable truth that peace is indeed the power of all the universes, that we flood our consciousness with that great power and, in so doing, cast the light of reason upon the shadows of our mind and begin to live a more full and abundant life.

Without the thought of I, there is no mental experience. That thought of I is the king of the mental world. You all know, from experiences that you have had, that others too have had similar experiences, that it has an impact upon you when you identify with it. To rise to higher levels of mind is to see more clearly. To rise above the levels of mind is to be totally freed from it.

So when you feel that your life is such a struggle, when you feel there are so many disasters for you to work with, remember, that feeling is the effect of the thought of I, that by changing from that thought (that thought of I) you will no longer, through the Law of Identification, experience that disaster and that despair. But that does take some effort on your part. And that effort cannot be now and then. It must become a constant effort, for your mind is constantly releasing energy. And that released energy returns to you as an experience on the very level in which it was released by you. All of life is intelligent energy. You are an intelligent being because of that intelligent energy.

When you separate yourselves from that intelligent energy, the burden of responsibility becomes more than you are willing to bear. To experience feelings of rejection is in keeping with that ancient story of Adam, for he felt rejected, for he experienced loneliness, for he judged and became the thought of I. Whenever we judge anything, we guarantee through that law, through that thought process, we guarantee the judgment to befall us. For each judgment made by our mind is a denial. And each denial is its own destiny and it always comes home.

How does man free himself from judgment? By flooding the consciousness with the divine, demonstrable truth that God, the intelligent energy called Love, sustains everything—and certainly has the right to do so. Our philosophy, founded upon the very principle of divine will, known to us as total acceptance—when we judge, my good students, we move from total acceptance to limited acceptance and must indeed pay the price.

I assure you that my greatest struggle was my judgments. And I assure you that it was not personally directed to me because I was a judge on Earth, for I have viewed and spoken with many, many, many souls and each soul, in its awakening, has begged forgiveness for their judgments. Your struggles in life are experienced by all. Because you judge that they are yours alone, then alone shall you suffer, for you have judged accordingly. Let us, my friends, in beginning this semester, let us consider making greater effort to forgive or give forth to God each judgment that we make that we may, in time, be freed from that that is robbing us of our peace, our happiness, our enjoyment of life.

You may feel free to ask your questions.

Thank you. Please give your understanding of discernment.

The ability to discern, a soul faculty, is ever dependent upon total consideration. For man to discern, man must use wisdom. To use wisdom, man must first gain understanding. And for man to first gain understanding, he must first demonstrate total consideration. For we cannot understand anything that we do not first fully consider.

Thank you. Please discuss the detriments of rigidity and how to discern the difference between when one should be flexible, in order to break addictive patterns of mind, and when one should unwaveringly fulfill a commitment.

The fulfillment of any commitment in life, based upon what we know to be divine love or total consideration, should always be fulfilled. For we should never permit our mind, our self, to be an obstruction to the divine flow of God's love. And so before we make commitments, we should make the effort to consider all.

When should man permit himself to be flexible or to be rigid? No man, nor animal, nor all creation, was designed to be rigid, for it is all receptive to divine energy and being receptive to divine energy, it is the dispenser of that divine energy. So flexibility is a demonstrable law, revealed in all of nature. That that is creation must ever be in keeping with the Law of Creation: be flexible that it may survive.

To stand firm is a spiritual principle and, being a spiritual principle, is expressed in spiritual realms of consciousness. When we are in our mental world, there is a constant flux and flow. When we are in our spiritual world, there is the principle, the rock of truth. That that is has been, shall always be. Though truth often crushed to earth, covered by the illusion of creation, ever rises back to the Light of which it is, in truth, an eternal part. Be flexible. Be flexible in the mental worlds, but do not make spiritual commitments in those worlds. For to do so is only to bring unto you experiences that are not beneficial.

Thank you. Counsel is frequently given for a person to be near the water, work in soil, play a musical instrument, paint, etc. Please share with us your understanding of this.

In reference to the question and deleting the "etc.," I will speak on the movement, which is beneficial—the movement of water, the movement of soil, the movement in music, the movement in art. My good students, the movement of which you, in mental realms, are an inseparable part is a flux and flow. And unless you permit, while in mental consciousness, this movement to harmoniously flow, then you experience discord in your lives.

Because there are so many discordant thoughts in these mental realms, there is great need for rhythm. There is great need to become, once again, receptive to the beauty, to the goodness, to the enjoyment of harmony, for that which is harmonious shall grow and flourish. For as you study, around your world, nature, though to some levels of mind there appears to be discord, in truth, there is a rhythmic flow. There is a rise and fall, a constant process of movement. And so it is this movement that we find in the water. It is this movement that we find in the earth and the soil. It is this movement that is in music and in art. It helps you, as a healing balm, to become free from the thought of I, which is a rigidity, which removes you, by judgment and denial, from the rhythmic flow of what you call God's goodness, love, or intelligent energy.

The ruler of the mental worlds is the ruler of rigidity, for in the thought of I there is no flux and there is no flow. There is no rhythm. There is only a stagnation. Many people—in fact, most will agree that they have changed perhaps in the past ten years or twenty. They will agree—some—that they have changed even in the past year. And to those who are more awakened, they will agree they have changed in the past month. And as we expand our consciousness, we see that we have indeed made changes in the past week, the past hour, the past moment.

The tree that bends shall never break. Though it may grow crooked, it shall grow and survive. It may not look like the trees around it, for nothing in creation is exactly the same.

You see, my friends, when you say "I," you declare the world of creation as your realm of consciousness. You establish, by that thought, your view, at the sacrifice of your soul faculties. For with the thought of I is the judgment and denial that is the mental world. But each judgment has its price tag; each denial its inevitable destiny. If you will work with those demonstrable laws of nature each day, your path in life will get brighter, your enjoyment of life will become the fullness of your life. But only you can make that effort. It must, in time, mean enough to you and when it does, you shall be transformed in the sense that you shall be free, free to do what you truly know you must do.

There's no escape. There is no escape. We all have a mind. Experiences are indelibly recorded in our memory par excellence. But we can choose which level of the mind we shall experience. You cannot erase that which is recorded. You may forgive it. And by forgiving, be free from it. You can only forget it when you're in the fullness of the Divine.

Good night

MAY 4, 1978

CONSCIOUSNESS CLASS 177

Greetings, students.

This evening we shall spend a few moments in discussion of peace and freedom. For we all are working, in our way, to return to that state of consciousness, for from that state of consciousness, through the Law of Identity, we have descended into the duality of creation. Because we are, in truth, formless and free, ever before us is a view of, once again, returning to that realm. And there are moments that we all experience when we can say to ourselves, "Indeed, I have had a moment of peace. I have once again experienced those moments of freedom."

My good friends, there is a simple exercise to use each and every day: an exercise to remind oneself to ever remember that you are not the form, but you are using the form; you are not the thought, but you have created the thought. Through a daily reminder of who you really are—formless and free spirit—you will surely, gradually become what you really are in expression. To remember you are not those things, to separate you (truth) from creation, separate yourself by becoming more aware of these vehicles that you are using. Use them. Do not become them. For when you become the vehicle of expression that you use, you descend from those realms of peace and harmony and you enter the limit, the bondage of creation.

In all of our teaching that we have yet shared with you, we have and continue to make the effort to help you to help yourselves to remind yourselves, for the mind is constantly bombarded with thoughts. We are constantly, in form, experiencing different feelings. But we must remember we are not the feeling, we are not the thought.

Do not misunderstand that simple exercise. We are responsible. We have the ability of responding to the thought we create, to the forms through which we express. Therefore, the responsibility is ever ours personally.

But to separate our awareness, to rise to levels of light and reason, we will trod, slowly but surely, on that path of reason, that path of light. For our purpose is clearly before us. The lessons in life are ever in keeping with what we have and continue to set into motion.

In one of our classes with you, we spoke on universal consciousness. All of the world is sustained by one, intelligent Energy. We are that intelligent Energy. We are not these many suits that we wear in this great eternal life. We are that formless, free Spirit. That is our true home, for it is our true being.

I am going to spend some time now in answering the questions you have prepared. It is most important to you, as students, to present your questions in these classes. For the questions that arise in your mind are important to you and whatever is important to you is important enough to speak forth. And so you may feel free to state your questions.

Thank you. Please give your understanding of how the soul faculty of freedom is unfolded.

In speaking on freedom—we spent a few moments doing so—we must not forget that freedom is something we have always had. It is something that is ever with us. It is when we identify with form, the form of thought, the form of anything, that we descend from those realms of freedom. And so, as we have stated before, freedom is an effect of self-control. It is an effect of the control of the thoughts and the feelings of our mind. Whenever the effort is made to control those thoughts, there is this wonderful experience that takes place within. We call that freedom. Freedom means not bound. It means without limit. It means without beginning and, therefore, without ending. Freedom, like truth, *is*. It is not something that can be given. Therefore, it is not something that can be taken. Freedom dawns within you when you take control of creation. You take control of all thought and your first experience is a great stillness and from that, a peace, from that, a freedom.

And so to the questioner, I say concern not yourself with how to attain. Be interested in the moment of now. For freedom is not tomorrow and freedom is not yesterday. It is in the moment of your own choice; it is in the moment of your effort. If you permit the mind to dictate that you will have freedom as a final effect of several steps that you must take, and that mind dictates to you it will take X number of years, then freedom is not what you will experience.

Thank you. Please explain the statement, "Justification is the defense of a personal desire made by a judgment."

Justification, commonly referred to by most people as excuses, is the defense of a judgment made by the human mind. In order to defend our judgments in life, we find it repeatedly necessary to justify the position, the throne of judgment upon which we place ourselves. This is a natural process of the human mind: to preserve what it has judged it has. Preservation is a very basic instinct in all creation. It is the very nature of form to ever work to preserve itself. That is why, in creation and in form, you will not experience freedom. You will often experience license, which is, in truth, the delusion of freedom, but it is not freedom. And so it is the mind ever works to defend whatever judgment that it has made. And as part of that defense mechanism, the mind is filled with excuses so that the judgment may be preserved, and that is known as justification.

Thank you. How does the general appearance or form and the response of the entities we create correspond to the physical manifestations or ailments occurring in our bodies? And how is the chemistry of the body affected by the action of these entities?

In reference to the eight questions that you have asked, I would like to say, first, that a so-called ailment or illness in the physical body is a revelation of a lack of energy properly flowing through that part of the human anatomy. In other words, there is an obstruction in that part of the body and that obstruction to the natural, harmonious flow of infinite intelligent energy, that obstruction is called by men as disease or discord. Whenever you experience an affliction, a so-called disease in any part of your body, through an objective study of the anatomy and what it represents, spiritually and mentally, you can easily determine where the problem lies in consciousness.

Now, the anatomy has been charted for you, to some extent, in this philosophy. And many of you students have found how quickly you recover from your conditions when you honestly begin to consider what that part of your anatomy truly represents. I have viewed for many years students who had patterns of throat conditions, of problems with their breathing, and when they became aware of what the throat represented, those problems slowly, but surely, and their effects began to disappear.

My students, there are forty sense functions and forty soul faculties. When they are in balance, when, by your choice, equal amount of energy is directed to the faculty and the function, there is a balance. There is a harmony of the divine flow of an intelligent energy through your body. Therefore, it behooves all people interested in the divine birthright of perfect health to become aware of these faculties and functions and to consciously make the effort to bring about a balance in their lives.

For without perfect health, there is not perfect life. And perfect health is not only your birthright in this the earth realm, but it is your duty and your responsibility to the vehicle that you are using to express your true being on Earth. For if a vehicle is not in good working order, then the soul using the vehicle cannot fully, wholly, and completely express.

Many times a student will ask, "How can I bring this function into balance when I do not yet know the balancing soul faculty?" Through your efforts to flood your consciousness with the power of God, known to us as peace, this balance, by the very law of nature, which ever seeks balance, comes into being for you. The great healing power, known as peace, not only brings balance and harmony into your physical and mental body, but it brings you into harmony with the universe.

For though the eyes of creation see duality, see war and disturbance, the eye of eternity sees the perfect balance, for the eye of eternity is the patience of the whole.

If you find difficulties, which many of you have found, in bringing about a harmonious abundant flow of goodness in your lives, stop and flood your consciousness with the only power that can bring about that harmony and that peace: flood your consciousness with the Divine Intelligence. But that's only possible, my friends, when you accept the power of peace.

Thank you. Most philosophies teach that change must first take place in the individual before it can become a mass change, where deep cultural prejudice exists toward an ethnic or local group. Would you please recommend how the appeal might be stimulated to affect individual tolerance of those who are different from us?

My good students, in the first place, the judgment in the question must be first removed. To permit the mind to judge that there is such and such in the world is to establish supremacy of a mental world. Working in a mental world, you are governed and controlled by the laws that govern that world. Therefore, it is wisdom that reveals to us that we must first rise to higher realms of consciousness. There, viewing clearly, we can accept the inseparability of Divine Intelligence, that we are, in truth, inseparable from that Intelligence, that there is one, united whole of which we are. When we enter that realm of light and we are flooded in our universe with its healing truth, then we start our descent down into the mental world.

But before us is that light of truth that we are all one. And with that great truth, we light the darkened world. No matter what others think, no matter what others do, we are a light in the world when we permit ourselves to be so. Therefore, when you are united in consciousness, you emanate that simple truth, that Divine Love. And if you continue to stand firm upon that principle of unity, those with whom you come into contact shall accept that peace that you are demonstrating. For they, too, are an inseparable part of that which you are now expressing. And their soul, their true being, which is greater than all the thoughts that cover them, will rise in keeping with the law that like attracts like.

It is said that God's greatest work is done in silence. And when you understand the simple unity of the spiritual realms, when you truly perceive that, you will speak your word forth into the universe, you will know that it shall not return to you void, but accomplish that which you have sent it to do.

First, my students, we must heal ourselves. Our faith must ever be the guiding light to light our path in this world and all worlds. And if you never let go of that lighted lamp, then you will live to see the day, while yet on Earth, that there is no power greater than peace, that there is no greater demonstration of truth than the faith that you stand firm upon.

Thank you. Would you please discuss the importance, or the reasons, for talking the patient's, or student's, language when trying to help them?

My good friends, in order to be an instrument in helping another, you must first establish a rapport with the person. If the person is on a level of consciousness that you are not on at that time, then there is no honest and true communication. In order to help another, we must first help ourselves. For we must first become aware, within ourselves, of the level of consciousness of the person that we are trying to help. We cannot become aware of level ten unless we have experienced and qualified ourselves on that level.

Now, what do I mean by becoming qualified on a level of consciousness? I mean, by being aware of the level, by being able to consciously and objectively descend or ascend to the level, never to lose sight of the faculty of objectivity while on the level. Because to lose sight of objectivity is to become trapped in the level. And therefore when opportunity presents itself to you—for unsolicited help is ever to no avail—but when opportunity presents itself, then pause to think more deeply within yourself that you may be guided by a greater intelligence than the limited mind to go into the level of consciousness to help lift a soul up where there's a brighter light, where there is more peace and harmony, there's more joy than they're experiencing.

But, my students, become aware—become most aware, for all of life is the effect of energy. When you are working with someone, there's an inner knowing that will tell you when your job is done. If, because of demands upon your time, created by your own thoughts, you listen to them—those demands—and you do not complete your job, then what happens—you have left a soul worse than you have found them. It would have been better not to have spoken to them in the first place. For your job was not complete, for it was not, in truth, motivated by a selfless motivation. And therefore, the price is indeed very, very high.

We meet many people in our lives. Each one attracted into our universe is attracted not by some whimsical accident. Oh, no, my friends, many you have met before and you did not complete your job then. And so they have come again to knock at your door, for there is a responsibility and a debt in evolution that you have incurred. Therefore, not only broaden your horizons about life, but expand your faculty of tolerance. For they will knock again and again and again. Have you not already viewed in your Earth experiences the repetition in your life of certain lessons? My good students, the law repeats itself until our dues, so to speak, are fully paid.

We attempt to escape many things in our lives, only to find someday there is no escape. So let us face each person that enters our life, let us face them honestly. Let us not put the blame upon them, for they are only fulfilling a law. Let us view that law. Let us grow up and face our responsibilities that we may be freed from it and move on to greater opportunities.

When the lesson is not accepted by us, it will continue to knock throughout eternity until finally we bow, we accept the lesson, we pass the test that we alone created, and we move on.

Thank you. Please explain how complaining establishes the Law of Greed.

Yes, my friends. Complaining and how it establishes the Law of Greed.

We understand that abundance or supply flows through the soul faculty of gratitude; that when we truly demonstrate gratitude for the crumbs of life, that those crumbs in time, they increase and grow and become the loaves of abundance that our minds so dearly seek; that the opposite of ingratitude—the opposite, ingratitude, establishes laws contrary to abundance and supply.

Each time that we complain, we direct intelligent energy to the function of ingratitude. As we continue to do that, a feeling rises within us: that we are lacking. And this feeling of lack increases in our consciousness. We cannot experience greed until we have registered the lack of something that we desire. As we record a lack of what we desire, we establish the Law of Greed. As we continue to complain, we continue to feed that level of consciousness and experience an ever-increasing amount of lack. The effects of those experiences are often known to man as frustration.

So often man decides, when people speak of greed, that they're speaking only of money. But how far from the truth is such thinking. The function of greed is not limited to money. It is not limited to anything, for it encompasses everything.

When we stop complaining, we will start experiencing what we desire.

Our mind is in a constant process of programming. It is in a constant process of defending the programs that are in it. My friends, why live in the delusion of lack when the reality of abundant good is demonstrated by the Divine Intelligence throughout all nature?

But how many times a day, when you pass a tree, do you declare the truth, "God is the source of my supply. Look at the abundance he has placed upon the tree"? How many times, when you look at a blade of grass, do you declare that truth? You see, my friends, man, the highest evolved animal on the Earth planet in form, man must make the effort to reprogram his mind, for it is filled with the errors of ignorance. The tree does not need to think, "God is the source of my supply," for the tree has only the truth for its acceptance. But man has not only truth, but denial, the opposite, for his experiences and acceptance.

Each denial that we make not only establishes our destiny, but each denial is a cloud between us, the true being, and the realm of truth. For, in truth, there is no denial, for to deny is to demonstrate the opposite of truth. Truth needs no defense for truth *is*. It is falsehood and error that need defense. "I am what I am," and this we can all accept. But in that statement let us broaden our awareness of who we truly are.

Good night.

MAY 11, 1978

CONSCIOUSNESS CLASS 178

Greetings, students.

Many times in our classes, in so very many different ways, we have spoken to you on the fullness of life and the success of living. And we should like to spend some time this evening in bringing a broader understanding of that simple law that states, "To speak forth one thing and manifest another is an absolute guarantee of failure."

We have spoken on the great power that is contained in the spoken word. But that power is manifest through you only when you become, in consciousness, a united whole. As we speak, our spoken word is seldom in harmony with the thought that we are entertaining in consciousness. And so it is our spoken word has lost the power that is rightfully within it. When you speak, you must use all of your being in order that your words spoken may not return unto you void. If you speak the word *success*, you must see the Law of Success in order for that unity to bring back to you what you are sending forth. You cannot speak one thing and permit your mind to believe the opposite and have what you desire in life. But to speak your word and to see the fullness of the word is to put the power of the Divine Intelligence in your life and it shall not return to you void, but it shall accomplish what you have sent it to do. For you are, in that moment, a united whole through which this impartial, intelligent energy goes forth into the universe.

As we all know, and cannot help but accept, all experiences are effects of what we alone are doing with our word and with our thought. To bring forth the word with the thought in total harmony is to release from your universe what you know as feeling. Therefore, all of that will return unto you and you shall know your tomorrows and your tomorrows shall be filled with goodness. For it is your divine right to know each moment, to not only become aware of impartial universal laws, but to use them, to use them wisely for your greater good. For not until you use these infinite, infallible laws for your good can you be qualified and be an instrument for the law to be used for the goodness of another. For, as we know, we cannot grant unto another what we have not first granted unto ourselves.

Do not be discouraged in your efforts, for there are areas in your life where you are demonstrating this simple Law of Unity. And in those areas, you experience success. For no one in any universe is a complete failure. And even if they were, in failure is the hidden ingredient of success. When you face these experiences and you permit your mind to dictate that you have tried everything to bring about the change, consider changing your desire. For the obstruction that you are meeting may well be a signpost guiding you on to greater things.

To flow with the universal consciousness is an experience of perfect rhythm and perfect harmony. That is our true purpose in life—is to flow with the natural laws that govern the universes.

Each moment and every moment is an important moment to you, for those moments, though they seem to be but a fraction of a second, in those moments laws are being sustained and set into motion. And so it is the moment that should be of your interest, not the yesterdays, nor the tomorrows, for the tomorrows are within your awareness when you take care of those moments, each moment. It is indeed worth your while. It is inevitable for all souls, for it is the destiny of so-called eternity.

Try to visualize, for a moment, that you, the being you, is inseparably united to everything that your eyes are viewing, to everything that your ears are hearing, to everything your senses are feeling. Then you will begin to have an awakening of who you are and what you are. To permit yourself to move in harmony with that truth is to flow in the abundant goodness of eternal life.

I have been with you before and I am with you now and I will be with you again, for there is no separation in truth.

To broaden one's horizon is to free oneself from the bondage of the Law of Identification. For each time we permit our mind to identify—and it does so in each and every moment—we put another link upon the chain of bondage. It is through identification that the soul has descended into the worlds of experience. But through the bondage of identification and through the struggle to free oneself, those laws of creation are, slowly but surely, being refined.

As the formless, you, the true being, formless and free, enters the bondage of identification, there is ever that insatiable urge to be free. You must ask yourselves where this urge truly comes from. It is not something that your world has educated you to. It is not something that someone else told you about. It is something that you have always known. And it is something that you will always know, for you, the true you, cannot be kept captive and the victim of mental worlds of restriction and limitation forever and ever.

Each change that takes place in your life is freeing you from something. So let the change be harmonious to you by the divine will of acceptance. For it is the will of Divine Intelligence that all be accepted. When you stop the battle of the mind, which insists on holding on to that which is passing, when you stop the battle of the mind that uses fear to protect its so-called holdings and possessions, you will experience harmoniously the changes taking place in your life.

To say that yesterday was better is to live in a world of delusion, created by those levels of consciousness, by those entities and form in the mental world who are crying out to once again receive energy and sustenance from you, your soul, the true being. That is not you that cries for yesterday. It is not you that rushes tomorrow. It is you that pauses in the moment and experiences the fullness of life. It is the moments in which you pause that you broaden your horizons. It is the moments in which you pause that you free your being. Let those moments increase in your life that you may be free from this mental world of form that ever cries and demands more time and energy from you.

He who shows no patience reveals the degree that he is controlled by mental forms of yesterday. He who experiences frustration is locked in the mental worlds of self, where the battles ever rage. Look at the world of this mental experience as you view the movies of your world, for that, in truth, is what they are. They are not eternal. They are born and die. But you are forever and forever. From forever you came, to forever you go. No ending, my friends, no beginning. Why spend so much of life's beauty by restricting that beauty by the dictates of mental thoughts?

As we awaken within ourselves, we very surely begin to walk upon that single path of light known as reason. To chase this world for the many forms that it offers and lose yourself in the process is no gain, in truth, at all. It only postpones the inevitable, which is facing the light of reason and humbly accepting the infallible Law of Personal Responsibility.

Everything that we send comes back home again and again and again until finally we pause and we accept the demonstrable truth that yes, yes, indeed, we and we alone are sending it forth into the universe and we and we alone are getting it back. I stated once that we always get what we really want. And, my good friends, that is daily the demonstrable truth. If we do not believe that we always get what we really want, it simply reveals to us that we have not yet accepted the personal responsibility of our thoughts, our acts, our deeds.

As each hair upon our head is counted, each thought is witnessed and recorded. We have not found in our worlds a God of judgment. We have not found in our worlds a God of form, for God is the formless, free, true Spirit, using form for its expression. But we have found the Halls of Records, where each thought you think, each word you speak, each feeling you experience is indelibly recorded. No one stands by to judge you. The law simply returns unto us. My good students, accept the experience that you may make the changes that you know are necessary for you. No one need tell you what those changes are, for you know what they are better than anyone in all the universes. Our purpose is, and has always been, to share with you our experiences, to share with you our understanding that perhaps, be it in the divine order, it may be helpful to you through your application of it.

To be controlled by feelings of regret or feelings and thoughts of guilt is only to keep yourself in the bondage of those realms of judgment. My friends, you cannot experience regret, you cannot experience guilt, unless you have first made [a] judgment. It is the judgments that cause us to suffer. And I know from those experiences so long ago that it takes a constant moment-by-moment effort to control that form that sits on the throne of judgment and orders the little eternal soul around and around and around. But I assure you it is the divine will that frees us from the throne of judgment and the divine will is total acceptance.

Think about that word, my friends, for a few moments. For, in so doing, all the defenses from the throne of judgment will rise up within your consciousness. View them—view them well. They were born in the errors of ignorance. They live in the dark recesses of the human mind. They are forms centuries old, primitive in many respects, using all of the intelligence of your mind. They cause you frustration. They cause you fear. They cause you failure. They cause you distress and hopelessness and despair. For that is the throne that they rule. They cause you discouragement and all the so-called negative experiences of life, for they are the kings of judgment and they demand their payments. But you need not be their slaves forever. You know the way. As God, the Divine Infinite Intelligence, accepts and sustains all forms, all thoughts, even those thoughts of judgment—God sustains them through your error of ignorance.

But you can neutralize all of that. It is your love of the divine intelligent Energy that will bring balance into your life, that will neutralize, as a great healing balm, all those mental things. But to experience the fullness of the Divine Light, called God, one must demonstrate, through his own efforts, the worthiness thereof. And so, my friends, when you grant the right to all, you have, in truth, granted the right to the allness of yourself.

Many people, I find, including myself, centuries ago, do not think much of the word *love*. I know, when I was on your realm of Earth, that word had no true meaning to me. The law, as I understood it, that had meaning. It had purpose. But it took me centuries in this other realm to realize that meaning, for law, to me had been dependent upon my love for it. You see, my friends, without love, there is no life. Without life, there is no Light. There is so much to that simple truth: to love all life and know the Light.

We all love something. I know some of you may disagree, for some of you may say, "Some people love other people." My friends, we all love some*thing*. For love, in truth, is the reflection in another of the goodness in oneself. And so my love was for the law, for the law, as I understood it, was that goodness in me. So let us take a different view of the word *love,* for there is the Divine Love, free from want, need, and desire. Divine Love is free from all those things, for being divine, it has total consideration, it has total acceptance.

But most of us are more familiar with what is called conjugal love, that has want, has need, and has desire. And so we find when those wants and those needs and those desires we judge are being fulfilled by another person, then that person we love. And therefore, it is some*thing* that we love. But there is a better way—to love all life because you are all life. And when you do that, that Light will shine as never before. But most of us don't want to love all life, for we are too busy loving the things in our mind. And so we experience limited love and have yet to be free with limitless love. But I assure you, my friends, without love, there is no form, for love is the great magnet of all the universes. And it is through love that Light brings life to form.

Wherever you may wander, you will always return to your life, to your light, to your love. For there is no form—be it plant, animal, human—there is no form without love. For it is not only the magnet, but it is the cohesive element that holds all things together.

And as your physical form, as your love for it begins to wane and is transformed to those finer ethereal forms, it returns to Mother Nature, who gave it birth from her love. And so it is with your seeming struggles in life. It is your limited love that binds you to those patterns that have long worn out their usefulness in your evolution. Learn to love the new that is yet to come. But to do that you must broaden the great faith that you already have.

Ofttimes a student will ask, "What is the true difference between the human form in evolution and the animal forms?" The human form, the intelligence expressing through it, has what is known as a self-awareness. It is aware that it is. But without the light of reason, it can indeed be a stumbling block along its path. But that self-awareness is the demonstration of faith. The human being has great power within it. It has the potential of experiencing the power of the universes the moment it bows to accept a higher order, a higher intelligence than its limited form.

When you speak your word and you see the fullness thereof, you demonstrate the power of God. And the fullness of God is ever present. No one can deny that. But you must take hold of the reins. And if you say it is difficult for you to visualize, pause in that thought, for that reveals to you, my friends, something is deeply hidden. And that which is deeply hidden is robbing you of the vital energy needed for the visualization process to take place in your life. Pause and go deep within yourself and you will find that hidden form that does not want you to see it. For you are evolved in a human form. And it is within the right of that human form to see, to hear, to sense, to feel, to visualize. That is the divine right of the form in which you are presently expressing. So let not the forms of delusion from the recesses of your mind deceive you. For I know there is no one within the sound of my voice who has not entertained a choice desire and had no problem in the process of visualization.

If you speak the word *peace,* then look at the word *peace.* See what it brings forth unto your mind. If you speak the word *success,* become aware of what your mind creates when you speak the word. Time and again I have stated that the strongest imprint in ectoplasmic substance in the world in which you, in embryo, live, the strongest imprint is the imprint of feeling and emotion. And, my friends, feeling and emotion is released from your aura when your thought and your word, in the fullness of imagery, is expressed.

Imagination, the doorway through which you must pass to enter higher realms of consciousness, is very important. For through it, through this realm of imagination, you are all experiencing.

Your word, my word, all word, the lost word, that word—an image is released with each word you speak. And only through your efforts to visualize will those images rise up into your mind's eye that you may see clearly what is going to return to you. You see, my friends, when you speak "success," you must look and see what image, what form, rises from your mental world when you speak that word. For it is that image that will reveal to you what your experience shall be. Because you have the power to change the word, you have no less the power to change the image that, through errors of ignorance, is related to your word.

It is time, in the many classes that most of you have received, it is time that you start a daily exercise. And you have been given a few. But that you start this exercise this moment to become aware of the image, the form, that is related to your word. For then you can truly see what is going out into the universe. You can see beyond a shadow of any doubt in which areas in your life you are still a house divided. Start now, my students, choose whatever word you wish, but choose one that has some meaning to you, and become aware of what images are related to it. And if you are not pleased with those images, begin at once to change them. Implant new images into your mind related to the word. Long, long ago we asked you to speak a word *beauty*, to repeat it thrice and become aware. Now, this evening perhaps you know the reason and you will make the change.

Oh, how I have thought and thought and thought. When I came over here and the experiences that I encountered, I did not know about the word and the image. But I did somehow, in my evolution, merit the voice of a guardian angel. And when you have tried everything, then there's nothing left but to listen.

Most of us hear and we hear very well, but we don't listen. And so I would like to share with you my understanding of the difference between the word *hear* and the word *listen*. To hear something is to hear it dependent upon your own censorship. But to listen is to be free from that throne of judgment called censorship. To listen is to be awake with the faculty of wisdom fully expressing. So let us listen, my friends. I give freely to you what it has taken me untold centuries to learn. And the reason that it took me centuries is because I heard—and I heard well—but I did not listen, for my love of law, the law that the mind offers, my throne of judgment, was very great. And so I could not listen, but I could hear.

And now I give to you this golden key that will open the doors of your life and put you into the beauty of eternal experience, to fill your life with the goodness that is waiting patiently for your recognition. Use the exercise of the word, become aware of the image, and take the necessary measures to bring the fullness, the goodness, and the successful joy of living to your being here and now.

Good night.

MAY 18, 1978

CONSCIOUSNESS CLASS 179

Good evening, class. The beauty of the Living Light philosophy is that it doesn't follow any set rigid pattern and you never know when the classes are going to take a turn in a different direction than what you might expect, like tonight and other nights that have passed before.

The philosophy teaches that exposure frees the soul. Are there any of my students present in the physical world that know how that really works? If so please raise your hand. How does exposure free the eternal being? Yes. Would you rise, please?

Yes, is exposure to the Light—and then we can understand it better?

Yes, whenever we have understanding, of course, that's going to free our soul.

Yes.

Thank you.

Well, I find that at the beginning, when I was exposed, that I was quite irritated, extremely irritated, into emotionalism, whether it was playing the rejection tape or whatever tape I was experiencing at that particular time. But through more exposure, it seems as though those particular levels become educated, through the process of repetition and the exposure. Then maybe a particular level that is particularly strong with us doesn't affect us as much. And therefore we recognize that particular level and perhaps it's educated a little bit more. That's not all eighty-one levels, because we're expressing on different levels at different times.

Thank you very much. Now, we have heard this teaching that fear is the mind's control over the eternal soul. Then, we've also heard the teaching that exposure frees the soul. When any level of consciousness, a pattern of mind, an attitude, rises up to get its energy for its own continuity and survival and it experiences what we call exposure, what takes place within the mind? Does anyone know? What takes place in the mind? What do you experience? Yes. Would you rise, please?

Anger.

Anger. Why—

Defensiveness.

Why do you know—yes. Defensiveness. Why do you experience anger?

Because I think that tape has control over you and it doesn't want to be dethroned.

It doesn't want to be dethroned. Thank you.

The pattern of mind that is at stake, that rises up and is exposed, causes the mind to experience what is known as fear. Now, we all understand, I am sure, that evolution is inevitable, that all form evolves. Whether we like it or not, it does evolve. Its process of evolving is known as the process of change. So all of us are in a process of changing our minds—not our eternal being, but the form that the being is using is in a constant process of change. Through exposure, this process is accelerated.

Now, many of you have been with us for years and you are very much aware that hundreds upon hundreds of people have come and gone in this school. Some of you have often questioned, "Why don't they stay?" But what you are not considering is that the patterns of mind that have control of them are the very patterns that take them out from the light from fear. Because fear is the mechanism that keeps control over our eternal being.

Now, when a pattern rises up, an attitude of mind, and that is exposed, the mind experiences—as a defense mechanism to perpetrate its level—it experiences what is known as fear. Practically all religions in the earth realm demonstrate and teach a process of fear: the fear of the wrath of God, the fear of hell. Why do you think, as students, that philosophies of old and even of today, that the major philosophies and religions of our world today are founded upon the fear of the wrath of God? [*After a short pause, the Teacher continues.*] Without that demonstration from religions, there are very few people that would make any changes. When we fear, we start to make changes.

This philosophy teaches very clearly that fear is nothing more and nothing less than faith directed to the negative or faith in the patterns of the human mind. It does not teach that you should fear God. It does not teach that you should fear anything. Because, you see, this philosophy doesn't need to teach you to fear, for fear is the very defense of your own mind. No one needs to teach you to fear. Fear is something that you cope with. Moment by moment each and every day of your life you are facing one fear upon another. Those fears are nothing more than the defenses of patterns of mind of yesteryear. This philosophy tries to show you that, through an effort to accept an infinite intelligence, that is ever present within you, that you may be free from that defense mechanism.

So, my friends, whenever you are exposed, remember to be grateful that there is someone somewhere that cares enough for you to help you to help yourself to face those levels of consciousness.

Now, I want to take a few moments to ask the student if she knows why she forgot the strawberries this evening. If she does, that's fine. If she doesn't, we will help share our understanding.

I'm a bit surprised.

Thank you. You realize that there has to be a judgment take place within our mind in order for us to forget anything. Does everyone understand that? First a judgment must take place. You see, we live and move constantly in a realm of priorities. Our priorities in life are the effects of our judgments. And so we are constantly shifting and reshifting the priorities that we face moment by moment by moment.

Now, therefore we have to ask ourselves, when we have made a commitment and we just forgot, somehow, to fulfill it, What really happened in our mind? What judgment did we make and upon what experience did we base the judgment to put on our priorities, a commitment, down at the bottom of the list? So far at the bottom that we totally forgot. This is what's important. You know, many years have been spent to try to explain to people the mechanism of the human mind, of how the mind really works. For once you understand your mind, then you are in a position to begin to control your mind. Our purpose is to help you, through an awakening from within, to see how the vehicle, that your little soul is supposed to be driving, how you can once again get in the driver's seat and not be driven around by these varying patterns of mind, by learning how your mind really works.

And so, would you [*the student who forgot the strawberries*] like to help us in this experience, for the benefit of yourself and the benefit of the class? When did you first become aware that you had a spiritual commitment by your choice? Was not your commitment voluntary?

No—well, I agreed to it voluntarily. I was asked to bring the item . . .

Does your mind feel that it was a voluntary commitment? That's important. Because, you see, to understand the mind, we must always go to the first step, for the first step is the most important step. For the first step in anything establishes the law that we, as souls, must follow. Therefore, is it my understanding that you voluntarily accepted because . . .

I agreed to what was suggested because I was doing my part.

Thank you. I did say "because," didn't I?

All right. Now, I don't want any student to take these things personally. We're trying to show you how the human mind works. The word *because* and the word *but* mean exactly the same thing to the emotional body. There is no difference between the word *but* and the word *because*. Now it's the buts and the becauses that cause us so many of the problems in our life. Because, because—what does the word *but* and what does the word *because* truly mean? It means subject to. Do any of my students know what it is subject to? Whenever you experience the word *but,* the word *because,* it is subject to something. Do you know what it's subject to? Would you rise, please?

Our personal desires—and justifying . . .

Subject to our personal desires and justification. It is subject to fear. All buts and all becauses are subject to fear.

Now, can the human mind experience fear without first experiencing judgment? No, it cannot. You cannot experience fear without first having experienced judgment. So judgment is the king that sits on the throne of our own mind. Judgment is what sends us down the so-called primrose path, for we are constantly,

constantly making judgments. Without judgment, there is no regret. Without judgment, there is no fear. All our experiences in life can be traced back through the path of the human mind to the throne of judgment.

The so-called descent of the angels of Light into the realms of darkness was when the human mind rose superior to the Intelligence that sustains it and experienced what is called judgment. There is no hell, there is no suffering, there is no pain, no sorrow until you pass through the doors of judgment. When you free yourself, through constant effort, from judgment, you will free yourself from the mental realms that offer you only the experiences of duality. For every high, there is a low in the mental realms. For every gain, there is a loss in the mental realms. So it is judgment that we should try to make some effort to become aware of. For from the throne of judgment the mental laws of the universe are established.

Now, you've all had the teaching that divine will, the will of the Infinite Intelligence—is known as what? What is it known as? You've all had the teaching.

Acceptance of something.

Total acceptance is known as what? [*After a short pause, the Teacher continues.*] As divine will. If you have total acceptance, can you have judgment? It is not possible. If you have total consideration, which we understand to be divine love or the love of God, can you experience judgment? So, you see, my friends, in your day-to-day experiences, you must ask yourself the question, "Am I in total consideration? Am I in total acceptance?" Your answer will come back immediately. "No, you're not in total acceptance." Because if you were in total acceptance, you would have no judgment. If you were in total consideration, you would not have these experiences of rejection. You can only experience rejection, you can only experience the struggle, while you are the victim and the slave of the king who sits on his throne of judgment. You cannot experience lack, limitation, pain, suffering, and all that that realm has to offer when you are free from judgment.

How does man really get himself free from judgment? By first accepting himself. You see, my friends, there are very few people here on Earth that have accepted themselves. Now, they've accepted maybe one, two, three, or four of the images that they have created of themselves. But when they judge that they are not moving and experiencing in one of the those images that their mind has created, then they do not accept themselves. In fact, they reject themselves. They deny themselves. And that denial establishes the very law of our own destiny.

You see, our denials are our destinies, because our denials are judgments. So everything you judge, you destine yourself to. If you judge that you will never be poor, that you will never be without, you destine your life experience into that very thing! Because you are not accepting in totality the right of all, you are denying and being the victim of the realm of judgment. And you must pay the price. Now, because we have had those errors of the moment before, that does not mean that we must stay in those errors today. Because our mind is constantly in movement, we can move into new areas, not by denying the old, for to deny the old is to guarantee its return.

You see, my friends, in the experiences of yesteryear, we have denied fatherhood and motherhood of those experiences because we have permitted our mind to blame outside what was truly taking place and caused inside. Each time you permit your mind to put the responsibility or blame for any experience in your life on anything outside of you, you establish the Law of Denial and begin to walk on the destiny of that denial to serve that judgment. This is very important on the path of your own freedom. The very foundation of the Living Light philosophy—its foundation stone is the Law of Personal Responsibility. When you begin to accept the ability that is your divine right—to respond to all of your experiences—when you begin to accept your birthright of the ability to respond to life and you free yourself from the delusion of giving that ability to things you blame outside of your own personal life, then you will free yourself from the destiny of denial and you will not perpetrate those experiences of yesterday.

Now, you noticed—all of you are well familiar with the repetition of yesterday's experiences. I assure you that you can free yourself from that treadmill the moment you truly accept responsibility for all experience in your life. When you truly accept responsibility for all experience in your life, your life will make a drastic change for the better. Remember, whenever your mind rises up and says, "If so and so hadn't done such and such, I wouldn't be where I am," you are only feeding the treadmill upon which you will repeat the experience again and again and again and again until repetition, the Law of Change, takes place.

Now, in all of this philosophy you see a great deal of repetition. Be rest assured, my friends, as the changes become more harmonious in your life, you will find less repetition in your philosophy. Because the repetition is ever in keeping with the battle of your mind in its denial and its refusal to accept the changes which are inevitable. We can never change what's outside, but we are in a constant process, as small as it may seem to be, in making the changes that are necessary inside.

You know, it certainly would be—and I've often said, and I say again—much easier—at least my mind likes to say—not to have to expose so much of these levels. Because each exposure guarantees, according to the law, a retaliation. That's just the way the human mind works. And we have to work through a mental realm, because we have a mental vehicle that we are using. But not to make the daily effort to expose those levels of consciousness, you would not have the school, the class, the philosophy, or the church that you now experience, for it would not be possible. Personal growth means exactly what the word implies: growth personally. And no one anywhere can grow personally without personal effort. And you can't make personal effort unless you have some awareness somewhere of what you're doing.

Now, that's what Serenity is all about—is helping you to help yourself to face yourself; to face yourself with a better attitude; to think well of yourself. You see, many words are spoken to try to help people to encourage themselves. If you tell yourself that things are getting worse, then you have established the law. You've established the Law of Denial and your destiny is guaranteed by your own spoken word. For many years, many, many, many years, I have spent my days in telling my mind how beautiful the world is, how great everything is, how good everything is. It is very difficult to program the mind when the mind has judged that it is experiencing the opposite. But I can assure you, if you have the wisdom of patience and if you make that effort, then you, *you* are the one who is going to benefit.

You see, in the Living Light, you are a divine incarnation. You, the true being, is whole, complete, and perfect. Any flaws that you say you have reveals only your own judgment. Your soul is a part of a perfect, whole, complete unit. It is inseparable. It is your mind that judges your so-called flaws. But to your soul, that has been evolving for eons of time, the vehicle that you are using is not imperfect to your soul. Oh, no, for your soul knows—it does not have to be told—that through that particular vehicle you are fulfilling the law. And you alone have the personal responsibility of it.

If you look at the vehicle your little soul is expressing through with distaste and you don't like it, then indeed it's a sad day. For it was the vehicle, and is the vehicle, that is necessary for your evolution—not someone else's vehicle, not someone else's body. No, that's your body. That is what you have *earned*. And through it, you can gain the goodness, the fullness of life if you free yourself from this error of ignorance called judgment.

Man long ago created a mental god of judgment. And many religions, unfortunately or fortunately, still teach this god, sitting up there judging all his children. We understand in this philosophy that that is a mental creation: a god created by the human mind. For I can assure you that only in the mental realms does judgment exist. You can only have judgment when you have duality. You can only have so-called right and so-called wrong in a mental realm. There is no right or wrong to the divine, neutral, infinite, intelligent Energy. There's no dark and there's no light to that Intelligence. There's no good and there is no bad, for that Intelligence is above and beyond the mental realms of judgment.

Now, when you accept that level of consciousness, then you will experience what is known as the spiritual realms. There, you will experience that there are things that are more developed, or less developed, as far as form is concerned, but there's no good and there is no bad.

Now, when you think of the word *peace,* if your mind still experiences the opposite, called war or struggle, then you have not yet attained the peace which is the power of the Divine. This philosophy does not imply, nor wish to imply, that man should have no feeling, for to have no feeling is to deny the very vehicle that your soul is using to express. And besides, in truth, there is no one expressing in form that is free from feeling. It is a matter of taking control of the vehicle that you may use it more wisely.

You know, I'm very pleased that I have been permitted to speak this evening in reference to this philosophy and to especially take a look to see what my students are doing while class is in session. I don't see anyone sleeping this evening and that pleases me a great deal, for there are some times that some of my students seem to feel they need to rest their eyes. Well, it's one thing to rest the eyes. It's something else to be consciously unaware of what's going on around and about a person. You see,

I can rest my eyes, but, then again, I do have some awareness. Let us remember that we are tired when we're overidentified with self.

Now, you know, it's so interesting, especially here—this is May. June's coming up. And, you know, it's kind of like the plague. It starts just a little bit, maybe in one little corner, but it always reveals that some of my students are becoming overidentified with self. And I can tell you how you can tell: the first thing you start hearing: "Let's see, June's coming up. I need a vacation." So—not that there's anything wrong with vacations! But why can't they talk about a vacation in November? It reveals that the programming is absolutely set! It's June. It's July. It's August. "I need a vacation." Now, are they thinking for themselves—those minds—or have they permitted themselves to be the victims of mass thought?

We've discussed before about mass thought and thought force. But remember, what is greater than thought and thought force is the power of your soul. Each moment our minds are being bombarded, like a hailstorm, with some kind of thoughts. The first step is to become aware of what those thoughts are saying to us. If they are not what we choose and like, as beneficial to our life, how easy do you find it to be for you to shut those thoughts off? I don't think you find it so easy. Why isn't it easy? As you experience the difficultly of telling those thoughts to be still and stop ordering you around—that you don't want those thoughts in your head—and you have great struggle to get them to stop, you can be rest assured that's how powerful you have permitted them to become.

Because I have accepted, from long ago recognizing that the mind is never still, that the mind is constantly broadcasting messages, thoughts into the universe, for many years I've made the effort to flood my mind with positive thoughts. Because it seemed to me a very practical, simple thing: that if I had to experience a mind that was constantly broadcasting, I would like to make some choice about what it's going to broadcast. Because whatever it broadcasts means that's what I have to experience.

So when I go off to sleep at night, I flood my consciousness. When I awake, I flood my consciousness. During the day, I flood my consciousness. All of you've had that teaching. But there are not too many of us doing it. We must ask ourselves, "Why?" Is it because we have not yet accepted that demonstrable truth that our mind is never still? The mind is never still. Only in meditation, true meditation, when you, through the power of concentration, rise your soul consciousness above and beyond the mental realms do you experience a peace that passeth all understanding. At any other time, your mind is constantly broadcasting a message out into the universe. Whether you like it or not, that is the nature of the human mind and you cannot change its basic nature.

So when your days are filled and it's time to retire or to rest, whatever you wish to call it—sleep, usually they call it—you ask yourself, "How did my day go?" Ask yourself that question. Usually your mind says, "Well, it could have been better." Why, of course, it could be better! It could always be better! Anything, everything could always be better in the mental world. Well, if it could have been better, why didn't you broadcast something better? Because what you experienced was exactly what you broadcast. And you have the choice to broadcast something better. So when you finish your day, you ask yourself that question. And if the answer is "It could have been better," then remember, you've got to broadcast something better. You've got to send out—see, whatever goes out, comes back.

Every philosophy teaches that basic truth: garbage in and garbage out. Anyone with any reason understands that truth. If you permit your mind to flood your universe with negativity and that vibration, well, that's the only thing that you can experience. You can't experience anything better. If you keep telling God how broke you are, you'll only get more broke, because you are establishing, through denial, the Law of Destiny. You are serving the king of judgment. He's not going to let you go so easy. But you are greater than him because only you created him. You are greater than any thought your mind entertains. You are greater than any experience that you have in life. It is when you forget that that you become the victim and the slave of those mental forms.

Now, also in keeping with this exposure, we also have that teaching that irritation wakes the soul. Exposure frees the soul and irritation wakes the soul. Is there anyone within the sound of my voice that has been free from irritation when they were getting one ounce of exposure? [*The Teacher names a student.*] Didn't you get just a split second of exposure when you told me you were just *great*? Now, I didn't talk to you from that level of consciousness. I was aware of what your judgments were doing to you and so I said, "Well, now, how are you feeling?" But that little judgment dude, he rose right up and he spit right back. I'm not trying to imply that all judges are Scorpios, but he was a bit stingy, you must admit that. But, you see—don't you see that affects you?

Oh, I survive. I survive. I get stung many times during the day. Many, many, many, many times. But I have always survived. Because I say to myself, "Well, yes, that's a tough level. I do remember that level. They will get free. That's not them. I know that is not them." Because I must remind myself that those stings from people's minds are not them, because if I permit myself to be deluded that that is the person, I will become a hermit. I'll go off to the mountains and I will only live with the animals. Because then, of course, my little mind will order them just what to do. And they will do exactly what I tell them to do and therefore I will love them. Because that's what the mental world offers, you see.

You see, as long as a person does exactly what you want them to do, then they're a wonderful person. But God forbid, if they do something that you don't want them to do, then they're a terrible person. And so we find difficulties in human relationships. We find difficulties in communication. The difficulty, of course, is in our own head. We tell that person to do that and they don't do that. And we don't demonstrate the tolerance. We don't understand the level. We don't want to waste the time to take three or four hours to try to show them what's going on inside of their head, as well as our own, you see. And yet, without those faculties of tolerance and understanding, we can't fulfill our lives with the goodness that we are truly seeking.

Now, it's like with the student this evening who wished to change her commitment. You see, it's interesting, don't you think, that your mind judged, "Well, a half hour early, not a half hour late. Therefore, a half hour early. There was a difference." Do you understand that? "Therefore Richard should have graciously accepted—Well, she wants to come a half hour early." But, you see, that would place me as a victim and a slave to a king of judgment who had made the judgment for a person to come a half hour early is better than a person who comes a half hour late. Well, the only difference, of course, would be, as far as the house is concerned, is that a half hour late would cost you $150, but a half hour early is costing you the exposure of that judge. Do you understand the difference?

Yes.

You see? Yes, all right. Now, this is important, because, you see, if—and we're getting here right down to what they call the nitty-gritty. You know, many of my students have been asking for the nitty-gritty. So prepare yourself. Your classes are getting better. I'm sure that's what you will consider—some of you.

Have you traced that total lack of consideration back to the source?

Yes, I believe. And I thought, "Oh, I will ask" ... I made that judgment.

But you—yes! Aha! Now, don't you see? You were willing to accept that lack of total consideration because you were doing it for someone else. Is that not correct?

Yes, that's right.

But is it not also correct that you are attached to the person that you wanted to do it for?

Oh, sure.

Therefore, on your priorities that person had a higher priority than your spiritual commitment.

Right.

Yes. Now, my friends, that's known as selling out. And don't think that she's the only one who does it. We do it all the time, you see. We sell out to personality and we're constantly making the effort—unfortunately, for many of us—we're constantly making the effort to please those people that we have judged we are attached to.

Why do we make such effort to please the people that we have judged we are attached to? [*After a short pause, the Teacher continues.*] Because we want to control them. So we make the judgment, well, as long as we please them, they will be our victims. They will be our little puppets and we can do with them exactly what we want to do. That's usually the first process that starts in a marriage. I'm not saying that people shouldn't be married. But great effort is usually made to, to go overboard to please the partner until full control is established in keeping with the judgment and the true motive, you see.

But remember, only our minds want to control someone else. Our soul knows better. It's not our soul that wants to control outside. Our soul rises up and it speaks in a humble voice and says, "You want freedom and the goodness of life? You must make the effort to control that vehicle that we are driving around or soon that vehicle will be driving us." But the little old mind projects that out there: to control something out there. Because it doesn't want to make any changes.

Even the Christian Bible says that least you leave your mother, your father, your brother, your sister, your son, and your daughter and follow the eternal Light, you cannot be free. What does that mean? When you make a commitment to you, your true inner being, then brother or sister, mother or father, husband or wife, they cannot stand in the way. For if they do, we have sold principle to the judge who rules on his realm of personality.

Thank you very much. Thank you.

MAY 25, 1978

CONSCIOUSNESS CLASS 180

Greetings, friends. We shall spend this evening on the questions that you have prepared.

Thank you. There is no attainment without payment. Is the payment higher when one steals something than when one earns something or is the energy exchange the same?

The Law of Payment and Attainment is an infallible law. Therefore, it is ever in keeping with that which one truly attains. If man, in his delusion, believes that he can steal and have no payment, then he is still in the realms of darkness. If a man feels that by work he may attain without a payment, except what he dictates is necessary as work, then he is still in the errors of ignorance. For payment and attainment, an infallible law, is ever equal and in keeping with energy expended.

Thank you. Please explain how the nervous system is a link between matter and spirit and why some people are so-called nervous.

People are nervous for many, many differing reasons. The so-called connection between the spirit world and the nervous system is ever in keeping with the Law of Vibration and Harmony. For example, that that is composed of finer substance is accelerating at a much more rapid speed, so to speak, than that of gross substance. And so it is that as our being is attuned to those higher rates of vibration, that we may perceive and understand the spirit world, which is indeed a much higher vibratory wave, there are times when one may *seem* to be a bit nervous. But do not, please, my students, entertain the thought that whoever appears nervous is in tune with the world of spirit, for that is rarely the case.

Thank you. Is it necessary for spiritual healers to possess a knowledge of anatomy or physiology in order to be effective healing channels?

Absolutely not. For the so-called spiritual healer is not in any way, sense, or form doing the healing. The spiritual healer, so to speak, their true purpose is to be free from self thought, to rise to higher realms of consciousness that they may be a clear channel through which the spiritual healing vibrations may pass through their aura and enter the aura of the patient. The purpose of spiritual healing is to awaken the soul within the person who is desiring the healing. If they do not awaken and establish new laws that are constructive and positive in keeping with nature's harmony, then the healing will not be lasting.

Thank you. Will you please discuss more deeply the importance of courage in making a decision when one is frustrated, so that it will not lead to fascination?

When one is in a state of so-called frustration, they are already under the control of the function of fascination. For without fascination, they could not experience the function of frustration. So when a person is having those experiences, it is in their best interest to make the concerted effort to pause and to experience, through the powers of concentration, a level of consciousness known as peace.

Thank you. Please explain if it is more effective for a healer to touch one's aura than to touch one's physical body.

It is not necessary for one called a spiritual healer to touch any physical body. The healing is not physically taking place. It is spiritually taking place. The soul, which is an inseparable part of the Allsoul, is the perfection of the Divine. It is the awakening of the soul within that emanates this perfect harmony in the mental and physical body. The healing takes place from within the person. It is not something that is coming from without. As like attracts like and becomes the Law of Attachment, so it is absolutely necessary for the spiritual healer to awaken their own soul and be in a vibratory wave of peace in order to attract that divine peace that is within the patient that the healing may take place by the soul that is within the body. It is not outside, my friends.

Whether your experiences are one seeking healing for a health problem or whether it is seeking material supply, which seems to plague your world each and every moment of every hour, it is inside. Not until you accept that demonstrable truth—that everything, your heaven, your hell, your happiness, your abundance, your good, the money, and the desires that you are seeking are inside of yourself. They are not outside. You will not find them outside. When you make that moment-by-moment effort to change your attitude, you will experience the fullness, the abundance, and the goodness of life. But not until you control the mind, which ever goes outward to place the blame and experiences outside, not until, through the powers of concentration and peace, you take and put the harness upon your mind and face the demonstrable truth: your heaven, your happiness, your goodness, your abundance is a level of consciousness that is within you. That, my friends, is the very foundation of this truth known as personal responsibility.

Thank you. What is the true purpose of the conscious mind? Are we always aware of our self-will choices?

We are always aware of our so-called self-will choices. Yes, my good friends, we are always aware. We do not like to often admit that we were aware, especially when we get caught or exposed with our little petty devices and games. It is when we suddenly become aware that we are now the victims of our own transgressions that we do not want to admit that we made a conscious choice. I assure you, we are always conscious of the laws we establish. But once having established those laws, they come under, through repetition, the Law of Habit. But even in the Law of Habit, there is that flicker of awareness at the moment we establish those laws.

Thank you. Would you please explain the origin of confusion and clutter?

From the realms of fascination are born the functions of frustration. And from all of that we go into the realms of confusion and regret: a total lack of organization. Because, you see, my friends, it is the living demonstration that we have lost control of our own mind. Our desires are swimming within our consciousness and there is no control upon them. And because we have fascinated with our own desires for so many, many, many centuries, we suddenly, seemingly so, find ourselves in a state of so-called confusion. And the confusion that we are in inside is revealed by the confusion and clutter that we find in our universe outside. For whatever is in our life outside only reveals what is being sent out from within.

But you have the moment, the moment of choice. You have the moment to work with to direct your thought, through the great power of peace, to bring about in your life some degree of control, for someday it shall come. But you can make it a bit easier by making the effort this moment today. Of what benefit is it to any soul to entertain a multitude of desires and rarely fulfill any of them? Is it not wiser to look upon these desires that your mind is spinning with and make a choice in the light of reason of the ones that, through the Law of Effort and the Law of Continuity, you will fulfill?

Often we have stated that just before the gates of victory, the fools lie down and quit. And so it is that man, in his experiencing of the pain of patience, he quits just before the victories in life, only to run over to something else and something else and something else. Ever blaming outside for his failures that he experiences in life because he did not demonstrate the Law of Effort, the Law of Continuity until he passed through the gates of victory. Nothing grows and matures in a healthy and successful way overnight, so to speak. It takes, in your dimension, time and effort. It takes an unwavering faith, of knowing beyond a shadow of any doubt, regardless of temporal experiences, that what you have to do is in the process of being done. Only through that positive attitude of mind will you pass through the gates of victory. Because, my friends, that is the Law of Life.

Whatever you put into anything in life, that is what you are going to experience and take out of life. If you find that life is marking you short on your desires, then you can be rest assured that you are marking life short. For you are only experiencing what you are putting in. You want your experiences to change, my students, then change your attitudes. Because your experiences cannot change as long as you insist upon the mental games of blaming someone else, someplace else.

We all know what we're doing. But we haven't all yet awakened to what the effects of what we're doing are going to be. But we shall all awaken to that truth. For whatever your motive is in life, that *is* your experience. And if you are not sure of your motive, then pause and do not move, that you may gain control of life, your life, and bring about some positive, beneficial results through experience in your earthly journey.

Do not be so quick to move to fulfill the multitudes of desires that plague your consciousness. Pause and make your choice wisely. In the spiritual awakening of all souls, there are these so-called tests. But these tests are not given by any law or anything that is outside of ourselves. These so-called tests are choices that we face in life to bring about a balance between the function that has control of us, with its desire, and the corresponding soul faculty.

You have been given, in these classes, sufficient awareness of these faculties and functions to bring you through these so-called tests that lie in your spiritual path. And the mighty magnetic pull of the functions is very great, but it is not greater than the power and the peace of the soul faculties.

And so in any school of spiritual awakening, you will find many who answer the call; you will find few who make the final walk through the gates of victory. It is because, my good friends, they are not yet ready. They are not yet ready to bring about a balance between the soul faculties and the sense functions. Remember as you face these so-called tests, which all of you are facing, remember, you're not giving up a function; you are only working to bring about a balance in the function.

We never know what really controls us until we begin to experience an obstruction to our desires in life. When we experience the obstructions to our desires, we, slowly but surely, begin to see what really is controlling our mind. And so the obstructions to our desires, in truth, serve a very good purpose. So often our attention is upon the obstruction. And because of that, we cannot see the light that is greater than the mental creation. We look in life to the experience of the effects and rarely do we trace them to the causes that we alone have set into motion.

If you were to leave your physical world this moment, of what good would your money be? Of what good would the things of the physical world be to you? They would be of no value, my friends. They would indeed be a great detriment to your evolution. You may say, "Well, but you are still in the physical earthly realm." But, my good students, you are working your way in other realms. And if your attention is so filled with the physical world, then you shall be a weak little child in entering these other dimensions. We must prepare ourselves today and truly live in the three worlds, which is, in truth, our home: physical, mental, and spiritual.

For the laws established this moment are very important laws. They are important to you to establish a law with a full awakening of your spirit, of your mind, of your body. You will take with you your mental attitudes. That's what you're taking with you today. Because you do not see this mental realm, because you do not hear these spiritual and astral realms, my friends, you still are living in them. They are controlling you because you have given them control of you. Each time you make the effort to change your attitude, you experience the struggle and return to the patterns of old.

And yet you know that you are stronger than that which you have created. But you cannot help, in the light of reason, to ask yourself the honest question, "I desire to have new, more beneficial experiences. And yet I continue to experience the things of yesterday which I find are not beneficial for me." That shows you, my students, that the attitude, you have yet to change.

What is it that keeps you from a state of constant prayer? What is it that keeps you from flooding your consciousness with peace? What is it that keeps pulling you down into realms of poverty, of lack, of limitation, of discord and disturbance, of poor health and all of those effects? It is not God. It is not spirits. It is attitude of mind.

When an affirmation is given to you to help flood your consciousness to bring about new experiences that are beneficial and beautiful, I find one, sometimes two, of my students make the effort for a few days—some even for a couple of weeks. What keeps you from the Law of Continuity when you know beyond a shadow of any doubt that it will reap a good harvest for you? It is the patterns of old, the attitudes of yesterday. They still rule. But their days are numbered, for they are created forms and, knowing birth and death, they cannot rule forever and ever.

Some time ago one of my students recommended to you students on Earth, when you were going through what is known as the forces, to take a hand mirror and look at your face that you may see the distorted form that was controlling your body, your very being. It is most beneficial, my friends, to make that effort, for indeed will you be surprised to see the distortion in your face when those mental forms have control of your mind. But how many, how many pick up the mirror to take a look?

The changes, they are coming. They are very slow, but they are very sure. Any desire that has risen in our consciousness to be supreme over the Divine Intelligence will repeatedly rise up in our path to so-called test us. We find our minds crying for many things. And it is those great cries of our mind that are revealing to us that our mental forms are still greater than the Divine Intelligence. When they rise within you, remember, you created them. You can begin to call to the true Source for peace.

It is not money that you need. It is not these things that you have deluded your minds with that you need. It is a reuniting with the source of life itself, a true acceptance, a reunion with your true being. That, my friends, is your great need. For that will bring you all the goodness that you can seek. But if you continue to cry for the effects, to cry for the forms, then you cry only in vain, for you are not speaking to the true source of your life.

Let us truly make some effort to become more aware of what we are crying to. For if we truly believe in an intelligent Energy, which is sustaining and available to all of us, then let us become in harmony with that intelligent Energy, called God. For by becoming in harmony with that Intelligence can we experience the fullness of life. But to cry for the fulfillment of our demanding desires is to cry in vain, for in that cry to the effect do we deny the cause and do we deny the source and, therefore, not only become a house divided, but live in discord and disharmony.

Thank you. Please explain the statement, "Duty becomes direction when you use wisdom." [*A saying from the Serenity Game.*]

Duty becomes direction when you use wisdom. The word *duty* is so frequently misunderstood by so many. What is man's true duty? Man cannot know his true duty unless the faculty of wisdom is awakened within. For wisdom, my good friends, is greater than knowledge; it is greater than all things. For wisdom sees clearly the beginnings and endings of all things and wisdom knows the principle, the essence of the law itself. So when we use wisdom, we walk upon the lighted path. Our direction, our duty is very clear, for each of us, in each moment of experience, has duty: the duty to our true being.

Our true being, we cannot know without wisdom. These many lessons in life that come and go are serving their purpose. It is true. But when we, through our errors, hold to these lessons that have served their purpose, then we are only standing in our own light. And to stand in our own light is to blind ourselves and experience what is known as the night.

Remove the thoughts in your mind from you. Become more objective that you may be less emotionally disturbed. Wisdom, may it reign supreme, for it is the faculty of the soul that opens the doors of reason and understanding, that transfigures your whole being, your whole life.

So often a student thinks, "I have studied this philosophy for years, but it doesn't work for me." My friends, that which works for one, works for everyone. Of course, it is dependent on whether or not we apply it. We can study many things in life, but the only thing that's going to work for us is that which we apply. I know that to some of my students it seems to be a bit of a struggle to apply this philosophy in certain areas of their life. But they cannot deny that the areas in their life that they have applied the philosophy here that they are studying, in those areas there has been change. So when we falter along the path and when we think something is not working for us, then we must give more consideration and application to it.

We know within our being where we really are. We all know where we really are. Ofttimes we don't like to be where we really are, but we do know how we got there. And because we do know how we got there, we know how to get out of there.

In a world of creation, you will always stumble because that is the Law of Creation, that duality. This philosophy is trying to show you how to use creation as the tool for which is was designed: to rise above creation, to use the vehicle of creation the way it should be used, the way it was designed to be used. But you must make the effort to separate yourself, the truth, which you are, from the creation, which you are not.

You are an intelligent being without beginning or ending. That is what you truly are. The thoughts that you experience, the life you experience is a passing panorama. Your soul is whole, complete, and perfect. There is nothing you can add or subtract from it. Your perfect being is encased in form that through the emanation of that perfection, known as the eternal soul, those vehicles of form may be refined as part of the eternal Law of the Evolution of Form. Your soul, your true being does not evolve, for there is nothing it can evolve to. The forms that are being used by you, the true being, are what are being evolved.

You have a purpose to serve in life: to serve the true light which is you. When you forget your true purpose, you experience the discord that is not you. Through your daily effort to remind yourself you are not the thought, you are not the form, you are not the experience, you are using the thought, the form, and the experience. Again and again we bring forth the simple teaching, separate truth from creation that you may know the heavenly paradise that is your true home.

Your mind, the vehicle, gathers and garners. Your mind, the vehicle, fears and possesses, not you. Take control of the vehicle for it is when you take control of the vehicles you are using that those vehicles are refined and the true purpose of your soul incarnation into form is truly served. That is the process of spiritualization or spiritual education through discipline of the forms.

The payment for not making that effort daily is very great. Because, my friends, your being is the intelligent energy. If you do not consciously direct it, by control of the vehicles, then you soon experience the delusion that you are the vehicles. And when you experience that which you all experience—the delusion that you are the thought, the delusion that you are the feeling, the delusion that you are the form—then you are the victim, you are the captive. And then life does not seem to have a meaningful, just, or good purpose.

We have spoken to you on the power of the word. We have shared with you how to use it. It's up to you to take those steps. It's up to you, my friends, to separate truth from creation, to free yourself from this illusion of forms. To become aware of when you speak or when a thought-pattern-form of your mind is speaking. For all of these things that you experience by feeling and do not yet see or hear, you shall see and you shall hear. And the day is not far off in this great eternity.

As you will recall when my guardian angel spoke to me and advised me to resist not. Had I resisted, the centuries would have been without number that I would have remained in those realms. For through that resistance would energy have been directed to the forms to make them, yea, even stronger.

One of the greatest lessons ever brought to your world is that energy follows attention. Energy follows attention. When your attention is upon the lack of anything, you create an ever increasing lack until it falls upon you in so-called disaster. You know the law, but you must daily remind yourself of the law in order that you may apply the law. Energy follows attention. Whatever your experience be, you may be rest assured your energy, through attention, is keeping it in your life.

Redirect your attention. If your thoughts are not feeling good for you, then you may be rest assured that you did not feel so good when you created them. Change your thought. And when you find great struggle and great difficulty in changing your thought, then say, "God grant me, yea, even greater strength that I may be free from the delusion of my own mind." Put your attention upon the abundant good in life and only then can you experience the abundant good of life. You cannot experience what you are not placing your attention upon.

My friends, I do sincerely pray that you will pay greater heed to that simple truth: Energy follows attention. All life is energy. All experience is attention.

Good night.

JUNE 1, 1978

CONSCIOUSNESS CLASS 181

Greetings, students.

This evening we shall spend some time in sharing with you the history of your planet Earth and the inhabitants upon it.

As you will recall, some time ago we stated to you that the so-called missing link in man's physical evolution would not be found upon your planet, for it did not originate upon your planet. And so it is that history, so-called, is ever repeating itself as all things physical, mental, and spiritual are destined to return to their source. As your Earth planet, the fifth in your solar system, was given birth from the Mother Sun in your solar system—as were all the other planets—so it is that your Sun was given birth from, yea, another solar system. And they are, in keeping with the Law of Return, the Law of Evolution, the Law of Expansion and Contraction, are in the process of returning to their source, the Sun, though it will be eons yet in your time dimension.

Your planet, the Earth, was long, long ago colonized by intelligent beings from other planets, as the planet is given birth, matures, passes, and returns to its source. And so in your present day, you are viewing this repetition of history, as the Earth inhabitants, in time to come, will colonize other planets in other solar systems.

It is important to you and your expansion in consciousness to understand the principle of evolution: to understand that all things—be they physical beings, be they thoughts or whatever they be—they go out into a so-called world to grow and to refine, only to return to their source. As you, your Earth inhabitants, go out into the universes in the times ahead, you will at first be greatly disappointed that you are not able, in those early stages of investigation, so to speak, to find intelligent beings. But it is only because your view is limited. It is because your judgments are ruling and you expect to find intelligent beings on the surface of the planets, as you, yourself, are presently living. But that I assure you, my friends, is not the case in many of the planets. For life exists within some of them as it exists on the surface of your own planet.

The guidance that you receive daily is ever in keeping, of course, with the Law of Effort that you alone establish. When intelligent beings were first transported to your planet, as their own home was slowly, but surely, dying, so to speak, they searched the universe and found the planet Earth. In your lifetime these intelligent guardians in physical form will once again become known to your world.

There is a great need upon the Earth planet to expand the limited consciousness of its inhabitants in order that they may become prepared, that they may adjust to the inevitability that is to be faced in time yet to be. Earth is not the least evolved, nor indeed is it the most evolved. As you have been given the guardianship and charge over the intelligent forms upon your planet, there are those who have been given the guardianship and charge over your own destiny as Earth beings.

And so, my friends, we have taught you much concerning the laws of identity, the Law of Total Consideration, the great need to open your minds and to let fresh air awaken your consciousness that you may see beyond a shadow of any doubt your true purpose in life, that you may face your responsibilities as intelligent beings. For each thought you think is a deposit in universal consciousness. It serves to help, to restore, to heal, to bring the great vibratory wave of harmony to your world or it serves the other realms of consciousness that are still in discord and disasters. In many different ways we have tried to show you the benefit of constructive and positive attitudes that you may gain the wisdom of patience to see that, through simple, daily moment-by-moment efforts, you are making a beneficial deposit in consciousness, not only for yourselves, for your world, but the many worlds that are within it.

To permit your minds to be so limited to mundane, trivial seeming problems is to close your view of the heaven that is with you in this, the eternal moment.

Man, as he entered the earth realm, as he was the instrument through which intelligent beings were to colonize it, brought with him a great responsibility. Man, in his conscious mind, has forgotten that responsibility. He has forgotten it because he has limited his view of life, through a restriction through the Law of Identity, and, in so doing, has brought upon himself the seeming struggles of day-to-day living. My good students, what is day-to-day living, when you have ever been, when you are and shall always be? Your forms have changed before. Your forms are changing now. Your forms will change again. For the form that blinds you is but a suit of clothes. Therefore it is necessary for you, in order to be free from the prison of the form that you have identified with, to pause more often to look—to look at the moment of great eternity, to joyously in the spirit of true gratitude face the responsibility and the reason for your journey on your earthly realm.

For what you do affects the multitudes in ways that your limited mind cannot imagine. For you are an instrument through which the Law of Vibration is established and that vibration is a responsibility. For from harmony you have come and to harmony you shall return. Therefore, you are the instrument through which the Law of Harmony may flow in your Earth. If you are not making that effort to be a free and clear instrument through which that vibration may become supreme upon your planet, then you are not facing your responsibility in evolution and not facing responsibility simply means a struggle and a continuous battle against the tides of eternity. That need not be so if you will pause more often. That need not be so if you will accept that you do have the ability to respond to life, for you are life and that that is contains the ability for what is necessary.

There is no experience that you can encounter or that you have ever encountered that is not in keeping with your own abilities to conquer. The conquering of experiences in one's life is the demonstration that you still are master and captain of your ship of destiny. It is your destiny and you sail upon that sea of time. But with you, in your little ship, you take many. And it is the many that you take—all those thousands of created children—that look to you for their guidance. For they are the children that you have created. You are their mother and their father. And your responsibility is greater as your children continue to grow. They grow, of course, in keeping with your attention, with your energy, but only you are making the choices in life.

So whatever, whatever you view your life as, it is from a level, of course, within you. And you know—and thousands upon thousands of words have been spoken—you know how to change. You know how to change graciously. For he who changes graciously reveals his own maturity.

Let us move in this great sea of time by pausing and letting the divine Law of Peace take control of our being. For in those moments of peace shall your ears open and your eyes awaken to the great truth that you are indeed the instrument of this great, intelligent Source that sees each thought before you think it, that knows each act before you do it, that whispers gently within you, "Peace and patience."

For that that is yours is facing you. If you do not see it this moment, it is because the throne of judgment stands between you and your own destiny. That which is inevitable is in keeping with what we alone have set into motion. But always remember that as you continue to establish laws in consciousness, you are never left without the power to change them. You are never left, in truth, without the courage that is necessary.

Untold millions of souls wait to incarnate upon your planet and some must wait for many centuries in keeping with the laws that they have established. For what is the benefit in waiting to express in form? What does man gain as he waits for that that he desires and knows that, for him, is inevitable? Man gains wisdom from the pain of patience. So when the pain of patience speaks within your mind, remember, your soul, in that moment, is being granted the opportunity to express the greatest faculty of all faculties: the faculty of wisdom. It is not often that the eternal soul receives the opportunity to express that faculty because when the pain of patience cries, it cries very loud. And so the intelligent energy that is flowing through the being goes to the screaming demons who know only what they do not have, who cannot see what is on its way to them.

It's over the mountain, my friends. It's always over the mountain to our minds, because the mountain, representative of the soul's aspiration, is blinded. It is blinded by our view for we look from below in the realms of creation and we look up to see how high the mountain is. But when we rise, through the power of peace, our soul looks down and sees how majestic, but how small, the mountain really is. So all of life, all obstructions, and all ways are ever in keeping with our view. And, of course, our view is ever in keeping with our attitude of mind.

There has been much interest in your world with what you refer to as cloning or duplicating the forms of your planet. I want to assure you, for in time upon your planet it shall come to pass, that these so-called duplicates—that are in some forms already being created—do not receive so-called different, or new, souls to animate them. Whenever a part of any form is taken, it is in the realm of possibility, through the laws of creation, for it to prosper and grow. The intelligent energy that is sustaining the so-called duplicate is the energy that is flowing through the original form. And so your questions in respect and regards to the cloning of the human species is simply an extension, so to speak, of the original. It is not a different soul. It is not even a same soul. It is the soul that is. Life eternal, in form, is something that already is. It is not something that is going to be.

But your questions rise in reference to life eternal in the form that you are presently identified with. Cloning will offer an extension of that particular form. It will not change the eternal being that you are. It simply gives a constant supply of forms through which the soul may express. But be rest assured, my friends, when that day comes in centuries yet to be, that those souls have merited in keeping with their evolution, those particular experiences and lessons in life—for the souls that are to inhabit those forms have long been waiting on your earth realm to enter.

Your so-called new inventions are new only to your physical world. They are not new to these many other worlds. They have just finally entered and finally been accepted by your world. You know how difficult it is for anyone to accept a new thought, an idea. This is why, in many ways, evolution is a slow, but indeed a sure process.

When your struggles seem so great, remember, with them, you have overidentified. Look another way. Identify with something good. Identify with something great. For that that you identify with, you become. If you are not happy with what you think you are, identify with something you desire to become. To some people, I am sure that teaching will seem like daydreaming. But I assure you, all of life is a dream. And therefore some time ago we stated, "Dreamer, dream a life of beauty before your dream starts dreaming you."

My students, when you lose control, when you lose control, you gain bondage and freedom is no longer existent for you. If it is true—and demonstrably it is—that life is a dream, that you are dreaming the dream—it is when the dream starts dreaming you that you suffer. And that means when you overidentify with anything, the thing you overidentify with, you become. You lose control and it gains control.

Now, this is what we mean when we speak about the separation of truth from creation. Your thought is a creation. It is something that you, by the powers of your mind, have created. When you overidentify with what your mind creates, that's when you lose control, that's when you go into bondage, that's when you begin to experience impatience and suffering and the many functions of the human mind.

But you don't have to overidentify. There is a law in the universe called the Law of Balance. There is a law in the universe—the Law of Loss and Gain, the Law of Positive and Negative, the Law of Day and Night. Those laws are. You have the intelligence to use those laws wisely. Instead of identifying with what you judge you're losing, stop in that moment and identify with what you are gaining. If you say you cannot see what you are gaining, it simply reveals that you have not made the effort to create it, that all of your attention is upon that that has been created by your mind that you now judge you are losing. To view the closed door, the losing in life, is to deny yourself from the experience of the gaining. For without the loss, there is no gain, and without the gain, there is no loss and, therefore, are you denied the experience of evolution itself.

In the worlds of creation you must learn to receive as graciously as you give. So often we delude ourselves by judging that we give and give and give and gain nothing. This is one of the very strong delusions of the human mind to defend the realm that absolutely refuses to give anything. And that is the realm of judgment.

This philosophy teaches that selfless service is the path to spiritual illumination. But you cannot have selfless service as long as you have judgment. The greatest gift that you can give, my friends, is the gift of self. And the gift of self is the throne of judgment. If you give without the gift of self, if you give without giving of the throne of judgment, then your gift goes in vain. For it is not a gift: it is a loan. For you, your throne of judgment still has it under its control, for it still thinks about it and, in so doing, is still attached to it. That, my friends, is not a gift, but it is a loan.

So let us not confuse, in our lives, let us not confuse giving with loaning. Loans incur debts; gifts are free from the soul. For a gift, truly given, comes from the infinite Source and is ever replenished; it is ever replaced. We need not be concerned—if we are truly giving, there is no concern. We are then the instruments of the infinite, divine, abundant Good that is everywhere, everywhere, everywhere. It is when we give begrudgingly that we haven't given at all; but we have loaned. You see, my friends, so often in our so-called giving, we make the judgment if we do this, we will gain that. And then time marches on and we don't have those experiences. We take a look and we do not see the gain, because all of our attention is upon what we have done. That is known as overidentification.

Be not concerned with what you do and you will be free from the doing. It is your concern that is your payment. For each concern you have in life reveals the authority and priority of your mind over all your experiences. Be not concerned. Do that which you know is right because it is right to do it. Give not so much of thought to your doing. Then, you will be able to experience a greater life than you have ever known in all your evolution. For you have come this far and much farther shall you go, for you have established those laws and those laws are the lights that are lighting your path.

Some will step aside, for they have overidentified with form and, therefore, shall be trapped by form. But some of you will stay upon the lighted path and you will move ever onward and upward in consciousness and you will see more clearly than ever before what the world really is—not the things your eyes and senses experience, but a great, powerful, peaceful intelligent Energy that ever waits to serve. Think of that, my friends. The intelligent Power that sustains your very being is a servant to you.

Choose more wisely how you use this great, serving God. Choose more wisely. For you have been given the intelligence, given the intelligence in keeping with your own evolution, given the intelligence to use this energy that is ever at your bidding. Do not cast your pearls before the swine of the human mind and its multitudes of temptation, for that only builds your own prison. Become more thoughtful of your words, your acts, and deeds. Become more objective. He who does not accept the Law of Personal Responsibility is denying the great power that is waiting to serve him.

Do not be so quick to judge. Do not be so quick to take the credit for everything you think is great. And then you'll begin to experience in your lives the greatness of the Power that sustains you. It denies you nothing. It's your mind that denies you. It's not the Intelligence. That is ever there to serve you. And you have a great responsibility to an intelligent Energy that is so humble, that is so willing. Use it wisely, that you may become what you are destined to become, not in some far distant future of time, but in the moment of now, in this moment. That, of course, is dependent upon your willingness to accept a better way: To expect the goodness and greatness that is yours and to demonstrate the faculty of wisdom and control the pain of patience.

Good night.

JUNE 8, 1978

CONSCIOUSNESS CLASS 182

Good evening, class.

We're going to have a little change in our classes. For you have all received many classes in this philosophy and we must take an assessment, personally, each of us, of course, to see in what way, if any, the philosophy is benefiting our lives. Of course, like anything, if we don't use it, it can't work for us.

And so we find with, of course, ourselves that in the early stages of study, we are usually a bit enthused, certainly a bit interested. And we find that, at times—of course, when we use it—that it works for us. Then we go on through the months and the days and the years—it looks like someone had lunch up here—the months, the days, and the years and when we face these so-called struggles in our life, we permit these old patterns of ours to have control again. And we use the philosophy less and less and less and revert back to that with which, of course, we are so familiar: the patterns of our life. This is not something that is uncommon in any study of any philosophy.

We are constantly facing, every day in every way, our mind and the patterns, of course, that we alone have created. Unless we really make the conscious, moment-by-moment effort to apply the philosophy that we spend our time studying, that we (our mind) may view the beneficial results, then, of course, these changes that we all know must be made in order for us to move on to more successful ways of living do not get so easily made.

In the years of sharing with you this understanding, I've viewed many students come, stay for varying times, and go. I've always felt good that they have received what they came for and let them go as graciously as they have come. Because every experience in life we encounter is recorded and can, and does, serve us when we permit it to do so.

It is interesting, especially in this type of religion and philosophy, to see how the mind accepts and rejects, denies and doubts, and goes through its many struggles, which, of course, is known to us as the battle or the war within. Now, we all have this war going on at all times. Sometimes, through a degree of objectivity, we are aware of it. For each pattern of mind that has been rigidly established within our consciousness that views our efforts to change is experiencing a threat, of course, to itself.

Our struggle, then, is when we permit our mind to tell us that we are those patterns. For in that moment, we do lose objectivity. And when you lose objectivity, there is no faculty of reason expressing. For the faculty of reason can only express through objectivity, through a total consideration, not through a limited one. So you must realize, in your journey on this spiritual path that you have chosen, that you will constantly face yourself. You will constantly face these patterns of mind that have enjoyed already a very long life. They will not bow easily. Some, of course, some that are not as strong, they do bow. They come back up periodically to express themselves, to receive energy from you through your attention to them.

Now, you must realize that a pattern of mind, a thought, is a form that is created in a mental world, that you, your soul, is moving through the mental world of your own creation. And a pattern of mind, which is a form, or forms, you have created, receives more energy through your identification with it than it does simply from your attention to it. So it is critically important to become more consciously aware of what you are identifying with.

Now, so often we'll wake up in the morning, we say we feel lousy or it's a lousy day or we meet someone and things didn't go the way we had judged they should or we thought they should or this didn't happen the way we felt that it should. All of those experiences reveal a reliance, a dependence, through attention and identification, to certain patterns of mind. It is not you, your soul, that is crying out in that respect. It is, however, those created forms.

Now, this philosophy has taught, and continues to teach and to make the effort to demonstrate, that life, of course, is an effect, not a cause. It is an effect. All experience in life is an effect. Therefore, we will have to, someday, make that constant effort. Now, when your mind says, "I don't want to be bothered to do that every day of my life. For how long will I have to do it?" Well, this is—I'm going into my thirty-eighth year of this work. A lot of people seem to be under some kind of an illusion that, for me, it must be easy. I mean, after all, I do have eighty-one souls who have founded this organization. And they make all the decisions governing it. Therefore, for me it must be easy. But, you see, that is not true.

I must work on my mind, which has created patterns. What you must realize is that these patterns of mind, these forms, they don't just disappear. They die off very slowly, for they were very slowly created. They have received a lot of energy. And they live on that energy even though you stop giving them any identification or attention. And they live for some time.

Now, Madame Blavatsky, the founder of Theosophy, she perceived a very simple truth concerning the astral realm—and she perceived correctly—that many people were—so-called mediums—were not communicating with the soul of the so-called departed. But they were communicating with their astral shell. Now, what we must understand is this: first of all, it must be the astral body of the individual in order to communicate with the astral shell. Well, what happens is, when you leave (your soul), the physical body, the body doesn't disintegrate immediately. It's a very slow process of disintegration. And so the same law that applies to the physical world also applies to the astral and mental worlds: that it is a slow, disintegrating process. Therefore, there are people, of course, who are communicating with astral forms that the soul has left. I bring this point up in order that you may become a bit more aware: that although, perhaps for years, you have not directed attention or identified with certain patterns of mind, they haven't died off. They slowly disintegrate.

Now, anytime that you permit your attention to go back to them and especially to identify with them, then you give them a regeneration, a charge of energy, for them, once again, to become active in your life and in your experiences.

Now, we all have experiences—we are experiencing them—that continue to repeat themselves, especially the ones that we don't like. Well, we must be honest with ourselves and we must say, "Why does this—or these combination of experiences, why do they continue to take place in my life? I am personally responsible. I know the Law of Personal Responsibility. I accept that demonstrable truth. Now, what is it inside of me that keeps creating this repetition of experiences?"

Well, it is known—a demonstrable truth—that the way to get out of anything in life is the way that we got into it. Now, if we get into a level, a state of consciousness that created forms by a law of repetition, then it's going to be a law of repetition to get us back out. I am not one of those people who believe in instantaneous miracles. I don't believe in miracles at all. It's just a lack of our understanding of laws of the universe: we haven't yet perceived how they work.

Now, we look around in our lives and we see that we're feeling pretty good or we're in the forces. We are either up or we're down. Well, we can be rest assured, of course, that we're over-identified with our own mind, because the human mind, being a part of creation, is up and it is down. You will not find peace, happiness, joy, success, and on through the list of abundant good in a mental realm. It does not exist there. For the mental realm is either up or it is down.

Now, if you think that money will cure all your ills, then you will face that delusion, which will, in time, prove to you it is not a cure-all. There is nothing that is a cure-all in a mental world of creation of duality.

The experience beyond the mental realm is when we bring this mental world of functions and faculties into some degree of balance so that we may experience higher levels of consciousness.

In working in this organization, it has always been interesting to me to note that the human mind denies the existence—or even the possible existence—of anything that is above and beyond its direct control. Many people, over the years, have asked, "Why, why has Spiritualism had such a struggle for thousands of year?" For it is the oldest philosophy and religion known to the human mind here on Earth. In the primitive cultures, you find Spiritualism practiced, and continuing to be practiced century upon century upon century. For the mental realm has not risen supreme in its authority. When our mind is the authority, it must, in order to maintain its position of authority, it must deny anything that is beyond its direct control. This is why we find here, as students, in this Spiritualistic philosophy, the mind—the acceptance and the denials.

Now, when things appear to our mind to be going the way our mind dictates they should be going, there is what is known as a false acceptance of something beyond the mind. I assure you, my good students, it is a false acceptance. When things are difficult and are not going the way that our minds have dictated, immediately, *immediately* there is no authority, there is no spiritual world, there is no soul, there is no Spirit. The denial is immediate. What we must face, ourselves, for ourselves, is, in our false acceptance, we must face that level of consciousness. For to deny one day and to accept the next reveals and demonstrates an expression of the human mind, not the soul and not the spirit.

For your philosophy to work for you, you must use it constantly. You must use it wisely. You must use it in the small ways first. For those are the ways that your mind will accept. It'll accept giving a crumb, oh, but never a whole loaf. So you must use it in the little ways in your life.

This philosophy teaches that man, his mind, is locked in what is called a mes, *m-e-s*. It's known as money, ego, and sex. Now, those are very strong, potent forces of the human mind. We all have them. We all experience them when we overidentify with self, the mind.

For many years, I have flooded my consciousness with affirmations. Because I have learned, hopefully, that unless I do, the experiences I encounter are not what I care to enjoy. The mind, which is constantly broadcasting, sending out these vibratory waves into the universe, brings back experiences into our life. If you really make the effort in the application of what you are studying here, if you are ready, if you are ready to flood your consciousness with the affirmations of your choice that are positive and constructive, then you will experience the good that is the effect of them. But you have to do it when you're feeling good and when you're feeling bad. You can't just wait to just before the trapdoor of disaster has opened and start to flood your consciousness. Because that's not the way that it works. You see, it takes time, it takes effort, it takes energy.

I mean, flooding my consciousness constantly doesn't mean that I have nothing but bummer experiences in my life. Not at all. In fact, I feel very good. I work to keep myself that way. And I work right around the clock to stay that way. Because I have been blessed, through my merit system, to have students and to witness the up and down, up and down, up and down—it's worse than being on a rollercoaster. And I have not chosen, in my life, to live that way. I don't care to live that way. And I have found a way so I don't have to live that way. But no one, of course, can do it for you. You have to have enough highs and enough lows and you have to go down far enough till finally you're willing to give whatever you think you've got—that is, up here—to get something, something better.

And I want to bring up that point on giving, because it's a very important point. We had a class once, some time ago, on giving. It seems that many of us still misunderstand the Law of Giving. We give things, it seems. And after we give things, we think, "Now, what are they doing with what I gave them?" or "What have they done with what I gave them?" You see, my friends, the difference between a gift and a loan is very simple: If you loan somebody something, you're constantly worried what they're doing with it. But if you give someone something, you no longer have any thought concerning it. Now, there's the basic difference between a gift and a loan. Now, we loan many things in our lives and we give very little. Because, you see, we're still thinking about it and that reveals the loan, instead of the gift.

But the giving is something much greater. You see, this philosophy teaches, The gift without the giver is worthless. Now, what does that mean? The gift without the giver is worthless. It means it's not a gift. It's a loan. You see, when you give and the giver goes with the gift, there's no attachment. Do you understand? It's those chains of attachment to your so-called giving that cause all your problems in life. So, if you choose to give, then make sure you go along with your gift. Because if you don't go along with your gift, it wasn't a gift at all: it was only a loan. And all loans demand their interest rate. Now think about that.

So when you accept, accept the giver along with the gift, because if you don't do that, you're going to pay mighty high interest. And the interest rates today are mighty high! Think about that, friends. But the giving I'm talking about is the greatest gift you have. And that's the gift of self. You see, this is what is really required to experience this so-called abundant good in life. You have a great gift. You have that. And it really takes something to give that gift to the divine Source.

But when you worry about money and when you worry about all the other functions, stop in that worrying, stop for a moment and say, "Well, Lord, what is it that I can do to free myself from these hounds that are driving me crazy? What can I do?" It's really very simple: If you will give the self—this—in that moment to the divine Source, along with that gift you give will go all those hounds, will go all of those problems. It will go right along with your gift, you see. That's what we all are going to learn to do someday.

It is when our minds, in their tenacity, insist upon being the final authority—and justifying all over the universe why they should be the final authority—that we have all these struggles and all these problems in life. Now, don't get me wrong. It doesn't mean that I haven't had to work on my own mind. I still do. It is a total illusion to think that you can work on your mind and—"Ah! I got through that now!"—and sit back on your haunches and relax. That isn't how it works. At least, it doesn't for me.

Whenever you have a thought to do something, put more into it than just the mental substance. Put your all into it. Now, if you put everything—your all—into it, then it cannot help but come back in a bountiful harvest if you demonstrate the soul faculties that you already know. These faculties that have been given to you folks were not given for something to fascinate your minds or entertain your minds with. They have been given to you to use and to use wisely.

This philosophy teaches that fools quit before the victory. And you look and you see how many people, just before the victory, they quit. But you must also remember that people who do that have a pattern. It isn't specific to that area or that. They have a pattern of quitting just before the victory. Because the mind rises up and says, "Well, now, I've been working on this for X number of months—or years—and I have not gotten out of it what I should have gotten out of it." That's where we have to start thinking. We have made a judgment. And we are paying the price of the judgment that we alone made. This is what we do in our life, whether it's in business or in relationships or in anything else. We set up all these judgments, all these dictates: how long this is going to take and what it's going to be like when it's finished. And how rarely is it really like that.

You know, I remember when I was back in Forest Knolls in a little, small place and I had to move. And the owner had lost the place and I had to move rather suddenly. And I remember saying, "Well, I don't know what I'm going to do, but I've got to do something. I mean, that's all there is to that." And my mother said to me, she said, "Richard, would you stay there when we have a mansion waiting for you?" Well, the place I finally moved into had two rooms, instead of one, and to me, it was a real mansion.

And so, what I'm telling you this for is that we, so frequently in our lives, we look at the dark side of everything. But why do we seem to enjoy looking at the dark side? It's kind of like a person that races to the freeway because five cars have just smashed up. It excites our senses! Think about that. You see, if you can look at the dark side and all this struggle and all this disaster and everything—it certainly does not, in any way, appeal to your faculties of peace and harmony, of joy. But it certainly does a lot of work on discord and disaster and all the excitement of the senses. Why, you can cry, you can scream, you can wail. You can do all of those things of the senses.

So, you see, you take a look at any mind that just seems to feed on negativity—it seems to feed on disaster—then you can understand that the mind is starving for the excitement of the senses. But now wouldn't it be better to turn on the television? They've got all kinds of excitement on the TV—or even the radio—and get your excitement that way, rather than put yourself through the Chinese torture chambers in life. Don't you see, my students? Energy follows attention.

Now, you can say, "Well, that's fine for him to say. Everything's going fine for him." Be that in divine order. I work on it constantly. But any of you that have been around, I don't think that you can say things are always going so great for Richard Goodwin. They're going as great as I will permit them to go. It's in my head. I didn't always know that. And because I didn't always know that, things didn't always go so great for me. Because, you see, I didn't know that teaching. I had to pay the price to receive that truth. I hope that your price will not be so great to receive that truth. Not that it hasn't been spoken to you. But, you see, truth is individually perceived. My, many words are spoken, but how many of them get accepted? Not too many.

But I assure you, it is definitely dependent upon our acceptance how our life will continue on. It's not dependent on anyone else. It's not dependent on the tax collector or the government or anything. It is dependent on what we personally, *personally*, choose to accept.

When we are in this realm of the human mind, we see the discord, the confusion, and the disasters in life. We cannot seem to see them as stepping-stones to attain something better, for our eyes constantly view the stepping-stones of payment. Well, my friends, I have my own stepping-stones in life and so do you and everyone else in the whole, wide world. And whenever there is a step forward for your organization, my mind takes a sly look at it and blinks immediately. Because the mind is well informed: there's a payment for every attainment. So, of course, my mind is not in any way or in any sense anxious to grow too much too soon. Because each step along the way must be paid for.

And because this body, this student body, and this organization *is* an organization, what one does has an effect, within the organization, upon the others. Because that's just the way that it is when you are in a body. It has an effect. Direct or indirect, it still has an effect. So there is more to consider when you are involved in an organization or a class than the self. For your thoughts, acts, and activities within the organization have an effect upon the whole.

As I told a group of students before the home was built for Serenity, I said, "When the body is 51 percent in the positive realm of consciousness, the home of the church will come to pass. But not until a minimum of 51 percent are demonstrating that vibratory wave." Because that *is* the way the law works: it has to be at least 51 percent.

In all of this and in the experiences you are having today, if the struggle is driving you out of the mind into realms that can bring into your life some degree of balance and harmony, then, of course, it's serving a good purpose. I mean, after all, there is a bottom to everything. Sometimes we seem to think it's made of elastic, because it keeps getting deeper. But there is a bottom to everything in this old world. And if you'll remember that in your mental struggles in life—when you reach that bottom, there's no place left to go but up—you're bound to reach it much sooner, instead of stretching it out year after year after year after year.

I feel that it is very important to the students to have some understanding in reference to what this organization, presenting this philosophy, is really all about. It has gone through many growth steps and continues to do so. The purpose of evolution is the refinement of all form. And so Serenity is in a constant process of change, growth, and refinement, as anything in form, of course, is. And that brings to my mind new rules and regulations that we are constantly growing through.

And to some of you who are not aware, rules and regulations are brought into force as an effect of transgressions of simple considerations within any organization. This is how you get laws. You see, you wouldn't have traffic lights on the streets if the pedestrians and the drivers considered each other. Then, you wouldn't have to spend all your tax dollars to put them all in. You wouldn't need them. Because the driver would be driving along the highway and he would see that somebody was waiting to cross and he would stop. And the person would walk across the street, you see. But because of the lack of consideration, you have laws in your land. And that's how you get laws—because of the self-interest, instead of the interest of the whole.

And so it is in Serenity. You get new rules, new regulations, new laws governing the church body. I've never been one that appreciated rules, regulations, and laws. I'm not too keen on them. And therefore I have had to learn to accept them. We have had some members and some students request leaves of absence. And the church has granted leaves of absence. But because that granting, from the church to those requesting leaves of absence, has been taken advantage of, new rules and new regulations have come into being this very day—this morning, in fact. Therefore, members of the organization who request leaves of absence must, before returning to the organization and to any of their spiritual duties within the organization, must have a spiritual counseling to discuss their responsibilities involved within the organization.

It always saddens me a bit—not as much as it used to—but a bit. You know, when you have a lot of experiences, you don't get as sad as much, as often. But it still always saddens me a bit that, once again, new rules and new regulations must be born and enforced. Now, why should the Council of your church establish this type of rule and regulation? Because—it's very simple—an increasing number of people, although there's only a very few, have taken advantage of a consideration offered to a member of the organization. Therefore, if that vibratory wave of self-interest over the good of the whole increases, then the good of the whole soon disappears. It is no longer existent.

Now, you, as students, should be very grateful. Because you come here to learn a philosophy that, I assure you, works. But you don't have to believe me. All you have to do is really try it. It works.

Everything in life is, in truth, vibration. If you have a student body that is making the effort to help themselves and you permit other students who are not making equal effort, or even in the ballpark of effort, to come and go, then that rate of vibration becomes predominant and is certainly not beneficial to those who are truly making the effort. And it's really that simple. And so, once again, Serenity, in its evolution, is tightening up the ship that it may sail more smoothly.

For many years I have said to the members and to my students, it is not numbers that we should ever be interested in. It is never quantity. It is always quality. For you can take one person in life in the right quality vibration and get more accomplished than you can with a thousand workers. For everything is vibration.

It's like building a house. If you are in the vibration of peace and harmony, if you are emanating and demonstrating that, then the house will be built of quality construction. It will be built in a shorter period of time because you have controlled those mental forms that are discordant. And the work progresses beautifully. But if you jump around and you get excited and you get upset and you get worried, then you'll have the opposite result, no matter what it is that you do in life. Now, think about that, friends—no matter what it is you do in life. I have found that more gets accomplished by taking the time to sit down with the person and have a cup of coffee and a discussion, than to scream at them to hurry up and get the job done. More gets accomplished because there's always more good that gets accomplished when there's consideration being expressed. You see, if a person does a job in life and they're in a level that is discordant, then the effect of that work will be most discordant. And if you're interested in quality, it will only have to be done over again and again and again and again. That certainly is not, surely—I'm sure we will all agree—that is not a key to success.

Now, do not be concerned, friends, about new rules and regulations. They will be *impartially* enforced, as rules and regulations always have been at Serenity.

The only thing that causes anyone to slip off the rock of principle, the only cause of moving off the rock of principle is the lack of controlling desire. When we educate desire that we may see clearly, then we can remain in life on the rock of principle. But if we don't make an effort to educate our desires, then we are constantly tempting, *constantly tempting,* personality.

One of the greatest things that upset me in opening up the doors of any church was my experiences with personality in the church of which I was already a member. Of course, I learned later I couldn't have experienced all the personality if I hadn't been in it myself. But, you see, you people are so fortunate. I did not know those laws in those days. So that was one of the things that I really didn't appreciate in opening up a church or any organization—is because of personalities, the experiences of personalities.

But how does personality get born in an organization? Personality gets born very simply: it gets born by desire, blind desire.

I've spoken to students, now, for several weeks in reference to when you choose to do anything within the organization, you must ask yourself one question: "How will this affect thirty other people?" For there are—of course, there are less members now. There are twenty-seven, which pleases me to no end. I never was interested in numbers anyway. The twenty-seven members—I am very grateful for the refinement and the quality keeps on growing. I'd rather have seven and have principle and have quality than to have 2,700.

How does this all get born, this personality? Because one takes a look and sees, "Ah, now, that one gets to do that. But I don't get to do that." Another one takes a look and says, "Well, so-and-so hasn't spoken to me properly lately." See, this is how all personality gets born: all out of desire, blind desire. In order to experience personality, of course, we have to be in the level to experience the level.

So let us stop and think of what we're here for. Let us take stock of that. I know we're not here to fill up the chairs. I know none of us come for that purpose, be rest assured of that. But we're here for something. I hope that it is to stand up and have the courage to make the necessary changes in your mind to take control of your mind. Because, I assure you, that's where it really exists. It exists—our experiences—within our own realm of consciousness. That's the only place it exists.

I am really grateful for the multitude of experiences in these past seven years or more and the effort that people have, and do, make. There is no question in my mind that each one here is sincerely interested in trying to better themselves. And you must realize that I am sincerely interested in trying to share with you the philosophy that has been granted to me that has worked for me. It works for me because I use it. If I don't use it, then it doesn't work for me. And when I say I use it, I don't mean that I study the book [*The Living Light*] every day. And I don't mean that I listen to the tapes every day. But you must realize that I have listened for many years. I still listen to the Spirit. But I try to pause and to think: to be aware of any thought swimming around in my mind that is not positive, that is not expressing abundant good for me.

In fact, it's most interesting to me because—I'll bring up this point. The founders of your church informed me, when we first started building, that the entire property line up the road would be covered someday with bamboo. Well, I said, "That's fine. That's going to take a lot of bamboo." But, anyway, we—they also had us put a little bamboo—many twenty or thirty—well, more than that—around these fishponds, which was nice. It helped blot out some of the buildings across the street down the hill. So, I guess it was a week or two ago, I was informed to order thirty-six bamboo trees. And, of course, with the order, I was also informed to raise the funds. Because I never get an order to spend the money that I don't get an order to raise the money. My mind did not appreciate that because I already had some experience with the cost of bamboo trees: $14.95 for 5-gallon trees. And I multiplied that immediately by thirty-six. But I went ahead to fulfill the order. I ordered the trees. I raised—I got a bamboo committee established, which I'm still working on, and it's coming along.

Well, just as it was coming along—and I think we had 14 commitments to buy a bamboo tree—14 out of 36—I thought, "Well, now, that's coming along. It won't be too long before I'll be halfway. And when you get halfway, you can start looking over the mountain." And I was feeling real good that evening. And the next morning, I got another order that we would complete—we had now planted those tress—that we would complete the roadway. And then I felt a little sick inside because I saw how far 36 bamboo trees went and I calculated another 36 wouldn't complete it. I was told to get 54. OK. Well, I went through my mental trauma and I ordered 54. I had no sooner ordered 54 when, an hour later, I was told the number was changed to 63.

[Mr. Goodwin coughs.] Excuse me. Which are being delivered tomorrow.

That, of course, meant, over the whole process, that there were 99 holes to dig, because that's how many trees there are. Well, fortunately, one of our students was very kind. I asked him if he would help: if he could give an hour a day after work until we got these holes dug. Well, really, it went quite well considering he dug 20 holes in one hour—Isn't that correct?

Yes.

Twenty holes in one hour and, of course, that still left 79 to go.

But, now, the question has to be asked, Why couldn't they tell me up front that there would, in truth, be 99 bamboo trees that I would have to get underway and get paid for, instead of telling me 36? And why did they have to, after telling me 36 and I got them planted, tell me, by the way, there'll be 54 more. And then, just a matter of an hour or so later, tell me there will now be 63. My mind says, "When are they going to stop?" That's an awful lot of trees—because I love trees anyway. Then, on top of that, of course, we're on well water. And then I calculated how many gallons of water that will take. But that's not so bad. I did get that calculated, but with some help.

But what I'm trying to say is, we are given in life exactly what we can bear and not one iota more. So don't ever think your cross is so heavy that you can't carry it, because, I assure you, you can. Although, of course, my ego doesn't appreciate that they had to give me 36, then 54, then 63. I'd rather just have had it right up front. But, of course, you must realize that's quite a shock. If you want to multiply 99—well, make it easy on yourself—multiply 100 times $14.95, plus tax. Make it very easy.

So, you see, I spoke to someone this evening in reference to the bamboo trees, the bamboo committee. I said, "You know, it's coming along. It's not too bad." I said—I think we've got about 22 committed. Is that right?

Yes.

Yes. So that leaves me 77—don't get upset or in fear. I'm not asking you for any money. So that leaves me 77. So I mentioned to someone, I said, "You know, we got 99 bamboo trees"—I'm trying to show you how the mind works, including my own. And they said, "Well, you overextended, didn't you?" [*Mr. Goodwin firmly hit the table once with his fist for emphasis.*] That's it! I tell you, my temper serves a wonderful purpose when I let it. I immediately went to work on my mind. Because, you see, to me, what that means, after working 38 years and after starting with $100 and 9 years later building a house and having assets in excess of over $600,000—"How could I have slipped so far into such stupidity that I had overextended, especially listening to the Friends, who have done so much?" Besides, it immediately put a damper on my mind, when I have 77 *more* to get underway!

However, I am very grateful for all these experiences. Because, you see, when those things—what I'm trying to show you, as students, is how to work on your mind when you have all these kinds of experiences, you see.

What rises up, when we're dealing in this material world, of course, is fear. Now, we all know that fear is the mind's control over our eternal being. Fear is a potent force. If I permitted my mind to experience fear in reference to the money department, I would have blown my brains out a year ago, facing the mortgage that you people, all you darling people have on your church home. Because I don't want to seem selfish and say it's all mine. Because it's not the truth anyway. It belongs, of course, to all of us—the bills, as well as the glory, if you want to call it glory.

But you must—we must learn to work on our mind, whether it's a bamboo tree—[*Mr. Goodwin coughs loudly.*]

Excuse me. Not that there's any resentment—there's a little condition. Whether it's a bamboo tree or anything else. Now, you know, it brings to my mind, too, a long time ago the archdiocese there in Los Angeles—the bishop made a statement once that he would like to spend more of his time in spiritual work and less of his time in fund-raising to build more churches. And I thought—that was years ago, back in the '50s—and I said, "Now, gee, that's very interesting. Why can't they have a business agent take care of that department and let the poor man do his spiritual work." I just couldn't understand how any religion could take their priest or their minister and have them involved in trying to raise funds, to raise money, to build churches, when they're supposed to be taking care of the spiritual needs of their congregation. But I can assure you that I lived to learn a little about it. I mean, if the minister is not involved with that level of consciousness—you know, it's really nice just to kind of float around and talk about spiritual matters, you know, and all of that, because he never has to face it himself. I think that's just great. But that isn't the way this church runs, you know. It never did.

So getting back to my bamboo committee—that committee I take very personal, very personal. I was never one to be short of getting any committee solvent. So I have no intention, of course, of being the chairman of a committee and find that I have not fulfilled the bill. Because then I would be setting a terrible example for my students who are also committee chairman of various committees.

So you can do your part very easily. You can change your level of thinking and say, "Well, God, they're your bamboos. And they're all getting paid for." And you can do your part to at least mention the bamboo committee to a friend or two—better make it three. My figures seem to require three. Each one mention it to three.

I don't want to have to go and put a name plaque on each bamboo tree. It will not look nice for the landscape. So I can assure you we're not going to do that, you see. And I know a lot of people myself, you know. So I will be talking to a lot of people, too. I have a lot of clients waiting for counseling. So I will be talking, of course, to everyone. I will not, however, make any announcement at the church service, because my mother doesn't feel that that is in keeping with the purpose of church service.

So let us stop and think, my friends, of how we're always bombarded with some negative shot. I got a nice negative shot just the other day from your vice-president. I think that's very important that you understand how my board of directors—your board of directors—sometimes think. It's very interesting. He said to me that I spend untold hours talking to people going around the mulberry bush, when he could just tell them right out and that was it. And I said, "Oh, that's very interesting. Yes, very interesting." What are the results? What *are* the results? What is the effect? Are there positive results in taking these untold hours of talking to people? And he agreed that there had been positive results—but couldn't understand why I took so much time, why I couldn't just get right to the point.

Well, let me tell you something about getting right to the point: If you want something kicked out real quick, rejected real fast, just come up to a person and say "Oh, you give $15 for a bamboo tree." Now, that kind of thinking, of course, that gets right to the point, you see, but it doesn't get the money, if that's what you're working on. It doesn't get the result.

So, anyway, I didn't appreciate what I considered to be an insult. Of course, if I hadn't been in self, I wouldn't have felt insulted. That's true. But that's not the point. The point is everybody's human. And I happen, at that moment, to be human, that is, my temper did. And I thought about that. And I thought about that. And I thought about that. And I thought about that longer than I should have been thinking about that because I got madder. I got very angry. And then finally I said to myself, "Now that's enough. I am wasting energy that I could constructively use to get my bamboo committee underway. And why am I wasting it on some knucklehead that has his own judgments"—and, of course, has his right to his judgments and who is a good soul—but who, obviously, after over six years in this organization, needs more exposure. You see, exposure frees the soul.

Now that reveals to me that this particular person has not been receiving sufficient exposure of those levels of consciousness and is, once again, permitting himself to be the servant of the king of kings called the judge of glory. Now, don't feel bad that it's only the vice-president of your church that gets that way. I'm working with people constantly that get in and out of that stuff.

So do you see how very important it is to make more effort to work on your mind more often that you may enjoy more good in life?

Many hundreds and thousands of words have been spoken on man's number one problem. And it seems that we just keep moving in and out of that problem. Does anyone present know of any problem greater than money? Anyone? No one has the sex priority over the money? [*After a short pause, the teacher continues.*] Well, that's good, then we can stick to one subject. But did you ever stop to think—now, seriously—did you ever stop to think how many times you think about money? Did you ever stop to think about that? Did you ever stop to think that every desire that you have plays the word *money* in your consciousness, your subconscious mind? If you drink a glass of water, the computer says, "Money." I mean, after all, you have to pay the bill, right? So everything we are doing in this mental world has this little red flag flashing of money. And that is going on right around the clock.

You can tell how free you're getting from its control when you judge that you are short of it. When your mind judges you are short of money, if you are not emotional, be rest assured God has blessed you, you finally got free. But if you are emotional—now, not when you have it, you understand, not when you judge you have it—only when you judge you don't have it. When you judge you don't have it and you are emotional, to the degree of your emotional expression reveals how much control it has over you. And I think if you will take that as a constant awareness, you will very soon realize what a great force that is not only in your universe, but in this whole mental world.

You see, if we had not judged that the fulfillment of our desires in life are dependent upon money, then we would not have so much emotion concerning it. But we have made that great judgment in our life. We have been so totally brainwashed to that illusion, from the time we entered this earth realm, that whenever our mind judges we are short, our emotions totally get torn apart. Now, is there anyone who would disagree with me? If so, just raise your hand.

How do you work on that kind of a level of consciousness and get freed from it? Well, I'm going to tell you what I've done myself. You know, when my mind, in its experiences, faced what it believed was disaster upon disaster upon disaster—and it seemed to me that they would never end. When I was told to get a book published [*The Living Light*] that, at that time, I think it was costing $6,000 and we didn't even have $600! [*Mr. Goodwin laughs.*] And it took a while, but it did get all paid off. I think what was so helpful to me in those days when my mind dictated that I was in such shortage and etc., that I visualized—I did make the conscious effort to visualize—"Well, if everything goes, where will I be? What, what will I be like if everything I think that I have"—and at that time, it was very little, if anything— "but if that all goes, am I going to pass on to another world? That's ridiculous. Am I going to lose my health? That is ridiculous." Because I wouldn't allow that, be it in divine order.

So let us pause and think, that we may get free from the control of the judgment that all the goodness in life is dependent upon the green paper that is created by man that we may reach a level in which we can say, with all honesty, that it needs us and we don't need it, that we may, through great effort, become free and no longer be the victim of that judge. Because I know there is no one who really enjoys being emotionally upset and being unhappy. I know that. And I can honestly say that as far as my peace of mind or my happiness in life, that happiness is not dependent upon a house or not a house. I appreciate a private bathroom. And I assure you that's all I ever asked for. Because, you see, when you ask for the crumb, you have a good chance of getting the loaf. So it's only common sense—and it's very practical—for whatever your desires may be in life, ask for the crumb. Because then, you can enjoy the wonderful surprise of receiving the loaf, though it may take quite a little while in coming.

Well, my friends, I do hope that somehow, in this discussion this evening, that it may be instrumental to help you to think more often, moment by moment, because whatever the experience is, that is yet to be, will be ever in keeping with your attitude. If you change your attitude, you'll change your experience. And if you don't like the experience you're having this moment, or the moment yet to come, change your attitude. That's all that it takes. If you change your attitude, you will change your experience. Because you will move out of that level of consciousness and you will experience something new, something different. And if the change of attitude is one that is more positive and constructive, then the experiences that you will have will be more positive and more constructive.

And please don't forget my bamboo committee. Thank you all very much.

JUNE 15, 1978

CONSCIOUSNESS CLASS 183

Before we begin our class this evening—Good evening, students—we'll take a few minutes here to discuss priorities, because, after all, that's the reason that we're here—is to first understand what our priorities are and, once having made the decision and the choice of our priority, whatever it may be, to have the courage of our convictions and commitments to gain some degree of control of our mind and fluctuating desires.

We all seek to get ahead in life. That is not something that is unusual or uncommon to the human race. And we strive to get ahead in our endeavors, whatever they may be, and then we seem to have all of these difficulties and all of these struggles. We must ask ourselves the question, Why do we have all these difficulties and all of these struggles when all we want out of life is the fullness and the goodness of life?

But we're going to have to understand, of course, the philosophy that we are studying. This philosophy does not teach, nor does it demonstrate, that whenever we have a desire that strikes a blow to our mind and our body reacts automatically, by habitual pattern, that we move with that desire. We must first consider, whenever we experience desire in our mind, "What is my priority in life?" And if we agree with our self that our priority is to be successful in life, to experience the goodness of life, then that means that we are looking for gain. We are looking for something that we are not presently experiencing and that is the choice and decision that we've made. So if we're looking for something, like getting ahead, that we now feel, or ofttimes feel, that we're not, then we have to demonstrate what we're teaching; we've got to demonstrate what we are studying. And to do that, we've got to gain some degree of control of our mind.

No matter what it is that you study in life and no matter what job you have, no matter what business you have, you cannot, *you cannot* desire one thing and then demonstrate a direct opposing desire and expect to be successful. It is contrary to natural, demonstrable law.

This philosophy teaches the Law of Giving. But what does giving mean? It also teaches the greatest gift you have to give is the gift of self. The gift of self has been clearly and fully explained. Self is the combination of all of the patterns, attitudes of mind, desires, experiences that we have, so far, had in our evolution. When you want something in life—and I've yet to find a person who didn't have want, need, and desire—then you have to pay the price. You want spiritual illumination? You want awakening? You want greater good in your life? Then you must pay that price. And that price is very personal; it is very individual to each person.

You cannot have the patterns and attitudes of yesterday and gain the changes of tomorrow. It just doesn't work. No one in life can have their cake and eat it, too. Now, as long as we insist—whoever we may be—in having our cake and eating it, too, we are not going to move ahead in life. We might as well face that today, my friends.

I am aware that some people, and some of my students, feel that the discipline, the rules, the regulations, the strictness of the Serenity Association is perhaps a little too much. Of course, we all understand it's only too much because we don't understand. If we understood, it wouldn't be too much at all. So that is the way it is also in our personal lives.

Now, for many years, we have had volunteer workers coming to our office, volunteer in the sense they alone made that choice. Not all members of this Association come to the office to work. They work in many different ways—some of them. But we have our rules and regulations governing those who will be permitted, for there is no law in the Association that says that every member will be permitted to come to the house, to the office, to work. There is nothing in the corporate structure, material or spiritual, that has that guarantee written in it. But those who do make that choice accept a responsibility. And the church has been as lenient as possible in reference to the commitments made by those volunteer members and friends of the Association. And there are times when the organization, the church, the office, has adjusted the schedules for their commitments that they have made outside of the organization.

But when those needs to change schedules and constantly adjust schedules begin to establish a pattern of license, it means that there is an increased workload in changing these fluctuating schedules of the volunteers. And when you look at it objectively and in a practical sense, those volunteers constantly changing their scheduling are taking more out than they are putting in. For an organization as small as this, for one person to keep changing their schedule of work means that someone else must take up the workload of the job that they normally do. Therefore, effective today, this day, there will be no more changing of schedules for those who have committed themselves to work at the office, with only these exceptions: a passing in their immediate family; a passing of themselves to another dimension or they're in the hospital and unable to get to the office to work.

I know that you will all agree that quality is the very principle upon which this organization was founded. We have never been interested in numbers. We are not interested in numbers today, for it is quality, not quantity, that moves us along the path of success, to serve the very purpose for which this organization was founded.

Now, I know that some feel that I am a very strict disciplinarian—a spit and polish stickler. But, then, that's my choice in life. I know that many of my members and students go through the fluctuating changes of attitude concerning what they think about me. But I also understand, having a mind, that that's only the mind. That's not their soul. But, my friends, this is your golden opportunity, your golden opportunity that once you make a decision in life, whatever it may be, you stick to it until you reap the success of the path upon which you have chosen to trod.

Personally, myself, I could have quit a hundred-thousand times. I don't entertain the thought as often as I used to, but my mind, like anyone's mind, has a realm known as justification, when there are conflicting desires rising, demanding their fulfillment. It is the control and the education of these desires, not the suppression, nor the attempted annihilation of them, that brings you what you are truly seeking in life.

Therefore, for those of you who have been with us for a number of years, you cannot help but see the rules, the regulations get stricter, the church—and its purpose to serve the Light to the world—continues to grow and to prosper. The membership seems to get less, but those who remain get stronger. So is it better to have a ship with a crew that can weather the storms of life or is it better to have a ship with a crew that is weak and will quit at that first port that it enters because it will not stand on the rock of principle? For we do right in life because it's right to do right. We must gain control of our own mind.

I know that some question many things. And I know that is, of course, their right. It is a divine right to question, for God sustains even the doubters. God sustains all of us. God sustains whatever thought we choose to entertain in our mind. The Power of the universe is sustaining that thought. And to me—and I've had many experiences and I'm sure I'll have a lot more, like everyone—to me, when those angels, who some of us seem to believe in and some don't, when those angels that I've seen for so many years of my life, work so hard to help us to be free from the illusions and delusions of a cloudy, misty mental world, when I feel that their efforts are questioned, I, unfortunately or fortunately, rise up in immediate defense, though I know that truth needs no defense. But I am sure, being human, that all of you would rise up, because in life, friends, if we have any common sense or any wisdom at all, we will give the seed a chance to grow and to prosper and we will look at the tree and see the fruit that it has to bear.

I am well aware that there are many levels that we all must work our way through. Don't ever delude yourself that you've gotten through that level, because the moment you make that judgment, you establish the law necessary to send you right back in. Because you didn't learn the lesson yet. So try not to fall into that pit: that you've learned the lesson. Try not to send yourself, by the Law of Repetition, back down again to make the changes that are necessary.

My friends, the teaching, Acceptance, the will of God, the divine will, is so clear and it is so very simple. It's such a simple teaching because it's such a truthful teaching. We must look, in life, at our patterns of mind that flatly and blatantly refuse to accept the possibility of anything else. I have always been a firm believer that wherever there is a will, there is a way. And I have yet to experience any student of mine that doesn't have plenty of will. We all have plenty of will. We all have equal faith, for God is not a partial God. Whatever ounce of faith that I may demonstrate, you, too, have that faith. You have that same power. Perhaps the difference is very clear to see: I choose to direct my faith, which your faith is as strong as mine, out of the limited computer, called my human self-image, to a universal Intelligence that I find demonstrably proves itself to be the only way to happiness in life. You, too, have that choice. And your faith is just as great as perhaps you may think mine may be. Your faith is equal. It is no less and, I assure you, it is no greater. For this God or this philosophy of this universe doesn't grant to one and deny another.

So we must ask ourselves very openly and very honestly with ourselves, "O God, what am I relying upon in my life? Am I relying upon self or am I relying upon a greater intelligent energy that will move away from my universe any obstruction that in the error of my ignorance I have created?"

When you give up a judgment of your mind—each and every time you give up a judgment, you open a door of opportunity. That law is so clear and so demonstrable if you will only make the effort to consciously remember it. Whenever you give up your judgment—no matter what your judgment concerns—the moment you give it up, the moment you give it forth—to give forth is to forgive—in that moment you have opened a door of opportunity: a door through which you may pass to experience what you really want in life. But if you do not give up the judgment in whatever area of life that you are struggling, then that door of opportunity cannot open.

We all knock at the door, but we usually quit before it opens. But why do we quit before it opens? Because we don't have the wisdom of patience to work and give up the judgment that has closed it in the first place. All closed doors in our life are closed by the king of judgment. All doors that open are opened by the divine law called acceptance.

Now, you have learned, "Acceptance, something good is happening;" to put into this, the eternal moment. My friends, only through your daily effort to take control of your mind, not someone else's mind—we all have a full-time job just with our own mind. Be not interested, nor concerned, with everybody else's mind and how you want them to be. Be interested in your mind. For I tell you it is a twenty-four hour, constant job just to keep a check on its own shenanigans. Because if we rest and we snooze for a few moments, that little mind of ours gets into all kinds of problems. And because we think that little vehicle, called our mind, is us, then we have all the pain and the experience of the problems that it keeps taking us into.

I know that each of you present knows deep inside of you that the philosophy that you are making the effort to learn works for you. I'm so pleased I get a chance to speak this evening, because I can see very clearly whose eyes are closed and whose are opened. I can see who's asleep and who is awake. And perhaps we ought to change the subject to something that will wake them up—very quickly. I've never been lost for words in that way. Perhaps we can speak about water. Please open that door so fresh air can come in. I don't want anyone to get sleepy. I don't know whether they're bored because I'm getting to talk or that it's stuffy in here, which it isn't, to me. And soon it won't be to everyone else, because there's a nice breeze coming in.

But I do know that energy follows attention and I have no intention of using up all my energy. You see, you folks, as students, have a responsibility to share some of your energy. And that sharing of energy takes place through what is known as the Law of Attention. So if I don't get your attention, then I have to use more of my energy to get the message across and perhaps in that respect I'd rather not say I'm selfish, but I am conservative.

Because, you see, my friends, I have spent many years of my life to try to share with you some of the things that I have learned. It is an absolute delusion of the human mind to think that all of this has come if there weren't some payment made for it. Because all you've got to do is look at your own lives. And for each step that you move ahead, you've got to give something; you have to pay the price. It's called the Law of Payment and Attainment. And I can assure you, in reference to spiritual matters, you'll pay up front. There's no credit on the other side of life. For everything you get, you have to pay in advance.

But why? Why is there no credit and pay later and no plastic cards in the world of spirit? Let's ask ourselves that question. Why is there no pay later? Well, it's very simple, my friends: If you get to pay later, you deny yourself the opportunity of faith in something greater than your mind when, when all these bills come in. Now think about that. If you have to pay up front, you then have to demonstrate your faith. And perhaps in that demonstration we accept. "Well, God, there has to be something greater because my little mind can't find any way out." Now, when our mind says that, we've established the Law of Judgment. We have locked the door of opportunity. There's always a way out, because there's always a way in. So whatever we get into in life, we might as well encourage ourselves. We did get in and we will get out.

You can't lock yourself in a closet and throw away the key, because while you're in the closet, there's the key. It's right with you. You see, the key's always inside. But if you permit your mind to say it's someplace else, then you'll keep chasing it all over the universe.

I spoke to someone the other day and I told him very clearly, I said, "You know, you can keep on searching, you can go to all of these"—What do they call them?—rebirth clinics—because that's quite popular these days, what they call rebirth clinics—"and you can go through all these psychological experiences and therapies, but you're not going to find out there what you are looking for." I said, "You won't even find it in Serenity unless you accept its very first teaching: Personal Responsibility—it's all inside you."

Serenity only serves to share with you a teaching that's proven and works. But it's worthless if you don't apply it. And I am sure that all of you present are applying some of it or you wouldn't even be here.

It's inside. I don't know how many different ways that the Friends can tell us: it's all inside. Everything's inside. The illusion, that we create, sends us outside for the answer, sends us outside for the joy of life, sends us outside for happiness and goodness and abundance. It keeps sending us outside. But that's not where it is. It's not outside. You will never find it outside, never. Every philosophy in the universe has taught that one simple truth: it's inside.

So our responsibility here and our job is to help you to get inside. I know that many of you have tried to get inside and you don't like what you see. But you have to remember there are levels in there that you're very happy with. So why not put your attention on some of those nice levels inside and some of the goodness that's in there? Because it does exist. And if you'll do that and work from a more positive vibration in life, then you'll have the transformation that is necessary for all of us.

Let us wake up. Let us be alert. Let us see, really, what it is we want. We know we can't have our cake and eat it, too. We all know that. None of us are so stupid to think that we can have our cake and eat it, too. We all agree, surely, that we have to work for what we receive, that we have to establish those laws in life. But let's work at it harmoniously and joyously.

You know, some of you are not used to any exposure. You don't get much because, then, you're not around the house up there, in Santa Venetia, very much. You know, I can always tell in reference to growth and control of one's mind in a student. For the ones who have the greatest emotional outbursts at the slightest ounce of exposure, they've got a long ways to grow, a long ways to grow, for truth has not yet been separated from creation. When you separate truth, *you*, the true you, from creation, then when some of these attitudes and these levels, they get exposed, you don't feel so bad. You say, "Darn it." And then you can trace it all the way back to when it first started. You can be objective about it. And you can tell yourself, while you are looking at it, "Well, I'm not such a bad person. This was created under these circumstances when I was very young, just a little girl or a little boy and I just wasn't aware. But now that I'm aware of this particular level, this judgment that I have in my head, now that I am aware, well, I can start working on it. Therefore, I am very grateful."

You see, that's how exposure frees the soul. It doesn't happen outside. It depends on what you do with the exposure.

If you get yourself all emotional, that is that particular level that is being exposed, that is rising up to defend itself. And you react along with that defense—because, you see, once you create a pattern of mind, once you create an attitude—you create this pattern—once you create that, you give it birth. Its only existence is when you give it attention. Now, if you don't give it any attention, you understand, it doesn't get any energy. If it doesn't get any energy, of course, then it dies. But the essence is always there. It's always waiting to get reborn, don't ever kid yourself. So, you see, exposure frees the soul to the soul who sees the light of reason during the exposure!

Now, we all must—open up that other door, please. So we can have some fresh air in here. I don't want my students going to sleep. We are here for class. That's why we are here. We are here to face the truth inside of ourselves. You must remember students, you are not here to agree or disagree with me. That is not your purpose for being here. That's not why we come to class. So don't ever be deceived by that. I never was one to win friends and influence people. But there are a few people that are still around me. I'm sure that they will be in the years to come.

Now, what are we going to do with these untold hundreds of thousands of words and classes that we've already had? I do know, if you play the tapes enough, it's bound to get into the consciousness. It's bound to get in there. I mean, you might have a few emotional experiences if there's a particular class that an attitude of mind, a level of consciousness, looks at and says, "Oh my God, that's a threat to my survival and I intend to survive!" You'll have that trauma. Sure, we all have that trauma. But let us remember we all are as great as we accept within ourselves.

This philosophy never ever taught to be crawling on the ground in humility. It teaches simply to think well of yourself. Think humble, yet well. Now, I think that's very important. It's important to me. I'm sure it's important to all of you. No one wants to think that they're a bad person. No one wants to think that they're a failure in life. No one wants to think that no one cares. No one really wants to think that way. No one, no one wants to feel rejected. No one truly enjoys that experience. Yet, we all know, we reject ourselves. We'll feel badly for ourselves. But those are levels of mind. That's not our true being.

And ofttimes if we spend some time to, to look at people, to pause long enough to understand why they retaliate, why they feel rejected, why they feel left out and on down all the list that comes under the heading of self and self-pity, if we care, we will make the effort to talk to them, to try to understand and to remember ourselves: It's only a level. It's not the person. And never to forget that whatever level we cannot tolerate in another, we are still waiting to educate it inside ourselves.

So whatever anyone says or thinks or does, you must remember: that potential exists inside of you, for all of us are a part of an inseparable whole. We have a mental body. We have a mind. And whatever is capable for one mind is capable for all minds. Now, if you will remember that in life, your chances of being free from that great throne of judgment are going to get very good. Just remember, you, too, have a mind and you, too, are capable—and very quickly—of doing the very thing you cannot tolerate that another is doing. Slowly but surely from that, we gain tolerance. Slowly but surely, climbing through those realms of judgment and intolerance, climbing on up through them, we start to gain some success.

You see, whatever it is you want to do in life, God has granted you the opportunity to do it. God, in his great wisdom and compassion, this great divine intelligent Energy, has denied you nothing, has granted you everything. The only thing that you can ever experience and say you don't have, whatever that is, you may be assured you have risen with that in judgment and it is that thought pattern that is denying what you want. God has given it to you. You already have it. You have it as much as I do and anyone else. You already have it! But if you won't make the effort to accept that you have it and if you insist upon reliance upon a mental realm that judges how you will have it, when you will have, and all the other conditions, then that's the path that you must trod. But that does not have to be that way. It doesn't have to be that way. We make it that way. We make it that way in our error. It is our error that makes it that way.

As you believeth, so you becometh is a very basic teaching. So whatever it is that we seem to be struggling with, we believe it. If we didn't believe it, it could not be. Now, to tell the human mind that simple truth, the human mind, in the realms of justification, will give you a twenty-hour discourse on why that can't be. For those levels are determined to survive.

Now, let's take, for example, say a person is in business. They have some good years; they have some poor years. And they say, "Well, I had three good years. So I've had three bad years. Well, it kind of balanced out. I don't feel too bad." Then the next year comes and they have another bad year. And they wonder why they had another bad year. But what did they say at the end of the third year of the bad years? They said, "Well, I've had three good years. And so now I have three bad years." What does that statement mean? That's the end of the bad years. Because they've made that judgment.

Now, these are the things, my friends, you want to think about in life if you want your success in life. If you talk to a person like that and they will say, "I didn't make any judgment that I was going to have four bad years! But what did I say? I said I had three good years. So now I have three bad years. Oh, well, everything balances out." That is a judgment. Now, for that judgment, it varies, of course. They're in the fourth year now and they have another bad year. And they say, "Now this is ridiculous." And then they—perhaps and there are many ways you can go with judgment. They say, "Well, the political situation and the financial picture for the country wasn't good this year." Now, they are in the fourth year now, see? OK.

They complete their fourth bad year and they're moving into the fifth year. The fifth year comes and things are still bad. They've already played the justification trip: the political situation and the finances of the country weren't too hot, you know. And they're in the fifth year, they say, "Well, this particular business of mine, it's been going downhill anyway." Another judgment gets established. They're now going into the sixth year. They're had five years of bad news. The sixth year, it slides even more, because they made even a stronger judgment. They now have made it very personal that this particular business wasn't any good anyway and it's really sliding down hill. So they go through seven years of bad news and they move into the eighth year.

Well, after so much, you know, tolerance goes so far. Then we start to think now, "I've got to get out of this." Now that's, that's wisdom speaking. But what it means is, "I've got to get out of this level of consciousness." Now, if it takes a trip to Saudi Arabia to get out of a level of consciousness that's detrimental to you, then, for God's sake, please everyone go to Saudi Arabia. Although it's very hot—I don't care to go myself. But, you see, they did get the message. The message is clear: "I've got to get out of this." That's true. Not that somebody out there has got to get out of this. "I am in it. I got to get out of it."

Friends, we make judgments so frequently in life. They have become so subtle in our thinking that we can no longer recognize them. And that's really sad because those judgments establish those laws. For every judgment is a denial and every denial is a destiny.

Now, someday before I leave this earth realm, this philosophy will all be put together in book form—all of it. And you will be able to sit and to really study and tie in each and every one of these hundreds of thousands of truths that have been brought to you and use them and use them wisely. But let me give you a moment of caution. Do not permit your minds to use such beautiful truths to justify the license of your desires, for that price is one of the greatest of all prices to pay.

Now, I think that I am, hopefully, as well versed in this philosophy as anyone else here. I hope. And I know how clever my mind is—just as clever as yours. And even the Lord's Prayer teaches us, "Lord, lead me not into temptation." Now, we understand that "Lord" means law, law of the universe. And so it says to the law, "Lead me not into temptation," for the law is within ourselves.

Some time ago, it was stated in our classes that he who tempts another is as guilty as the one whom is tempted. Now, why is it that he who tempts another is as guilty as the one who is tempted? For he who tempts another is already tempted. They are tempted to tempt another. So that's why, you see, my friends, they're just as guilty. They're guilty of that Law of Temptation. We tempt ourselves to many things. But remember one thing about temptation: it's so short-lived. If that wasn't true, you wouldn't have business flourishing the way it does. People are tempted to buy this and tempted to buy that and tempted to buy something else. And sometimes the temptation doesn't even last long enough until they get it home in their house. And because the temptation doesn't last very long, they take a look at it to find that that's not really what they wanted anyway. And then they run it back to the store.

So, you see, my friends, temptation, in truth, it has a very short life. The only thing is, it rises very frequently, very frequently. Let us not be tempted by passing desires that flood into our mind. And if we will make that effort not to be tempted by all these passing desires, then we'll live to see the day, right here on Earth, when we will have the fullness of life. There's one thing about temptation: it always has an empty void. That's the end of temptation. And just to be tempted again to another void and another and another and another and on and on and on and on.

But that's not the way it is with the fullness of life. The fullness of life—you pay the price of temptation to gain the fullness of life, for you must pay the price of those senses. But the fullness of life is something that's always with you. It's with you when you're up and it's with you when you're down. It's with you when your desires are not fulfilled and it is with you when your desires are fulfilled. Now, how could you ask for anything better than that? You are never without it once you have accepted and experienced it. But you must pay the price. You must take all these little desires that pound on your head—of course, some of them, I admit, are sledgehammers and some of them are even jackhammers. But remember, it's your head. It's your jackhammer. It's your sledgehammer. It's not someone else's. Because it's yours, you can always do something with it.

So let's do something, do something with the philosophy that we're studying. Let's do a little something more. I know we're doing something: at least, we're here in class. And I am very pleased that many of my students are extremely well versed in the philosophy, extremely well versed. And that, of course, pleases me very much. But what would even please me more is to see if only 10 percent of how well versed we are in the philosophy we put into demonstration to improve our lives, *to improve our lives*.

And so we're speaking on exposure. And so this evening, I would like to speak to one student. Because that's what this church is all about, you know: a little bit of exposure. I mean, after all, I do believe it was another student who got exposed on the strawberries. In fact, one of my students said they have their classes all categorized with headings. And they named one the Strawberry Class and the class the other week, the Bamboo Class. So I think it's interesting that we have such lovely names for classes.

Now, you recall last Tuesday, I spoke to you and said, "You're cutting this time business too close to the wire." In other words, it was twenty seconds to the hour when you arrived at the house for your regular commitment. And the Friends feel that twenty seconds to the hour is really a little too close to the wire. So therefore, as she well knows, she was forewarned. Is that not correct?

Yes.

Tonight, she was how many seconds late for choir rehearsal?
Twenty to thirty. [The choir director responds.]

Twenty to thirty seconds late. That means that if she did get the message, she did not heed it. Because the demonstration, of course, in our life is the revelation. And so, therefore, we've given you just an ounce—no, a half an ounce, I'm sorry. My mother says a half an ounce of exposure in hopes that you may make some effort in reference to that particular area in your life. Now, they do feel—and I'm sure you will agree—this teaching that you have already studied and continue to study: promptness considers the rights of another and is the true mark of one's character.

Now, I know that your little soul is working day and night on a sterling character. But remember, the demonstration is the revelation. And I do hope that you will stop cutting it so close to the wire. Do you know what cutting it that close to the wire truly reveals? *[After a short pause, the Teacher continues.]* It reveals, in reference to your personal desires, your spiritual commitment is very close to the wire. It is there, but it is so close it is dangerous because you were twenty seconds late tonight. You made it to the house twenty seconds before your commitment. So, you see, that reveals, in reference to those priorities, when you're in those levels, it's just barely close to the wire. And I wouldn't want you to get any closer, you might get electrocuted from it. You know me and that just may happen. All right. Now, I think that's very little exposure. Didn't you think so? *[This question was directed to another student, one who was not exposed.]*

[The student cleared her throat.]

Oh, you have no thoughts on that. Well, my friends, as these classes progress, we're going to have more and more exposure. Because if we don't have exposure, then we do not have growth. Because we're not facing the levels of consciousness. [*The Teacher now addresses the student who was exposed.*] Now, wouldn't you rather face the level and get through it than to have that go on year after year after year? Because someday you may be so close to the wire when you go to the bank that the door gets locked just as you're opening it up. Isn't that true? And you wouldn't want to have that experience, would you?

But, you see, the principle gets established, my friends. I mean, the difference is—you see, there's a principle involved. Now, if you establish the principle of, in any area, just getting close, so close to the wire, then the day comes you do not have control to use that only in that particular area. The day comes when you are supposed to get something you desire very much and because you have established that close-to-the-wire principle, when you get there, it's gone. Do you understand? Now, that's very important. I would think that's important to me in life. I would think that would be important to all of my students in life.

Now, we will delete these personal names. [*The personal names have been deleted from this transcription.*] So don't feel bad about it all. [*The Teacher now addresses a student with whom he has not yet spoken during this class.*] Was it not true that I asked you if you could spare your crew in reference to a very serious matter that involved not only your church and yourself, but other students as well?

Yes.

And did you or did you not agree to have your crew there, under this emergency situation, to take care of this particular thing?

Yes, I did.

All right. Then, I have to ask your son what was the problem. You see, my friends, if any of you noticed me being tardy this evening, I was working for your church right out front. Yes, perhaps you can explain first to the class, because every exposure helps to free all of us. What seemed to be the problem when that was the agreement reached between you and the Council of your church?

Well, I knew it was a priority. And when the Friends move—
Yes.

They don't hesitate or procrastinate in anything that they do. Otherwise, the success will not, will not be guaranteed.

All right. Now this is very important, *very* important. I'll come back to that. Otherwise, the success of the project is not guaranteed. This is a very important lesson for all of us. All right. Now, you did make the agreement—Is that not correct?—with the Council of your church to have your crew there? That was what the request was.

Yes. And I did ask one of my crew and my son if he could make it tomorrow. And that it was important and that it was a priority situation. And he said that, well, he had another commitment. And I—

But it's your crew and it's a regular workday.

Yes, it is—yes, it was. I mean, I have no control over his desires and he has a desire to do something else, I think I've—

But was it not—this is important for, because, you see, through this—don't get into personality with these experiences or you've lost the lesson and the great truth that is involved, just like the strawberries one week. The situation is really very simple. It was a scheduled workday. He had, already, an understanding that he would work for you on that day. Is that correct?

Yes.

Fine. Now, [*The Teacher addresses the son of the foreman.*] what was your problem this evening before class that the

Friends felt was so critical and important that they kept me outside to one minute past eight o'clock?

Well, I was told at work today that I had the day off. So I made a commitment to work and—

I see.

There was a lack of communication. I could have accepted it much easier if I hadn't already made a commitment.

All right. So what this does reveal—which is very important. Now, friends, just prepare yourselves, because this is the way your philosophy gets into demonstration so you, yourself, can apply it. There's a lack of communication. Is that right?

Yes.

Between who?

My employer and myself.

All right. Fine. All right. Now, you see, my friends, when it comes right down to it in life, we have a great lack of communication. And without clear communication in life, we don't have understanding. Without understanding, we don't have anything worthwhile to work for. We must have clear communication.

Does anyone have any problems with the clarity of my communication? And I'm not speaking about the phase of my mediumship. I'm talking about myself, personally. Does anyone have any problems? If you do, please raise your hands. So I can clarify it. I don't consider, honestly, that I have had, in my life, problems in the reference of communication. Now, I don't know—I don't think that it's because I talk so much. I mean, after all, there are many times I don't talk at all. I don't think it's because I am able to talk easily, necessarily. But what is the difference? What is it that brings about clarity of communication with people? Yes, what is it?

Getting to the point.

Oh, definitely getting to the point. Thank you. And that's a very important point. Of course, most of us, unfortunately, we do seem to enjoy playing with our little minds and fascinating with all those little thoughts up there. But what is really, what is really at stake?

I think you have to be honest with yourself as well as the other person. [Another student speaks.]

That's getting very close, very close. We must care for the person with whom we are communicating. We must care enough that we are willing to bow our self-thoughts, to bow our self-interest long enough to consider, and to care enough for, the individual with whom we are communicating. So that we know beyond a shadow of any doubt that they've gotten the message loud and clear. Then, you see, my friends, you'll be amazed. We will eliminate, through that effort of care—to care for the person with whom we are communicating at the moment, to have that much care—we will then eliminate 90 percent of all our problems in life. Just through the soul faculty of care. Because when we care enough, we consider the whole. When we care enough, we have total consideration. And when we have total consideration—I'm sure you all know that of the philosophy—you have the love of God. That's what total consideration offers. And if you have the love of God expressed, what can ever stand in the way? There's nothing that can stand in the way, absolutely nothing.

Now, we are bringing up these few little points, little simple things, so that you all can be stronger. I mean, after all, no one has asked that you come up here and sit on the podium and face all of the student body while you are discussing these things. And don't think for a moment that any of us is better or lesser than anyone else. For the foreman has great care; it's just a matter—I'm sure he will agree—of expanding it. It isn't that it doesn't exist, because we know it does.

And then we have to ask his son, How come, when he gets a message, he doesn't get it clear? Isn't that right? I mean, because I'm sure that he will agree with all of us here, that it happens rather frequently. Right?

Yes, it does.

Do you have difficulty in communicating with people?

Some people.

Ah, they are limited, right? I mean, there are certain people. Is that correct?

Yes, it seems to be. But that's for myself, though. It's not them.

Oh, I understand that. But what is it, do you think, inside that causes a difficulty in communicating with certain people?

Judgments.

Thank you very much. I am so happy that—you see, you see, my students do know the philosophy. They do know the truth. We all do know the truth. And you ought to spend a little more time encouraging yourselves. You should spend a little more time on saying, "Thank you, God, I really am a good person. I really am, deep inside, a happy person. And I'm so grateful because I am getting happier every moment." See?

Why, why should we live contrary to the very will of God: the fullness and joy of life? Why should we do that to ourselves when we don't have to do that to ourselves? Everything your heart could possibly desire is waiting for your recognition. It's waiting for you to bow whatever thought stands in the way. It's waiting for you. I really mean that. It's right in front of you and it's so close to you. The mind cannot see it, for the mind has clouded your view with all of its dictates. But when you bring peace to the mind, when you bring it under control, then you will see. "Thank you, God, the great feast of life is in front of me. It's here now. I don't need to chase anywhere. It's wherever I go. It always has been and it always will be. It is only my mind that tells me it's out there. It's only my mind that tells me how I must struggle to get it." But, you see, we, we alone and only we alone, can do that. But don't you all think it's time that we started to do that?

We are very fortunate—all of us—to be in a philosophical school that not only brings forth these truths, but grants to all of us the opportunity to see how they work. And, of course, it is so much easier for us to see the transgressions of another. It is so much easier for us to see and to say, "Well, why don't they change their thinking? Why don't they just make a change of their attitude?" Because, you see, we are not emotionally in it. And whatever we are not emotionally into, we can take a look with a little bit more objectivity. But then, don't let us ever forget that when we're in it and our emotions are as black as the blackest of clouds, there are others who may well be thinking the same of us.

But, you know, through all of these ups-and-downs and ins-and-outs and all these trips and—it's very interesting to me. Because even though, sometimes, my mind gets active, it doesn't get to stay active very long. But sometimes it gets active and then I'm always reminded, "Richard, that's not their soul. And it's not your soul that's looking at their soul." So don't ever forget, whatever they do or don't do, that is not their soul. And if you don't remember that, then it's not your soul that's looking. It's our mind.

And if you remember who you're really working for in life, you'll never have a problem: if you just remember you are not working for the passing panorama of creation. That is not what you're really working for in life. We have come here to Earth to learn the lessons that are necessary to free our soul. No matter what you call it is immaterial. We have come for that purpose. This is the planet—the fifth in this solar system—this is the planet that offers you the great lessons of the power of faith. This, in your Earth life, is the lesson to learn. When this great power called faith is directed to reliance upon our mind, we experience the horrors of fear. And when it is directed to the very source that sustains the universe, we experience the peace, the goodness, and all that God has to offer to his children. We can make that choice this moment: to direct it to that something greater that will never fail.

We cannot tell it what to do, be rest assured of that. Millions have tried. They have cried and they have beseeched and they have ordered and they have damned. But that intelligent energy does not work that way. It works by immutable, natural, unwavering, unchanging law. If we accept that law, we can walk along that path and have that experience. We cannot change—our form, our limited mind—we cannot change what we know as God. It is useless and a total waste of energy to even attempt to do so.

Now, we can give the Infinite Intelligence, God, a million names. We can get on our knees and pray. We can stand and pray. We can get on our backs and pray. And many people even meditate on their backs and pray. Do whatever you want. Prayer is the soul's aspiration to the Oversoul. But the human mind must bow. It must bow that the obstructions that the human mind has created in the way of this Divine, they must fall. But as they fall, you may be rest assured *you* will rise. And you will live to see the day when you are so much better and so much happier. For the senses, they are only pleased for a time. They're never pleased forever. I'm sure you'll all agree with that. For the mind, it's never enough. No matter what it is, you know, for the human mind, it's never enough. For a moment, you might say, "Oh, well, I have my full." Oh, but the very next moment, off again it goes.

Perhaps in another area, now. I mean, you know, you go out and you work and work and work. And you get money. And it's possible, though rare, the mind says, "I've got enough." But I can assure you, if it ever does say that, there are many other functions that it's screaming that it doesn't have any. So for the human mind, whatever it is after, you may be rest assured, it is never going to be enough. I don't care what you give it. You cannot feed it to fulfillment. It is not possible. It is contrary to the great empty vacuum of the mental realms. They're in a constant process of creating untold limitless forms and thoughts. It's never, never ever enough.

So how does man get free from this insatiable need? By rising up above and beyond what he calls the human mind. There's no other way.

[*Addressing yet another student, the Teacher continues.*] Did you get free from your judgment earlier this evening?

Which one was that?

Well, you didn't speak to me about it. But the one concerning Monday.

Oh, yes, yes.

Didn't you find that it was very interesting that you made an instantaneous judgment and that you justified it with every excuse that your little mind could create why you shouldn't have to do that? Didn't you find that interesting?

Not at the time, no.

Oh, you mean you were in the forces at the time your mind was—

Oh, after I had quit that. Yes, it's interesting

You see, I'm interested in the law after you are out of the forces, because then, when a person is out of the forces, you can have a more intelligent discussion with them. When they're in the forces, I mean, you're not talking to an intelligent person. I mean, you might as well get that through your head. [*The Teacher laughs.*] I'm sure we all agree, if a person is in the forces, why waste your energy? You're not going to get anywhere until the tape has fulfilled itself and played and played and played and finally, from exhaustion, the stop button is put on.

Now, what do you think freed you from that tenacity of that judgment you made this evening? I was very well aware of it, you know, before it was even discussed with you. I'm sure you are aware of that—I mean, that you were going to go into judgment.

Oh, I'm, I'm—

Based solely upon experience. Based solely upon experience, yes.

What got me free from that judgment?

Yes.

Well, a little bit of reason and balancing it out with something I could accept.

Now, see how the mind works. Now, your mind works the same way—all of you. Just the way his mind just worked. To find a way for the mind to accept the change. Isn't that right? Now, it could not accept the change the way it was presented by your wife. Is that correct?

Yes, it wasn't my idea.

[*The Teacher laughs.*] Oh, isn't that beautiful. See, even though that's his wife—I'm sure you will agree that was your idea, wouldn't you?

Yes.

I mean, after all, you're the one that courted her since school days. Is that not correct?

That's correct.

Therefore, it was your idea. Even though it was a long time coming, it was your idea.

But isn't it interesting, my friends, how our minds work. Because everyone of us, our minds work the same way. And I find that so beautiful. This is why we discussed this little microscopic exposure here. I think he has done very well. Because I well remember how he'd go totally into the forces at one ounce of exposure.

What's at stake in exposure, do you think? Why is it our minds rise up and don't want any exposure? What you think? What is that called?

Protection. They're trying to . . .

Protect pride. See the great price of pride, my friends. It's unbelievable how costly pride is. It's probably one of the most expensive, if not the most expensive, function that we entertain:

the human pride. All religions have taught the sin of it. All philosophies have taught to bow it. It is the most expensive human function that we can possibly feed. It isn't pride we need. It's gratitude for the opportunity that we already have. To feel good inside is the way man should feel and to be grateful that he feels that way is only right and just.

But what is it that pride does? Pride lift us in its illusion that we're a little bit better than anyone else. At least in this particular area or that particular area, we are a little bit superior. But, you see, my friends, we wouldn't need that feeling and that necessity to feel superior if we accepted the superiority of the goodness that is in us here, this very moment. We wouldn't need that delusion. We wouldn't need that so-called false pride. There would be no need for it, because we would've accepted what we truly are and not be deluded by what other people think we are.

Thank you very much. Thank you.

JUNE 22, 1978

CONSCIOUSNESS CLASS 184

Greetings, friends.

This evening, I should like to share with you some of my experiences on this side of the curtain, especially at a time in my evolution when I was in such great despair. And my guardian angel guided me, at that time, to an awareness of the benefit of removing from my consciousness the thought of I. Many centuries have passed since that time, but, I can assure you, from that long, long journey that the only obstruction to the goodness and greatness of life is a simple thought known to man as the thought of I.

When man entertains the thought of I, he establishes, by the Law of Identity, the Law of Destiny—the destiny of denial. For the mind cannot experience the broadness and goodness of life whenever the Law of Denial is expressed. As man moves along that path of denial by the thought of I, he destines himself to a multitude of experiences, each and every experience, the child of judgment. And so we are indeed our best friend or indeed our worst enemy.

To remove from the consciousness the illusion of that thought was not for me, at that time, an easy thing to do. It took me centuries to truly accomplish that. But it need not take you centuries or years or, yea, even months. For from that path I was granted an understanding of the laws involved. It is in the use of that understanding that we may quickly and surely free ourselves from the destiny that we are presently experiencing.

The affirmations and the truths that you have been given are of no benefit without your use of them. To stand guardian at the portal of thought is not something that man can do once a day. It is something that we must learn to do constantly. And in so doing, we shall awaken to the laws that we alone are setting into motion. From the thought of I, we are restricted by that Law of Identity to all of the limits that exist within our mind. We therefore find in our lives a repetition in principle of the experiences of yesteryear. Again and again, they knock at our door. Perhaps a bit different in form, but ever the same in principle. As these repetitions—of course, in time the change shall come, for repetition is the law through which change is made possible. But if you are presently weary of the repetition of certain experiences, then you must make the effort to remove the thought of I whenever those experiences enter your consciousness.

As you, in your lives, begin to take stock of what your mind is doing, as you pause when you experience, pause and remove the thought of I, you will see a great change take place: you will no longer be distressed and distraught and filled with fear. For without the thought of I, you cannot experience fear. To be fearless, to be courageous is ever dependent upon your removal of the illusion of the thought of I. Let us honestly ask ourselves, "What does this thought of I do for me that I should constantly be flooding my consciousness with it?" Ask yourselves the question and the answer, from the very depths of your being, will rise with its silent whisper and tell you the truth. Born in the dark realms of fear, it rose. For fear is the great weapon that the mind has to keep you its worker, its victim, and its slave.

Without fear, you are free. But we cannot be without fear until we apply the simple truth in all experience. And the simple truth is clear to all of us: within each one is the divine intelligent Energy. We alone choose how it shall be directed through our being. But, my goods students, we often choose through errors of ignorance.

When we stated to you some time ago that acceptance is the will of God—to accept the right of everything, to deny nothing is to be free. It is when you deny that you battle. But you cannot deny without entertaining the thought of I. You move and breathe in the will of God. All things in all worlds move and breathe in the will of God. To accept that truth is to permit your eternal being to rise to higher levels of consciousness. The struggle will only last as long as you live in denial. We all know nothing outside denies us. We all know it is that something inside ourselves that does the denying.

And as the years and centuries have passed for me and I have come, once again, to your earth realm to share with you what, through my years of experience, has brought a bit of understanding, perhaps, to me. You in your evolution have earned a great deal. But the earning of it is of no benefit without the application, my friends. The obvious need for constant watchfulness over the human mind is indeed most demonstrable. It seems that one is going along quite well for perhaps a day or two—perhaps even a week or two—and then it seems, all of a sudden, something happens. Something robs us of our peace and harmony, of our joy of living. But it was working silently all the time, but we were not on guard. We must remain guardian at the door.

As I spoke to you recently that each judgment you permit your mind to make closes a door of opportunity. And we all look for the opportunity of something better in our life. Therefore, my friends, we must give to gain. We must give up the patterns of mind that flood our lives with judgments. But in giving them up, opportunity upon opportunity upon opportunity will open for you. For each one you give, you shall gain something greater, something better. You need not question what; you need but demonstrate the wisdom of patience and you shall see beyond a shadow of a doubt.

The goodness and the greatness of life of which we speak so much is always waiting for your recognition. But you cannot recognize what has been denied, for it comes in so many varied garments.

I'm sure that you, as students, will all agree that we, our minds, yet to be educated, are always searching and always seeking to support, of course, what is already in the mind. Why do the thoughts and thought patterns of the human mind, why do they need to be supported? They need energy to survive. Therefore, they ever seek energy not only from yourself, but from the universe as a whole.

So they rise up within you and they bang at the door for your attention. You give them attention. They receive the energy necessary for their survival. But because they are ever hungry, because they are ever thirsty, because they are never satisfied, they not only rob you of your energy, they work day and night to rob everything and everyone with whom they come in contact. Have you not experienced the seeming difficulties in changing an attitude that you have given attention to? It rises up and causes you great distress.

The mind is like a great, empty, bottomless pit: you can never fill it. No matter how many centuries you try to do it, it will never be filled. For it is designed by a great Divine Architect that it may ever, it may ever receive all experience and send it out to receive even more. You cannot fill the human mind, but you can, *you can* educate it.

The education of the human mind is ever dependent upon the soul faculty of reason. You can cast upon it that great light that you may see clearly in all the dark recesses of it. The teaching to "Keep faith with reason; she will transfigure thee," means exactly, of course, what it says. Our faith is the faith of the Divine. All of us, as children of the Divine, have an equal amount of it. It is ever flowing through our being. It is our choice what we do with it. If we permit this great power called faith to support our human vehicle called the mind, then we must pay the price of the multitudes of judgments that are rising constantly within our mind. But we can choose to direct it to the very Source from whence it comes and, in so doing, rise supreme above and beyond the conflicting dual law of the human mind. And in so doing, the mind, slowly but surely, becomes educated, for the faculty of reason is in control.

This is the moment to work with, in the spirit of peace and harmony. For the abundant good of life is dependent upon your peace and dependent upon your harmony. If a thought disturbs you, then pluck it out. If it brings you peace and a feeling of good, then entertain it. Surely that is a simple thing and within the power of all men to accomplish.

How negative is your thinking? The negativity of one's thinking is ever dependent upon their judgments. The more judgments our mind entertains, the more negative is our thinking. Of what value is so much judgment? It brings no good. Think, my friends, are you permitting your mind to judge before the fact? If so, then you are the victim of prejudice. Do you prejudge what is yet to be? Is your mind so out of control that you are living this moment a victim of the king of prejudice? If so, then your suffering must be great, for the denial is ever equal. There is no reason to suffer and struggle. If you say that's the way it is for you, then you must pay the price for that thought. You can change any thought, for it's your thought. And each thought that you have is a form that goes out into the world. You can be free from it. You have been given the way many, many times.

And remember, my friends, when you attend these classes, if you feel sleepy and tired, then you know the reason. It's not your job. It's nothing outside. You are finding yourself grounded in self and, being so, you are tired and sleepy. But to go to a class and to experience a broader horizon, you must make the effort to free yourself from yourself. No one can make that effort for you, but you can make that effort when it means enough. Adjusting our priorities in life is a full-time job.

And as I stated to you some time ago, man always gets what he really wants. And so whether we like it or not, we are getting today what we really want. Perhaps we do not understand it, but as experience continues to bang at our door of consciousness, we, slowly but surely, gain the awareness and realize the truth: We always get what we really want.

Remember that, my friends. To some of you, I already see the irritation and anger rise. But it can serve for you a good purpose if you permit it to do so. The functions are not designed to be something detrimental to your well-being. They can be used as they were designed to be used: for balance and good in your life. It is the abuse of things that is detrimental to our good. It's never the use of them. For before you the Infinite Intelligence has placed all good. It's your view, your judgment that makes it so-called bad.

And now, you may feel free to ask your questions.

Thank you. Would you please discuss biofeedback and its potential in facilitating the natural healing processes?

Well, my good friends, this so-called gadget called biofeedback will, of course, serve its purpose to many people. It will help them to become aware that it is their mind and their attitude that is the true and only cause of their problems in life. And in that respect, it will indeed serve a good purpose, wisely used. As each attitude and each thought is instrumental in the chemical balance of the human body, so it is the thought, the attitude, that must be understood.

Thank you. If we have been the instrument of darkness in another person's life, must we necessarily, someday in eternity, be the instrument of light to the same person in order for both of us to progress spiritually? Or may we help a different person in a similar situation, thereby facing our own tapes and be free to go on, although the first person may remain in darkness?

My good friends, there is no need to concern yourself with such things, for the law is infallible. If you, through an error of ignorance, have been an instrument of darkness in anyone's life, you guarantee by the law established to be an instrument of light in someone's life. That may or may not be the very same person. You need not be concerned for the law, the divine law, the divine justice shall ever and forever be fulfilled.

Thank you. Please give your understanding of the word collaboration, *a word given much emphasis in one of the Eastern philosophies. Does it have any positive significance for us?*

The word *collaboration* indeed can have a positive significance. The meaning of the word, in and of itself, is not something that is necessarily detrimental to a person's life. Ofttimes people collaborate and agree upon a most useful and beneficial project for the good of humanity.

Thank you. Is there any spiritual significance attached to the astrological signs of earth, water, and air?

There most certainly is a spiritual significance to water, air, and earth and fire, for they are the basic elements. Without them, life on your planet, as it is known, would not exist. Perhaps, my friends, we can consider broadening our horizon to consider the various spirits of the elements, these little nature spirits who work so diligently to keep life, as you know it on your planet, going on and on and on.

As each thought you entertain, be it harmonious or discordant, has a direct effect upon your physical and, of course, mental body, so each and every thought and attitude that you entertain that is discordant or harmonious has a direct effect upon the nature spirits of the elements who are responsible in keeping your body, your physical body, in good working order. Certain thoughts deprive the various elements of the necessary energy for them to do their work harmoniously. And so this disturbance causes a war between the elements, for there is an imbalance. This imbalance, of course, is the effect of your attitudes in life.

Your responsibility as human beings is very great, for your responsibility not only is the responsibility unto yourself but as a part of the whole of nature. When you see a plant or a tree, you emanate a thought of love and peace and harmony, that brings balance to the very aura of that plant. My friends, whatever you view, whatever you sense with your senses, remember, remember your responsibility. For love, divine love is the great healing balm.

Now, we have all been given the teaching that total consideration is the love of God. We view each moment this great total consideration. Everything is sustained and supported by this infinite intelligent Energy. Therefore, God's love, the divine love in its consideration is absolutely total. Every thought you think, be it harmonious or discordant, is sustained by the total consideration called the love of God. There is no greater love, there is no greater healing balm than total consideration.

When you find yourself in an attitude of mind that is discordant, stop in that moment. Pause for a minute and remind yourself that God, in his great love and mercy, is sustaining the attitude that you have chosen, because the love of God is so great and so total. Though the Divine Intelligence knows before you entertain the thought what you are going to entertain, though it knows that it is discordant and disturbing, that it will bring no benefit to you or those around and about you or to the plants and the trees and the elements of nature that are affected by it, still the consideration of God is so total that it sustains your discordant attitude of mind. With a love so great, man cannot help but, in time, to bow this throne of judgment, which even *that* is sustained by the love and energy of God.

With such great power constantly available to man, does it not behoove man to choose wisely what he shall think? To stop, to pause, and to remember: the very intelligence, wisely used to set you free—unwisely used will bind you. For you have been given—by the law of your own evolution, you have earned the so-called right of choice. If you are miserable, in lack, want, need, and desire, remember, that great God is sustaining the thoughts that you choose. Don't ever forget, my friends, you alone choose the thought. And because you alone choose the thought, you alone may choose another. Let us choose today, let us choose the path of peace. Let us choose the light of reason. Let us choose to experience something greater, something better. And let us never forget that is the choice of wisdom.

Good night.

JUNE 29, 1978

CONSCIOUSNESS CLASS 185

Good evening, class.

Now, we have all been studying this philosophy now for some time and we're all aware that without the effort to apply it, it has no value for us. And so we're going to spend a little more time, in the coming classes, on application and also on the very principle upon which this philosophy stands: that principle being the principle of personal responsibility.

We must realize within ourselves that each and every time that we blame outside for what is going on inside, that is, inside our own mind, our own head, we deny the very foundation of the philosophy that we are making some effort to understand. Therefore, that, of course, is a demonstration and a revelation that we are not accepting the very principle of the Living Light philosophy: that principle, as I said, being personal responsibility.

Personal responsibility means, very simply, the acceptance, the willing, joyful acceptance that whatever happens to us, as individuals, is directly and personally caused by us. This philosophy teaches that like attracts like and becomes the Law of Attachment. So whatever we find ourselves attached to, then, of course, we realize that it is like kind that is within our own mind.

As we go through our activities in life, we sooner or later become aware that we are indeed not only victims, but slaves of the bondage of prejudice. To be prejudiced simply means to prejudge any experience in life or one yet to happen. As we prejudge how our lives are going to be, we establish for ourselves the Law of Denial. It is our denials that make our destinies in life. And so we find ourselves destined to a constant repetition of certain experiences that we have judged are distasteful and not pleasing to us. We can never change those experiences until we first accept the Law of Personal Responsibility. As long as we permit our mind to blame anything or anyone outside, we are going to remain upon that destiny path of denial, of judgment, and we are going to suffer the consequences of our own errors in life.

There is a part, however, of all of us, known to us as the conscience. It is a spiritual sensibility with a dual capacity. It knows right from wrong; it does not have to be told. And each and every one of us has a conscience. And when we're blaming outside for what we are really doing inside, we can only sustain and maintain that delusion for a certain period of time. Because it does wear thin and the voice of conscience within us does speak to us.

In the many years of this work, it is indeed evident to me, from experiences in life, that man's greatest struggle in life is his prejudices. We're prejudiced concerning politics, concerning the weather, concerning our material supply, concerning our spiritual supply. There is no area in life that we do not prejudge the outcome for us. But by so doing, by so prejudging, we establish those laws and experience exactly what we have set into motion.

Now, in this philosophy the effort is made to reveal to you those very simple truths. But unless you do something with those truths, those truths can do nothing for you. To learn anything and not apply it is a waste. It's a terrible waste of time and effort and energy. You wouldn't go and study mathematics and then never use addition or subtraction. We study the things in life that we want to study. If we are practical—and I'm sure that we all are to some extent—then we use it. You see, use, not abuse, is the path of freedom. When you study this philosophy and do not make the effort to apply the laws that are revealed in it, you are not using this philosophy: you are abusing it. For the lack of use is abuse.

Now, that Law of Abuse—no matter who sets it into motion, it's going to return to them. Whatever you abuse in life shall in your life abuse you, for you have established that law, that Law of Denial. For when you do not use that that you have received, you establish once again the Law of Denial.

And so, my good friends, let us take some time, as this semester comes to its close in a couple of weeks, to become more aware of what we're doing to ourselves. We all know that it is our divine right—divine meaning the right that God has granted unto us; that's what divine right means—that it is our divine right to experience perfect health, perfect wealth, and perfect happiness. If we are not experiencing this perfect health, wealth, and happiness, then we have got to take an honest appraisal of how we are thinking and what our thoughts are doing to us. It is our thoughts—it is not people, it is not this little church that's doing anything detrimental to us. It is our thoughts and our attitude concerning whatever we choose to think about that is detrimental or beneficial to us.

Now, when we accept that demonstrable truth—that it is our thoughts and our thoughts alone that bring unto us the health, the wealth, and the happiness that is our divine right—it's our thought. We are the ones who create that thought. It's our own attitude. Our thoughts create our thought patterns. Our thought patterns become our attitude of mind. Our attitude of mind establishes the law upon which we, having established it, must experience it. So without the effort to become aware of our thoughts, then we cannot expect to change our attitudes.

You have to begin with the beginnings of things. And the beginning of an attitude of mind is a thought. And that thought calls forth its own kind and it multiplies, as like attracts like and becomes the Law of Attachment. It increases and it grows until it becomes, within our mental universe, an established pattern. Once becoming an established pattern, it is known as an attitude of mind. So ask yourselves, in any area of your interest, what your attitude is.

Many of you have heard me say many times, the soul within us rises and it tells us the truth. It says, "You must control yourself, oh, mind, that you may be wisely used. For lack of wise use is abuse, to that which sustains the mind." The mind takes ahold of that voice from the soul and that simple truth and it looks outside, for it has, by its own attitudes and patterns, spent many, many years looking outside for the cause of things. It looks outside and tries to control anything that is around and about it. Whether it's a human or an animal, it doesn't matter what. But it knows that it must make effort to control. But the control is the control of our own mind, not the control of someone else's, not the control of things outside.

When we blame outside, we not only reveal our denial of the basic demonstrable principle of personal responsibility, we also reveal our great need to control—that it is being directed outside of our life, for we are yet not willing to face the need to control our thoughts that are going on inside. So when you blame your families, your friends, the politicians, and everything around and about you for your problems in life, it is a very clear and evident demonstration that you are trying to control the very things you are blaming for your problems.

I know—and it was stated when these doors first opened—that here in the Serenity school and church, we will grow or we will go. Some have chosen to grow. But that choice is made each and every moment. It is not a choice you make and then you sit back and relax. It's a choice that has to be made consciously, moment by moment. Because if you don't make it consciously, moment by moment, then those attitudes of mind to which you have become habituated, they rise up. They don't want to change. They don't want to lose. And if you're not alert and awake, you find yourself going off into something else and something else and something else. It's just like a job or any endeavor in life. If we keep moving from one to the other again and again and again and again, it's not the job. It's not the school. It's that something inside of ourselves, that certain attitude of mind, unwilling to bow, demanding it have its own way and experiencing, by the Law of Repetition, again and again and again—something wrong out there: something wrong with the job, something wrong with the people, something wrong with the church.

I never yet in my life have found any person, let alone any church, that is in a state of perfection. I don't know how it could be in a state of perfection, considering that a church is not just a name or a building: it is the people who compose it. It is the people who are working for the purpose for which it was founded. So when we blame our church for our problems in life, what we are, in truth, doing is blaming all of the people not only in the physical realm who compose the body called a church, but the founders from the spiritual realm and all of those dedicated workers. So let us, in this blaming outside and especially this humble church, let us, in our blaming, ask to speak individually and collectively to the body which the church really is. That's all of the people who are working to fulfill its purpose. If we do that, we will then at least start on the path of honesty.

And I can assure you, speaking to the people of this church and those who are working for it, I am sure we will soon get freed from that delusion, that error in our thinking of blaming anything outside for our so-called problems that are inside, that are the direct effect of our unwillingness to change our attitudes in life.

Remember that all of the goodness, all of the joy of life, is already yours. And that power that brings it to you is called simply acceptance. We already have accepted the patterns, the attitudes of mind that we have. We don't, in honesty, deny that we have accepted those attitudes, because we are the ones experiencing through those attitudes. But we accept something greater, something greater than what we already have.

Now, if we truly accept something greater than what we already have, we will soon begin to experience something greater. The time that it takes for us to experience something greater than what we already think we have is ever dependent upon the patterns of mind that we're already addicted to. And the energy directed to them must balance out in our new acceptance.

I'm so very pleased this evening that I am consciously, with my eyes open—that I may see clearly which of my students come to sleep and which of my students come to learn. Because, you see, I don't give sleep-learning classes. I leave those up to the gadgets and the machines that man has created. And I sincerely question if those who feel a great sleep, like a warm comfortable blanket that comes over to them, when they are exposed to truth, do they ever question their mind? Do they ever stop to think, why—please open the side door. So some of the students can awaken, please. It is, of course, only in our best interest to ask ourselves, "What is this feeing and this sensation that comes over me that I find as a frequent pattern when I go to school, when I go to learn to benefit my own personal life?"

We know, all of us, that energy follows attention. If our attention is on sleeping, then that, of course, is where our energy is going. And I have said before, and I say again, if the students' interest is on sleep, I shall not burden myself with an extra load of energy to help keep them awake. Because I believe in being practical. If we do not find that our classes are of a sufficient interest to us to stay awake, then I can assure you, ever in keeping with the law established, we will find soon there are no more classes. For who, in their right mind of common sense, would bother to give classes to those who are not interested? And so the demonstration once again in life, the demonstration is the revelation.

I can assure you, my good students, that if the percentage of those students sleeping during class continues to increase, there will be no more of these public classes. There will only be private classes, as there has been in the years passed. And only private classes for those who are alert, awake, and do not sleep, for those are the ones who are showing true interest—sufficient to keep themselves alert and awake.

Now, in one of our classes here recently, we had a discussion concerning those who are privileged, by the laws that they had established, to come to the house and to benefit from a few hours, or more, of work on a consistent basis. For the church has experienced many, many students who come and go. And someday they find that they have closed the very door that they showed a periodic interest in. It's kind of like the well. You know, we never miss the water until the well runs dry. Then all of sudden, we have value, we have appreciation, and we apply that appreciation and that's called gratitude. And then we are thankful for the water in life that we have. For without water, there would be no life on this planet as we know it.

And so it is, my friends, in reference to your classes and in reference to this school, quality not quantity is the foundation upon which this church stands. It is the foundation upon which it was built. It will continue on, on that foundation of quality, not quantity. So when you hear a fellow student complain and blame outside for what's going on inside, where is your responsibility? You must ask yourself the question, "Is it my church or am I a visitor who has come to take, to learn, and to go?" You must ask *yourself* that question. For you, my friends, you and those angels who are amidst us are the ones who are the church. It's not just a name that we can pick out of a hat to blame for our problems in life.

If we're having problems with our health and our wealth, then let us begin to apply what we have spent so many hours listening to. Let us begin to apply the laws that are revealed in the philosophy. And if we truly apply them, the changes in our life will come ever in keeping with the effort that we are making. But in so doing, remember the wisdom of patience. So many quit just before the victories in life and they move on to something else. And they keep going on and on and on. But a rolling stone gathers no moss. And so they gather little or nothing unto themselves to awaken to make the necessary changes.

We all know the attitudes of mind that we alone must make an effort to change. We know that. How do we know which attitudes we must change? Well, it's very simple: take a look at the experiences in life you don't like. That's all you have to do: look at those experiences; see that they are effects. They are effects of your attitude. We all know which attitudes have to go.

You know, in these years, many have come, many have gone, and a few have stayed. And it's interesting, to me, of some who feel that the philosophy offered is a wonderful philosophy and it certainly does work, but there's too much discipline. They're not quite ready for it yet. Stop and think, my friends. What do you mean by discipline? Does that mean a control of your thoughts? We all must agree it certainly does. So we have to make a choice in our life. To experience something better, we must control that which is creating what we don't want and that takes a little bit of self-discipline. And it takes a little self-discipline on a daily effort, not just now and then.

Some, it is said, are ready. And some are not ready. But who makes a person ready or not ready for the truth? We make ourselves ready or not ready. It's not something outside that does it to us.

In order for a philosophy to have an effect, in order to speak the word and not have it return to you void, you must demonstrate the meaning or the principle of the word. You cannot go out into the world and speak this philosophy to the world if you have not demonstrated the principle upon which it is founded. And that's called personal responsibility. For otherwise, you will find yourself speaking many words—beautiful words, all kinds of words—but they return unto you void. Our word returns to us void when we do not demonstrate, by the Law of Application, the very meaning of the word that we speak. You can say that God is the source of your supply ten-hundred times a day—it will not have any effect unless the meaning is demonstrated: the very principle of that truth.

Only you can demonstrate it. How do you demonstrate it? Well, you can't demonstrate what you don't accept. And so the answer is very simple: you must first accept. We all have belief and we all have a great and phenomenal faith. But it's where we direct this great power. We either direct it to God, the true source, from whence it comes, or we direct it to the vehicle of our mind that is temporal and that returns unto the realms from whence it was created. If we direct this great power to our mind, then we soon find out that we are the slave of that mind that we have directed this great faith to.

Now, that mind, that we all have, must be controlled before it controls us. And so you must ask yourself the question, "Do I control my mind or does my mind control me?" You can find the answer very quickly: pause for a few moments and see if you have any prejudice. If you have any prejudice, any prejudgment, then you can answer very honestly, "Oh, no, I am the victim of my mind. I do not control my mind. My mind controls me. I move and breathe and do what it says and it gets me into all kinds of trouble. I experience poor health and limitation and lack and all that that mind has to offer." Now, who in their *right* mind wants to be a servant to a mind that's constantly getting them into trouble, that's constantly denying them the goodness, the abundance, the joy, the health, and the wealth that God has offered to all his children? Our mind does that.

Now that doesn't mean that our mind is a bad vehicle. It will serve the purpose for which it has been designed by the great Architect of the universe if we will keep it under control. Now, I don't know how anyone is going to control a mind without some daily effort of discipline.

Without control of the mind, the faculties of the soul cannot express. Now this philosophy teaches a balance between the soul faculties and the sense functions. How can we express the balance of the soul faculty of tolerance if our mind is in control? For there are many things in our mind that our mind has judged are intolerable. Therefore, we cannot express in those areas the soul faculty of tolerance. When we gain control once again of the vehicle called the human mind—for we had control of it before—when we once again gain control of the human mind, we will be freed from worry, we will be freed from illness, we will be free from discord, we will be in the spiritual vibratory wave of harmony, through which the goodness of life there is a never-ending flow.

And in the process of gaining control of the mind, how many times do we view nature and declare the truth of the infinite abundance? Those are the things, my friends, that we can work on every day in every way. Are there any amongst us who enjoys poor health? Are there any amongst us who enjoys poverty and the lack of the goodness of life? I am sure there are none amongst us who enjoy those things. Yet, we find ourselves the victims of them. And why do we find ourselves the victims of those things? Simply because the effort is not being made on a daily basis to control the mind and it is controlling us. It's telling us what to do and where to go. It's telling us all of the bad and negative things of life, when there's so much goodness that is waiting for all of us.

And so remember, when you hear the minds of men blame outside for the problems inside, remember, if you don't speak up, then by your silence are you supporting that illusion. It not only has an effect upon you, it has an effect upon the universe. And, you see, it has a special effect upon the one who hears and experiences the illusion, because, by a law established, it has come to us. It has come to us to be corrected, to be illumined, to be transformed into the truth. For the essence of truth lies in all things. And because it has come to us ever in keeping with the law, we bear the personal responsibility to speak up. And if we don't, we have once again established the Law of Denial. If you find someone coming to you frequently complaining, then go inside your computer and look at every area of your life to see if the law has been established at any time within you. And speak up the truth that you may be an instrument not only to free your own soul from that type of illusion, but an instrument to free the soul that is speaking to you.

Here we have this wonderful opportunity to gain control of our mind. When our mind tries to put us to sleep because certain patterns within our mind do not want to hear the truth, that's the time to use that will that is within you. I can assure you, as I said earlier in this class this evening, there will be no more public classes as long as students come to sleep.

Thank you very much. Thank you

JULY 6, 1978

CONSCIOUSNESS CLASS 186

Greetings, students. Indeed, it is heartwarming to see the effort, the steps, that the students are making. Though they may seem very small, they are sure.

And so it is in concluding this semester with you we should like to spend the time in answering as many of the questions you have prepared as possible. Remember that encouragement is not only a soul faculty, but it is a lifeline to lift your soul to the realms of light and reason.

You may ask the questions you have at this time.

Thank you. Would you please discuss more deeply the importance of courage in making a decision when one is frustrated so that it will not lead to fascination?

Courage, a soul faculty, cannot be expressed without control of the human mind. Whenever one reaches a decision, there is always the pull in the human mind, in keeping with the Law of Duality, there's always the doubt—and the doubt and the fear that it uses to support itself. To express courage, one must first control the human mind and reach a state of concentration. Concentration, as you know, is placing the mind pointedly and fixedly upon the object of your choice until only the essence remains. And so it is in expressing courage, once your mind is fixed, once you are concentrated, the hissing hounds of the poles of the opposites, the doubts and the fears, they disappear and you accomplish that which you set out to do.

Thank you. Please give your understanding of the decision-making process. What part does surrender play?

In speaking to that question, concerning the human mind and surrender, whenever a choice is made, for every expression made by the human mind there is the process of surrender of the opposite. For example, each time the human mind entertains the thought of white, immediately the thought of black rises. Each time it thinks of good, the opposite rises, for that is the nature of the human mind. And in using the human mind, one must be able to express the power of concentration. There is something far greater than the vehicle of the human mind. And when man, willingly, by his own voluntary choice, surrenders the pairs of opposites offered by the mind, then he reaches the spiritual realms of essence.

For example, as we have told you many times, concentration [is] placing the mind pointedly and fixedly upon the object of your choice until only the essence remains. The essence is the principle. The essence is the spirit of whatever you choose to direct your consciousness to. When you, through the power of concentration, experience the essence beyond the object of your choice, you are then in rapport with the cause of the object of your choice. Being in rapport with the cause, you may direct your life through the mental realms in a more peaceful and harmonious way. But that is not something that is done and then finished with. It is something that involves each and every thought you entertain.

Go beyond your thought, which is form and governed by a dual opposing law. Go to the essence, which is singular. This is what is meant when it is spoken "To keep thine eye single." In other words, to see not the realms of duality, but beyond to the very cause to the realms of the spirit. For there, formless and free, you may direct this great power into the form in the mental worlds of your choice.

Thank you. What is the difference between forgiveness and making an apology?

To forgive is to free. To free from the boundaries and limits of one's own mental universe. To apologize is to, so to speak, save face. It is indeed much easier for an uneducated ego to apologize than it is to make the effort to forgive. One can apologize unto themselves or to someone they feel they have offended, but the apology does not reach the depths of one's being. Therefore, it ever lies waiting to rise again in another way on another day. In other words, forgiveness reaches the very soul of the person and they give it forth to the divine, eternal Source. An apology is entertained in the mental realms and remains there, ever recorded and waiting to rise again and again and again. And so it is that you view different people and you see that they readily, readily apologize, only to do the same thing over and over and over, again and again and again because the cause of the transgression has not been faced. And not having been faced within, it is not given forth through the faculty of forgiveness.

Thank you. You have stated that within the 81 levels of consciousness, there are 40 soul faculties, 40 functions, and the Divine Intelligence, and that the first soul faculty is duty, gratitude, and tolerance and the second, faith, poise, and humility. Does the first soul faculty account for 1 or 3 of the 81 levels? And what are the principles that apply to each of the 2 groups of 3?

The soul faculty of faith, poise, and humility, of duty, gratitude, and tolerance is a triune faculty. And it is 1 of the 40. The underlining principle of all of the faculties and the functions is known as the foundation stone of understanding.

Everywhere, throughout the ages it is taught in all your getting, get understanding. For it is understood that the human mind is a getting vehicle. It is constantly, by its very nature, gathering and garnering unto itself, in a constant process of getting something. But the getting that it needs more than anything that it can ever experience is the getting of understanding.

Why does it seem so difficult for man to get understanding? It simply reveals that the faculty of care needs expansion. In all of these soul faculties, you will find that all people are expressing them to some extent and to some degree. It is the broadening of the horizon of man's universe that is necessary. For man cares for the things that he has judged or decided are in his best interests. And he expresses the faculty of care in those limited areas of his life. But the faculty of care, like any faculty, must be broadened to encompass the whole.

When man begins to express a broadening horizon, he gains the understanding that will free his eternal being. But we cannot understand what we do not place interest, attention, and energy into. We must first in this getting and gaining vibration, we must first, slowly but surely, see the value of something that is beyond what we have already accepted. Once having viewed that value, we will start the very simple, natural process of the human mind to work in that area. And we will start the getting.

We understand some of the patterns that we spend much time in. What we do not seem to understand is that everyone, everywhere has those patterns of mind or attitudes. They're expressed, perhaps, in varying and different ways than we are expressing them, but in principle they are the same level of consciousness. In order for us to see clearly that it is the same level of consciousness that we ourselves are expressing in other areas of life, we must care enough for truth. This is where the faculty of care will broaden our horizons. When we care enough for truth, then we will begin to see what is beyond the mountains of obstructions that our minds have created for us.

Thank you. When someone in a negative level begins to bombard us with negativity or is in the forces, how can we prevent ourselves from slipping into their vibration and yet be effective in helping them?

Yes. A most important question. A most important question, especially in your world where the king mind is still the great ruler of the universe. Someone comes to us in the levels of negativity and the destructive forces to the harmony, the beauty, the goodness, and the graciousness of life—we first must understand that the level they are expressing exists within us. We have in that moment the divine right of choice. If we do not wisely exercise that divine right of choice, we soon find that the negative, destructive, discordant level that is being expressed to us soon rises within us.

I have always been, in the many centuries on this side of the veil, though I wasn't on your earthly realm, a person who is willing to help those who are willing to help themselves. Now, we must understand what we mean by *willing* or *willingness*. If we find negative, discordant levels of consciousness being expressed, it reveals that the will of the individual has chosen to express in those levels and it is the willingness of that individual that is continuing to direct intelligent energy to express those discordant, negative levels. Reason dictates to a person, to the listener, reason dictates, one: "How often has this level been expressed to me by this particular person? Have I spent time in compassion and understanding, tolerance and duty and gratitude to try to show the individual a better way, a way that, by their voluntary choice, they can be free from those discordant vibrations? Have I first made that effort?" Number two: "How many times have I truly made that effort with that particular person?" Number three: "Have they made any effort? Visibly or invisibly, has any effort been made on their part to make a change of attitude and redirect God's infinite, intelligent energy?"

If the answer is affirmative, then one follows the Light and does what they feel they can to help the person to help themselves. If, however, the pattern of discord continues to express itself and the effort is not being made by the individual to help themselves, then all you are doing in your efforts, if that is the case, is to support that discordant level of consciousness that needs a listening ear.

You see, my good friends, misery, as I have stated many times, doesn't just love company: company is indispensable to the existence of the level of consciousness known as misery. Now, a person will be miserable by themselves for not too extended a period of time. The level demands, and is very greedy in its getting, every bit of energy that it can find. Now, you will note, if you'll recall, for we've all had those levels expressing within us at times, whenever you have been miserable, grounded in self-thought and self-pity, judging the universe is the cause of your problems and everyone in it, you know after that entertaining of thought has passed through your mind, there is a feeling of exhaustion. You're very tired. That reveals to you how much energy it takes to sustain the discordant levels of misery and self-pity. Therefore, for the level of misery to continue to exist after having totally drained the energy of the individual who has chosen to express the level, it goes out into the universe, uses every device that it can possibly think of for a listening ear in order that it may receive more energy and perpetrate itself.

Now, in helping people to help themselves, you must become very well aware of that demonstrable truth. And if they insist, those attitudes of misery, to come to your door, think deeply within yourself and pray for forgiveness, for that level is waiting to rise within you. One must learn to be firm, but never fail to be kind.

And what is kindness? Kindness is a consideration of the *whole* person, not just the particular level that they are expressing at the moment. Ofttimes, my friends, people are kind to us and we mistake that kindness for a weakness in their character. We mistake that kindness because we ourselves are not expressing consideration of the whole. Our consideration, or what we know in this philosophy as Divine or God's love, is limited to a very small universe that we have created.

But we are, slowly but surely, we are expanding those walls that we have built around us. And remember that all these walls, these so-called security walls, those walls were built out of fear, out of ignorance, that we may lose something that we cherished. We can't lose what we never had. Everything that you experience in life, every thought, every feeling, every object that you have is on loan to you. It's only loaned to you by the great compassion of the Divine Intelligence called God. And it will all be recalled and you never know the day or the hour.

Let it go graciously from your universe, my friends. For if you let it go graciously, it will come unto you graciously. It has served its purpose and it's time for it to go, be it a thought, a feeling, a person, an animal, or an object. Remember, it has served its purpose. Do not hold to that which has entered your universe and has served its purpose. And let not your mind be the judge, for if you let your mind be the judge, then you'll pay a dear, a very dear price. There is something above and beyond the mind. Be receptive to that and then you will have no problem in receiving, having eliminated the problem, through an error of ignorance, in your giving.

Many people give many things. But, in truth, they give nothing, for the gift, the gift of the self is not with it. Therefore, it is no gift at all. And it is so important—and we have discussed before in these classes—the gift without the giver is ever worthless, for there's still an attachment. And the payment is the attachment.

Let your thoughts that you cherish, when they have served their purpose—and the God within you knows that moment—let them go. Let the things you have garnered go when the time for going has come. And then you will see the new. Whenever you turn your sight away from what is leaving, you see in that moment what is coming. And so if you will practice that simple level of consciousness in all your daily activities, then you can move smoothly with dignity with the spirit of joy, you can move through the great beauty of evolution for everything is in a process of change.

But unless you free yourself from attachment, then you cannot move graciously through those beautiful realms of evolution. Everything you think you have is in your universe in keeping with the divine law. It—everything—shall leave your universe in keeping with that same law. You are not the one (your mind) to make the decision. That is beyond the power and right of your mind. So when it goes, thank God for its going. Then you will be able to see, in that moment, and thank God for the coming of the new. No matter how hard you try to swim against the tide, you will only defeat yourself, for what is shall be. Man's peace is in knowing the difference. And the knowing of the difference is beyond the limits of his mind.

Thank you. It is taught that we change through our heart, never our head. Then, why are we encouraged to think and think more deeply?

My friends, when you begin to think and think and think more deeply, the deeper you think, the more you remove from your consciousness in the sense that you are passing through the various levels of the human mind. For example, view the human mind as a vast compartment of accumulated so-called knowledge and experience. As you begin to think, you begin to pass through these untold chambers and vaults that you alone have created. Now, the more you think, the more weary your mind becomes. And you will reach a state, in passing through these vast chambers, where you will pause. And when you pause, you will finally free yourself from the bondage of the mental realm and enter the door of wisdom that leads to the chambers of your own heart.

Thank you. Please explain the effect of there being no time in both your dimension and ours.

The effect is so varied and so multiplied in your so-called realms of time, I would much prefer to speak of the cause. To become aware of an eternal moment, formless, timeless, and free, there can be no thought of the things past; there can be no hope of that to come. It is stated that hope is eternal and truth is inevitable. But man must ask himself, "What is it within us that hopes?" Does our soul hope? That that knows does not hope, for it is truth. So it's not our soul that hopes. It is our mind that hopes. And because it is our mind that hopes, we must still the mind that it may not regret the past, that it may not hope for the future in order that we may experience the eternal moment of truth.

I am with you this moment. And this moment is every moment, for there is no future and there is no past. There is no longer the illusion and the veil of time. Therefore, I am here and I am there for I am everywhere in this, the moment of truth. When you, through the efforts of controlling your hopes and your regrets, stilling all that your mind has to offer, in that moment of truth everything, everything *is*. There is no longer desire, for you cannot desire what you already are. There's no desire. There is no want. There is no need. That, my friends, is the moment of pure, unadulterated meditation.

That is what you, in your efforts, shall in time attain. Once having attained it, that is your moment of truth. Being your moment of truth, it is everyone's moment of truth. And when the veil of the illusion of time is lifted, everyone, everything, everywhere shall know. Once having opened your eyes to the great eternity, it is difficult to permit the mind in its pettiness to entertain itself as a wild and reckless little child. That is the effect of control. That is the freedom that waits for your acceptance. All that you give to attain it shall be returned and multiplied unto you, for what you have to give is microscopic in comparison to what you have to gain.

Good night.

JULY 13, 1978

APPENDIX

The Divine Healing Prayer

I accept that the Divine Healing Power
Is removing all obstructions
From my mind and body
And is restoring me
To perfect health, wealth, and happiness.
My heart is filled with gratitude
For the Divine Law of Acceptance
That is healing both present and absent ones
Who are in need of help.
Peace, the power that healeth,
Is guiding my thoughts, acts, and deeds
As God and I go hand in hand
Living a life of joyful abundance.

The Total Consideration Affirmation

I am the manifestation of Divine Intelligence. Formless and free. Whole and complete. Peace, Poise, and Power are my birthright.

The Law of Harmony is my thought and guarantees Unity in all my acts and activities, expressing perfect Rhythm and limitless flow throughout my entire being.

Without beginning or ending, eternity is my true awareness and sees the tides of creation, as a captain sees his ship.

As the Light of Truth is sustained by the faculty of Reason, I pause to think and claim my Divine right.

    Right Thought. Right Action. Total Consideration.

        Amen. Amen. Amen.

Divine Abundance

Thank
(Gratitude)

You
(Principle)

God
(Divine Intelligence)

I'm
(Individualizing)

Moving
(Rhythm)

In
(Unity)

Your
(Realization)

Divine
(Total)

Flow
(Consideration)

www.ingramcontent.com/pod-product-compliance
Lightning Source LLC
Chambersburg PA
CBHW020634300426
44112CB00007B/105